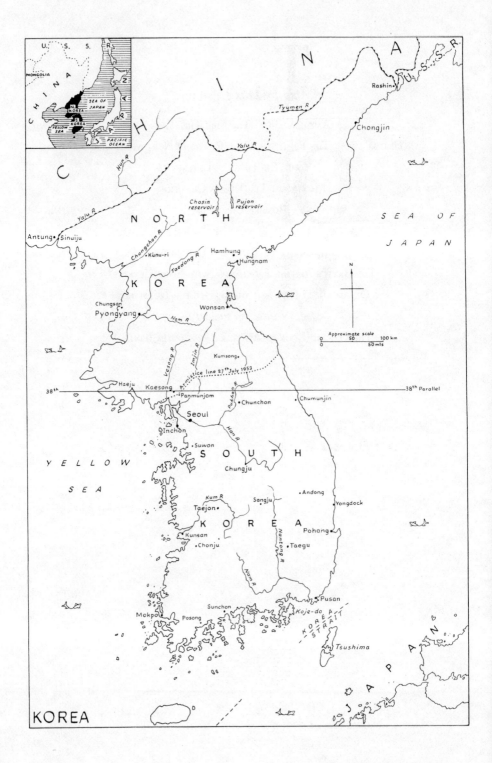

KOREA

THE

KOREAN

WAR

Max Hastings

SIMON AND SCHUSTER
New York   London   Toronto   Sydney   Tokyo

Published by Simon and Schuster
A Division of Simon & Schuster, Inc.
Simon & Schuster Building
Rockefeller Center
1230 Avenue of the Americas
New York, NY 10020
SIMON AND SCHUSTER and colophon are registered trademarks of Simon & Schuster, Inc.
Maps by Boris Weltman
Designed by Eve Kirch
Manufactured in the United States of America

10 9 8 7 6 5 4 3 2 1

Library of Congress Cataloging in Publication Data
Hastings, Max.
    The Korean War.

    Bibliography: p.
    Includes index.
    1. Korean War, 1950–1953. 2. Korean War, 1950–1953—
United States. I. Title.
DS918.H34   1987   951.9'042   87-16547
ISBN 0-671-52823-8

For permission to reprint excerpts, the author is grateful to the following:
David Higham Associates Limited for *Point of Departure* by James Cameron
Princeton University Press for *Origins of the Korean War* by Bruce Cumings
Don Congdon Associates for *MacArthur: American Caesar* by William Manchester
P. J. Kavanagh for *The Perfect Stranger* by P. J. Kavanagh
Harcourt Brace Jovanovich Inc. for *The Korean War: An Oral History* by Donald Knox
Cornell University Press for *The Wrong War* by Rosemary Foot
Doubleday and Co. Inc. for *The Korean War* by Matthew B. Ridgway

To Charlotte

CONTENTS

LIST OF MAPS

THE KOREAN WAR

FOREWORD

In the past twenty years the public fascination with military history has become a minor literary phenomenon on both sides of the Atlantic. It has centered overwhelmingly upon the Second World War. Indeed, at the extremities of the popular market, perceptions of the struggle between the Western Allies and the Germans long ago parted company with reality and took on the mantle of fantasy borne a generation earlier by cowboys and Indians. In the past decade, more surprisingly, Vietnam has also given birth to a major publishing industry. Some new books seek seriously to examine why the United States lost the war. Others, like the films they inspire, attempt to rewrite history, to present aspects of that sordid, doomed struggle in an heroic light.

How is it, then, that the other great mid-twentieth-century conflict with communism, Korea, remains so neglected? Popular awareness of the Korean war today centers upon the television comedy show *M.A.S.H.*, which dismays most veterans because it projects an image of the struggle infinitely less savage than that which they recall. The United Nations suffered 142,000 casualties in the war to save South Korea from Communist domination. The Koreans themselves lost at least a million people. United States losses in three years were only narrowly outstripped by those suffered in Vietnam over more than ten. Korea cost the British three times as many dead as the Falklands War. Chinese casualties remain uncertain, perhaps even in Peking, but they run into many hundreds of thousands.

9

Since 1945 only the Cuban missile crisis has created a greater risk of nuclear war between East and West. As some recent scholarly researchers have pointed out, notable among them Dr. Rosemary Foot in her fascinating *The Wrong War*, in Korea the American military displayed a private enthusiasm for using atomic weapons against the Chinese far greater than the Western world perceived, even a generation later. Korea remains the only conflict since 1945 in which the armies of two great powers—for surely China's size confers that title—have met on the battlefield.

Many Westerners were happy to forget Korea for a generation after the war ended, soured by the taste of costly stalemate, robbed of any hint of glory. Yet consider the extraordinary cast of American characters that came together to determine the fate of that barren Asian peninsula: Truman and Acheson, Marshall and MacArthur, Ridgway and Bradley. Then add the succession of great military dramas—the destruction of Task Force Smith, the defense of the Pusan Perimeter, Inchon, the drive to the Yalu, the shattering winter advance of the Chinese. A host of lesser epics followed, which may be allowed to include the stand of the British 27th Brigade on the Imjin in April 1951, an action relatively minor in scale, whose ferocity yet caught the imagination of the world. The fascination of Korea centers, above all, upon the battlefield confrontation between the armies of China and the United States. But the tragedy of the Korean people, the principal sufferers in the three-year struggle across their land, deserves far more attention than it has been granted.

Above all, perhaps, Korea merits close consideration as a military rehearsal for the subsequent disaster in Vietnam. So many of the ingredients of the Indochina tragedy were already visible a decade or two earlier in Korea: the political difficulty of sustaining an unpopular and autocratic regime; the problems of creating a credible local army in a corrupt society; the fateful cost of underestimating the power of an Asian Communist army. For all the undoubted benefits of air superiority and close support, Korea vividly displayed the difficulties of using air power effectively against a primitive economy, a peasant army. The war also demonstrated the problem of deploying a highly mechanized Western army in broken country against a lightly equipped foe. Many of the American professional soldiers who served under MacArthur or Ridgway did so later under Westmoreland or Abrams. When they reminisce about the campaigns of 1950–53, it is striking how frequently slips of the tongue cause them to substitute "Vietnam" for "Korea" in their conversation.

Yet because it proved possible finally to stabilize the battle in Korea on terms which allowed the United Nations—or more realistically, the United States—to deploy its vast firepower from fixed positions, to defeat the advance of the massed Communist armies, many of the lessons of Korea were misunderstood, or not learned at all. For instance, Pentagon studies showed during Korea, just as they had during World War II, that it was America's lower socioeconomic groups which bore the chief burden of fighting the war, and above all of filling the ranks of the infantry. Yet the same phenomenon would recur in Vietnam, and the serious shortcomings of the American footsoldier—the man at the tip of the spear—would once more have serious consequences. In Korea the Communists enjoyed the opportunity to learn a great deal about the limits of Western patience, the difficulties of maintaining popular enthusiasm for an uncertain cause in a democracy. By the time the armistice was signed at Panmunjom in August 1953, after a mere three years of hostilities, the Western allies had become desperate to extricate themselves from a war that offered so little prospect of glory or clear-cut victory. Yet in Korea the Communists had provided the most ruthlessly simple *casus belli,* the most incontrovertible provocation by aggression, to be offered to the West at any period between 1945 and this time of writing.

As in my past books, I have sought to explore the Korean War through a combination of personal interviews with surviving participants and archival research in London and Washington. In the course of writing it, I have met more than 200 American, Canadian, British, and Korean veterans of the conflict. Perhaps the most exciting aspect of my research has been the opportunity to talk to Chinese veterans, granted to me in 1985 through the good offices of the Peking Institute of Strategic Studies, and the help of the late and much-lamented Colonel Jonathan Alford of the International Institute of Strategic Studies in London. One of the possibilities that first attracted me to the project was that, in the new mood of détente between China and the West, it might be possible to gain some access to a Peking perspective upon the Korean War. After months of discussion and correspondence, this indeed proved to be so.

There are no German or Japanese triumphal museums commemorating World War II. It is an eerie experience for a Westerner to walk through the great halls of the Peking Military Museum, gazing upon the trophies of captured British bren guns and regimental flashes, American .50-caliber machine guns, helmets, and aircraft remains. Yet if my visit was a measure of how much has changed between China and the West, it was also a reminder of how much remains the same. There is still a great display given over to America's supposed 1952 "bacteriological warfare campaign" against North Korea. China claims to have inflicted 1,090,000 casualties on the U.S. armed forces in Korea, a figure one assumes was arrived at by adding a few thousands to the total Chinese casualties claimed by the U.S. I spent some fascinating days and nights in Peking and Shanghai listening to Chinese veterans describing their battlefield experience in Korea. Yet it must be said that none deviated for a moment from strict Party orthodoxy in describing their enthusiasm for the war and satisfaction with the manner in which it was conducted. There is no comparison with the experience of interviewing British and American veterans, whose views reflect such a wide and forthright range of opinion. In Peking senior officers gave me some fascinating explanations of Chinese behavior. At their Command and Staff College, I had some glimpses of the PLA's military perspective upon various battles. But there remains, of course, no opportunity to check official assertions against archives or written evidence. In a totalitarian state, such as China remains, it is debatable whether even those at the summit of power can discover the historical truth about events in the recent past, even should they wish to do so. In the same fashion, when Mr. Gorbachev claims in a speech that the Soviet Union won the Second World War effectively unaided, it seems rash to assume that he is perpetrating a conscious untruth. It may yet be that he, like the vast majority of his people, simply does not know any better.

During my researches in Korea, I must acknowledge an important debt to the U.S. Commander in Chief there, General Paul Livsey, who also served during the war as a young platoon commander; to British and American officers who provided me with facilities to visit key locations such as Panmunjom and Gloucester Hill; and, above all, to Brigadier Brian Burditt, who stayed on in Korea after the end of his tour of duty as British Military Attaché to act as my mentor and guide and to arrange some fascinating interviews with Korean veterans of the war. I made a decision at the outset to make no approaches to Pyongyang while writing the book. If truth remains an elusive commodity in China, in North Korea it is entirely displaced by fantasy. It seems impossible to gain any worthwhile insights into the North Korean view of the war as long as Kim Il Sung presides over a society in which the private possession of a bicycle is considered a threat to national security.

General Sir Anthony Farrar-Hockley was himself writing the British official history of the Korean War while I was working on my own book. With characteristic generosity, he arranged for me to have access to some of the key official files in his care. He himself remains, of course, one of the most fascinating witnesses of the Korean drama. Not only did he win a Distinguished Service Order as adjutant of the Gloucesters in their stand on the Imjin in April 1951, but he returned from two years' Chinese captivity with a reputation for indomitable courage and determination. His official history will clarify a host of details about British participation in the war, and no doubt add new revelations.

In Britain and the United States, I interviewed as wide a cross section as possible of officers and men of all three services. I did not, because of their great age, seek meetings with a handful of the most senior officers who survive. From past experience I have found that very elderly veterans have long ago said and written all that they wish about their great campaigns. To discuss these again merely starts a conversational train running upon familiar railway lines. It becomes fraudulent to acknowledge their assistance because it is so rare that they wish to say anything of substance. After thirty-five years, with very rare exceptions, the most helpful witnesses about the conduct of a campaign are those who held regimental and battalion commands, and staff officers who served under the principal commanders, whose memories are often remarkable. I shall always cherish the four-hour word portrait of MacArthur's headquarters at the Dai Ichi drawn for me by that great and wholly delightful American soldier who served there in 1950, Colonel Fred Ladd. Likewise, I am much indebted to Brigadier General Ed Simmonds, U.S.M.C., who is not only director of the Marine Corps Museum in Washington, but also a veteran of the Chosin campaign, and an uncommonly shrewd critic of the Korean experience.

This book, like those I have written upon other campaigns, does not purport to be a comprehensive history. The most scholarly account of prewar Korea is that of Bruce Cumings. Even after twenty-five years the British author David Rees's *Korea: The Limited War* remains the best overall narrative, above all, about the American political aspects. More recently, Joseph Goulden uncovered new American archival sources for his *Korea: The Untold Story*. Dr. Rosemary Foot of the University of Sussex, author of *The Wrong War* and another pioneer researcher, was characteristically generous in discussing her own reflections and sources about the political dimensions of the war. To all these authors and books, I acknowledge my indebtedness for important lines of thought. I have not attempted to emulate them. I have written relatively little about aspects of the Korean conflict, such as MacArthur's dismissal, which have been exhaustively discussed elsewhere. Instead, I have sought to paint a portrait of the war, focusing upon some human and military aspects less familiar to readers on both sides of the Atlantic. But it seems reasonable to suggest that a British officer's or private soldier's recollection of the experience of fighting the Chinese in Korea is no less valid, as a contribution to understanding what the struggle was like, than that of an American, a Canadian, an Australian, a Frenchman. The ranks attributed to officers and men in the text are those they held at the dates concerned. I have retained old-fashioned spellings of Chinese names, which are likely to be more familiar to Western readers than the newer versions.

In one important respect I must be numbered among the revisionists. Many writers about Korea in the 1950s, not to mention politicians and voters, looked back on the war with bitter distaste for the long stalemate, the growing tensions between allies that it generated, and the inconclusive truce that brought it to an end. Misgivings about Western wars in Asia were intensified by the long misery of Vietnam. Yet whatever obvious criticisms must be made of MacArthur's excesses, of the West's handling of Peking, of the conduct of the winter campaign of 1950, I remain convinced of the rightness of the American commitment to Korea in June 1950. The regimes of Syngman Rhee and his successors possessed massive shortcomings. Yet who can doubt, looking at Korea today, that the people of the South enjoy incomparably more fulfilling lives than those of the inhabitants of the North? Civil libertarians may justly remark that the freedom of the South's

35 million people remains relative. Yet few would deny that relative freedom, to pursue personal prosperity or private professions, remains preferable to absolute tyranny. North Korea is still among the most wretched, ruthless, restrictive, impenitent Stalinist societies in the world. South Korea is one of the most dynamic industrial societies even Asia has spawned in the past generation. The 1950–53 Korean War, which confirmed the shape of the two Koreas as they are today, remains one of the most significant, compelling clashes of arms in this century. Those who experienced it have long been irked by a sense of the world's neglect of what they endured, and of what they achieved. I hope this book will make at least a modest contribution toward remedying the omission.

Max Hastings
Guilsborough Lodge,
Northamptonshire

January 1987

PROLOGUE:
TASK FORCE SMITH

In the early hours of July 5, 1950, 403 bewildered, damp, disoriented Americans sat in their hastily dug foxholes on three Korean hills looking down upon the main road between Suwon and Osan. The men of 1/21st Infantry had been in the country just four days, since the big C-54 transports had flown them from Itasuki in Japan to the southern airfield at Pusan. Ever since they had been moving north in fits and starts—by train and truck, sleeping in sidings and schoolhouses, amid great throngs of refugees crowding roads and stations. Some men were sick from the local water. Lieutenant Fox was injured on the train, before they heard their first shot fired, by an inglorious stray cinder from the engine blowing into his eye. All of them were savaged by mosquitoes. They learned that Korea stank—literally—of the human manure with which the nation's farmers fertilized their rice paddies. They watched earnest roadside rendezvous between their own officers and the smattering of U.S. generals in the country. General William Dean, commanding the 24th Division, told the 1/21st commanding officer, Lieutenant Colonel Charles "Brad" Smith, "I'm sorry—I just don't have much information to give you."

They knew that the Communist North Koreans had invaded the anti-Communist South on June 25, and had been striking ruthlessly southward ever since, meeting little opposition from Syngman Rhee's shattered army. They were told that they themselves would be taking up defensive positions somewhere in the path of the enemy, as far north as possible. But after years of occupation duty in

Japan, the notion of battle, of injury and sudden death, seemed infinitely remote. Their unit, like all those of the Occupation Army in Japan, was badly under-strength and poorly equipped. Their own A and D Companies, together with many of their supporting elements, were still at sea between Japan and Pusan. On the night of July 4 they were ordered to take up a blocking position on the Suwon road, some fifty miles south of the capital, Seoul, which was already in Communist hands. In a country of mountains, the paths open to a modern army were few and obvious. The enemy sweeping south must make for Osan. The 1/21st, the first unit of the United States Army available to be committed to battle in Korea, must do what it could to meet them. "They looked like a bunch of Boy Scouts," said Colonel George Masters, one of the men who watched the battalion moving to the front. "I said to Brad Smith, 'You're facing tried combat soldiers out there.' There was nothing he could answer."[1]

They moved forward, as most soldiers move forward to battle in most wars, in drizzle and darkness. The South Korean drivers of some of the commandeered vehicles flatly refused to go farther toward the battlefield, so the Americans drove themselves. They unloaded from their trucks behind the hills that Colonel Smith had briefly reconnoitered that day and began to climb, by platoons, through the rock and scrub amid much tired, muffled cursing and clanking of equipment. Their officers were as confused as the men, for they had been told to expect to meet a South Korean Army unit to which to anchor their own positions. In reality, there was no one on the hill. Smith's company commanders deployed their men as best they could, and ordered them to start digging. At once, for the first time, Americans discovered the difficulty of hewing shelter from the unyielding Korean hillsides. For some hours, working clumsily in their poncho capes in the rain, they scraped among the rocks. Below them on the road, signalers laid telephone lines to their single battery of supporting 105-mm howitzers, a thousand yards to the rear. A few truckloads of ammunition were off-loaded by the roadside, but no one thought to insist that this was lugged up the hills in the dark to the company positions. Then, for an uneasy hour or two, most of the Americans lay beside their weapons and packs, sodden clothes clinging clammily to their bodies, and slept.

Blinking and shuffling in the first light of dawn, the men of Task Force Smith—the grandiose title their little force had been granted in a Tokyo map room—looked down from their positions. They were just south of Suwon airfield, three miles north of the little town of Osan. They began to pick out familiar faces: "Brad" Smith himself, a slightly built West Pointer of thirty-four with a competent record in the Pacific in World War II; his executive officer, "Mother" Martain, now demanding some changes in positions chosen in darkness. Major Floyd Martain was a New Yorker who had served in the National Guard from 1926 until he was called to active duty in 1940, then spent the war in Alaska. Unkind spirits considered Martain something of a fussy old woman, hence his nickname.

Yet he also earned it by looking after his men, many of whom felt a real affection for him. Corporal Ezra Burke was the son of a Mississippi sawmiller who was drafted in time to see a little action at the tail end of the Pacific campaign, then stayed on to share the heady pleasures of Japan occupation duty. Burke was one of many Southerners in the unit, young men whose hometowns in the late 1940s could offer neither a paycheck nor a life-style as attractive as that of MacArthur's army. Now, as a medical orderly, Corporal Burke and his team were laying out their field kits in a hollow behind the battalion position. They had "figured to be a week in Korea, settle the gook thing, then back to Japan." Now, uneasy, they were less confident of this timetable.

Lieutenant Carl Bernard, a twenty-four-year-old Texan, had served as an enlisted Marine in World War II. Quickly bored by civilian life when it ended, he enlisted in the 82nd Airborne Division and was commissioned into the 24th Division in 1949. When the Korean crisis broke, as one of the few Airborne-qualified officers in the division, he spent some days at the airfield in Japan supervising the loading of the transports. Now he was put in command of 2nd Platoon of B Company, where he knew nobody, after rejoining the battalion a few hours earlier.

Corporal Robert Fountain, of the Communications Platoon, watched Colonel Smith scanning the black smoke columns on the horizon through binoculars, his shoulders draped in an army blanket against the rain. The colonel looked like an Indian chieftain, thought Fountain. He himself, a nineteen-year-old farmboy from Macon, Georgia, was chiefly concerned whether the telephone lines would hold up. They had been unwound, used, spliced, rewound repeatedly on maneuvers in Japan. Yet they were now the battalion's principal means of communication, with so many of the radios rendered unserviceable by the rain. Fountain had found the experiences of the past few days deeply bewildering. With his parents divorced and jobs hard to come by, he had joined the army at sixteen because he could think of nothing else to do. He had never thought much about fighting. For himself, like many of the men, the flight to Korea was a first-ever trip in an airplane. In the days since they had been strafed by presumed North Korean Yaks, which they later discovered were Australian Mustangs. They had watched an ammunition train explode and a South Korean officer force one of his own men to his knees without explanation and shoot him in the back of the neck. There had been scares of enemy tanks that turned into friendly caterpillar tractors. Fountain and his comrades left Japan under the impression that they would be away only five days: "When the gooks hear who we are, they'll quit and go home." They left clothes, possessions, money in their barrack rooms. Yet now the vainglory of their departure had faded. Fountain ate a can of cold C rations and asked if anybody had any water left in their canteens. He felt cold, wet, and confused.

A few minutes after 7 A.M., Sergeant Loren Chambers of B Company called to his platoon commander, "Hey, look over there, Lieutenant. Can you believe?" Advancing toward them down the open plain from Suwon was a column of eight green-painted tanks. Lieutenant Day asked what they were. "Those are T-34 tanks, sir," answered the sergeant, "and I don't think they're going to be friendly toward us." All along the crest line, men chattered excitedly as they peered forward at this first glimpse of the enemy. Officers hastened forward to confirm the threat. Captain Dashner, B Company commander, said, "Let's get some artillery on them."[2] The forward observation officer of the 58th Field Artillery Battalion cranked his handset. A few moments later, rounds began to gusher into the paddy fields around the road. But still the tanks came on. The guns of the 58th possessed no armor-piercing capability.

Lieutenant Philip Day and one of the battalion's two 75-mm recoilless rifle sections manhandled their clumsy weapon to a position overlooking the road and fired. Inexpert, they had sited on a forward slope. The round did no visible damage to the enemy, but the ferocious backblast slammed into the hill, provoking an eruption of mud which deluged the crew and jammed the gun. Urgently, they began to strip and clear it.

At the roadside, Lieutenant Ollie Connors clutched one of the unit's principal antitank weapons, a hand-held 2.36-inch bazooka. In 1945 the serious defect of the bazooka rocket was well known—its inability to penetrate most tanks' main armor. Yet even now, five years later, the new and more powerful 3.5-inch rocket launcher had not been issued to MacArthur's Far East Army. As the first T-34 clattered toward the narrow pass between the American positions, Connors put up his bazooka and fired. There was an explosion on the tank hull. But the T-34, probably the outstanding tank of World War II and still a formidable weapon, did not check. It roared on through the pass and down the road toward the American gun line. As its successors followed, with remarkable courage Connors fired again and again at close range, twenty-two rockets in all. One tank stopped, appearing to have thrown a track. But it continued to fire with both its main armament and coaxial machine gun. The others disappeared toward Osan, to be followed a few minutes later by another armored platoon. A single 105-mm gun possessed a few rounds of armor-piercing ammunition. One of these halted another T-34, which halted and caught fire. A crewman emerged from the turret firing a burp gun as he came. The Korean's first burst, before he was shot down, granted one of the gunners the unhappy distinction of becoming the first American soldier to die by enemy action in Korea. Lieutenant Day's recoilless rifle began to fire again, but its flash made it an easy target. An 85-mm tank shell disabled the gun and left Day reeling from the blast, blood pouring out of his ears. Between 7 A.M. and 9:30 some thirty North Korean tanks drove through Task Force Smith's "blocking position," killing or wounding some twenty of the defenders by shell and machine-gun fire. The Americans could think of nothing to do to stop them.

Around 11 A.M. a long column of trucks led by three more tanks appeared on the road from the north. They halted bumper to bumper and began to disgorge North Korean infantry who scattered east and west into the paddies beside the road. Some of the mustard-colored tunics began to advance steadily toward the Americans amid desultory mortar and small-arms fire. Others worked patiently toward the flanks. Since Task Force Smith occupied only a 400-yard front, and no other American infantry units were deployed for many miles behind them, it was immediately obvious that this action must eventually end in only one fashion. As the hours passed, Communist fire intensified and American casualties mounted. Colonel Smith called C Company's officers, west of the road, to the company CP. The entire force would now consolidate in a circular perimeter on the east side, he said. The 150 or so men of Charlie Company left their positions platoon by platoon, filed down to the road, clambered up among the scrub on the other side, and began to hack foxholes and fields of fire for themselves as best they could.

Smith's choices were not enviable. His unit was achieving very little where it stood. But if he chose to withdraw immediately from the position, put his men into their surviving trucks, and head south, sooner or later the column was likely to meet the Communist tanks that had gone before them. He would gain little, with his small force, by abandoning the high ground to launch a counterattack against the enemy infantry. Yet, if they remained in place, they could expect neither reinforcement nor relief. Here was an extraordinary situation. This was the year 1950, when vast economic wealth, possession of the atomic bomb, and the legacy of victory in the Second World War caused America to be perceived as the greatest power the world had ever seen, mightier than the Roman Empire at its zenith or the British a century before. Here, on a hill in Korea, the first representatives of United States military power to meet Communist aggression on the battlefield were the men of a mere understrength infantry battalion which now faced annihilation as a military unit. Not all the B-29s on the airfields of the United States, nor the army divisions in Europe, the fleets at sea from the Taiwan Strait to the Mediterranean, could mitigate the absolute loneliness and vulnerability of Task Force Smith. Those in Tokyo or Washington who supposed that the mere symbolic commitment of this token of American military might would suffice to frighten the North Koreans into retreat were confounded. Subsequent interrogation of North Korean officers suggested that the encounter between their 4th Division and Task Force Smith provided Pyongyang with its first inkling of American ground-force intervention, which had not been anticipated. Neither side on the Osan road was troubled by political implications.

The Communists were using mortars now, to some effect. American small-arms ammunition was growing short, as men stumbled up the slippery paths worn into the mud to the forward positions, dragging crates and steel boxes. Among the boulders below the position, the wounded lay in widening rows, the medics toiling among them, hampered by lack of whole blood. Captain Richard Dashner, the Texan World War II veteran commanding C Company, said abruptly to Major Martain, "We've got to get out of here." Lieutenant Berthoff, commanding Headquarter Company, agreed. At first, Smith said there would be no immediate pullback. But as the fire from the flanks intensified, he changed his mind. "I guess we'll have to," he told his officers. Then he added unhappily, "This is a decision I'll probably regret the rest of my days." C Company was to go first. Within minutes the first of its men were slipping down the rear of the position and into the paddy fields beyond, stumbling and cursing at the stench and the enemy fire. There was no question of escaping along the road, open and vulnerable to raking machine guns as far as the eye could see. They could only scramble through the fields, balancing precariously on the intervening dikes, down the farm tracks as fast and as best they could, until they met friendly forces.

It was during the withdrawal of Task Force Smith that its imperfections as a fighting unit became apparent. There is no more testing military maneuver than disengagement in the face of the enemy. The Americans were softened by years of inadequate training and military neglect, bewildered by the shock of combat, dismayed by the readiness with which the Communists had overwhelmed them, and the isolation in which they found themselves. As men saw others leaving the hills, they hastened to join them, fearful of being left behind. "It was every man for himself," said Lieutenant Day. "When we moved out, we began taking more and more casualties. . . . Guys fell around me. Mortar rounds hit here and there. One of my young guys got it in the middle. My platoon sergeant, Harvey Vann, ran over to him. I followed. 'No way he's gonna live, Lieutenant.' Oh, Jesus, the guy was moaning and groaning. There wasn't much I could do but pat him on the head and say, 'Hang in there.' Another of the platoon sergeants got it in the throat. He began spitting blood. I thought he had had it for sure . . . For the rest of the day he held his throat together with his hand. He survived, too."[3] The retreating Americans abandoned arms, equipment, sometimes even helmets, boots, personal weapons. Cohesion quickly vanished. The debris of retreat lay strewn behind them as they went. In ones and twos and handfuls, they scrambled southward through the fields.

C Company, first off the positions, fared better than B in holding its men together. Captain Dashner reached Taejon after two days' hard marching with more than half his men still under command. Floyd Martain and the little team in the battalion command post struggled to burn their confidential papers, but found them too wet to catch fire. They dug a hole and buried them, then started walking, following the railroad tracks south. After some hours, Martain's little group saw some trucks and hastily took cover. Then, to their overwhelming relief, they found that these were American vehicles carrying some gunners—who had blown up their pieces rather than attempt to get them out, an action which infuriated some officers—and Colonel Smith himself. After a night of nerve-racking hide-and-seek with enemy tanks as they crossed country, they reached positions of the 34th Infantry at Ansong.

Corporal Robert Fountain never heard any order to withdraw—he simply saw men streaming past him who glanced an answer to his shouted question about what was happening: "We're pulling back." Fountain joined them. He scrambled past an American sitting upright against a dike wall, stone dead. Suddenly he found himself face-to-face with two baled-out North Korean tank crewmen. The next man shot one, Fountain killed the other as he ran toward a house. Then the American stumbled away through the waterlogged paddies amid machine-gun fire from the positions the battalion had abandoned. In a wood, he met a group of sixteen other Americans. He took out a knife and cut off the tops of his combat boots so that he could get the water out. Two sergeants organized the group. They set off again, attempting to carry the wounded among them. One man, a Japanese-American, was shot in the stomach. When they reached a deserted village, they left him there, dying. Fountain found a turnip root and ate it. They walked on through the darkness for many hours, following a group of South Korean soldiers they encountered. They reached a Korean command post in a schoolhouse where they slept for a while. Then somebody shouted, "Tanks coming!" They piled into a truck and drove for some miles until the truck blundered into a ditch and stayed there. They began walking again, and eventually found themselves in the lines of the 34th Infantry.

Lieutenant Carl Bernard was still on the hill with his platoon of B Company when he sensed the fire from the other American positions slackening and sent a runner to find out what was going on. The man returned a few minutes later in some consternation to report, "They've all gone!" Command and control frankly collapsed in the last stages of the action. Bernard, wounded in face and hands by grenade fragments, hastily led his men to beat their own retreat. At the base of the hill they found the medical orderlies still coping with a large group of wounded. They took with them such men as could walk, and left the remainder to be taken prisoner. The lieutenant divided the survivors of his platoon into two groups, sending one with a private soldier who had been a scout and taking the other himself. He had no compass, but in an abandoned schoolhouse he found a child's atlas. He tore out the page showing Korea and used it to navigate. In the hours that followed, his group survived a series of close encounters with enemy tanks. Bernard bartered a gold Longines watch that he had won playing poker on the boat from San Francisco for an old Korean's handcart on which to push a wounded NCO.

Ezra Burke came off the hill with four of his medical team, two stretcher cases, and one walking wounded. As they staggered onward with their burdens, they kept halting and glancing back, hoping to have outdistanced their pursuers.

But all that afternoon they could see files of North Koreans padding remorsefully behind them. At last, they decided to split. Burke headed southwestward with two others. They were soaking wet, exhausted, and above all desperately anxious to be reunited with their unit and their officers, with anyone who could tell them where to go and what to do. They huddled miserably together through the hours of darkness, and at first light began to walk again. On a hill above Pyontaek, they met Lieutenant Bernard and his seven-strong group and continued south with them. Thenceforward, they hid most of the day and walked by night. Starving, they risked creeping into a village and bartering possessions with a mama-san for a few potatoes. They met two Korean soldiers with whom they walked for a time. Then a South Korean lieutenant who talked to them declared his conviction that the men were Communists. The two ran off across a rice paddy. Burke fired at them with a carbine and missed. Bernard caught them with a BAR just before they reached a wood.

They reached American positions on July 10, five days after the battle at Osan, utterly exhausted, their feet agonizingly swollen. The next day Burke was found to be suffering from a kidney stone and was evacuated by air from Taejon to Osaka. Carl Bernard spent some painful hours in a field hospital, where the grenade fragments were picked out of his face and hands. Then he slept the sleep of utter exhaustion for an entire day.

Most of Task Force Smith trickled back to American positions in something like this fashion in the week that followed their little action at Osan. After the battle 185 men of the battalion mustered. Some, like Sergeant William F. Smith, who escaped by fishing boat a fortnight later, made their way to the American lines after epic adventures. Lieutenant Connors received a Silver Star for his brave endeavors with the bazooka by the roadside on July 5. The official figures showed that Task Force Smith had suffered 155 casualties in the action at Osan. By the time they returned, they discovered that any shortcomings in their own unit's performance on July 5 had already been outstripped by far less honorable, indeed positively shameful, humiliations suffered by other elements of the American 24th Division in its first days of war, as the North Korean invaders swept all before them on their bloody procession south down the peninsula. And all this flowed, inexorably, from the sudden decision of the United States to commit itself to the least expected of wars, in the least predicted of places, under the most unfavorable possible military conditions. Had the men of Task Force Smith, on the road south of Suwon, known that they were striking the first armed blow for that new force in world order, the United Nations, it might have made their confused, unhappy, almost pathetic little battle on July 5 seem more dignified. On the other hand, it might have made it appear more incomprehensible than ever.

1

ORIGINS OF A TRAGEDY

Seldom in the course of history has a nation been so rapidly propelled from obscurity to a central place in the world's affairs as Korea. The first significant contact between "The Land of the Morning Calm" and the West took place one morning in September 1945 when an advance party of the American Army, in full battle gear, landed at the western harbor of Inchon, to be met by a delegation of Japanese officials in top hats and tailcoats. This was the inauguration of Operation "Black List Forty," the United States' occupation of South Korea.

These first American officers found the city of Inchon, fearful and uncertain of its future, shuttered and closed. After a hunt through the streets, glimpsing occasional faces peering curiously at their liberators from windows and corners, they came upon a solitary Chinese restaurant bearing the sign "Welcome U.S." Then, from the moment the Americans boarded the train for Seoul, they met uninhibited rejoicing. A little crowd of Koreans waving gleeful flags stood by the tracks in every village they passed. At Seoul railway station, the group had planned to take a truck to their objective, the city post office. Instead, on their arrival, they decided to walk. To their bewilderment, they found themselves at the center of a vast throng of cheering, milling, exultant Koreans, cramming the streets and sidewalks, hanging from buildings, standing on carts. The Americans were at a loss. They had arrived without any conception of what the end of the Japanese war meant to the people of this obscure peninsula.[1]

23

Throughout its history until the end of the nineteenth century, Korea was an overwhelmingly rural society which sought successfully to maintain its isolation from the outside world. Ruled since 1392 by the Yi Dynasty, it suffered two major invasions from Japan in the sixteenth century. When the Japanese departed, Korea returned to its harsh traditional existence, frozen in winter and baked in summer, its ruling families feuding among each other from generation to generation. By the Confucian convention that regarded foreign policy as an extension of family relations, Korea admitted an historic loyalty to China, "the elder brother nation." Until 1876 her near neighbor Japan was regarded as a friendly equal. But early that January, in an early surge of the expansionism that was to dominate Japanese history for the next seventy years, Tokyo dispatched a military expedition to Korea "to establish a treaty of friendship and commerce." On February 26, after a brief and ineffectual resistance, the Koreans signed. They granted the Japanese open ports, their citizens extraterritorial rights.

The embittered Koreans sought advice from their other neighbors about the best means of undoing this humiliating surrender. The Chinese advised that they should come to an arrangement with one of the Western powers "in order to check the poison with an antidote." They suggested the Americans, who had shown no signs of possessing territorial ambitions on the Asian mainland. On May 22, 1882, Korea signed a treaty of "amity and commerce" with the United States. In the words of a leading American historian of the period, this "set Korea adrift on an ocean of intrigue which it was quite helpless to control." The infuriated Japanese now engaged themselves increasingly closely in Korea's internal power struggles. The British took an interest, for they were eager to maintain China's standing as Korea's "elder brother" to counter Russian influence in the Far East. By 1893, Korea had signed a succession of trade treaties with every major European power. The Japanese were perfectly clear about their objective. Their Foreign Minister declared openly that Korea "should be made a part of the Japanese map." Tokyo hesitated only about how to achieve this without a confrontation with one or another great power.

The Chinese solved the problem. Peking's increasingly heavy-handed meddling in Korea's affairs, asserting claims to some measure of authority over Seoul, provoked a wave of anti-Chinese feeling and a corresponding surge of enthusiasm for the Japanese, who could now claim popular support from at least a faction within Korea. In 1894, Japan seized her opportunity and landed an army in Korea to force the issue. The government in Seoul, confused and panicky, asked Peking to send its own troops to help suppress a rebellion. The Japanese responded by dispatching a contingent of marines direct to the capital. The Korean government, by now hopelessly out of its depth, begged that all the foreign troops should depart. But the Japanese scented victory. They reinforced their army.

The last years of Korea's national independence took on a Gilbertian absurdity. The nation's leaders, artless in the business of diplomacy and modern power politics, squirmed and floundered in the net that was inexorably closing around them. The Chinese recognized their military inability to confront the Japanese in Korea. Tokyo's grasp on Korea's internal government tightened until, in 1896, the King tried to escape thralldom by taking refuge at the Russian Legation in Seoul. From this sanctuary he issued orders for the execution of all his pro-Japanese ministers. The Japanese temporarily backed down.

In the next seven years Moscow and Tokyo competed for power and concessions in Seoul. The devastating Japanese victory at Tsushima, a few miles off Pusan, decided the outcome. In February 1904 the Japanese moved a large army into Korea. In November of the following year the nation became a Japanese protectorate. In a characteristic exercise of the colonial cynicism of the period, the British accepted Japanese support for their rule in India in exchange for blessing Tokyo's takeover of Korea. Whitehall acknowledged Japan's right "to take such measure of guidance, control, and protection in Corea [sic] as she may deem proper and necessary" to promote her "paramount political, military and economic interests."

Korean independence thus became a dead letter. In the years that followed a steady stream of Japanese officials and immigrants moved into the country. Japanese education, roads, railways, sanitation were introduced. Yet none of these gained the slightest gratitude from the fiercely nationalistic Koreans. Armed resistance grew steadily in the hands of a strange alliance of Confucian scholars, traditional bandits, Christians, and peasants with local grievances against the colonial power. The anti-Japanese guerrilla army rose to a peak of an estimated 70,000 men in 1908. Thereafter, ruthless Japanese repression broke it down. Korea became an armed camp, in which mass executions and wholesale imprisonments were commonplace and all dissent forbidden. On August 22, 1910, the Korean emperor signed away all his rights of sovereignty. The Japanese introduced their own titles of nobility and imposed their own military government. For the next thirty-five years, despite persistent armed resistance from mountain bands of nationalists, many of them Communist, the Japanese maintained their ruthless, detested rule in Korea, which also became an important base for their expansion north into Manchuria in the 1930s.

Yet despite the decline of China into a society of competing warlords, and the preoccupation of Russia with her own revolution, even before the Second World War it was apparent that Korea's geographical position, as the nearest meeting place of three great nations, would make her a permanent focus of tension and competition. The American Tyler Dennett wrote presciently in 1945, months before the Far Eastern war ended:

"Many of the international factors which led to the fall of Korea are either unchanged from what they were half a century ago, or are likely to recur the moment peace is restored to the East. Japan's hunger for power will have been extinguished for a period, but not forever. In another generation probably Japan will again be a very important influence in the Pacific. Meanwhile the Russian interest in the peninsula is likely to remain what it was forty years ago. Quite possibly that factor will be more important than ever before. The Chinese also may be expected to continue their traditional concern in the affairs of that area."[2]

And now, suddenly, the war was over, and the Japanese Empire was in the hands of the broker's men. Koreans found themselves freed from Japanese domination, looking for fulfillment of the promise of the leaders of the Grand Alliance in the 1943 Cairo Declaration—that Korea should become free and independent "in due course."

The American decision to land troops to play a part in the occupation of Korea was taken only at the very end of the war. The Japanese colony had been excluded from the complex 1943–45 negotiations about occupation zones between the partners of the Grand Alliance. The Americans had always been enamored of the concept of "trusteeship" for Korea, along with Indochina and some other colonial possessions in the Far East. They liked the idea of a period during which a committee of Great Powers—in this case, China, the U.S., and the U.S.S.R.—would "prepare and educate" the dependent peoples for self-government and "protect them from exploitation." This concept never found much favor among the British or French, mindful of their own empires. And as the war progressed, concern about the future internal structure of Korea was overtaken by deepening alarm about the external forces that might determine this. As early as November 1943 a State Department subcommittee expressed fears that when the Soviets entered the Far East war, they might seize the opportunity to include Korea in their sphere of influence: "Korea may appear to offer a tempting opportunity to apply the Soviet conception of the proper treatment of colonial peoples, to strengthen enormously the economic resources of the Soviet Far East, to acquire ice-free ports, and to occupy a dominating strategic position in relation both to China and to Japan. . . . A Soviet occupation of Korea would create an entirely new strategic situation in the Far East, and its repercussions within China and Japan might be far reaching."[3]

As the American historian Bruce Cumings has aptly pointed out, "What created 'an entirely new strategic situation in the Far East' was not that Russia was interested in Korea—it had been for decades—but that the United States was interested."[4] Yet by the time of the Potsdam Conference of July 1945, the United States military was overwhelmingly preoccupied with the perceived difficulties of mounting an invasion of mainland Japan. They regarded the Japanese armies still deployed in Korea and Manchuria as a tough nut for the Red Army to crack and were only too happy to leave the problem, and the expected casualties, to the Russians. The Pentagon had anyway adopted a consistent view that Korea was of no long-term strategic interest to the United States.

Yet three weeks later the American perception of Korea had altered dramatically. The explosion of the two atomic bombs on Japan on August 6 and 9 brought Japan to the brink of surrender. The Red Army was sweeping through Manchuria without meeting important resistance. Suddenly, Washington's view of both the desirability and feasibility of denying at least a substantial part of Korea to the Soviets was transformed. Late on the night of August 10, 1945, barely twenty-four hours after the dropping of the Nagasaki bomb, the State-War-Navy Coordinating Committee reached a hasty, unilateral decision that the United States should participate in the occupation of Korea. The two officers drafting orders for the committee pored over their small-scale wall map of the Far East and observed that the 38th Parallel ran broadly across the middle of the country. South of this line lay the capital, the best of the agriculture and light industry, and more than half the population. Some members of the committee—including Dean Rusk, a future Secretary of State—pointed out that if the Russians chose to reject this proposal, the Red Army sweeping south through Manchuria could overrun all Korea before the first GI could be landed at Inchon. In these weeks, when the first uncertain skirmishes of the Cold War were being fought, the sudden American proposal for the divided occupation of Korea represented an important test of Soviet intentions in the Far East.

To the relief of the committee in Washington, the Russians readily accepted the 38th Parallel as the limit of their advance. Almost a month before the first Americans could be landed in South Korea, the Red Army reached the new divide—and halted there. It is worth remarking that, if Moscow had declined the American plan and occupied all Korea, it is unlikely that the Americans could or would have forced a major diplomatic issue. To neither side, at this period, did the peninsula seem to possess any inherent value, except as a testing ground of mutual intentions. The struggle for political control of China herself was beginning in earnest. Beside the fates and boundaries of great nations that were now being decided, Korea counted for little. Stalin was content to settle for half. At no time in the five years that followed did the Russians show any desire to stake Moscow's power and prestige upon a direct contest with the Americans for the extension of Soviet influence south of the Parallel.

Thus it was, late in August 1945, that the unhappy men of the U.S. XXIV Corps—some veterans of months of desperate fighting in the Pacific, others green replacements fresh from training camps—found themselves under orders to embark not for home, as they so desperately wished, but for unknown Korea. They were given little information to guide their behavior once they got there. Their commander, General John R. Hodge, received only a confusing succession of signals at his headquarters on Okinawa. On August 14, General Stilwell told him that the occupation could be considered "semifriendly"—in other words, that he need regard as hostile only a small minority of collaborators. At the end of the month the Supreme Commander, General MacArthur himself, decreed that the

Koreans should be treated as "liberated people." From Washington the Secretary of State for War and the Navy Coordinating Committee dispatched a hasty directive to Okinawa ordering Hodge to "create a government in harmony with U.S. policies." But what were U.S. policies toward Korea? Since the State Department knew little more about the country than that its Nationalists hungered for unity and independence, they had little to tell Hodge. As a straightforward military man, the general determined to approach the problem in a straightforward, no-nonsense fashion. On September 4 he briefed his own officers to regard Korea as "an enemy of the United States," subject to the terms of the Japanese surrender. On September 8, when the American occupation convoy was still twenty miles out from Inchon in the Yellow Sea, its ships encountered three neatly dressed figures in a small boat who presented themselves to the general as representatives of "the Korean government." Hodge sent them packing. He did likewise with every other Korean he met on his arrival who laid claim to a political mandate. The XXIV Corps' intention was to seize and maintain control of the country. The U.S. Army, understandably, wished to avoid precipitate entanglement with any of the scores of competing local political factions who already, in those first days, were struggling to build a power base amid the ruin of the Japanese empire.

The fourteen-strong advance party who were the first Americans to reach Seoul were fascinated and bemused by what they found: a city of horse-drawn carts, with only the occasional charcoal-powered motor vehicle. They saw three Europeans in a shop and hastened to greet them, only to discover that they were part of the little local Turkish community, who spoke no English. They met White Russians, refugees in Korea since 1920, who demanded somewhat tactlessly, *"Sprechen sie Deutsch?"* The first English-speaker they met was a local Japanese who had lived in the United States before the war. His wife, like all the Japanese community, eager to ingratiate herself with the new rulers, pressed on them a cake and two pounds of real butter—the first they had seen for months. That night they slept on the floor of Seoul Post Office. The next morning they transferred their headquarters to the Banda Hotel.[5]

In the days that followed the major units of XXIV Corps disembarked at Inchon, and dispersed by truck and train around the country, to take up positions from Pusan to the 38th Parallel. General Hodge and his staff were initially bewildered by the clamor of unknown Koreans competing for their political attention and by the disorders in the provinces, which threatened to escalate into serious rioting if the situation was not controlled. There was also the difficulty that no Korean they encountered appeared to speak English, and the only Korean-speaker on the staff, Commander Williams of the U.S. Navy, was insufficiently fluent to conduct negotiations.

Amid all this confusion and uncertainty, the occupiers could identify only one local stabilizing force upon whom they could rely: the Japanese. In those first days the Japanese made themselves indispensable to Hodge and his men. One of the American commander's first acts was to confirm Japanese colonial officials in their positions, for the time being. Japanese remained the principal language of communication. Japanese soldiers and police retained chief responsibility for maintaining law and order. As early as September 11, MacArthur signaled instructions to Hodge that Japanese officials must at once be removed from office. But even when this process began to take place, many retained their influence for weeks as unofficial advisers to the Americans.

Within days of that first euphoric encounter between the liberators and the liberated, patriotic Koreans were affronted by the open camaraderie between Japanese and American officers, the respect shown by former enemies to each other, in contrast to the thinly veiled contempt offered to the Koreans. "It does seem that from the beginning many Americans simply liked the Japanese better than the Koreans," the foremost American historian of this period has written. "The Japanese were viewed as cooperative, orderly and docile, while the Koreans were seen as headstrong, unruly, and obstreperous."[6] The Americans knew nothing—or chose to ignore what they did know—of the ruthless behavior of the Japanese in the three weeks between their official surrender and the coming of XXIV Corps—the looting of warehouses, the systematic ruin of the economy by printing debased currency, the sale of every available immovable asset.

To a later generation, familiar with the dreadful brutality of the Japanese in the Second World War, it may seem extraordinary that Americans could so readily make common cause with their late enemies—as strange as the conduct of Allied intelligence organizations in Europe, which befriended and recruited former Nazi war criminals and Gestapo agents. Yet the strongest influence of war upon most of those who endure it is to blur their belief in absolute moral values and to foster a sense of common experience with those who have shared it, even a barbarous enemy. There was a vast sense of relief among the men of the armies who still survived in 1945, an instinctive reluctance for more killing, even in the cause of just revenge. There was also a rapidly growing suspicion among some prominent American soldiers—Patton notable among them—that they might have been fighting the wrong enemy for these four years. McCarthyism was yet unborn. But a sense of the evil of communism was very strong and already outweighed in the minds of some men their revulsion toward Nazism or Japanese imperialism. In Tokyo the American Supreme Commander himself was already setting an extraordinary pattern of postwar reconciliation with the defeated enemy. In Seoul in the autumn of 1945, General Hodge and his colleagues found it much more comfortable to deal with the impeccable correctness of fellow soldiers, albeit recent enemies, than with the anarchic rivalries of the Koreans. The senior officers of XXIV Corps possessed no training or expertise of any kind for exercising civilian government—they were merely professional military men, obliged to improvise as they went along. In the light of subsequent events, their blunders and political clumsiness have attracted the unfavorable attention of history. But it is only just to observe that at this period many of the same mistakes were being made by their counterparts in Allied armies all over the world.

"South Korea can best be described as a powder keg ready to explode at the application of a spark," Hodge's State Department political adviser H. Merell Benninghoff reported to Washington on September 15. "There is great disappointment that immediate independence and sweeping out of the Japanese did not eventuate. Although the hatred of the Koreans for the Japanese is unbelievably bitter, it is not thought that they will resort to violence as long as American troops are in surveillance. . . . The removal of Japanese officials is desirable from the public opinion standpoint, but difficult to bring about for some time. They can be relieved in name but must be made to continue in work. There are no qualified Koreans for other than the low-ranking positions, either in government or in public utilities and communications."[7]

The pressures upon the Americans in Korea to dispense with the aid of their newfound Japanese allies became irresistible. In four months 70,000 Japanese colonial civil servants and more than 600,000 Japanese soldiers and civilians were shipped home to their own islands. Many were compelled to abandon homes, factories, possessions. Yet the damage to American relations with the Koreans was already done. Lieutenant Ferris Miller, U.S. Navy, who had been one of the first Americans to land in the country, and subsequently enjoyed a lifelong association with Korea, said, "Our misunderstanding of local feelings about the Japanese, and our own close association with them, was one of the most expensive mistakes we ever made there."[8]

In the months that followed the expulsion of the Japanese, the Koreans who replaced them as agents of the American military government were, for the most part, long-serving collaborators, detested by their own fellow countrymen for their service to the colonial power. A ranking American of the period wrote later of his colleagues' "abysmal ignorance of Korea and things Korean, the inelasticity of the military bureaucracy and the avoidance of it by the few highly qualified Koreans, who could afford neither to be associated with such an unpopular government, nor to work for the low wages it offered."[9]

Before their enforced departure, the Japanese had been at pains to alert the Americans to the pervasive influence of communism among South Korea's embryo political groupings. Their warnings fell upon fertile soil. In the light of events in Europe, the occupiers were entirely ready to believe that Communists were at the root of political disturbances, their cells working energetically to seize control of the country. Benninghoff reported, "Communists advocate the seizure *now* of Japanese properties and may be a threat to law and order. It is probable that well-trained agitators are attempting to bring about chaos in our area so as to cause the Koreans to repudiate the United States in favor of Soviet 'freedom' and control.''[10]

The principal losers in the political competition that now developed, to discover which Koreans could prove themselves most hostile to communism and most sympathetic to the ideals of the United States, were the members of the so-called Korean People's Republic, the KPR. In Korea in 1945 the phrase ''people's republic'' had not yet taken on the pejorative association it would so soon acquire. The KPR was a grouping of nationalists and prominent members of the anti-Japanese resistance who, before the Americans arrived, sought to make themselves a credible future leadership for Korea. More than half of the eighty-seven leaders chosen by a several-hundred-strong assembly at Kyonggi Girls' High School on September 6 had served terms of imprisonment under the Japanese. At least half also could be identified as leftists or Communists. But prominent exiles such as Syngman Rhee, Mu Chong, Kim Ku, and Kim Il Sung were granted places in absentia, though few subsequently accepted the roles for which they had been chosen. It is significant that the men of the right nominated to the KPR leadership were, on average, almost twenty years older than those of the left.

It was not surprising that the Americans, on their arrival, knew nothing of the KPR. The chaotic struggle to fill the political vacuum in Korea was further confused by the arrival from Chungking of the self-proclaimed Korean Provisional Government, an exile grouping which included some nominated members of the KPR. In the weeks that followed the military government's skepticism about the KPR—energetically fostered by the Japanese—grew apace. Here there was more than a little in common with Western attitudes to Ho Chi Minh and his colleagues in Vietnam of the same period. There was no attempt to examine closely the Communist ideology of the leftists, to discover how far they were the creatures of Moscow and how far they were merely vague Socialists and Nationalists who found traditional landlordism repugnant. No allowance was made for the prestige earned by the Communists' dominant role in armed resistance to the Japanese. Hodge and his men saw no merit in the KPR's militant sense of Korean nationalism—this merely represented an obstacle to smooth American military government. It would be naive to suppose that such a grouping as the KPR could have formed an instantly harmonious leadership for an independent Korea. The group included too many irreconcilable factions. But it also represented the only genuine cross section of Korean nationalist opinion ever to come together under one roof, however briefly. Given time and encouragement, it might have offered South Korea some prospect of building a genuine democracy.

But the strident tones in which the KPR addressed the American military government ensured that the group was rapidly identified as a threat and a problem. "There is evidence [wrote Benninghoff on October 10] that the [KPR] group receives support and direction from the Soviet Union [perhaps from Koreans formerly resident in Siberia]. In any event, it is the most aggressive party; its newspaper has compared American methods of occupation [with those of the Russians] in a manner that may be interpreted as unfavorable to the United States."[11]

It was another group, which could call upon only a fraction of the KPR's likely political support, that seemed infinitely more congenial to Hodge and his advisers: ". . . the so-called democratic or conservative group, which numbers among its members many of the professional and educational leaders who were educated in the United States or in American missionary institutions in Korea. In their aims and policies they demonstrate a desire to follow the western democracies, and they almost unanimously desire the early return of Dr. Syngman Rhee and the 'Provisional Government' at Chungking."[12] Barely three weeks after the American landings in Korea, official thinking in Seoul was already focusing upon the creation of a new government for the South around the person of one of the nation's most prominent exiles.

Syngman Rhee was born in 1875, the son of a genealogical scholar. He failed the civil service exams several times before becoming a student of English. Between 1899 and 1904 he was imprisoned for political activities. On his release, he went to the United States, where he studied for some years, earning an M.A. at Harvard and a Ph.D. at Princeton—the first Korean to receive an American doctorate. After a brief return to his homeland in 1910, Rhee once more settled in America. He remained there for the next thirty-five years, lobbying relentlessly for American support for Korean independence, financed by the contributions of Korean patriots. If he was despised by some of his fellow countrymen for his egoism, his ceaseless self-promotion, his absence from the armed struggle that engaged other courageous nationalists, his extraordinary determination and patriotism could not be denied. His iron will was exerted as ruthlessly against rival factions of expatriates as against colonial occupation. He could boast an element of prescience in his own world vision. As early as 1944, when the United States government still cherished all manner of delusions about the postwar prospect of working harmoniously with Stalin, Rhee was telling officials in Washington, "The only possibility of avoiding the ultimate conflict between the United States and the Soviet Union is to build up all democratic, non-communistic elements wherever possible."[13]

Rhee had gained one great advantage by his absence from his own country for so long. Many of his rivals disliked each other as much as the Japanese. But against Rhee, little of substance was known. He was free from the taint of collaboration. While the Americans struggled to come to terms with a culture and a society that were alien to them, Rhee was a comfortingly comprehensible figure:

fluent in the small talk of democracy, able to converse about America and American institutions with easy familiarity, above all at home in the English language. Rhee was acerbic, prickly, uncompromising. But to Hodge and his advisers this obsessive, ruthless nationalist and anti-Communist seemed a plausible father figure for the new Korea. On October 20 the general was present at an official welcoming ceremony for the Americans in Seoul, stage-managed by the so-called Korean Democratic Party, the KDP—in reality a highly conservative grouping. On the platform stood a large ebony screen inlaid with mother-of-pearl. In a grand moment of theater, the screen was pulled aside. The bony, venerable figure of Dr. Syngman Rhee was revealed to the Korean people. The crowd cheered uproariously. Rhee delivered a rousingly anti-Soviet speech, and disconcerted even his sponsors by denouncing American complicity in the Soviet occupation of the North. The doctor was triumphantly launched upon his career as South Korea's most celebrated—or notorious—politician.

Overwhelmingly the strongest card that Rhee possessed was the visible support of the Americans. Roger Makins, a senior official in the British Foreign Office throughout the early Cold War period, remarks upon "the American propensity to go for a man, rather than a movement—Giraud among the French in 1942, Chiang Kai Shek in China. Americans have always liked the idea of dealing with a foreign leader who can be identified and perceived as 'their man.' They are much less comfortable with movements."[14] So it was in Korea with Syngman Rhee.

In an Asian society, where politics are often dominated by an instinctive desire to fall in behind the strongest force, Rhee's backing from the Military Government was a decisive force in his rise to power. When Benninghoff identified Rhee with the Korean "Provisional Government" in Chungking, he blithely ignored the open hostility between the two that had persisted for twenty years, despite Rhee's continuing claim to be the "Provisional Government's" representative in Washington. The State Department, with long and close experience of Rhee, regarded him as a dangerous mischief-maker. There is no murkier episode in the history of the American occupation than the return of Rhee to Seoul. The Military Government firmly denied not only complicity but prior knowledge of this. Yet all the evidence now suggests that General Hodge and his staff participated in a carefully orchestrated conspiracy to bring back Rhee, despite the refusal of the State Department to grant him a passport. A former deputy director of the wartime OSS, Preston Goodfellow, prevailed upon the State Department to provide Rhee with documentation. There appears to have been at least a measure of corruption in this transaction. Rhee got to know Goodfellow during the war, when the Korean mendaciously suggested to the American that he could provide agents for operations behind the Japanese lines. After the war it seems almost certain that Goodfellow assisted and raised money for Rhee in return

for the promise of commercial concessions in Korea when the doctor gained
power. Rhee flew to Seoul in one of MacArthur's aircraft. Despite the vigorous
denials of the U.S. Army in the Far East, it seems likely that he met secretly with
both the Supreme Commander and Hodge during his stopover in Tokyo. Rhee, it
is apparent, was their nominee for the leadership of a Korean civilian government.

Why did not Washington, undeluded about Rhee's shortcomings, simply call
a halt to the policies being pursued in Seoul? John Carter Vincent, director of the
State Department's Office of Far Eastern Affairs, indeed sought to remind the War
Department that the United States was seeking to avoid taking sides, far less
promoting factions, in Korean politics. But his memorandum of November 7 on
these issues provoked a response from John J. McCloy, the Assistant Secretary of
War, which goes as far as any document of the period to explain the course of
events in postwar Korea.

"Vincent's memorandum [wrote McCloy] seems to me to avoid in large part
the really pressing realities facing us in Korea. . . . From talking with General
Hodge I believe that his concern is that the Communists will seize by direct means
the government in our area. If this were done, it would seriously prejudice our
intention to permit the people of Korea freely to choose their own form of
government. There is no question but that Communist action is actively and
intelligently being carried out through our zone. . . . It would seem that the best
way to approach it in the overall is to build up on our own a reasonable and
respectable government or group of advisers which will be able under General
Hodge to bring some order out of the political, social, and economic chaos that
now exist south of the 38th Parallel and so provide the basis for, at some later date,
a really free and uncoerced election by the people. . . . To get back to Vincent's
memorandum—does it not add up to asking us to tell Hodge that we really repose
little confidence in him, that we are not prepared to let him do the few things
which, on the spot—and what a spot—he feels can be useful towards achieving
our aims? Let us ask for his views on the Communist problem and his thoughts as
to how to keep it from wrecking our objectives, but let us also let him use as many
exiled Koreans as he can, depending on his discretion not to go too far."[15]

The essence of McCloy's argument, which would serve as the justification for
all that was done in Korea in the three years that followed, was that it was an
idealistic fantasy to suppose that the United States could merely hold the ring,
serve as neutral umpires while Koreans worked out their own destiny. Some
Korean leaders must be singled out from the mob of contending factions and
assisted to win and retain power. It must surely be the men on the spot, Hodge and
his staff, who were best qualified to decide which Koreans these should be. The
American military rulers employed no further deceits to dignify the process by
which they now set about installing a congenial regime. Just as the Russians, at
this period, were securing control of North Korea for a Communist regime, so the

only credentials that the Americans sought to establish for the prospective masters of South Korea were their hostility to communism and willingness to do business with the Americans. If this appears a simplistic view of American policy, the policy itself could scarcely have been less subtle.

In October 1945 the Americans created an eleven-man Korean "Advisory Council" to their military governor, Major General Arnold. Although the membership purported to be representative of the South Korean political spectrum, in reality only one nominee, Yo Un-hyong, was a man of the Left. Yo initially declined to have anything to do with the Council, declaring contemptuously that its very creation "reverses the fact of who is guest and who is host in Korea." Then, having succumbed to Hodge's personal request to participate, Yo took one look around the room at the Council's first session and swept out. He later asked Hodge if the American believed that a group which included only one nonconservative could possibly be considered representative of anything. An eleventh nominated member, a well-known Nationalist named Cho Man-sik, who had been working in the North, never troubled to show his face.

The Council was doomed from the outset. It reminded most Koreans far too vividly of their recent colonial experience—its chairman had been a member of the Japanese governor-general's advisory body and an enthusiastic supporter of the Japanese war effort. Yet Yo Un-hyong's "unhelpful" behavior, contrasted with the "cooperative" attitude of the conservatives who joined the Council, reinforced the American conviction that the conservatives—above all, the members of the Korean Democratic Party—were the men to work with. But what now was to be done about the reality in the countryside—that reports reaching Hodge declared that while the KPR was "organized into a government at all levels," the KDP was "poorly organized or unorganized in most places?"[16]

Hodge's answer was that the KPR must be fought and destroyed to provide the KDP with the opportunity for survival and growth. On November 10, as a warning to the Korean press, the most prominent Seoul newspaper sympathetic to the KPR was shut down, ostensibly for accountancy irregularities. On November 25, Hodge cabled MacArthur about his intention to denounce the KPR: "This will constitute in effect a 'declaration of war' upon the Communistic elements in Korea, and may result in temporary disorders. It will also bring charges of political discrimination in a 'free' country, both by local pinkos and by pinko press. If activities of the Korean People's Republic continue as in the past, they will greatly delay time when Korea can be said to be ready for independence. Request comment." MacArthur answered simply, like McCloy before him, confirming Hodge's absolute discretion: "Use your own best judgement. . . . I am not sufficiently familiar with the local situation to advise you intelligently, but I will support whatever decision you may take in this matter."[17]

Throughout the winter of 1945–46 the Military Government waged a campaign to suppress both the KPR and resurgent labor unions, which were adjudged an inevitable focus of Communist subversion. And even as this struggle was taking place, a new controversy was growing in intensity. In a fit of benevolent reforming zeal after their arrival, the Americans greatly eased the burdensome conditions of landholding for the peasants—a highly popular measure—and also introduced a free market in rice. The traditional rice surplus was the strong point of the Korean economy. Now, suddenly, by a measure introduced with the best of intentions, the Americans unleashed a wave of speculation, hoarding, and profiteering on a scale the country had never seen. The price of a bushel of rice soared from 9.4 yen in September 1945 to 2,800 yen just a year later. Officials were making vast fortunes through rice smuggling and speculation. By February 1946, not only was the free market rescinded, but stringent rationing had been introduced. Tough quotas were introduced for peasant farmers to fulfill, enforced by local police and officials.

In the winter of 1945 the Americans ruling South Korea harbored no delusions that they had made much progress toward creating an ordered and democratic society. They understood that they presided over a seething, unhappy country ripe for major disorders. They saw that Koreans' hunger for unity and independence surpassed all other ideology and sentiment. They perceived that the drifting policies of the military government, contrasted with the coherent if ruthless socialization now taking place north of the 38th Parallel, could only increase Korean respect for Soviet strength and diminish still further American popularity. On December 16, Hodge submitted a grim report to MacArthur in Tokyo, which subsequently reached the desk of President Truman. His summary of the situation he faced concluded, "Under present conditions with no corrective action forthcoming, I would go so far as to recommend we give serious consideration to an agreement with Russia that both the U.S. and Russia withdraw forces from Korea simultaneously and leave Korea to its own devices and an inevitable internal upheaval for its self-purification."[18]

Hodge and his colleagues placed the overwhelming burden of blame for their difficulties upon the Russians: Soviet-directed internal policies in the North and skillful subversion in the South. The Americans detected the organizing hand of Moscow in a host of political groups in South Korea. In this they greatly overestimated both Soviet will and capability in the South at this period. There is no doubt that Communists throughout Korea wished to create a united nation under their own control. But many non-Communist Koreans also incurred American animosity by their enthusiasm for national unification, merely because Hodge and his colleagues considered this unattainable under non-Communist rule. The U.S. military government in Korea—like its counterparts in other areas of the world at this period—dismissed the possibility that its own manipulation of conservative forces in a society was comparable, morally and politically, with the

Soviets' sponsorship of Communist groups in their own zone. Western historians support the ultimate benevolence of American influence upon the postwar political settlement in the developed societies that came under their control, above all, those in Europe. But in Korea, as in other less-developed nations, it was infinitely less easy to discover any prospective anti-Communist leadership possessed of the political maturity, the commitment to tolerable moral and political standards, which would render it truly worthy of the support of the United States.

On December 27, 1945, the Three-Power Foreign Ministers' Conference ended in Moscow with an important agreement. The Russians had accepted an American proposal for Korea: the nation was to become the object of a Four-Power "International Trusteeship" for five years, paving the way to independence as a unified state. Four-Power Trusteeship represented a concession by Moscow, cramping immediate progress toward a Communist state in Korea. The Russians probably anticipated that the Left in Korea was sufficiently strong to ensure its own ultimate triumph under any arrangement. But the Moscow Accords also reflected the low priority that Stalin gave to Korea. He was willing to appease Western fears in the Far East, no doubt in the expectation that in return Washington would less vigorously oppose Soviet policies in Europe.

In the weeks that followed the Moscow meeting, there was political turmoil in South Korea. Right-wing factions expressed their passionate hostility to the trusteeship proposals, backed by strikes and demonstrations. So too did Hodge and his advisers, who raged against the unknown State Department "experts" who had made the agreement with the Soviets. On January 28 the general offered his resignation in protest. It was refused. More than that, the tide in Washington now began to turn strongly in favor of the American group in Seoul. No less shrewd a diplomat than Averell Harriman visited Korea in February and returned to report most favorably upon Hodge's "ability and diplomacy." The Americans themselves now stood their own proposal on its head, and indeed revoked their assent to it. In the wake of the Moscow meeting, President Truman determined that Secretary of State Byrnes had given away far too much; that the time had come for a determined stand against Soviet expansionism; that Stalin should be confronted on a range of critical fronts. Of these, Korea was now identified among the foremost. All Asia understood the nature of the struggle taking place there. "The Korean question," declared an editorial in the Chinese newspaper *Ta-Kung-Pao,* "is in effect the political battleground for Russo-American mutual animosities, parrying and struggling for mastery."

Hodge's new proposal was that an indigenous Korean political body should be hastened into existence before the first meeting of the American-Soviet Joint Commission, intended to supervise the Trusteeship arrangements. On February 14 the Representative Democratic Council held its first meeting in Seoul's Capitol Building. Of its twenty-eight members, twenty-four were drawn from rightist

political parties. Syngman Rhee declared, "Hereafter, the Council will represent
the Korean people in its dealings with General Hodge and the Military Government." Limited as were the powers of the Council, it provided the Americans with
a core of acceptable Korean leaders to match the Russian-sponsored Communist
leadership now established in the North under Kim Il Sung. When the Joint
Commission began its meetings on March 20, each side focused its attention and
complaints upon the lack of facilities afforded to the sympathizers of the other for
political campaigning in their own zone.

American policy was now set upon the course from which it would not again
be deflected: to create, as speedily as possible, a plausible machinery of
government in South Korea that could survive as a bastion against the Communist
North. On December 12, 1946, the first meeting was held of a provisional South
Korean Legislature, whose membership was once again dominated by the men of
the Right, though such was their obduracy that they boycotted the first sessions in
protest against American intervention in the elections, which had vainly sought to
prevent absolute rightist manipulation of the results. A growing body of Korean
officials now controlled the central bureaucracy of SKIG—the South Korean
Interim Government. In 1947 a random sample of 115 of these revealed that
seventy were former officeholders under the Japanese. Only eleven showed any
evidence of anti-Japanese activity during the Korean period.

The suspicions of many Korean Nationalists about the conduct of the
American military government were redoubled by the fashion in which the
National Police, the most detested instrument of Japanese tyranny, was not merely
retained but strengthened. It was the American official historians of the occupation
who wrote that "the Japanese police in Korea possessed a breadth of function and
an extent of power equalled in few countries in the modern world."[19] The 12,000
Japanese in their ranks were sent home. But the 8,000 Koreans who remained—
the loyal servants of a brutal tyranny in which torture and judicial murder had been
basic instruments of government—found themselves promoted to fill the higher
ranks, while total police strength in South Korea doubled. Equipped with
American arms, jeeps, and radio communications, the police became the major
enforcement arm of American military government and its chief source of political
intelligence. A man like Yi Ku-bom, one of the most notorious police officers of
the Japanese regime, who feared for his life in August 1945, was a year later chief
of a major ward station in Seoul. A long roll call of prominent torturers and
anti-Nationalist fighters under the colonial power found themselves in positions of
unprecedented authority. In 1948, 53 percent of officers and 25 percent of
rank-and-file police were Japanese-trained. By a supreme irony, when the
development began of a Constabulary force, from which the South Korean Army
would grow, the Americans specifically excluded any recruit who had been
imprisoned by the Japanese—and thus any member of the anti-Japanese resistance.

The first chief of staff of the South Korean Army in 1947 was a former colonel in the Japanese Army.

Paek Sun Yup, who was to prove one of the few competent soldiers in Rhee's army in the 1950–53 war, rising to become its Chief of Staff while still in his early thirties, was a typical product of the system. A North Korean landlord's son, he attended Pyongyang High School, then Mukden Military Academy. He served as a young officer with the Japanese Army in Manchuria. "We thought nothing about Japanese influence," he said, shrugging, years later. "Every young man takes the status quo for granted. At that time, the Japanese were Number One. They were winning. We had never seen any British or Americans."[20] Paek's unit was fighting the Russians when the war ended. He walked for a month to reach his home. He quickly disliked what he saw of the new Communist regime in the North. On December 28, 1945, he escaped across the 38th Parallel, leaving his wife behind in the North. She joined him later. Two months later, he joined the Constabulary as a lieutenant. He rose rapidly, to become director of intelligence in the embryo South Korean Army and a divisional commander a few weeks before the 1950 invasion. No man could have attained Paek's position without demonstrating absolute loyalty to the regime of Syngman Rhee, and all that implied. But in every Asian society there is an overwhelming instinct in favor of serving the strongest force. The worst that can be said of Paek is that he was a tough, ambitious product of his environment.

But some young South Koreans did express their hostility to Rhee . . . and paid the price. Beyond those who were imprisoned, many more became "unpeople." Minh Pyong Kyu was a Seoul bank clerk's son who went to medical college in 1946 but found himself expelled in 1948 for belonging to a left-wing student organization. "There was an intellectual vacuum in the country at that time," he said. "The only interesting books seemed to be those from North Korea, and the Communists had a very effective distribution system. We thought the Americans were nice people who just didn't understand anything about Korea."[21] Minh's family of eight lived in genteel poverty. His father had lost his job with a mining company in 1945, for its assets lay north of the 38th Parallel. Minh threw himself into antigovernment activity: pasting up political posters by night, demonstrating, distributing Communist tracts. Then one morning he was arrested and imprisoned for ten days. The leaders of his group were tried and sentenced to long terms. He himself was released but expelled from his university, to his father's deep chagrin. Like hundreds of thousands of others, Minh yearned desperately for the fall of Syngman Rhee.

Kap Chong Chi, a landowner's son and another university student, felt far better disposed toward the Americans, and toward his own government, than Minh. But even as an unusually sophisticated and educated Korean, he shared the general ignorance and uncertainty about the politics of his own country: "In those days, we did not know what democracy was. For a long time after the Americans came, we did not know what the Communists were, or who Syngman Rhee was. So many of the students from the countryside, farmers' children, called themselves Communists. There was so much political passion among them, but also so much ignorance."[22] Korean society was struggling to come to terms with a political system, when it had possessed none for almost half a century. Not surprisingly, the tensions and hostilities became simplistic: between haves and have-nots; between those who shared the privileges of power and those who did not; between landlord and peasant, intellectual and pragmatist. The luxury of civilized political debate was denied to South Korea, as it was to the North.

Ferris Miller, the naval officer who was one of the advance party at Inchon in September 1945, left the country at the end of that year. But he was that rare creature—an American deeply attracted by Korea: "Somehow, it had got into my blood. I liked the place, the food, the people." In February 1947 he returned to Seoul as a civilian contract employee of the Military Government. He was dismayed by what he found: "Everything had gone downhill. Nothing worked— the pipes were frozen, the electricity kept going off. The corruption was there for anybody to see. A lot of genuine patriots in the South were being seduced by the blandishments of the North. There were Korean exiles coming home from everywhere—Manchuria, China, Japan. Everybody was struggling, even the Americans. The PX was almost bare of goods. Most of our own people hated the country. There were men who came, stayed a week, and just got out. There were Koreans wearing clothes made of army blankets; orphans hanging around the railway stations; people chopping wood on the hills above Seoul, the transport system crumbling. It was a pretty bad time."[23]

The conditions Miller discovered in Seoul might as readily have been observed in Berlin, Vienna, Hamburg—any of the war-ruined cities of Europe that winter. Even in London and Paris, cold and shortages were a way of life in 1947. But whereas in Europe democratic political life was reviving with remarkable vigor, in South Korea a fundamentally corrupt society was being created. Power was being transferred by the Americans to a Korean conservative faction indifferent to the concept of popular freedom, representative only of ambition for power and wealth. The administration and policing of the country had been placed in the hands of men who were willing tools of a tyranny that a world war had just been fought to destroy. Their only discernible claim to office was their hostility to communism.

    Between 1945 and 1947 the foreign political patrons of North and South Korea became permanently committed to their respective protégés. The course of events thereafter is more simply described. In September 1947, despite Russian objections, the United States referred the future of Korea to the United Nations.

Moscow made a proposal to Washington remarkably similar to that which General Hodge had advanced almost two years earlier: both great powers should simultaneously withdraw their forces, leaving the Koreans to resolve their own destinies. The Russians were plainly confident—with good reason—that left to their own devices, the forces of the Left in both Koreas would prevail. The Americans, making the same calculation, rejected the Russian plan. On November 14 their own proposal was accepted by the General Assembly: there was to be UN supervision of elections to a Korean government, followed by Korean independence and the withdrawal of all foreign forces. The Eastern bloc abstained from the vote on the American plan, which was carried by 46 votes to 0.

The United Nations Temporary Commission on Korea met for the first time in Seoul on January 12, 1948. The Russians and North Koreans utterly rejected UN participation in deciding the future of Korea. Thus it was apparent from the outset that any decision the Commission reached would be implemented only south of the 38th Parallel. The General Assembly's Interim Committee brooded for a time on this problem. Dr. Rhee was strongly in favor of immediate elections for as much of Korea as was willing to hold them. But every Korean opposition party argued against holding a vote in the face of the Communist boycott. Not only would this make genuinely "free" elections impossible—it would doom for years, if not forever, the national unity so many Koreans still cherished. It would be a formal recognition of the divided status of Korea.

The Australian and Canadian members of the UN Temporary Commission shared these misgivings. But a majority of its members—France, the Philippines, Chiang Kai Shek's China, El Salvador, and India—supported elections in the South. The Interim Committee agreed that elections should go ahead. Campaigning for election to South Korea's first government was held in a climate of mounting political repression. William F. Dean, the American military governor, replied to a question from the UN Commission about political prisoners: "I have yet to find a man in jail because his ideology is different from anyone else's." Yet it was he who authorized the Korean police to deputize bands of "loyal citizens" into "Community Protective Organizations." These quickly became known colloquially among Americans as "Rhee's goon squads." Their purpose was frankly terroristic—to drive not only Communists, but any group unsympathetic to the Right, from South Korean life. In the six weeks before polling, 589 people were killed in disturbances and 10,000 "processed" at police stations.

On election day, out of a total population of 20 million, 95 percent of the 7.8 million registered voters went to the polls. The UN commissioners declared that the vote represented a "valid expression of the free will of the people." America's Ambassador to the UN, John Foster Dulles, told the General Assembly that the elections "constituted a magnificent demonstration of the capacity of the Korean people to establish a representative and responsible government." Syngman

Rhee's "Association for the Rapid Realization of Independence" gained 55 of the 200 seats in South Korea's new constitutional assembly. The Conservative Hanguk Democratic Party won 29, and two other right-wing groups gained 12 and 6 seats respectively. The Right therefore commanded an effective majority of the 200 seats. The Left boycotted the election. The North Koreans, invited to send delegates, unsurprisingly made no response. Rhee and his supporters instituted a presidential system of government. He himself was inaugurated as South Korea's first elected leader on July 24, 1948. On August 14, the third anniversary of VJ day, amid the wailing tones of the Great Bell of Chongno, the U.S. flag was lowered over the Capitol Building in Seoul and that of the new South Korean Republic was hoisted. General MacArthur delivered a bellicose speech in which he told Koreans, "an artificial barrier has divided your land. This barrier must and shall be torn down."

In the months that followed Syngman Rhee addressed himself to the creation of a ruthless dictatorship in South Korea. Any minister who showed symptoms of independence was dismissed. The President took steps to bind the police and Constabulary under his personal control. Each new manifestation of left-wing opposition provided provocation for a renewed surge of government repression. There were frequent clashes along the 38th Parallel with North Korean border units, for which blame seemed about evenly divided. The most serious internal upheaval began on October 19, 1948, when an army unit sent to deal with Communist rebels on Cheju Island mutinied at Yosu, on the southwest tip of Korea. They won local civilian support by urging vengeance upon oppressive local police and marched against the town of Sunchon. Here, they were checked. By the end of the month the uprising had been defeated, at a cost of a thousand lives. But a climate of oppression, intolerance, and political ruthlessness was deepening. Ferociously hostile radio propaganda from Pyongyang fed rumors of imminent invasion from the North. In November press restrictions were imposed, and more than 700 political arrests carried out. Between September 1948 and April 1949 there were a total of 89,710 police arrests in South Korea. Only 28,404 of the victims were released without charge. Kim Ku, the seventy-four-year-old veteran of the "Provisional Government" who had suffered grievously for his opposition to Japanese rule and still commanded widespread respect in South Korea as the President's most credible rival, was assassinated in his study by one of Rhee's creatures in June 1949. In the same month the last United States occupation troops, excepting a 500-man assistance and training group—the KMAG—left Korea. Rhee pleaded desperately for a continued American military presence. But the Russians had already pulled their army out of the North, and Washington was anyway reluctant to allow its forces to linger longer in Korea, whose occupation had cost so much pain and so many dollars. The United States had done all that it believed possible. With so many other demands upon America's resources as the

Cold War intensified, its leaders were unwilling to allow Korea to assume a disproportionate importance. It was a measure of Washington's determination to limit the mischief that could come out of Korea, that Dr. Rhee's new army was denied armor and heavy artillery. The intention was to provide South Korea solely with the means for her own defense, above all against mounting internal guerrilla activity.

The peaceful departure of the Red Army from North Korea diminished American fears of overt Communist aggression in the peninsula. North of the 38th Parallel, the Soviets left behind a ruthlessly disciplined, totalitarian Stalinist society in the hands of their protégé, Kim Il Sung. Russian advisers helped to set up a national network of "people's" committees, and a central government based upon a "Provisional People's Committee." In November 1946 the first election to membership was held, based upon a single list of candidates, all members of a "Democratic Front." Moscow reported that Kim Il Sung's grouping collected 97 percent of votes cast. In February 1947 a "Convention of People's" Committees met for the final time in Pyongyang and established the "People's Assembly of North Korea." The "Democratic People's Republic of Korea" was proclaimed on September 9, 1948. But North Korea was an undeveloped society. The prospect that it might embark upon a war without the direct support of its Russian sponsors still appeared remote. Among those in the Pentagon and the State Department conscious of Korea's existence, there were considerable misgivings about what had been done and what had been created in the South in America's name. Yet there was also the feeling that the best had been made of an impossible situation. Diplomatically, it was a considerable achievement that the United States had been able to maintain the support of the Western allies for her anti-Communist program. The United Nations Commission on Korea, charged with pursuing the eventual objective of supervising the unification of the divided nation, now maintained a permanent presence in the South, monitoring the mutually hostile activities of Seoul and Pyongyang and seeking "to observe and report any developments which might lead to or otherwise involve military conflict in Korea." It is a backhanded tribute to the vestiges of democracy that persisted in the South that, in the elections for a new National Assembly in May 1950, Syngman Rhee's bitter unpopularity was fully reflected. The parties of the Right gained only 49 seats against 130 seats won by Independents and 44 by other parties.

With the advantage of hindsight, it is evident that United States policy in postwar Korea was clumsy and ill conceived. It reflected not only a lack of understanding, but a lack of interest in the country and its people beyond their potential as bricks in the wall against Communist aggression. This failure, it may be suggested, lay close to the heart of the United States' difficulties not only with Korea, but also with China and subsequently with Vietnam. The occupiers' enthusiasm for the reproduction of American political and bureaucratic institutions in Asia held little charm for Koreans with different attitudes and priorities. Japan, alone in Asia, represented in the 1940s, as it represents today, the single glittering example of a society in which American political transplants took firm root. Only Japan was sufficiently educated and homogeneous to adapt the new institutions successfully. In Japan alone the traditional leaders of society were not identified by their poorer compatriots with an intolerable measure of injustice, corruption, and collaboration with foreign oppressors. In those parts of Asia where they exerted influence, the Americans honorably attempted to mitigate the worst excesses of landlordism and social oppression. But they never acknowledged how grievously these evils damaged their perpetrators as credible rulers in a democratic society. Again and again in Asia, America aligned herself alongside social forces which possessed no hope of holding power by consent. Chiang Kai Shek's followers, like those of Syngman Rhee, could maintain themselves in office only by the successful application of oppressive force.

Yet the United States is also entitled to argue before the bar of history that a more enlightened and idealistic policy in postwar Korea would have caused the country to fall to the Communists. The local Communists' credentials as fighters against the Japanese, their freedom from the embarrassments of landlordism and corruption, would almost certainly have enabled them to gain some popular mandate in 1945–46. Whatever their initial willingness to form a coalition with Koreans of the Center and Right, would the moderates not have suffered the same inexorable fate of death or impotence that befell so many Eastern European politicians of that period, not to mention those of North Korea? Diplomatic historians have convincingly shown that in 1945–46, contrary to American belief at the time, South Korea did not form part of the Soviet expansion plan. Yet how were the contemporary leaders of the West to know or to guess that this was so, that Stalin had indulgently decided to exclude Korea from the fate that had befallen Czechoslovakia, Poland, Yugoslavia, Romania, Hungary? In the late 1940s it seemed, upon sufficient evidence, that the purpose of the Soviet Union was to test the strength of the West at every possible point and to advance wherever weakness was detected. Dr. Syngman Rhee and his followers appeared at least to represent strength and determination at a period when these were at a premium. In historical assessments of the postwar period, it is sometimes forgotten that the Russians were as deeply feared by many Europeans as the Germans a few years earlier. The appeasers of Hitler had become objects of derision and contempt. Those who observed the Red Army's dreadful record of rape and pillage in Eastern Europe, the unquestionable readiness of Moscow to employ murder as an instrument of policy, felt nothing but scorn for the would-be appeasers of Stalin in Europe or in Asia.

Nor did American manipulation of South Korean politics seem anything like as awful a matter, even in liberal circles, in 1945 as it might forty years later. In the course of the Second World War, none of the partners of the Grand Alliance had shown any greater sensitivity toward the human rights and feelings of Asian peoples than the chiefs of the Military Government displayed in Seoul from 1945 to 1948. If Korean policemen sometimes tortured or killed civilians, if their leaders accepted bribes, if their politicians behaved like mafiosi—was not this the way "these people" had always done things? Was it not merely a higher form of Western arrogance to seek to impose Western ideas of humanity upon a society in which dog was a culinary delicacy—customarily strangled and depilated with a pine taper in the course of preparation—and where fried crickets and boiled silkworms featured prominently in local good-food guides? The American record in Korea between 1945 and 1950 must be judged against the indisputable reality of Soviet expansionism, of Stalin's bottomless malevolence. No charge against the Rhee regime can blunt the force of one simple truth: that while the United States deliberately declined to provide South Korea with the means to conduct armed aggression, the Soviet Union supplied North Korea with a large arsenal of tanks, artillery, and military aircraft. The events that unfolded in the summer of 1950 demonstrated that American fears for the peninsula were entirely well founded, whatever the shortcomings of Washington's political response to the situation.

2

INVASION

In the course of 1949, relations between North and South Korea, the tempo of mutual propaganda hysteria, rose sharply. In the South constant military pressure eroded the strength of the Communist guerrillas in the mountains. In April 1949, Pyongyang invited South Korea's anti-Rhee leaders to attend a "coalition conference." Of 545 delegates present, 240 were from the South. Rhee denounced them, not unreasonably, as "Communist stooges." In August a new Communist "Supreme People's Assembly" met in Haiju, just north of the 38th Parallel. At this a "People's Democratic Republic" embracing both North and South Korea was announced. A South Korean was its nominated Foreign Minister. But on the 38th Parallel, responsibility for border incidents was by no means a monopoly of Pyongyang. In May 1949, in one of the most serious incidents, South Korean forces penetrated up to 2.5 miles into North Korean territory and attacked local villages. In a climate of intense mutual mistrust, in December the British Foreign Office asked the War Office for a military assessment of the situation in Korea. It received an interesting response:

"In the past [wrote Major J. R. Ferguson Innes] it had always been our view that irrespective of strengths the North Korean forces would have little difficulty in dealing effectively with the forces of South Korea should full-scale hostilities break out. This somewhat naturally (since they raised, equipped and trained South Korean forces) was not the American view. Recently, however, they have been

46

coming round to our way of thinking regarding the capabilities of the respective forces. . . .

"On the question of aggression by the North, there can be no doubt whatever that their ultimate objective is to overrun the South; and I think in the long term there is no doubt that they will do so, in which case, as you so aptly remark, the Americans will have made a rather handsome contribution of equipment to the military strength of Asiatic Communism. As to their method of achieving their object, short of World War III beginning, I think they will adopt the well-tried tactics of preparing the country from within rather than resort to open aggression, although 'frontier incidents' will doubtless continue. . . .

"Regarding American policy, if in fact one exists, towards South Korea, I can only say we know little, and of their future intentions even less. . . . Whilst being in no doubt about future North Korean (or Soviet) plans regarding South Korea, we think an invasion is unlikely in the immediate view; however, if it did take place, I think it improbable that the Americans would become involved. The possession of South Korea is not essential for Allied strategic plans, and though it would obviously be desirable to deny it to the enemy, it would not be of sufficient importance to make it the cause of World War III. Meanwhile, we must accept an uneasy status quo and hope for the best."[1]

Brigadier General W. L. Roberts, commanding officer of the American KMAG Military Assistance Group in Korea, not surprisingly took a more sanguine view of the South Korean Army than the British officer quoted above. In a letter to General Charles Bolté, Director of Plans at the Pentagon, in March 1950 he urged that Americans should play a prominent role in stiffening ROK formations:

"If South Korea is called upon to defend itself against aggression from the North, its ground army is capable of doing an excellent job. If American advisers are present (even on Regimental and Division level) it will do an even better job, for we have found Americans are leaned on heavily the rougher it gets. In other words, the advisers will almost command except in name."

Here, of course, was the root of many delusions that were to plague the U.S. Army in Asia for the next generation. The belief that American officers could, in effect, officer Asian troops to the same effect that the British had achieved with their Indian army for two hundred years persisted into Indochina. Worse, there was the notion that they could temper control with politeness by accompanying units merely as "advisers." Later, as the ROK Army expanded in the course of war, this principle of giving Koreans American support would be extended so that Korean formations were integrated with American ones. The Koreans' knowledge of the absolute lack of confidence with which they were regarded by their allies and mentors contributed materially to justifying this. But in March 1950, despite his optimistic view of ROK capabilities, Roberts acknowledged that the strategic perspective did not favor Seoul's forces:

"All G-2 sources tell that the North Koreans have up to 100 Russian planes and a training program for pilots. You know and I know what 100 planes can do to troops, to towns and to transport on roads.

"So, if South Korea were attacked today by the inferior [sic] ground forces of North Korea plus their Air Corps, I feel that South Korea would take a bloody nose. Again then, knowing these people somewhat, I feel they would follow the apparent winner and South Korea would be gobbled up to be added to the rest of Red Asia.

"This is a fat nation now with all its ECA goods, with warehouses bulging with plenty of rice from a good crop even if their finances are shaky with great inflationary tendencies. It is getting into the position of an excellent prize of war; strategically it points right into the heart of Japan and into the hands of an enemy it weakens the Japanese bastion of Western defence."[2]

Washington's view of the importance of Korea to the anti-Communist cause was changing. But the Administration's thinking remained confused, and so did the signals that it sent out across the world. The critical force in United States policy toward the Far East by the summer of 1950 was the deep bitterness and frustration of the American people about the "loss" of China to the Communists. The defeat of Chiang Kai Shek's American-sponsored Nationalist armies had been a profound shock and source of sorrow not only to the legendary "China lobby" but to many Americans who had grown up all their lives with a sense of missionary commitment to China. The vast Asian society had been a central force in the lives of such men as Henry Luce, who put Chiang on the cover of *Time* magazine a record seven times. In the case of great industrialists such as Alfred Kohlberg, economic interest marched hand in hand with a real personal passion for China. America's cash investment in Chiang's creakingly corrupt regime had been enormous: $645 million in aid and $826 million in Lend-Lease during World War II, followed by another $2 billion in the years that followed. Asia in general, and China in particular, called deeply to many Americans in a manner that Europe did not. Europe was a fully fashioned society, often ungrateful for American influence and aid. Yet Asia seemed to lie half-made, half-civilized, wide open for all the cultural, religious, and democratic improvements that the United States could offer. Throughout the Second World War, America retained delusions about the virtue and power of Chiang Kai Shek's regime that were shared by none of her allies. When the State Department's admirable "old China hands" warned persistently of the hopeless corruption and incompetence of the Nationalists, of the irresistible power of Mao Tse Tung's Communists, their reports served only to damn them long afterward. Davies, Vincent, and the others became, for conservative America, not the faithful prophets of disaster, but the agents who had contributed to bring this about. "China asked for a sword, and we gave her a dull paring knife," declared Senator Bridges of New Hampshire. Senator Taft damned the appeasers of the State Department, "guided by a left-wing group who obviously wanted to get rid of Chiang, and were willing at least to turn China over to the Communists for that purpose." The fall of China to the Communists, far from convincing Americans of the need to ensure that the regimes they supported possessed some validity within their own societies, merely persuaded much of the United States that anti-Communist regimes must be sustained and supported, however unpopular within their own societies. George Kennan sought to suggest that "a certain sentimentality toward the Chinese" among Americans "was both patronizing and dangerously naive." Dean Acheson, Truman's Secretary of State, was doing his utmost through 1949 to reconcile Americans to accepting the probable fall of Chiang's last bastion, the island of Formosa.

"The unfortunate but inescapable fact is that the ominous result of the civil war in China was beyond the control of the government of the United States," Acheson wrote, eminently sanely, in an August 1949 white paper. "Nothing that this country did or could have done within the reasonable limits of its capabilities could have changed that result; nothing that was left undone by this country has contributed to it. It was the product of internal Chinese forces, forces which this country tried to influence, but could not. A decision was arrived at within China, if only a decision by default."

But this was now the day of Senator Joseph McCarthy. Gallup suggested that 39 percent of Americans believed in the Wisconsin Republican's red witch hunt, that his hounding of the State Department officials who had "betrayed" China to the Communists was "a good thing." In the words of McCarthy's best biographer, "the political atmosphere in the spring of 1950 was such that evidence and logic were often avoided." Senators Bridges, Knowland, and McCarran issued a statement denouncing Acheson's China white paper as "a 1,054 page whitewash of a wishful, do-nothing policy which has succeeded only in placing Asia in danger of Soviet conquest, with its ultimate threat to the peace of the world and our own national security. . . . Growing numbers of Republicans were convinced that McCarthyism was their ticket to political power, and were determined to back Joe's Red hunt as long as the headlines continued to bombard the Administration." By this mid-term of Truman's second Administration, he was already a belea-guered President, under immense domestic pressures for his alleged weakness in confronting the Communist threat at home and abroad.

Truman himself was increasingly convinced that the Soviets were risk-takers, opportunists who would press forward on every front where they detected weakness. In 1950 the memory of the 1930s was not merely vivid but a dominant force in the thinking of most Western politicians. At this historic period, when the closest advisers of the American President were men whose minds focused upon Europe as the cockpit of world affairs, the failure of the policy of appeasement of the dictators lay close to the heart of their political thought. "We are losing the Cold War," Bernard Baruch warned Truman in April 1950. John Foster Dulles accepted office in the Administration that month, only on condition that "some early affirmative action" would be taken against "the Communist menace." The joint State-Defense study group headed by Paul Nitze which produced the critical study of American foreign policy objectives, NSC-68, in the first months of 1950, urged much greater defense expenditure. It defined the Soviet purpose as "the complete subversion or forcible destruction of the machinery of government and structure of society in the non-Soviet world, and their replacement by an apparatus and structure subservient to and controlled by the Kremlin." George Kennan and Chip Bohlen, two of America's most prominent experts on the Soviets, opposed the National Security Council's paper. They argued that Moscow was, in reality, far more cautious than the document suggested. But Acheson accepted NSC-68. Its principal conclusion—that the Soviets should be challenged wherever in the world they next embarked upon an assault on freedom—became part of the policy of the Truman Administration.

Yet whatever the validity of Washington's assessment of Soviet intentions, the gravest charge against the United States government in 1950 was that it made a precipitate commitment to an end before it had begun to will the means. In the aftermath of World War II, the nation's armed forces had not merely been reduced—they had been allowed to crumble to the brink of collapse. Again and again between 1947 and 1950 the Joint Chiefs of Staff warned the President that he was extending America's diplomatic commitments beyond her military means to defend them. Among the glittering cluster of intellects around the President, by far the least impressive figure was the Defense Secretary, Louis Johnson. A political operator, a fund-raiser, an electoral grandstander, Johnson had made much political capital from his dramatic savings in the military budget. Yet it was a direct consequence of Johnson's policies, approved by Truman, that by June 1950 MacArthur's divisions in Korea lacked 62 percent of their infantry firepower and 14 percent of their tanks, that 80 percent of the army's sixty-day reserve was unusable, and the army in Japan possessed only forty-five days' supply of ammunition. It was in recognition of the desperate shortcomings of MacArthur's army that the Defense Department agreed that Korea could be removed from the general's theater responsibilities.

The first and most obvious manifestation of the commitment to NSC-68 was that the United States began to give active support to the French in their struggle against the Communist Vietminh in Indochina. Washington felt a growing concern that the Russians might consider some move against Japan, the centerpiece of the

American defense of the Pacific basin. While Acheson remained unwilling to commit the United States to the protection of Formosa, his Assistant Secretary for the Far East, Dean Rusk, was increasingly anxious to do so.

Yet in June 1950 the hardening of attitudes within the Administration remained little understood within the United States, and scarcely at all outside it. NSC-68 has been cited as a classic example of a document whose secrecy destroyed its very purpose. Its conclusions remained unpublished for more than twenty years after they were drafted. The public signals reaching Moscow about American intentions thus remained unchanged and uncertain. Had the Russians possessed any inkling of the strength of Washington's newfound determination to seek a battleground upon which to challenge Communist expansion, it is profoundly unlikely that Moscow would ever have allowed the North Korean invasion of June 1950 to take place.

To this day there remains no explicit, trustworthy evidence about the circumstances in which Kim Il Sung made his decision to invade South Korea in June 1950. But the circumstantial evidence is strong that the Russians sanctioned rather than instigated the attack. Plainly, it would have been impossible for Kim to act at all without the active assistance of Moscow in providing arms and supplies, and the connivance of Peking in allowing rail movements through Chinese territory. In addition, in the months before the invasion many thousands of Communist veterans who had fought with Mao Tse Tung's armies, but were Korean by birth, returned to their homeland in the North. In sending the Koreans back, the Chinese may well have been inspired more by the urgent need to demobilize their vast forces than by any desire to reinforce Kim Il Sung's divisions. But the effect was the same. Pyongyang's army was strengthened by large numbers of combat veterans.

The memoirs of Nikita Khrushchev, a heavily tainted source, nonetheless offer a plausible version of the events leading up to the invasion. According to Khrushchev, Kim Il Sung came to Moscow to seek Stalin's acquiescence in his plans for war, and the North Korean was successful in convincing the Russian that he could gain a speedy victory. Mao Tse Tung agreed that the United States would not intervene, "since the war would be an internal matter which the Korean people would decide for themselves."[3] The behavior of Moscow in the months following the outbreak of war suggested Soviet reluctance to identify wholeheartedly with Kim Il Sung's adventure, to stake everything upon his victory. The Soviets appear to have satisfied themselves that the Korean could make his attempt to unify the country under communism without intolerable political or military risk to themselves. They were probably encouraged in this view by their knowledge of the widespread Communist support within the South, which might be expected to rally when the Northerners swept across the country.

One of the foremost historians of this period, Allen S. Whiting, concludes that there was "no agreement . . . nor . . . any direct evidence on the degree to which Communist China participated in the planning. It is possible that Stalin did not even inform Mao of the forthcoming attack during their weeks of conference in Moscow, although this is highly unlikely."[4] The Chinese, the overwhelming probability suggests, were passive if acquiescent parties to North Korea's intentions. Peking, that first summer after attaining final victory in its own civil war, had ample national problems at home, without seeking any share in those of Korea.

In the summer of 1950 a wave of intelligence reports reached both American headquarters in Tokyo, and the CIA in Washington, suggesting that the North Koreans were preparing an invasion of the south. One CIA report, of March 10, 1950, even pinpointed June as the chosen date. Later that month MacArthur's intelligence department even prepared a report predicting a war in Korea by early summer.[5] Yet, as so often on the eve of twentieth-century crises, those at the summit of power showed no sign of expecting real trouble. MacArthur repeatedly declared his disbelief in the imminence of war. His absolute lack of attention to the combat training of his divisions in Japan can be explained only by his conviction that they would not be called upon to fight. The most serious contingency Far East Command recognized was likely escalation of the Communist guerrilla struggle against Syngman Rhee, which had been in progress for many months.

But only historians can focus with such clarity on the intelligence warnings of war. The few flimsy sheets upon which these were provided reached the desks of MacArthur's officers and the departments of Defense and State in Washington among a vast paper harvest of contradictory, confusing, often obviously unreliable information and analysis. It was the familiar intelligence problem of distinguishing "signals" from "noise." The "noise," that summer of 1950, came in the form of Communist threats that seemed to touch every quarter of the globe: on the occupation boundaries in Europe, at Trieste and in the oil fields of the Middle East, among the Huk guerrillas of the Philippines, on the borders of Greece and Yugoslavia. Korea was indeed recognized, in the war departments of the West, as a possible point of confrontation with the Communists. But it lay near the bottom of a long list of prospective battlefields.

The devastating North Korean artillery and mortar barrage opened at 4 A.M. on the morning of June 25, 1950. In Washington it was early afternoon on Saturday, June 24. The Communist attack, masked by a skilful deception plan in the preceding weeks, achieved complete strategic and tactical surprise. The Korean People's Army possessed seven combat-ready divisions, an armored brigade equipped with Russian T-34 tanks, three newly activated divisions, and ample supporting artillery. Since Kim Il Sung's army was founded in February 1948, it had been welded into an intensely motivated, well-equipped fighting force of 135,000 men.

The air force, of some 200 Yak-9 fighters and Il-10 ground-attack bombers, was negligible by Western standards but sufficed to provide formidable close support for the North Korean assault and to wipe out Seoul's pitiful handful of T-6 trainers on the ground in the first hours of war. Syngman Rhee's 95,000 strong army had been deliberately denied armor, antitank weapons, and artillery heavier than 105 mm. In the summer of 1950 more than a third of the ROK Army's vehicles were immobilized in want of repair. Spare parts were almost nonexistent. There were just six days' ammunition reserve in the country. Only around a third of Rhee's army was deployed in the line confronting the Communist assault on June 25. Like its parent regime, the ROK Army was a corrupt, demoralized body entirely devoid of the motivation that was so quickly apparent in the Communist formations.

Four Communist spearheads were soon driving south, led by their almost invulnerable armor, checked more by terrain and natural obstacles than by the ROK forces as they forged through the gaps in the hills. Ten Communist divisions, supported by 1,643 guns, streamed over the Parallel. The town of Ongin fell within hours to the KPA 6th Division. The Communist 1st Division drove for Kaesong, while in the east the 3rd and 4th Divisions took the Uijongbu corridor. Farther eastward the 5th Division mounted its own attack, supported by amphibious landings along the coast behind the collapsing ROK front. The fighting, such as it was in those first hours and day, involved only isolated stands by pockets of ROK troops. Faced by an assault of such formidable power and decision, Syngman Rhee's army was wholly unable to mount a coherent defense by formations. Reeling, its battered and broken companies began to straggle southward, often abandoning their equipment, hastening to keep a brief bound ahead of the bleak, mustard-drab battalions of Kim Il Sung's victorious army. At 9:30 A.M., Kim himself broadcast the version of events along the 38th Parallel which would form the basis for the public posture on Korea throughout the Communist world from 1950 until the present day:

"The South Korean puppet clique has rejected all methods for peaceful reunification proposed by the Democratic People's Republic of Korea and dared to commit armed aggression . . . north of the 38th parallel. The Democratic People's Republic of Korea ordered a counterattack to repel the invading troops. The South Korean puppet clique will be held responsible for whatever results may be brought about by this development."

Four hours after the North Korean onslaught began, it was evident in Seoul that this was no new border raid. The American Ambassador in Seoul, John J. Muccio, cabled the State Department in Washington, "North Korean forces invaded Republic of Korea at several places this morning. . . . It would appear from the nature of the attack and the manner in which it was launched that it constitutes an all-out offensive against the Republic of Korea."

3

THE WEST'S RIPOSTE

Washington

Han Pyo Wook, the thirty-four-year-old First Secretary at the South Korean Embassy in Washington, was at home in Tacoma, Maryland, on Saturday night, June 24, when a journalist acquaintance from United Press International telephoned him. "Philip"—the name Han had long ago adopted for his American life—"you know your country's been invaded?"[1] No indeed, "Philip" did not know. He called the Associated Press to confirm the news, then the State Department. The Administration, like Han, had received its first news of the invasion from the agency wires. But this was now being confirmed from Muccio's office in Seoul. Han was told to come at once to Foggy Bottom with his ambassador, whom he telephoned. Wretched and silent, the two men drove themselves into the city. Han had lived in America since 1938 and was a devoted adherent of Syngman Rhee, whom he had come to know well. He was embittered by the chronic criticism of his President in the State Department, the complaints that he was dictatorial. "Sure, he's dictatorial compared with President Truman," Han said, shrugging. He hated always to go to the Far East Department at State as a supplicant. In May 1949, when Rhee personally requested him to explain to the Americans that his army lacked ammunition to train, Han was deeply wounded when John Williams, on the Korean desk, answered lightly, "Well, Philip, I guess you must be using too many bullets back there."

54

This Saturday night the two little Koreans were shown at once into the office of Dean Rusk, the Assistant Secretary of State. They found him standing grimly among a little cluster of his officials, all in dinner jackets. Rusk said, "We have received cables from Ambassador Muccio indicating that there is no doubt that an armed attack has occurred. Do you have any information?" The Koreans shook their heads. They made an immediate plea for American military assistance. Rusk's reply was inaudible, but plainly noncommittal. The Koreans were merely thankful that the possibility was not ruled out. Twenty minutes after their arrival, they drove home through the darkness to the ambassador's residence. It was there, less than an hour later, that they took a call direct from Syngman Rhee in Seoul.

Rhee's voice was remarkably clear, but in the background they could hear a babble of voices from his Cabinet. "The Communists have invaded," said the doctor calmly. "Our soldiers are fighting courageously, but they lack weapons. Please ask the government of the United States to hasten the delivery of arms to us." In reality, even as Rhee spoke he was preparing to flee with all the speed he could muster for the southern city of Taejon. But his representatives in Washington hastened to do his bidding. At 1 A.M. on Sunday morning they were back in Rusk's office at the State Department, with the same group of American officials. "This is plainly a serious matter," said Rusk, "a large-scale attack. This is a matter that should be the concern of the United Nations." America's ambassador to the UN was away in Vermont for the weekend, but his deputy had been contacted. The UN Secretary-General, Trygve Lie, had been requested to summon a meeting of the Security Council. But the Koreans still received no clear answer about military aid.

The next morning they flew from Andrews Air Force Base to New York with two State Department officials, alongside whom they worked through the flight, preparing a short statement for the United Nations Security Council. At the UN's temporary home at Lake Success that Sunday afternoon, the Council met. Some members protested about the short notice, which had prevented them receiving instructions from their governments. The Yugoslavs demanded that if the South Koreans were to be heard by the Council, no resolution should be passed until the North Koreans had also attended to put their case. They were outvoted. On January 13 the Soviet delegate, Yakov Malik, had walked out of the Security Council in protest against the UN's refusal to seat Communist China in place of the Nationalists. On June 25 he was still absent. In these extraordinary circumstances, at 6 P.M. a UN resolution condemning the North Korean attack, and calling for the withdrawal of Kim Il Sung's forces south of the 38th Parallel, was passed by a 9-0 vote.

The UN resolution on Korea passed into history. It was a landmark event, probably never to be repeated in the history of this or any other world body. Here, for once, was no mere vote for a peacekeeping force, a body to intervene between two warring parties, but unequivocal support for one combatant against another. Many times since 1950 nations have committed flagrant acts of armed intervention in the affairs of others. In many cases the victim has appealed to the United Nations for military protection and heard this refused. Whatever excesses states commit against their neighbors—South Africa in Angola, Libya in Chad, Israel in Lebanon—the issues are adjudged too confused, the tangle of international loyalties and hostilities too great, ever to achieve a consensus for international military action. The UN intervention in Korea was a fluke of history made possible by the unique accident of the Russian boycott. In the absence of the Soviets, the United Nations in 1950 was still overwhelmingly the instrument of the Western democracies and their clients. In that last period before the rush of colonies to independence multiplied the UN's size and its dissensions, it possessed only fifty-eight members. Many of these cherished a sincere crusading enthusiasm that the new body should prove capable of more than the sterile debates of the inter-war League of Nations.

Most international disputes are shrouded in such a fog of claim and counterclaim, outrage and reprisal, that it is difficult to subject them to any absolute moral judgment. In less dangerous times, the questionable legitimacy and obvious unpleasantness of Syngman Rhee's regime in Seoul would have made many nations reluctant to come to his aid. There were few illusions about this in informed circles in the United States. "The unpopularity of the Syngman Rhee government and the questionable political and military reliability of the army and police force," wrote Hanson Baldwin in The New York Times on June 27, "are the greatest weakness of the defending forces." But it was not only the United States, in the summer of 1950, which saw in Korea an extraordinary opportunity to draw the line against Communist aggression. In Europe, in Asia, in the Middle East, in Latin America, the advance of communism—nourished if not directed by the agents of Stalin—was perceived not as an abstract problem but an immediate physical menace. The spectacle of Eastern Europe, the heart of such gaiety and culture for centuries, disappearing into the dark fog of totalitarianism had not only dismayed but frightened a host of citizens of free nations. Not merely Greece, but France and Italy also, seemed close to falling under Communist rule. The vision of Russian armies storming across the postwar occupation lines to assault Western Europe appeared perfectly plausible. It was a British Socialist Member of Parliament of that period who said, thirty-five years later, "People have forgotten just how indescribably bloody the Russians were at that time. Because the Soviets have now become more reasonable, less frightening, we should not lose sight of how ruthless and immediate a threat they then seemed."[2]

The miscalculation of Kim Il Sung was to launch so blatant an act of aggression that even the least warlike spectators around the world found it difficult to take refuge in equivocation. The most ruthless Stalinist takeovers in Eastern

Europe had been protected by a cloak of legitimacy, however threadbare. The most successful Communist acts of expansionism around the world, both before and after Korea, were achieved in a fog of moral and political confusion. Not even the tatters of a pretext had been erected along the 38th Parallel. Kim Il Sung set himself simply to seize South Korea by the exercise of naked military force. Even viewed from a Communist perspective, it was a huge act of folly. A former senior South Korean officer remarked many years later, "If Kim really wanted to get the South, by far his best course would have been to do nothing. His biggest mistake was to attack us." The speaker meant, of course, that by 1950 Syngman Rhee's regime was in deep internal political trouble. A few more years of discreet subversion could have ensured its collapse from within. But by precipitating his invasion, Kim gave Rhee what the South Korean President could never have gained on his own in a thousand years—a just cause and a banner of moral legitimacy. To these the United Nations rallied on June 25, 1950.

Dean Acheson met President Truman at Washington airport on Sunday evening with news of the UN vote. Truman returned from his troubled weekend at home in Independence, Missouri, to host a dinner at Blair House attended by all his most senior defense and foreign-policy advisers. For twenty-four hours Acheson and his officials had been examining every aspect of the Korean thunderbolt. It continued to surprise and confuse them. For months it had been thought likely that the Soviets would launch an operation to test the West's will. Korea had been listed as a possible, but not a probable, battlefield. Berlin, Greece, Turkey, Iran all appeared far more vulnerable. Korea was geographically easy for America to reinforce, difficult for the Soviets. Yet now they had gone to war for it. "Plainly," wrote Acheson later, "this attack did not amount to a *casus belli* against the Soviet Union. Equally plainly, it was an open, undisguised challenge to our internationally accepted position as the protector of South Korea, an area of great importance to the security of American-occupied Japan. To back away from this challenge, in view of our capacity for meeting it, would be highly destructive of the power and prestige of the United States."[3]

If the first and last of these assertions were unchallenged by most of the President's advisers, Acheson's intermediate remarks were to be bitterly contested by his contemporaries . . . and by history. The Secretary of State was held largely to blame for sending the misleading signals to Pyongyang and Moscow which made the Communists believe they could attack with impunity. His statement to the Washington National Press Club in January 1950, when he so carelessly excluded South Korea from the defined perimeter of American vital interests in the Far East, has been fixed as a critical landmark on the road to war. Today there remains no shred of evidence from either Russia or North Korea to indicate what influence, if any, Acheson's remarks had upon Stalin and Kim Il Sung. But

Ambassador Muccio had warned for months from Seoul of the dangers of appearing to exclude South Korea from the declared interests of the United States. The withdrawal of American forces from South Korea, the visible lack of enthusiasm within the United States for Syngman Rhee's regime, the opposition of right-wing Republicans to financial aid of any kind for his country combined with such public statements as that of Acheson to create an overwhelming impression of American indifference to Rhee's fate.

And beyond the misjudgments made in the past, there now also existed the utmost uncertainty among the military men assembled at Blair House concerning Acheson's easy assurance about "our capacity for meeting" the North Korean threat. By the summer of 1950 the American armed forces were at the lowest point of the great postwar rundown undertaken by the Administration. Their numbers had shrunk from 12 million men in 1945 to 1.6 million. Spending was down from $82 billion to $13 billion, just 5 percent of GNP. Nearly every unit in the army was understrength, undertrained, and underequipped. Almost every regiment in the four divisions of MacArthur's occupation army in Japan had been stripped of a battalion or a battery, every company of a platoon, and so on. Their training and readiness for war—for whose shortcomings MacArthur would later seek to blame everyone but himself, their Supreme Commander—were lamentable. Admiral Forrest Sherman, the Navy's Chief of Operations, declared later, "I was fully aware of the hazards involved in fighting Asiatics on the Asiatic mainland, which is something that, as a naval officer, I have grown up to believe should be avoided if possible."[4]

Yet from the outset Truman's Administration was determined to resist the North Korean aggression. "The symbolic significance of its [South Korea's] preservation is tremendous, especially in Japan," George Kennan told the British Ambassador in Washington, Sir Oliver Franks. The President and his advisers were convinced that, even if the Communist invasion did not signal Moscow's readiness to risk all-out war with the United States, it represented a challenge to the will of the non-Communist world that had to be met. "The invasion of the Republic of Korea by the North Korean Army was undoubtedly undertaken at Soviet direction," declared a CIA report of June 28, "and Soviet material support is unquestionably being provided. The Soviet objective is the elimination of the last remaining anti-Communist bridgehead on the mainland of northern Asia, thereby undermining the position of the United States and the Western Powers throughout the Far East."[5]

At that first Blair House meeting Truman made three immediate decisions. First, MacArthur would be told to evacuate the 2,000 Americans in Korea, covering the operation with fighter aircraft from his command. Second, the Supreme Commander Allied Powers—SCAP—would be ordered to provide the South Koreans with every available item of equipment and round of ammunition that could be dispatched from Japan. Third, his area of command would be extended to include Formosa. The Seventh Fleet would deploy immediately between the island and the Chinese mainland to "quarantine" the Korean struggle and discourage either Mao Tse Tung or Chiang Kai Shek from embarking upon a dangerous escalation of Asian hostilities. Throughout those first days of the crisis Washington's thinking was profoundly influenced by fears that the Communist powers were now embarking upon an orchestrated offensive that might be scheduled to extend at any moment to other flash points around the globe. Seldom has mutual ignorance between the superpowers seemed so dangerous, or the absence of solid political intelligence posed a greater threat.

At noon on June 26 the Korean Mission in Washington received yet another call from Syngman Rhee, this time audibly shaken. "Things are not going well militarily," he said. "Please see President Truman and ask him for immediate supplies of arms, for help of any kind." That afternoon at 3 P.M., distraught and weeping, the Koreans were shown into the Oval Office at the White House to meet President Truman and his Secretary of State. Han was impressed by Truman. Like some Americans and many foreigners, he had formed a picture of a somewhat homespun President, a hick from the sticks. Instead, now, in the flesh he saw a smiling, self-assured statesman. "We admire your people and their struggle in adversity," Truman told the visitors. "Your soldiers are fighting bravely. Please convey my appreciation of this to President Rhee. I tell you two things: many years ago, when Americans were fighting for their independence, at Valley Forge, our soldiers lacked food, medicine, clothing. Then some friends came and helped." The Koreans, with a somewhat sketchy grasp of American history, were bemused by this. The President continued, "In 1917, Western Europe was about to fall to pieces, Europeans were in despair, but some friends went over and helped them." The meeting lasted thirty minutes, during which Acheson said nothing. But as Han and his ambassador left, the Secretary of State handed them a statement promising full United States support for the United Nations resolution. This the ambassador read to the great throng of reporters on the White House lawn. But the Koreans went away confused and unhappy about the President's failure to give them an unequivocal assurance of American military support.

Early the next day, June 27, the Korean Ambassador and his First Secretary were at Washington airport, preparing to take a commercial flight to La Guardia for another meeting at the United Nations, when they were paged. They heard on the telephone that President Truman had promised immediate United States air and naval support for the Korean armed forces. Then the Koreans wept again.

Douglas MacArthur later wrote, "I could not help being amazed at the manner in which this great decision was being made. With no submission to

Congress, whose duty it is to declare war, and without even consulting the field commander involved, the members of the executive branch . . . agreed to enter the Korean War. . . . All the risks inherent in this decision—including the possibility of Chinese and Russian involvement—applied then just as much as they applied later."[6]

All this was perfectly true. The bewilderment caused in Moscow and Peking by the American intervention, against the background of the signals the Administration had sent in the past two years suggested such a different attitude, was remarkable. The British Ambassador in Peking cabled to London a few days later, "The strength and extent of American reaction has been a shocking surprise, and will prove a grave embarrassment to the People's Government."

Of all the decisions taken by the White House in those days, it was the declaration of interest in Formosa—which caused little heart-searching for the President and his advisers—that was to have the most profound long-term consequences. At a stroke it bound the United States more closely than ever before to Chiang and his Nationalists, and it signaled that commitment with dismaying clarity to Peking. The movement of the Seventh Fleet, and the extension of MacArthur's theater to include Formosa, alarmed and angered Mao Tse Tung's government far more than the other early American decision, to provide air and naval support for the South Koreans.

At 10:45 P.M. on Tuesday, June 27, a resolution sponsored by the U.S. Ambassador, Warren Austin, was passed by the United Nations Security Council calling upon member nations to "render such assistance to the Republic of Korea as may be necessary to repel the armed attack and to restore international peace and security to the area." It was carried by a vote of 7-1, with Yugoslavia abstaining. At a press conference in the aftermath, Truman agreed with a reporter who asked, "Would it be correct to call it a police action under the United Nations?" This was a phrase that would later haunt Truman. Thousands of young Americans fighting and dying in Korea through the years that followed, and their families and friends at home, would laugh bitterly at the suggestion that they were conducting a "police action" against the massed waves of Communist infantry. But the immediate consequence of the United Nations vote on June 27 was that the President prepared himself to provide whatever military resources proved necessary to stem the Communist invasion. Truman had been accused of weakness in his stand against communism by his Republican opponents. Suddenly his beleaguered Administration had been provided with the opportunity to demonstrate, once and for all, the strength of its will. Truman seized upon it. The State Department also began a hasty round of calls upon its principal allies. The British were contacted for the first time since the North Korean invasion, with apologies from Acheson that there had been no time to contact them sooner. Would the British government consider, as a matter of urgency, what forces it might commit to the support of the United Nations? The earliest possible gesture would be welcomed. In a similar vein, Acheson's officials talked to the Canadians, the French, the Australians, and every other non-Communist power with the resources to make even a token commitment to a great armed demonstration in the cause of freedom.

And MacArthur was to be their commander. In the light of the Administration's subsequent difficulties with their general, it is remarkable how great was its almost mystic faith, in those first days of war, that SCAP could salvage the fortunes of the anti-Communist cause in Korea. If his appointment, as the man on the spot, afterward seemed entirely natural, even in those dramatic days there were skeptics who predicted with remarkable accuracy the risks of placing the direction of the United Nations forces in his hands. "At seventy," wrote James Reston in *The New York Times,* "General Douglas MacArthur . . . is being asked to be not only a great soldier but a great statesman; not only to direct the battle, but to satisfy the Pentagon, the State Department and the United Nations in the process." MacArthur had never been regarded as an Eisenhower, with the Kansan's genius for international teamwork. SCAP, noted Reston, "is a sovereign power in his own right, with stubborn confidence in his own judgment. Diplomacy and a vast concern for the opinions and sensitivities of others are the political qualities essential to this new assignment, and these are precisely the qualities General MacArthur has been accused of lacking in the past."[7] It was impossible for anyone subsequently to suggest that the perils of appointing MacArthur had gone unnoticed.

But there was little doubt about the enthusiasm of the American people for the course their President had adopted. A lead article in *The New York Times* on June 30 was headlined "Democracy Takes Its Stand." It praised Truman's "momentous and courageous act" and welcomed the revision of the American policy in the Far East that "helped to lose China." Wall Street fell sharply in a fit of war nerves, and an unholy alliance of the *Daily Worker, The Wall Street Journal,* and Colonel McCormick's Chicago *Tribune* opposed American intervention in another foreign war. But Washington and Middle America seemed uncommonly united in support of the Administration. "The average American is pleased that the United States has for once boldly taken the initiative," the British Ambassador Oliver Franks cabled to London, "proud that it has called the Soviet bluff and 'won't let them get away with it.' Virtually all shades of opinion wholeheartedly support the President." An hour after Truman's announcement of the American military commitment, Congress passed a bill extending the draft, by 314 votes to 4. On June 30 the Military Assistance Program for Korea passed the Senate by 66 votes to 0. Fueled by the warmth of genuine outrage, the first American response to Communist aggression in Korea enjoyed overwhelming popular support. "I have lived and worked in and out of Washington for twenty years," wrote Joseph

Harsch in *The Christian Science Monitor* the morning after the announcement of
American intervention in Korea. "Never before in that time have I felt such a
sense of relief and unity pass through this city."

Oliver Franks, Britain's envoy, was a close personal friend of Dean Acheson. The
two men spent much time together, at Acheson's house in Georgetown or at Sandy
Springs. If their business was very secret, they would talk it out in the midst of the
fields, where in those innocent days they could not be "bugged." Franks
sometimes received letters from right-wing senators, disgusted with the Anglo-
philia of the American Secretary of State and some of those around him, saying
"Take your Acheson and your Marshall back to England with you." By 1950
more and more conservative Americans were unhappy about an Administration
that still revealed such a strong preoccupation with decadent Europe. But to a
European the quality of those men never seemed in doubt. More than thirty years
later,[8] almost the last living witness close to the very center of events in the
American capital in the summer of 1950, Franks remarked upon the extraordinary
accident that, at this moment of history, such a group of Americans occupied the
principal positions of power in the Truman Administration: the President himself—
"a man of wider outlook than you might think; he had read and enjoyed a lot of
history, especially of Europe and of the American Civil War; he had a background
of depth"; Acheson—"a natural First Class in any university"; Marshall—"he
was looking at the big world all the time, a cool, definite mind which looked for
solutions to problems rather than simply worrying about them"; Bradley—"very,
very high class"; Lovett; and in the second rank, George Kennan, Chip Bohlen,
Dean Rusk. Franks's strongest personal enthusiasm, of course, was for the
Secretary of State: "He came to believe that the United States had an appointment
with destiny, from which there was no way out but for the nation to lead and bend
its whole energies to ordering the world. He could be irascible, romantic,
short-tempered. But he was a blade of steel." To that group of men, Kim Il Sung's
invasion represented a watershed.

"Their thinking [said Franks] moved from the Czech coup in February 1948, to
the Berlin airlift, to Korea. These were seen as stages in Soviet risk-taking that
would culminate in their armed forces crossing boundaries. It is hard now to
remember the shudder about the Russian seizure of Czechoslovakia and the
ghastly memories that it evoked of 1938. There was the feeling that 'we couldn't
do anything in '38, and we find we can't do anything now.' There was the sense
of not knowing where the Russians would break out next. I myself saw Korea as
the last in a series of events. I favoured countering the North Korean invasion,
because I thought that if any army could cross any frontier when it chose, then
chaos had come. Looking back, I don't think I disagree with myself in 1950. It

was one of those moments when *people*—the presence of that extraordinary group in the Administration—made a decisive difference to history.''[9]

Tokyo

MacArthur first learned of the North Korean invasion when a duty officer telephoned from his headquarters, ''General, we have received a dispatch from Seoul, advising that the North Koreans have struck in great strength south across the 38th Parallel.'' To the old general, it seemed an extraordinary rewriting of personal history. Here he was once more, in the Philippines in December 1941: ''An uncanny feeling of nightmare . . . it was the same fell note of the war cry that was again ringing in my ears. It couldn't be, I told myself. Not again! I must still be asleep and dreaming. Not again!

''Barring urgent developments, the Supreme Commander said, he wanted to be left alone with his own reflections. Stepping into his slippers and his frayed robe, he began striding back and forth in his bedroom. Presently Jean stepped in from her room. 'I heard you pacing up and down,' she said. 'Are you all right?' He told her the news, and she paled. Later Blackie bounded in, tried to divert his master with coaxing barks, and failing, slunk off. Then Arthur appeared for his morning romp with his father. Jean intercepted him and told him there would be no frolicking today. MacArthur put his arm around his son's shoulders, paused, thrust his hands in the pockets of his robe, and renewed his strides.''[10]

When MacArthur at last emerged from Olympian seclusion to drive to his headquarters and begin to take up the web of vast new problems and responsibilities that now encircled him, his moods fluctuated. Some of those who saw him believed that ten years had fallen away, as a new crisis lent him new vigor. The extraordinary prospect that now, when it had seemed that the balance of his career could offer only dignified decline, he was once more to play a leading part in the destiny of the world mantled him in serenity, almost euphoria. At first he seemed slow to acknowledge that the North Korean action was more than a border incident. Even when events forced him to do so, he continued to declare his belief that the South Korean Army could hold them. While the general was still wavering about the seriousness of the threat, it was John Foster Dulles, unconvinced by MacArthur's view that Rhee's forces could look after themselves, who cabled Acheson, ''Believe that if it appears the South Koreans cannot contain or repulse the attack, United States forces should be used even though this risks Russian countermoves. To sit by while Korea is overrun by unprovoked armed attack would start a world war.''

But if MacArthur was slow to grasp the climactic nature of the crisis, once he had done so he showed no further hesitation. For years he had watched with dismay and disgust while the Administration focused its overseas attention overwhelmingly upon Europe. It had always been his fundamental conviction that America's destiny lay in the Pacific. He declared that he was almost as astonished that the Administration was showing the will to intervene in Korea as he was by the Communist invasion. But he was deeply gratified by Washington's decision when it came.

Yet from the very beginning the Supreme Commander, entrusted with the execution of the American, and United Nations, response to the Communist invasion, revealed the gulf between his own attitude and the policy of Washington. The Administration's purpose was to conduct a limited war. Communist aggression was to be repelled by whatever means proved necessary. But the struggle was to be confined to the Korean peninsula. The "quarantining" of Formosa, the diplomatic signals sent to Moscow were intended to demonstrate America's determination to prevent an Asian incident from escalating into a global conflict.

From June 1950 until his dismissal ten months later, MacArthur displayed a wholly different perception of the Korean conflict, which he never concealed from his superiors, and scarcely at all from the world. He considered that it was the historic destiny of the United States, as the greatest capitalist power on earth, sooner or later to confront communism on the battlefield. He believed the immense advantage granted to America by her monopolistic possession of effective nuclear forces could not last. It was therefore strongly in America's interests to conduct a decisive struggle against worldwide communism sooner rather than later. The conflict between Washington and MacArthur that was to become one of the most dangerous and divisive factors in the Korean War was essentially a simple one. MacArthur did not believe in the concept of limited war. He acknowledged the Thomist doctrine of just wars. As his biographer William Manchester has written, he "believed that if the battlefield was the last resort of governments, then the struggle must be waged until one side had been vanquished." Furthermore, and far more alarming in its implications, had Washington chosen to grasp them, MacArthur took the view that once hostilities had begun, the general in the field became the central force in decision-making. If he was being entrusted with the direction of United States forces in the Far East in time of war, he expected to be granted the widest discretion in determining their employment. In World War II he had enjoyed extraordinary policy-making powers in the Pacific. He now expected to exercise such powers again, in the age of the new superpowers and of the atomic bomb.

From the beginning the Administration felt uneasy about MacArthur, the aging titan, the "overmighty subject," in command in Tokyo. It was unthinkable to replace America's greatest living field commander at a moment such as this. But given the convictions of the principal player in the drama, what was remarkable was not that Korea precipitated a crisis between the President of the United States and his Supreme Commander in the theater of war, but that the climax was delayed until the struggle was so far advanced.

*   *   *

Even the warmest admirers of General of the Army Douglas MacArthur have conceded his huge aberrations and defects of character. "His paranoia was almost certifiable," wrote William Manchester.[11] "He hated an entire continent: Europe." Another recent American study of MacArthur revealed some hitherto unknown details about his private life when Chief of Staff of the U.S. Army before the Second World War: his penchant for histrionic threats of suicide; his enthusiasm for the platonic attentions of prostitutes, as an audience to boost his titanic ego. The author of this work suggested that, had these facts been widely known, they would have provided sufficient evidence of instability to disqualify him from high command, either in World War II or Korea. This seems a hasty judgment. A moment's reflection upon great commanders of recent history shows that many have possessed eccentricities, to say the least: Patton, Montgomery, Stilwell spring to mind. Humility and the higher peaks of intellectualism are also doubtful assets to great captains. A sense of destiny may be shown to have been mistaken in the case of certain commanders, in whose ranks Hitler might be included. But the same attribute has guided others to marvelous achievements on the battlefield. MacArthur's role in the Korean War can be viewed as a tragedy, or as a case history of the overmighty subject in a democratic society, or as an example of unchallenged military authority leading to megalomania. But it is not enough merely to paint a portrait of an aging general ruling a Byzantine court in postwar Tokyo and to argue that his nature and behavior made all that followed inevitable. There was a greatness about MacArthur which all his own efforts from the autumn of 1950 until his death have been unable to destroy.

Throughout his life he acted on the assumption that the rules made for lesser men had no relevance to himself. Few commanders of any nationality could have borne so large a responsibility for the United States military debacle in the Philippines in 1941–42 yet escaped any share of it. Fewer still could have abandoned his doomed command on Bataan and escaped to safety with his own court, complete even unto personal servants, and made good the claim that his own value to his country surpassed that of a symbolic sacrifice alongside his men. Even less so could they have escaped public censure for accepting a vast personal financial gift from the Philippines President at the very hour when the battle for his country was being lost. There remains considerable controversy about MacArthur's achievement as Supreme Commander in the Southern Pacific, forever struggling with the U.S. Navy for greater personal authority, surrounding himself with sycophantic staff officers—"the Bataan gang"—sometimes slow to grasp tactical opportunities.

Yet no one could deny his stature as a symbol of American authority and the will to prevail, presiding over the vast military might deployed to destroy the Japanese Empire in Asia. His military achievement in the Second World War was very real. Even his pomposity, his studied grandeur suited the role in his country's affairs that he had been called upon to fulfill. Then, when the Japanese surrender came, MacArthur was the architect of that supremely imaginative gesture, the pardoning of Japan. Only a regal figure could have dared to do it when the starving skeletons of the Allied servicemen who survived were still being released from Japan's prisoner-of-war camps, when the people of the United States had been impressed for four years with the baseness and animality of their Japanese enemies. By 1950 MacArthur was seventy years of age. He had gained heroic status in the eyes of the Japanese people, who believed—perhaps not entirely incorrectly—that he had saved them from slavery, while his unsuccessful flirtation with the 1948 Republican nomination for the presidency failed to diminish his position in the eyes of America—the homeland he had not lived in since 1936— as her greatest warrior of the Second World War.

For a young officer to join the staff of the Supreme Commander Allied Powers in Tokyo was an experience akin to becoming a page at the court of a seventeenth-century European monarch. His palace was the squat concrete mass of the old Dai Ichi insurance building. The restoration of self-government to Japan had scarcely diminished SCAP's authority over the nation he had first conquered, then resurrected. MacArthur remained the most powerful man in Japan, a legend not merely to Americans but to the Japanese people who still crowded outside his headquarters each day to watch his ceremonious arrivals and departures. The ruler worked an unusual routine: arrival at the office at 10 A.M., departure at 2 P.M. for lunch at home, return at 4:30 P.M., when he might remain until 9 P.M. or later. Weekends and public holidays meant nothing to him. The more cynical members of his staff disputed his need for their assistance since, in the words of one, "he made every goddamn decision himself."[12] But the "Bataan gang" still dominated the court. Willoughby, his intelligence officer, was nicknamed "Sir Charles" by the staff for his pomposity. Of his key men only General Almond, the Chief of Staff, was not a Bataan man, and very conscious of it. MacArthur liked and trusted Almond, for reasons unclear to some of his staff, who did not. They respected the Southerner's energy and dedication, but they disliked his fierce temper and arrogance. Almond could never take the liberties with the Supreme Commander that, say, Willoughby might. If Willoughby wanted to buttonhole MacArthur, he might lurk ready to catch him, apparently by chance, as he walked down the corridor past the honor guard to take the elevator.

"Well, Charles"—that deep, sonorous, actor's voice.

"Oh—you're going home?"

"Oh, no, Charles"—taking Willoughby's upper arm in that characteristic gesture—"come back in."[13]

The curious group of men around the Supreme Commander could not be said to create a happy, relaxed atmosphere—rather, one of strained, ambitious professionalism. Almond never took time off, because MacArthur did not. Staff officers rode, shot skeet, played a round at the Far East Golf Club, worked out how many more months they must suffer on the rota before it became their turn to be allowed to have their wives come out to join them. But there was not a great deal of laughter, even at the big formal parties of which there were so many, in a country where servants were two for a nickel and any man with the right connections could buy a case of Canadian Club for $25.

Many of the staff were at just such a party, in the garden of one of the spacious villas every senior American in Tokyo possessed, late on the Sunday morning of June 25, 1950. MacArthur himself was not, of course, for he never attended mere social functions. He was already at the Dai Ichi. Almond called his aide, Captain Fred Ladd, and murmured discreetly to him:

"Get two or three of the cars lined up—we're going back to the office."

"Are we coming back here?"

"No."

They left the wives at the party, drove across the city, and took the elevator to the top floor of the Dai Ichi, where they found a ferment of conferences and briefings already in progress. What units were available? What could be done to bring them up to strength? What equipment did they lack? How could they be transported to Korea? The answers to all these questions were much less than satisfactory. The Supreme Commander developed an early rage on Monday afternoon when he heard staff officers discussing the difficulties of finding quarters in Tokyo for some American personnel already evacuated from Seoul with their families.

"What do you mean—find space for the husbands? Why aren't they at their posts? I want them all rounded up—use the military police if you have to—and sent back to their posts in Korea where they are supposed to be."[14]

While the evacuation aircraft were landing at Kyushu all through Tuesday, June 27, the military reconnaissance party, detailed by SCAP to fly from Japan to Korea to make an urgent investigation of the military situation, waited at the airfield. At last, at twilight, the group of fifteen officers headed by Brigadier John Church boarded the transport and took off for Korea. They were met at Suwon by U.S. Ambassador John Muccio, standing with a cluster of Koreans alongside the abandoned Chevrolets of the embassy evacuees. They drove to a nearby school, where they were briefed on the situation, as far as anybody knew it: "The location of enemy forces was unknown, in short," said Lieutenant Colonel George Masters, an ordnance officer from Far East Command who was among Church's group. "But it was reckoned that they would be in Seoul at any time."[15] In reality, the enemy had taken the city that day.

The next day, the twenty-ninth, intermittent American aircraft landed at the strip. Some, from Japan, carried ammunition. Clusters of South Korean troops appeared from nowhere on the tarmac, hastily unloaded the cargo, and once more vanished. Two Japanese-based U.S.A.F. B-26s set down, damaged while carrying out strafing runs. The crews were sent off to headquarters. A few minutes after they had gone, two Communist Yaks appeared overhead and machine-gunned the tarmac and the cripples before making off. Scarcely had these vanished when another aircraft arrived from Japan. This one carried MacArthur himself, together with a clutch of press correspondents. He had come to be photographed and reported inspecting the scene of battle.

MacArthur's brief visit was characteristic. His Constellation, christened the *Bataan,* was bounced in flight by a Communist fighter, which had to be driven off by the escorting Mustangs. MacArthur alone of its passengers watched the drama with keen curiosity, unencumbered by fear. He landed to be met by Ambassador Muccio, a distraught Syngman Rhee, and Brigadier Church. In a nearby schoolhouse, Church briefed the visitors on the military situation. Then, for eight hours, MacArthur drove by jeep through the rear areas of the battlefield. He saw the great columns of terror-stricken refugees pouring south, streams of South Korean soldiers among them. He watched the smoke from artillery and mortar bombardment pockmark the horizon, gazed upon the distant buildings of Seoul, already in enemy hands. He later declared that it was there, at that moment, that he conceived the notion of a great amphibious landing behind the enemy flank. Then he drove back to the *Bataan.*

On the airstrip, to the deep dismay of Brigadier Church's mission, he told the fourteen American officers that they were to remain "and put some backbone into the Koreans." Then he strode up the steps and ordered his pilot back to Tokyo. He sat puffing his corncob pipe through the flight back, scribbling notes for his report to Washington. He declared unequivocally that the situation in South Korea could only conceivably be restored by the commitment of United States ground forces. Men must be thrown in as fast as they could be shipped aboard ships and aircraft. He acknowledged the shortcomings of his Occupation Army for immediate combat, but saw no possibility of waiting until they were trained or re-equipped. Days, hours were now vital. He urged the Administration that the American commitment should be made on the most powerful possible scale: "Unless provision is made for the full utilization of the Army-Navy-Air team in this shattered area, our mission will at best be needlessly costly in life, money, and prestige. At worst, it might even be doomed to failure." Even now MacArthur was not sketching a plan for the expulsion of the North Koreans from the South. He was demanding resources sufficient to inflict absolute defeat upon North Korea. He saw no lesser purpose for which it was worthwhile, or even conceivable, to wage war.

It was still the early hours of the morning of June 29 in Washington when MacArthur's report began to rattle off the printer in the Pentagon. The Army Chief of Staff, General Lawton J. Collins, "Lightning Joe," who had been Bradley's ablest corps commander in Northwest Europe, was wakened from his makeshift bed in an anteroom to the Joint Chiefs' quarters. Collins proposed to see the President with the report as soon as the White House could decently be disturbed. No, said MacArthur. Truman must be seen at once. With every passing hour, the North Korean T-34s were driving deeper and deeper into South Korea. At 5 A.M. Truman was in the Oval Office, ready to act upon MacArthur's recommendations.

This was still 1950, less than ten years after Pearl Harbor and more than ten before the Tonkin Gulf Resolution became the cornerstone of an impassioned debate about the rights of Presidents to make war. Truman, like Roosevelt before him, considered it his function to make executive decisions in defense of the interests of the United States around the world, without need for prior reference to Congress. In his own mind, before MacArthur's report arrived, he knew what he would do. There was some discussion with Acheson about a proposal that had come in the previous evening from Chiang Kai Shek. The Nationalist leader offered 33,000 men to the UN cause in Korea. Truman liked the idea of involving as many of America's allies in the war as possible. He wanted to accept. Acheson was appalled, recognizing the likelihood that war with North Korea would at once become war with Mao's China. The Chiefs of Staff then cast a deciding vote against the proposal, on the purely pragmatic grounds that they doubted the training and usefulness on the battlefield of Chiang's divisions.

So it must be Americans, at first alone, who sought to check the Communists. Truman approved MacArthur's request for authority to commit men drawn from the Occupation Army in Japan. From the White House the order passed through Frank Pace, the Army Secretary, to Collins at the Pentagon, and thence back to the Dai Ichi. Its substance was declared to the world within hours: a naval blockade of the entire Korean coast had been ordered; the United States Air Force in the Far East was to be committed to the war against the Communists. And "General MacArthur has been authorized to use certain ground units." Within hours the first men of the 24th Division were enplaning for Korea. American forces in Japan, jerked unceremoniously from the ease and, indeed, unashamed sloth of occupation life, began the painful struggle to adapt themselves to a war footing. MacArthur and his staff at the Dai Ichi, with one of the least impressive armies the United States had ever put into the field, immersed themselves in the huge task of intervention in a campaign against a ruthless and victorious enemy.

An aide to Almond, MacArthur's Chief of Staff, Captain Fred Ladd, later became one of the most respected American soldiers and advisers in Vietnam. Looking back on Korea many years later, he believed that even in those first days of the war at the Dai Ichi, the roots of all the later disappointments and disasters were there to be seen:

"All those officers, those generals: they really thought that they were going to go over there and 'stop the gooks'—just the same as in Vietnam. Just who 'the gooks' were, they didn't know, and didn't want to know. You could have asked any American senior officer in Korea: 'Who commands the Korean 42nd division—ROK or Communist—and what's his background?' He wouldn't have known what you were talking about. A gook is a gook. But if the Germans had been the enemy, he'd have known.''[16]

Yet MacArthur would have said, What was the choice? If he, or America, stayed their hands until the nation was militarily ready, South Korea would have been gone. Better, surely, to stake out and defend some claim upon the soil of South Korea, however precarious, than discuss from Tokyo how to recover a peninsula entirely fallen to the Communists. And whatever the virtues of Kim Il Sung's hordes, the defects of the 24th Division and its sister formations in Japan, American soldiers could surely somehow prevail against a barefoot Asian army.

Whatever the next Communist move, the Truman Administration was now committed to use whatever measure of force proved necessary to restore the independence and integrity of South Korea. It remained only to discover how many of America's allies and members of the United Nations would lend tangible aid for the cause to which they had voted commitment.

To the enormous relief of Washington, Britain immediately dispatched her Far East fleet—a light fleet carrier, two cruisers, and five escorts—to join America's warships in operations against North Korea; a token land force in brigade strength followed shortly thereafter. The Ministry of Defense cabled to Air Marshal Lord Tedder, then leading a British delegation in Washington, ''We consider such demonstrations of solidarity are more important than the actual strength of the forces deployed, and we hope other members of the United Nations will quickly follow suit.''

Tedder's hopes were fulfilled, in that more than a dozen major nations dispatched small contingents of men, ships, and aircraft to support the United Nations cause. But none showed any enthusiasm to provide substantial help in greater than battalion or brigade strength. Each in turn pleaded impoverishment of military resources to justify their reluctance to send major forces to Korea.

The direct consequences of Korea for Britain included the extension of National Service to two years and a mounting balance-of-payments deficit as a result of rearmament. But even most left-wing Socialists conceded the justice of the American cause in Korea. There was almost a euphoria among Members of Parliament about the raising of the banner of the United Nations. ''I should like to remark,'' said Mr. Harry Hopkins, MP for Taunton, ''that we are, in fact, witnessing something quite unique in the enforcement by arms of collective security by a world organisation. . . . That is something that has never before occurred in the history of the world and it is, at least, a consolation that we are

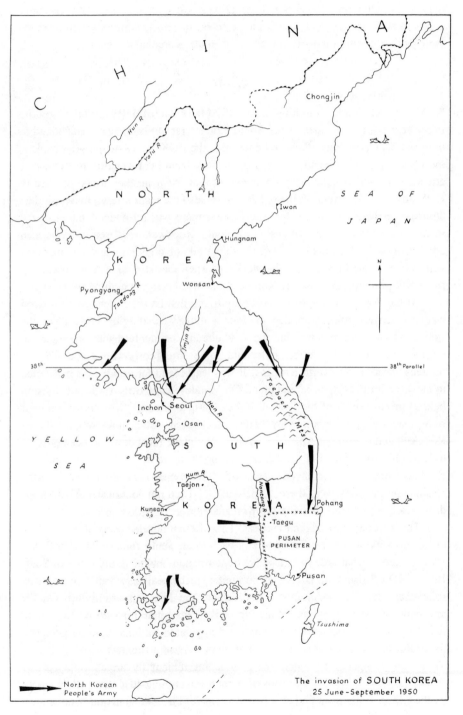

North Korean
People's Army

The invasion of SOUTH KOREA
25 June - September 1950

moving along the lines towards an international police force.'' Thus, full of wordy
ideals as well as economic and strategic fears, the British and other allies made
their modest commitments to the cause of South Korea.

Seoul

At 7 A.M. on Sunday morning, June 25, Major General Paek Sun Yup, the
thirty-year-old commander of the South Korean 1st Division, was telephoned at
home by his Operations officer to be told that the ROK forces on the west bank of
the Imjin had been overrun. He had been away from his formation for ten days,
attending a course at the army command school. Now he took a taxi at once to
ROK army headquarters, in the old Japanese headquarters building in Seoul. The
atmosphere there was still surprisingly calm: there was no understanding of the
scale of the Communist offensive. Colonel Rockwell, his senior American
adviser, took Paek in his own jeep to collect one of his regimental commanders
who was at home in Seoul for the weekend. Then the three men drove north, up
roads still peaceful, because the Korean public had been told nothing of the crisis.

At the divisional command post they found that half the men were away on
weekend leave. Officers trickled in. Paek's units were digging in south of the
Imjin, but they had no wire, and they had already lost contact with one regiment
north of the river. The commander and some stragglers escaped south a few
minutes ahead of the North Koreans. It was learned that the engineers had failed
to blow the Imjin bridges behind them. On Monday, the twenty-sixth, the division
held its ground south of the river. But they learned that the 7th Division, on their
right, had collapsed completely. They received a bitter blow when Colonel
Rockwell and their other American advisers announced that they had been ordered
to leave the front. Some of the Americans shed tears in their embarrassment. The
Koreans were utterly dismayed. Paek said, ''We thought that it was for this kind
of situation that they were there, to help us.''[17] Then the American KMAG jeeps
drove away southward, leaving the Koreans alone.

The next day they began to retreat. That afternoon Paek received orders from
one of his superiors immediately to pull back to the south bank of the Han River,
south of Seoul. That order was hastily countermanded by the Army Chief of Staff.
But the ROK 3rd and 5th Divisions, committed piecemeal to the battle, were being
rolled back by the Communists. Everywhere the line was crumbling. On the
afternoon of the twenty-eighth, the North Koreans broke through on their right
flank. By now American aircraft were overflying the front, looking for targets. But
the ROKs possessed no forward air controllers and had no contact with the planes.
They were compelled to watch many unloading their ordnance on empty paddy
fields. Far worse, hundreds of tons of ordnance were unloaded upon ROK troops
by the U.S.A.F. in those first chaotic days. One of Paek's regimental commanders

announced that he knew a place where they might get a ferry across the Han. Paek told his men to make their way out as best they could and head for a rendezvous north of Suwon. Then, in small groups, they made for the river, crossed at the ferry, and started walking south—colonels, generals, and privates alike. After one week of war, Syngman Rhee's army could account for only 54,000 of its men. The remaining 44,000 had merely disappeared, many of them never to be seen again. "South Korean casualties as an index to fighting have not shown adequate resistance capabilities or the will to fight," MacArthur signaled bluntly to Washington, ."and our best estimate is that complete collapse is imminent."

Ferris Miller, the American who had first come to Seoul as a naval officer in 1945, and was now an economic aid adviser working from an office in the Banda Hotel, spent the night of Saturday, June 24, playing mahjongg at the Nationalist Chinese Embassy across from the Catholic cathedral. On Sunday morning he rose late, heard the news, and hastened to wake up a Korean politician friend. "It's only a skirmish," he told Miller casually. "It won't amount to much."[18] Through the hours that followed Miller watched the tempo of panic rise: vehicles careering through the streets at reckless speed, radio appeals for military personnel. From a hotel room he watched Communist planes strafing. Yet still Miller could not escape a sense of ridicule, of fantasy, about what he was seeing.

That evening he attended a long-scheduled dinner party at the U.S. Army compound. Here he found growing signs of nervousness. By Monday night, looking out of his apartment window, he could see the gun flashes on the northern horizon. Then he heard on the U.S. Armed Forces radio that the situation was stabilizing. Emergency feeding arrangements would be suspended. As of Tuesday all U.S. personnel would once again be required to pay for meals in the mess. Miller went to bed somewhat reassured.

But in the early hours of the morning there was a fierce banging on his door. An American officer told him to bring a toothbrush and pajamas to U.S. headquarters in the Banda Hotel. Amid a total blackout, he packed his possessions in two footlockers and drove to the U.S. Embassy. Here he found chaos: men burning documents in great heaps on the street outside, Koreans besieging the building for help in making their escapes. Inside, Miller saw a Korean woman sobbing helplessly amid officials hastening to and fro. "Help me, help me," she begged him. "My husband is in the States." Miller could do nothing. At dawn buses came to take the staff out to Kimpo for evacuation. Miller was one of the last to leave. He felt guilty as he pushed his footlockers into the hold of a C-47, conscious of all the men and women around him who had salvaged nothing. The ambassador's secretary climbed aboard with a dog under one arm, a bottle of scotch under the other. Then they started the engines and taxied bumpily across the tarmac for takeoff. Only when they landed in Japan did they discover holes in the fuselage from stray Communist ground fire. Only later did they learn of those left behind: the mining adviser who overslept in his billet and was never heard of again, the party of Americans who had been attending a wedding in Kaeson and became prisoners in North Korea for three long years.

Lee Chien Ho, a twenty-one-year-old tax collector's son studying chemical engineering at National University, was in a barber's shop having his hair cut on the morning of June 25 when the news of the North Korean invasion came through on the radio. His father was away in Inchon. Unlike many Koreans, Lee was eager to take some part in the defense of his country. He and a few score like-minded students spent much of the next two days at their university campus east of the city, pathetically standing guard armed with broomsticks. On the second night of their vigil, South Korean Army stragglers began to come through from Uijambu. "What do you kids think you're doing?" demanded one. They told him they were defending the university. "You're out of your minds," the soldier said. "Go home." Bewildered, they drifted away in ones and twos toward the city, among the dejected military fugitives. Lee slept that night at the School of Liberal Arts, by the streetcar terminal. Walking out the next morning, he saw a long row of large, shiny government cars abandoned neatly in front of the railway station. It was his first tremor of understanding of the scale of the disaster.[19]

Lee went home and told his mother that he was sure they should leave. At first she was bitterly reluctant to abandon all their household possessions. The banks were closed, so they had no means of recovering their money. But at last he persuaded her. On Tuesday afternoon, carrying a sack of rice on his back and leading his two younger brothers, Lee led his mother through the streets toward the Han River bridge. Curiously enough, he found few others going their way and many reentering the city from the south. They laughed at the family, burdened with their possessions: "What are you so worried about?" That night they slept in a schoolhouse, disturbed by the thunder of heavy rain on the roof and distant guns. The next morning, as they walked on southward, they heard the huge explosion as the Han River bridge was blown by Rhee's retreating army. They struggled on amid a growing army of panic-stricken soldiers and frantic civilians, a confusion of abandoned possessions on the road and low-flying aircraft sweeping overhead— the wreckage of defeat.

To Suk Bun Yoon, a thirteen-year-old middle school pupil, the son of a merchant, the North Koreans looked more like a defeated army than a victorious one as they straggled into Seoul.[20] Suk and his family had spent much of the previous two days hiding in a sewage pipe. On the twenty-seventh they struggled through the seething mass of refugees toward the Han River. But the press, the hysteria, the screaming mass of humanity fighting to reach the ferries was too great.

Despondent and frightened, they returned home to await their fate. On the morning of the twenty-eighth, as the first Communists arrived, civilians in red arm bands hastened through the streets, urging the watching citizens to cheer their liberators. Some did so. But most of the older people slipped away to their houses, from whose windows they peered nervously out into the street at the solemn, olive-clad files padding past, some still wearing camouflage foliage in their helmets.

Many hundreds of thousands of the small men and women of Korean society, whose names featured on no lists, whose lives had merely been a struggle for survival, were unsure what to make of the Communists' coming. Won Jung Kil was a peasant's son who had grown up in Inchon as the breadwinner of a family of eight. Their father was dead, Won had no fixed employment: "We thought about food—nothing else."[21] Inchon was a stronghold of Communist sympathies of a primitive kind: Won and his kind hated Syngman Rhee because he did nothing for the working man, and loathed the police for their privileges. He was in Seoul the day war broke out. He hastened home, uncertain what to think. He found the local Communists running, exulting, through the street, preparing a grand welcome for the North Korean Army. The family talked. They decided that it was safer to go. There might be fighting in the town. They gathered up saucepans, blankets, children, and began walking southward. They expected that it would be safe to come home in a week. In reality they were embarking on a three-year odyssey shared by millions of their fellow countrymen, that would cost them their home—a shack carelessly destroyed by the warring armies—their freedom, for the young men of the family were conscripted and spent three years barely subsisting in uniform, and enormous hardship for the women, who would exist chiefly upon American milk powder and herbs picked from the mountains until many months after the war ended. For the nations of the West, the war that had now come to Korea represented a challenge to the principles of freedom and anticommunism. The democracies were to endure huge anxieties and frustrations in the course of seeking to meet this. But for the people of Korea, three years of unspeakable tragedy, privation, and sacrifice had begun, from which scarcely a family in that unhappy land would be spared.

4

WALKER'S WAR

Retreat to the Naktong

South of Seoul, Kim Il Sung's army paused. The North Koreans needed time to regroup and allow their logistic "tail," such as it was, to catch up. Yet the week that they lingered, however essential to enable them to consolidate their hold on the capital and prepare for the next thrust, was critical in the development of the war. When their advance began once more on July 5, the Communists encountered Task Force Smith, north of Osan. Smith's battalion, committed under the most unfavorable circumstances, inflicted only the merest check upon the Communists. But behind the 1/21st Infantry the remainder of the U.S. 24th Division was deploying.

Major General William Dean, its commander, a big man of fifty-one with a reputation as something of a martinet, set up his headquarters in Taejon as the South Korean Army appointed its third chief of staff in less than three weeks of war. For all the South Korean assertions that their army was fighting desperately, the Americans could see evidence only of chaos and retreat. Subsequent evidence from Communist sources suggests that, in reality, in those weeks some South Korean units inflicted substantial damage and important delay upon the invaders. But the only useful intelligence about Communist movements came from the American aircraft now flying constant interdiction missions. These in turn were critically hampered by lack of general knowledge of the North Korean forces and specific information on targets. No effective system of forward air control existed. In those first weeks of war, the U.S.A.F. poured thousands of tons of bombs onto Korea. There is little evidence that these proved more than an irritant to Communist operations in the first stage of the war, however important they became in August and September.

The next unit of the 24th Division to face the enemy assault was the 34th Infantry, moving up behind Lieutenant Colonel Smith's battalion. The 34th, 1981 men strong, devoid of tanks or effective antitank weapons, was transported from Japan under conditions of haste and confusion, and was no more prepared in mind, training, or equipment to arrest the North Korean advance than Task Force Smith. But Major General Dean could give its commander only the simplest and most straightforward of orders: to deploy his men in blocking positions across the key routes southward, at Ansong and Pyongtaek. It was to these positions, late on the night of July 5, that the stragglers and survivors of Task Force Smith began to drift in, bearing their bleak and confused tale of being overrun by a Communist armored host. The disarray within the 24th Division was compounded by almost total lack of communications: telephone wires were repeatedly cut, radios were defeated by distance and mountains between units. In the rain and mist of early morning on July 6, the 1/34th found itself facing North Korean infantry and armor swarming south across the shallow river line they were defending.

The brief action that followed was considerably more inglorious than that of Task Force Smith. The Americans engaged the Communists with mortars and machine guns, but quickly found the enemy closing in upon them. The battalion commander, Lieutenant Colonel Harold Ayres, saw no alternative to retreat, if his men were not to be isolated and cut off. He had earlier been advised by General George Barth that, come what might, he was "not to end up like Brad Smith," left irretrievably exposed behind the Communist advance. A few minutes ahead of the enemy's T-34s, amid a frenzied stream of Korean refugees, their carts and baggage and animals, the Americans hastened southward, discarding equipment as they went. By the time General Dean had learned that his point battalion was in full retreat, and hurried forward in his jeep to check the movement, the 34th Infantry was south of Chonan. A furious scene ensued between the divisional commander and the senior field officers of the 34th. They had offered no significant resistance to the enemy and had withdrawn without orders. Dean expressed his disgust. He now had no alternative but to order them to dig in where they stood. He also relieved the commanding officer of the 34th Infantry and replaced him by an officer with experience of regimental command in World War II. It was the first of a long procession of sackings in the field which proved necessary in those early, traumatic weeks. Martin, the 34th's new commander, survived just forty-eight hours before his death in action at Chonan.

*   *   *

"As daylight broke on July 8 [recorded Private First Class Robert Harper of the 34th Infantry's Headquarters Company] we heard this loud clanking noise off on the left. We understood now what was happening—their tanks were coming. Eventually I could see them dimly, moving through the morning mist. I counted them. When I got to nine, an order was given to pull back off the railroad tracks and set up in the first row of houses behind the sewage ditch. From there I saw the North Korean infantry moving to my right across the field in front of the railroad depot. I could hear occasional small-arms and machine-gun fire. Mortar rounds began falling nearby. The tanks continued to roll down the road toward us. We had no way of stopping them. They came to the end of the road and I could hear them firing. I did not know which of our companies were down there but knew they were catching hell. We were ordered back to a narrow street, where we waited to see what would happen next. I heard the new CO, Colonel Martin, tried to take on one of the tanks with a bazooka. The tank scored a direct hit on the colonel, and he was killed on the spot. We began receiving real heavy mortar and tank fire. . . . We ran down some alleys and met some more GIs who said orders had been issued to evacuate the town. I could hear a lot of small-arms and mortar fire behind me. We went to the east edge of town, worked our way through rice paddies and got to the road. There were quite a few civilians still on the road. We joined them in heading south. We drew heavy artillery fire and began to lose a lot of people."[1]

"Resistance had disintegrated, and now our troops were bugging out," wrote Dean.[2] Through the wretched weeks that followed, among the gloomiest in the history of the United States Army, the pattern of Chonan was repeated again and again. An uncertain and unhappy American infantry unit would be hustled into a defensive position, its officers unwilling or unable to conceal their own confusion and dismay. The flood of refugees would slow to a trickle, then halt altogether. There would be a tense silence, men peering up the empty road, until they heard the tortured squeal and clatter of advancing armor. The North Korean tanks would come forward until they met American fire. Then they halted to allow infantry to swarm past them, infiltrating the American positions and working around their flanks. The Americans then withdrew, often in undignified haste, abandoning vehicles and equipment as they escaped as best they might amid the swelling columns of civilian refugees. "We knew that we weren't doing very well," Major Floyd Martain, one of the survivors of Task Force Smith, declared wryly. "But we kept saying to ourselves, 'Well, here we are, and we've been here a month, and where the hell is the rest of the United States Army?' "[3] They felt profoundly lonely.

The essential criticism of the performance of the 24th Division at this period centers not upon the fact that its units repeatedly withdrew, for had they not done so, they would assuredly have been bypassed and eventually destroyed. It was their failure to inflict significant damage or delay upon the enemy before disengaging that so embarrassed their commanders. Neither MacArthur nor his subordinates could reasonably have expected the scanty American forces deployed thus far to halt the Communist invasion. But well-handled regimental combat teams could have hit and run, punished the North Koreans for a few hours with mortar and machine-gun fire, then pulled back to the next obstacle suitable for defense. In reality, American officers seem to have had neither will nor skill to create antitank obstacles, to use mines even when these became available, or to employ the support weapons they had against the North Korean infantry. Terrain, logistics, poor communications, and refugees did more to delay the North Korean advance in the first weeks of July than the American infantry in their path.

On July 10, General Douglas MacArthur was formally appointed Commander in Chief of the United Nations Command. The United States rejected the UN Secretary-General's proposal that the war should be directed by the "Committee on Co-Ordination for the Assistance of Korea," as the British, French, and Norwegians seemed to favor. Since the U.S. was bearing the overwhelming burden of war—and directly contributing most of its cost—Washington insisted upon direct military control and got its way with its allies. "In the military field," the principal diplomatic historian of the UN has written, "the control of the United States government was complete; in the political field, consultations with the United Nations and some contributing nations were more frequent. On occasion the UN made various recommendations. In the final analysis, however, a large range of political decisions was taken by the United States government as the United Command."[4] On July 13, General Walton Walker, a corps commander under Patton in Northwest Europe, established his Eighth Army headquarters in Korea, with operational responsibility for UN ground forces in the field. The stubby, rugged, impatient little Texan could scarcely enthuse about the material he was being asked to work with. His forces were exclusively now, as they would remain principally for many weeks, men of the American Occupation Army in Japan. The only available reinforcement for the crumbling forces of Syngman Rhee must come from Japan, where the 25th and 1st Cavalry Divisions were being hastily mobilized for war. Until they came it was essential for Dean's 24th to delay the Communist advance, to give ground only yard by yard between Osan and the next natural defensive line, forty miles southward on the Kum River.

The North Koreans brushed past the two regiments of Dean's shaken force deployed along the Kum with almost contemptuous ease. At its low, almost barren summer level, the river presented no significant threat to T-34s. The 19th Infantry found itself compelled to fight its way out of encirclement, with the loss of almost one man in five, more than half of its 1st Battalion. With his flanks turned, Dean was driven back into Taejon. The Communists began their assault on the city on

July 19. Dean directed its defense with furious energy. Antitank teams armed with the newly arrived 3.5-inch bazooka scored a string of successes against the Communist T-34s. Dean himself led one team, stalking a tank through the streets for more than an hour before successfully destroying it. But within a few hours North Korean armor and infantry had broken through, and the survivors of the 24th were retreating southward once more. Dean himself remained a fugitive in the hills for a month before he was captured, the senior American officer to be taken by the Communists in the Korean War.

It was a period when there was a desperate need for heroes, and Dean was represented as one across the United States. At the end of the war he was decorated with the Congressional Medal of Honor. His courage was never in doubt. Yet some expert soldiers in Korea were dismayed, even disgusted, by the collapse of leadership in the 24th Division even before the Taejon battle. "Why any general would tolerate the chaos at his headquarters in the fashion that Dean did, I never understood," said Colonel John Michaelis, a distinguished World War II combat veteran who witnessed it. "There was a sense of hysteria. Nobody seemed to want to go and kick somebody in the butt. I never knew what Dean thought he was doing, as a divisional commander, to grab a bazooka and go off hunting tanks."[5] Michaelis was among those who considered Dean's behavior the negation of his responsibility as a commander. He was not alone in his opinion. "Dean was very personable," said Lieutenant Colonel George Masters, "but he still did not know what war was. Fundamentally, he was a silly man." If these seem harsh judgments, they are those by men who watched the agony of the 24th Division. It was difficult to pass any less cruel verdict upon the performance of most of the American units in the battle. "We had the conceited opinion that we were trained soldiers," said Colonel Masters. "Yet what we did in Korea, as we do quite frequently in our history, was to try to use civilians as soldiers and expect them to be combat-effective. We are usually disappointed."[6]

Between July 10 and 15 the U.S. 25th Division landed in Korea. On July 18 the 1st Cavalry—paradoxically, an infantry division—came ashore at Pohang-dong. By July 22 they were deployed. The remains of the battered, indeed almost ruined, 24th Division were able to withdraw through their positions and at last catch their breath. In seventeen days the 24th had lost some 30 percent of their strength, more than 2,400 men reported missing in action. Yet the reinforcing formations gave little ground for confidence on their first appearances in action. On July 20 the 24th Infantry of 25th Division broke and fled after their first few hours in battle at Yechon. The 24th was an all-black unit, a relic of the U.S. Army's ill-fated segregation policy. The pattern of the 24th's first action was repeated in the days that followed, with men streaming toward the rear as soon as darkness provided cover for their retreat. An inexplicable panic overcame the 1/24th on July 29 after facing a Communist mortar barrage. It became necessary to set up roadblocks behind the 24th's positions, to halt deserters and stragglers leaving the line. The U.S. Army's official history castigates the regiment: "The tendency to panic continued in nearly all the 24th Infantry operations west of Sangju. . . ." By the end of July, Walker recognized that it was possible to use the 24th only as an outpost force, a trip wire in the face of Communist assaults. It proved necessary to maintain another regiment in reserve behind the front, to conduct serious resistance when the 24th broke.* In Washington, Collins, the Army Chief of Staff, recognized the failure of the concept of all-black units. At the earliest possible moment, black soldiers must be integrated into white units. But there was no time for that in Korea in July.

Even for the better American regiments, the first encounter with the Communist manner of making war in Korea was disturbing, confusing, demoralizing, brutalizing. It was a common experience to see a herd of refugees shuffle toward an American position, then sweep aside at the last moment to reveal the North Korean infantrymen sheltering among them. Even for GIs who had seen combat against the Japanese in the Pacific in World War II, it was a frightening experience to meet a North Korean enemy willing to hurl away his life in suicidal "human wave" charges at point-blank range. Later, when the Chinese came in, these tactics would be translated to a vastly greater scale, even more unnerving in their fanaticism. The Communists acknowledged no claim of treachery or breach of the rules of war in their use of soldiers in civilian clothes or pretended surrenders to mask attacks. Most shocking of all to American sensibilities in Korea and at home in the United States, the Communists proved ruthlessly indifferent to the taking of prisoners. A shudder of revulsion ran through the American nation at the discovery, in Korea, of the first groups of American prisoners shot dead by the roadside, their hands tied behind their backs with barbed wire. It rapidly became apparent that the North Koreans served prisoners in such fashion whenever they had no explicit need for them alive, for propaganda or intelligence purposes.

Bleakly, American commanders perceived a certain advantage when news of Communist atrocities spread through their formations. Some soldiers who had hitherto made little show of wanting to fight were now brought face-to-face with the likely consequence of capture. There was no salvation to be sought in a comfortable POW compound. Yet, conversely, fear of being outflanked and cut off became an obsession in many units. "Bugout fever," the urge to withdraw precipitately in the face of the slightest threat from the flank, was already a serious problem. "I saw young Americans turn and bolt in battle," wrote Marguerite Higgins of the New York *Herald Tribune,* "or throw down their arms, cursing their government for what they thought was embroilment in a hopeless cause." Americans trained and conditioned to fight as part of a large army of mutually

* This account is disputed by members of the 24th Infantry. The U.S. Army's official history is currently under review.

supporting elements were deeply ill at ease holding isolated positions with their flanks in the air, with the knowledge of perhaps twenty or thirty miles of mountains between themselves and the next allied formation in the line.

Beyond this, the terrible shocks of the first weeks of war, the sense of facing a merciless Asian enemy caused many Americans to extend their fears and suspicions to the entire people of Korea: "the gooks" meant not merely the Communists, but all Koreans. Communist atrocities provoked callousness in many Americans, fighting a desperate struggle for survival, toward the Asians around them, creatures from another planet whose language they could not understand, whose customs bewildered them, whose country seemed most vividly represented by the universal stench of human excrement manuring the fields.

Yet whatever the shortcomings of the American military performance in those weeks, it narrowly sufficed. And for all the bitter criticisms of the South Korean Army, the ROK, whose battered and demoralized remnants were falling back alongside the Americans, its struggle had not been in vain. Amid the pain of withdrawal and defeat in July, America and her allies were disposed to dwell upon the sufferings of their own armed forces. Yet in those first weeks of fighting, surprised and facing overwhelming odds, the South Koreans and their American allies inflicted heavier losses upon the Communists than was understood at the time. It later emerged that the North Koreans had suffered some 58,000 casualties between June 25 and early August. At the moment when the confidence of Walker and his army was at its lowest ebb, when they saw defeat staring them in the face in southeast Korea, the UN forces in the peninsula by now outnumbered their Communist enemies.

The 25th Division held its positions in the center of the country until July 30 before being compelled to begin falling back. The 1st Cavalry, outflanked around Yongdong, began retreating on July 29 toward Kumchong. And even as the Americans fought the threat from the north, in the west an even more dangerous Communist movement was under way. A North Korean division had hooked around Taejon and hastened through the defenseless countryside southward. By August 1 its leading elements were near Masan, just thirty miles short of the southeastern port of Pusan. If the North Koreans could reach Pusan, the Americans would be encircled with little chance of escape. Their predicament was desperate. Walker was able to rush units of the 25th Division down to Masan, with hours to spare, to block the advance. By now the Eighth Army's commander knew that both his men and the North Koreans had run out of room for grand maneuvers. The defenders must stand and fight. On the high ground behind the great loop of the Naktong River they would command positions of great natural strength. In the first days of August the long files of dusty, exhausted Americans and their overloaded vehicles trudged doggedly south and east, to the new line. Here, on the last mountain mass before the sea, the fate of Walker's army, of the United Nations in Korea, would be decided.

Dressing Ranks

Even as the men from that soft, ill-prepared American Occupation Army struggled to improvise their perimeter against the Communist assault, the Western powers were gathering forces to reinforce them. From the outset it was apparent that MacArthur would need every man who could be spared from the democracies' worldwide commitments if he was to hold the North Koreans. At the Pentagon, the War Office in London, the war departments of Canada, France, Australia, New Zealand, politicians and staff officers pored earnestly over their orders of battle and staff tables, seeking to determine what could be spared for Korea. From far and wide, reservists were being recalled from their civilian occupations and tranquil domestic lives; draftees hustled through basic training; cadre formations built up to strength with whatever men could be found to fill their ranks, and equipment to stock their inventories. Only five years after the end of World War II, the victors found themselves embarrassingly, absurdly pressed to find the resources with which to fight a limited war in Asia.

MacArthur's initial optimism about the scale of resources required to halt the Communists in Korea was replaced by mid-July with demands for men on a scale that thoroughly alarmed the Joint Chiefs in Washington. On July 5 he sought—and received agreement for—the deployment of the 2nd Infantry Division, a regiment of the crack 82nd Airborne, and the 2nd Engineer Special Brigade. On July 20 four National Guard divisions were activated. Within days of the outbreak of war, Congress rushed through a one-year extension of the newly lapsed Selective Service Act. The Defense Department declared a requirement for 50,000 conscripts in September, the same again in October, 70,000 in November. Caught in the contemporary mood of war fever, Congress voted the President an $11 billion emergency defense appropriation. Yet even the vast economic strength of the United States did not make it possible, by a mere national act of will, instantly to transform a demobilized, almost decayed military machine into an instrument of war capable of fighting effectively in Korea while maintaining combat readiness for a greater struggle elsewhere in the world. For months to come, as America mobilized, her military effort in the Far East would be a patchwork of expedience and improvisation.

Some young Americans, matching the mood of the time in their country, saw the war in genuinely idealistic terms, as an opportunity to take a heroic part in the crusade against communism—that and perhaps a hint of boredom with postwar life in a small town. Bill Patterson was the tall, lanky, twenty-year-old son of an industrial worker in Stillwater, New York. He and a group of friends became passionately excited by the cause—forty-five of them marched in a group to enlist: "They had a problem over there. We wanted to do something about it. And I guess I didn't have a lot to do at home. We started preaching around the town, saying—

'Come down to Albany! Join the service!' I remember driving one kid of seventeen home to his parents to sign the papers.''[7]

Private Warren Avery was a bus driver's son from Virginia, a high school dropout who had "bummed around" for a year before joining the Army in June 1949. He volunteered for Korea because the war sounded exciting. He was issued with a brand-new M-1 rifle, pushed onto a Pan Am airliner to make the first flight of his life to the Far East, and posted to the 29th Infantry on line on the Pusan Perimeter just ten days after he put in his name for Korea.[8]

Corporal Selwyn Handler was called to active duty with the 1st Marines after two years as a reservist, a few days after returning from summer camp. He found the intense, purposeful bustle at Camp Pendleton entirely romantic: "To me, it was a great adventure.''[9] A few reservists with young families were unhappy, but most exulted in the intensive training that continued every day on the ships on which they sailed for Japan. Marine Bill Sorensen had always bitterly regretted missing World War II, not least because his idolized elder brother had won the Congressional Medal of Honor as a sergeant. He was thrilled to be recalled from the reserves and shipped to join the 7th Marines. As they practiced firing their rifles over the fantail of the transport in mid-Pacific, the young man from Michigan enthused like a schoolboy about the prospect of combat. But an old sweat said to him, "Sorensen, as soon as that first shell goes over your head, you'll wish you'd never seen a war.''[10] And, of course, it was true.

But many men still believed that whatever was happening in Korea—and whatever Korea was—it would "never be any big deal." Private Clyde Alton, from Indiana, a World War II veteran of thirty, found himself drafted to a battalion of the 2nd Division alongside the same top sergeant with whom he had gone through the North African campaign. He and Alton agreed that Korea was unlikely to amount to much: "This is going to be no war, cos these people are natives.''[11]

The Pusan Perimeter

The six-week series of actions that came to be known as the battle of the Pusan Perimeter began on the night of July 31 when the last of Walker's retreating army crossed the Naktong eastward. "There will be no more retreating, withdrawal, readjustment of lines or whatever you call it," the Eighth Army's commander declared in a ringing order of the day following the fall of Chinju. "There are no lines behind which we can retreat. This is not going to be a Dunkirk or Bataan. A retreat to Pusan would result in one of the greatest butcheries in history. We must fight to the end. We must fight as a team. If some of us die, we will die fighting together." If it was corn, this was an hour when corn, as well as courage, was called for.

The Naktong River itself created an obstacle between a quarter and half a mile wide in its lower reaches defended by the Eighth Army but was shallow enough to be forded in many places. More important for Walker, it was commanded by steep hill ranges on both banks. Half the length of the American perimeter lay along the river line. On the south side the Americans were now dug into positions of great natural strength. Armor, heavy artillery, and support equipment was being unloaded in quantity at Pusan. As the fighting stabilized, forward air control and clearer identification of positions made fighter bomber strikes increasingly effective against Communist concentrations. Walker's most serious problems, his chronic difficulties throughout the Perimeter battle, were the poor morale and training of many of his men together with the shortage of manpower which made it impossible for him to hold his entire 130-mile front in strength. At the end of July, Walker disposed of a paper strength of some 95,000 men. Most of his 47,000 American combat troops were deployed in three infantry divisions of the Japan Occupation army, some of whose units were already badly mauled. Week by week this number was increasing as reinforcements reached Korea—the Marine Brigade, the British 27 Brigade. Walker could also call upon 45,000 South Koreans, though the combat value of these men was very limited indeed. Most were entirely untrained levies, dragged at gunpoint from their villages days before being sent to the front.

In August 1950 the men on the Pusan Perimeter saw themselves as a beleaguered army, clinging to the United Nations' last toehold in Korea amid the onslaught of massed ranks of Communist fanatics. Beleaguered Walker's army indeed was. But it is a measure of the psychological dominance the Communists had achieved at this time that most Americans would have been frankly disbelieving had they been told that the UN forces by now outnumbered the North Koreans significantly, and outgunned them overwhelmingly. The ferocity and suicidal recklessness of the massed attacks of Kim Il Sung's units, night after night through those weeks, gave the defenders the impression of an Asian horde with limitless reserves of manpower. In reality, the North Koreans were squandering their dwindling reserves of armor, ammunition, and trained men. But again and again the Communist gamble came close to success. Enemy attackers broke through Walker's line, began pushing forward to open a chasm in the front, and were halted only by the last-ditch movement of one of his handful of reliable "fire-brigade" units to stop the gap.

The battle for the Pusan Perimeter was marked by an almost daily succession of crises for the Eighth Army, in which disaster was averted by the narrowest of margins. Kim Il Sung and his commanders fully grasped the urgency of smashing through to Pusan before the UN buildup made their task impossible. The North Korean 4th Division mounted one of the first big attacks against the U.S. 24th— the battle of the Naktong Bulge. On the night of August 5 they successfully pushed forward across the river with tanks and guns, overrunning American outpost positions. In the days that followed they built up strength on the east bank, gaining ground steadily.

On August 17 the Marine Provisional Brigade was committed to counter-attack. Two days later, after bitter fighting, the Communists were driven back across the Naktong. And even as the 24th Division was being hard pressed, farther north the 1st Cavalry and ROK 1st and 6th Divisions faced a succession of thrusts aimed to break through to Taegu, where Eighth Army headquarters was sited. By August 15 they had come within fifteen miles of the town. Three Communist divisions were poised for the assault. But when two further enemy formations, the 3rd and 10th Divisions, sought to force the Naktong eastward to link up with the assault, in a week of intense action between August 8 and 15, they were thrown back with massive losses. American air and artillery concentrations hammered their crossing points by day and night. The Naktong's defensive value was diminishing as the river fell to its lowest summer level. Some of the 1st Cavalry's forward positions east of the river were overrun. But the North Koreans proved unable to reinforce their leading elements. The attack was repulsed. Walker could turn his attention to the northwestern threat to Taegu.

The 15th Division bore the brunt of the fighting in "the Bowling Alley," as it became known, the sheer-sided valley in which a week-long tank battle—one of the rare armored encounters of the war—raged as the Communists strove to break through. The defenders watched in awe as the glowing armor-piercing shells of the T-34s streaked down the valley through the night, searching out the American Pershings. Again and again the Communists pushed forward, yet each time their assaults broke upon the barrier of American firepower. By August 24 the northwestern thrust had burned itself out. The sector was left in ROK hands, while the 25th Division was withdrawn.

At the northeastern end of the perimeter, the ROK 3rd Division was pushed back through Yongdock to Changsa-dong. On August 10 the North Koreans worked through the mountains to cut the road south behind the South Korean positions. The 3rd Division was successfully evacuated by sea, but the town of Pohang-dong was lost, and Walker's resources were stretched to the limit to fill the hole in his line. Scratch American task forces were dispatched to support ROK units in the northeastern sector. To their relief, they began to perceive that the Communist effort and manpower in the area were almost spent. Pushing cautiously north again, by August 20 they had retaken Pohang-dong. Walker was confident that he faced no further serious threat in this quarter.

Most men's first impression of Korea was of the stench, drifting out from the land to the sea—of human excrement and unidentifiable oriental exotica, mostly disagreeable. Replacements and new formations filed down the gangplanks at the pierside amid the disturbing spectacle of casualties being loaded alongside. There was no shortage of black jokes about the most likely fashion of leaving the country. Pusan was a grossly overcrowded shambles of corrugated iron, street markets, refugees, military convoys, beggars, prostitutes, and organized crime. Most American units had been organized and reorganized, stripped of specialists and reinforced with drafts so often since early July that officers, NCOs, and men scarcely knew each other. "We realized something was radically wrong the moment we arrived," said Lieutenant Clyde Fore of the 29th RCT. "We could see our advance party sitting on the quay, silent and unmoving. Our unit really was unfit to go at all. We had been told we would have three or four months in country to train before we were committed to combat. Instead, on the quayside we were just told to uncrate the weapons and get ready to go in the line."[12]

When Lieutenant Colonel Robert Taplett, commanding the 3/5th Marines of the 1st Marine Provisional Brigade, landed on August 1, "everything seemed in turmoil—there were too many people with a wild stare in their eyes. The whole story of the army at this period is a very unsavory one."[13] The Marines were dismayed by meeting army units that had abandoned their dead, and even wounded, on the field, by units that, indeed, did not linger to fight at all. There were tales of officers who had found it convenient to make their own way back to Japan, and of the black battalion of the 9th Infantry, which had failed to distinguish itself, to put the matter politely, by its determination in combat.

When Private James Waters reported with two other replacements to the 1/35th Infantry of the 25th Division on August 28, his company commander welcomed them bluntly: "This isn't a police action—it's a war. You'd better get it into your heads that you can get killed at any second."[14] Waters's companions were indeed killed within weeks. The seventeen-year-old Missourian found the nervous strain of the night battles, the constant uncertainty about where and when the enemy would come almost intolerable. He and his comrades came to hate even the cowbells tinkling in front of the positions, for the North Koreans sometimes used them to mask their movements. The low moment of the day came toward evening, when section by section they filed back down the hill to the chow jeep, knowing that night was approaching. The high moment followed in early morning, when once again they went to get their chow, knowing that they had survived the hours of darkness.

"Everything I had read about Bataan, I felt in the first few hours after landing at Pusan," said Sergeant John Pearson of the 9th Infantry. "People were just completely demoralized. We were told right off that the front had collapsed. As we were taken forward on the train, we could see GIs on flatcars, without weapons, going the other way—stragglers getting out."[15] Pearson was dismayed to learn that his raw recruits would not even be given time to zero their weapons. They were dumped out in the countryside by trucks that turned and drove back toward the city at once to fetch more men. They were filling their canteens in a stream when a furious officer drove up in a jeep, jumped out, and began demanding what they were doing. It was Walton Walker himself. They said they were taking on water. "What are you thinking of?" shouted the Eighth Army commander. "I want your asses forward."

Without reconnaissance, they were launched into a counterattack to recover a lost position, advancing in a skirmishing line across open paddy fields toward high ground held by the enemy. Their battalion commander was wounded within a few minutes, while men dropped right and left from the Communist fire. But they reached their objective. In the days that followed Pearson began to marvel at the incompetence of the North Koreans, as much as the shortcomings of his own side: "They just threw their tanks away, coming at us head on again and again."

Pearson was twenty-seven, a veteran of the Pacific campaign who had found life in the postwar army an anticlimax—"I couldn't stand all the peace and quiet." He had married a German girl while stationed in Frankfurt, and the very night after that first action in Korea he received a letter reporting her safe arrival in New York. Pearson was the son of British immigrants and a keen student of military history. He cherished a sepia photograph on the wall at home, of his Uncle Charlie, a Lancashire Fusilier in the First World War. In Korea he was dismayed to see how far the U.S. Army had declined since 1945: "Somehow, the whole thing had come unglued." There were too few West Point officers, too few trained men. They became accustomed to the sudden appearance of North Korea infiltration parties behind the front, to sudden movements from position to position to meet Communist night attacks, to the chronic shortage of tank and artillery support on their own side. One morning Pearson was an awed spectator as the 1st Provisional Marine Brigade launched its legendary assault in the battle of No Name Hill. "They went up in column of companies. They came back on stretchers in column of platoons," he said. "It was a magnificent thing, but out of another era—a typical Marine frontal attack."

That night the 9th Infantry were committed to the battle. After fighting all through the hours of darkness, the men stood up on their positions and cheered as the Australian P-51 Mustangs came in rocketing and machine-gunning the North Korean trenches at first light. Again and again as the infantry met Communist attacks and approached their last reserves of ammunition, they were saved at the last moment by resupply from the patient files of Korean porters trudging up the reverse slopes, their backs bent over their A-frames laden with ammunition. "We couldn't have fought the war without those Korean litter bearers," said Pearson. "There were a lot of complaints about them, but I guess there were a lot of complaints about Gunga Din, too."

Sergeant Pearson was walking the line of his platoon's positions when a new Communist assault began, and he was slow jumping for a foxhole. A bullet entered his thigh, turned on his message book, and stopped at the base of his spine.

He suffered instant trauma, and lay thinking himself dead, wondering dimly what would happen to his wife. Then a man gave him a drink from his canteen, which made him feel even worse. Semiconscious, he endured the agony of being bumped and jolted down the hill on a stretcher, along an endless track by jeep. At the aid station, the orderly who stripped off his boots asked if he could keep them: "You won't be needing them." He made the first helicopter trip of his life to an operating table from which he looked up at an exhausted, blood-spattered surgeon who said, "This is not going to hurt. We'll give you a spinal." Then he pulled Pearson's bowels up, and the sergeant was torn by excruciating pain. They left the bullet and the scraps of his message pad inside him. Next he remembered a train, and hearing a grenade explosion, and the hammer of quad .50-caliber machine guns. Was this the reality of a guerrilla attack or a comatose fantasy? He never knew. In Pusan a priest gave him the last rites. He murmured that he was an Anglican. "That's all right," said his comforter reassuringly. "It all counts upstairs." A British hospital ship bore him to Japan. Thence, after almost six months of medical care, he was returned to the United States in March 1951.

It was only with the deepest reluctance that the British government and chiefs of staff at last agreed to send a token ground force to Korea. In response to Washington's urgent pleas, 27 Brigade, part of the Hong Kong garrison, was dispatched posthaste to join the defenders of the Pusan Perimeter.

The Brigade's arrival at Pusan was not auspicious. Their brigadier, a sound, steady, competent professional named Basil Coad, was met by an American officer with the cheerful greeting, "Glad you British have arrived—you're the real experts at retreating." When Coad and his staff were taken on an introductory tour of the line by an American general, the British were disconcerted to find that their movements were stage-managed for the benefit of the accompanying photographers. They were staggered by the lack of military security, above all by the freedom with which men could telephone on civilian circuits from the perimeter to girlfriends in Japan. And the British had ample problems of their own. Many of their men were young conscripts, bewildered to find their service abruptly extended to go to war.

For many South Koreans the process of discovering the meaning of Communist liberation was extended through the four months that Kim Il Sung's army occupied their country. It is difficult to overemphasize the importance of this period in the subsequent history of Korea. In the years between 1945 and 1950, many of those living under the regime of Syngman Rhee were dismayed and disgusted by the corruption and injustice that the old President came to represent. For all the rumors filtering down from the North, about land reform and political education, there seemed no reason to imagine that life under Kim Il Sung was any worse than under

Syngman Rhee. The two vicious totalitarians appeared to have much in common. Even when the invasion came in June 1950, in the words of the young bank clerk's son Minh Pyong Kyu, "We still did not realize that this was a catastrophe for us."[16] Syngman Rhee's creatures conducted some odious killings of alleged Communist sympathizers as they fled south. Yet the behavior of the North Koreans in their four months of dominance of the South, their ghastly brutalities and wholesale murders of their enemies, decisively persuaded most inhabitants of the country that whatever the shortcomings of Syngman Rhee, nothing could be as appalling as Communist tyranny. In 1950, and in the years that followed, many distinguished Western journalists such as the British James Cameron were so disgusted by the excesses of Rhee's lackeys that they became opponents of the UN presence in Korea. Not a few UN soldiers were appalled by the acts they witnessed, committed by South Korean soldiers and police. Yet the attitude of such observers as Cameron reflected a Western liberal conscience that shrunk from facing the relative moral issues that Korea posited. Something will be said below about the crimes of Syngman Rhee's minions. But to this day not a shred of evidence has been discovered of crimes by the Seoul regime on the scale which the North Koreans committed during their rule in the South: the awful mass murders, of which the 5,000 bodies discovered in Taejon alone were only a sample. The UN Command later estimated that some 26,000 South Korean civilians were slaughtered in cold blood by the North Koreans between June and September 1950. The arrival of the Communists unleashed a reign of terror which gave the United Nations cause in Korea a moral legitimacy that has survived to this day.

Young Minh Pyong Kyu and his family lived near the West Gate prison in Seoul. They watched the arriving Communist army unloose its doors, spilling out into the streets thousands of captives, common criminals, and political prisoners who ran forth yelling "Long Live the Fatherland!" Minh said, "In the beginning, it was an atmosphere of unrestrained happiness, of true liberation. Everybody was running through the streets, leaping for joy." Minh's family found themselves penniless. But they had relations in the country. His father decided to travel to visit them with his younger brothers, in the hope of getting food. Minh went back to his medical school. He found most of the teachers still in residence, having declared decisively for the cause of socialism. Minh and other students who had been expelled for political activity were readmitted. But there were no classes. Only the hospital was functioning, under North Korean military supervision. Minh was impressed by the Communists' tough discipline. They kept themselves to themselves, they committed no excesses. "Then, in the days that followed, we heard that the Communists were rounding up 'reactionaries.' Slowly, the atmosphere of terror set in."

Kap Chong Chi, a twenty-two-year-old student, knew from the beginning that, as the son of a landowner, his position and that of his family was perilous. He spent the night after the Communist seizure of Seoul deep in thought about what he should do. He had still reached no decision the next morning, when he walked out into the street to see the bodies of two policemen, their identity cards laid neatly upon their chests. Yet, foolishly, he went to the house of a friend in the police force to ask his advice. The man had gone, but two strangers carrying rifles stopped him by the door and demanded to know who he was. His answers did not satisfy them. He was taken away to police headquarters near the Capitol Building and held alone with his fear all that day and night. Early the next morning he was marched through the courtyard, past the bodies of men already executed, and taken up to the third floor. He joined a long procession of men and women awaiting interrogation, their wrists tied together with strips of cloth. After an endless, wretched wait, he found himself before the People's Court. The judges, in white civilian clothes, were themselves newly released from Syngman Rhee's prisons. To his dismay, he identified one as an acquaintance of his older brother. This man said, "I know your family. Landowners. Your life is finished." Kap was taken away to join some thirty others, mostly South Korean soldiers or policemen, in a basement cell.

The captives said little to each other through the hours and days that followed, each one fearful of willing his own death by identification with another. A succession of different Communist officials took their names and asked further questions. Kap, in desperation, tried a new tactic. He told his interrogators that, like his cousin, he had always been a secret sympathizer. His answers to new, probing questions about his Communist convictions sounded pathetically unconvincing. But one of his interrogators proved surprisingly sympathetic. He prompted Kap with some ideological answers. At last, at 4 A.M. five days after his arrest, this official gave him a chit to present to the desk officer responsible for the prisoners.

The little student suffered a further agonizing delay in the central hall of the headquarters building, sitting amid a throng of officials, guards, and prisoners coming and going while his papers were processed. He shrank against the wall, hiding his face, terrified of being identified by a new denunciator. But at last he was casually told that he might go. He walked home through the early morning Seoul streets, decked with huge posters of Stalin and Kim Il Sung. For a few hours he hid, listening to the Voice of America, desperate to discover what was happening in the south of the country. Then, ravenously hungry, he went to the house of a fellow student. He found his friend in the same case as himself. They discussed what to do. No young man could leave the city, yet somehow they must. They considered stealing a boat, rowing out to the American Fleet. They lingered for days, not daring to venture onto the streets. Only when they became convinced that if they remained, they must face rearrest did they summon up the courage to join the great throng of refugees crowding the approaches to the improvised ferry crossings south across the Han River. They had forged themselves crude passes to get past the Communist checkpoints. In the confusion at the river, they bluffed their way through.

Like hundreds of thousands of Koreans in those days, they walked for weeks, hither and thither amid the Communist troop columns and incessant American strafing, which killed many hundreds of civilians along with the North Koreans. They sought in vain to get through to the UN perimeter in the southeast. Despairing of this, they set out for the family home at Kwangju. Kap was arrested again, held overnight, and escaped during a bombing raid. From a friend outside Kwangju he heard that all his family had been arrested and were believed to be dead. Kap could think of nowhere else to go: "I began to travel aimlessly, merely waiting for something to happen."[17]

Thousands, even millions, of South Koreans lived on the brink of animality in those months, roaming the countryside, fighting off fellow stragglers for survival with increasingly ruthless desperation, existing partly on peasant charity, but more generally by plundering the fields of whatever crops and scraps and domestic animals they could reach in darkness. Suk Bun Yoon was a thirteen-year-old middle school pupil, the son of a Seoul merchant. Many of his fellow students, urged by their teachers to volunteer for Kim Il Sung's army, did so. But Suk's father knew that sooner or later the Communists would find his name on the rolls of several Rhee-sponsored political organizations. The family hid in their home for weeks while Suk and his younger brothers walked out into the countryside to buy food, each trip a longer search becoming necessary, sometimes twenty, thirty, forty miles. Then they struggled back to the city. One day Suk was stopped on the road and pressed into joining an army forced-labor group, humping ammunition. It took the boy twelve hours to carry his huge load six miles to the station where it was wanted. Then he was detailed to dig slit trenches, a task interrupted by repeated flights to a nearby sewer during air attacks. Once he found himself within a few yards of a bridge that blew up before his eyes, beneath the bombs of a B-26. At last he was able to slip away and walk home to the city. He found that his father had gone, seeking refuge in the countryside. The rest of the family lingered in the house, exhausted by hunger and fear. They could think of nowhere to go, but they knew that if they remained, sooner or later the Communists must come for them. They prayed for a miracle.

There are those who might argue that the families of such young men as Suk Bun Yoon or Kap Chong Chi had willed their own misery by their support for the regime of Syngman Rhee; that their own terrors at the hands of the Communists were matched by those of left-wing sympathizers in the hands of Rhee's police in the years that went before. Yet if Rhee's regime had been a relative tyranny, that of Kim Il Sung proved absolute. There are no more striking testimonials to the political development of Korea at war than those of such young men as Minh Pyong Kyu, who were avowed left-wing sympathizers before the North Korean invasion, yet who abruptly ceased to be so when they saw the manner in which the regime of Kim Il Sung exercised its power.

The men of the Eighth Army strung out along the mountains above the Naktong were entirely unconscious of the terrors and nightmares of many South Koreans at the hands of their occupiers. They could measure something of the reluctance of thousands of people to join the ranks of Kim Il Sung by the vast drift of refugees into the Perimeter. But the Americans had come to this war too speedily to have any chance of indoctrination about its higher purposes, and their cause still lacked any remotely grand grievance in the manner of Pearl Harbor. They were told that they were fighting Asian communism at the gates of the Pacific. Most were aware only of the desperate need to survive against the cluster of ''gooks'' working up the defile below them, the T-34 grinding down the road toward their position. The struggle for the Pusan Perimeter attained its historical coherence only to those who wrote about it afterward. In those autumn weeks of 1950 it was an interminable series of short, fierce, encounter battles in which the defenders' units had known each other, had fought together, for too brief a period to be called an army in any meaningful sense.

''There was no point where the line began [wrote the British correspondent James Cameron] because naturally there was no line—except at rear on the briefing-room map: a doubtful chalk-mark between established positions; it had no meaning on the ground. What line there was, was this road, winding up from security in Taegu northwards into the hills until it stopped, only for fear of its own length. A mile or two outside town no part of it was safe; you would meet nothing on the road, but the hillsides were full of invisible people, and when you turned back along the track there would be a barrier between you and your rear. It might be only a machine-gun roadblock, but for a while it would dislocate the whole crawling vertebrae of the column, which could move only in one plane, forwards or back, and never to the side. One drove trying to look behind; the dangerous place was always one corner away, at the back of your head.

''Bit by bit the front materialized, the tanks squatted on the flats of the river-beds, the road grew dense with traffic, and soon, where it ran in a kind of cutting between wooded slopes, were the groups of men, like picnickers, crouching on the verge with automatic guns, huddling in the dust of the passing wheels among a litter of ration-cans ('The Ripe Flavor of Nutty Home-Grown Corn Enriched with Body-Building Viadose') or heads buried under the hood of a jeep. The air was alive with a tinny whispering from field-telephones and the radios of tanks, a thin erratic chattering like insects, the ceaseless indiscriminate gossip of an army. Up and down the road, weaving through the traffic, bare-legged

Koreans humped loads of food or mortar ammunition on their porters' frameworks of wood, like men with easels on their backs.''[18]

"In many ways, it seemed a tougher war than Europe," said Lieutenant Walt Mayo, an artillery forward observer with the 8th Cavalry. Mayo had fought as an enlisted draftee with the 106th Division at the Battle of the Bulge.

"Things were so disorganized and depressing—I remember going back to the battery to get some clean clothes, to find them evacuating our ammunition dump. We were rationed to twenty-five rounds a tube a day, and one was constantly fighting to get extra rounds—it became a game as to which FOO could lie best to the Fire Direction Officer. There were days when one lay there for hours on end under incoming mortar fire, but could get no rounds at all to send back. You fought for a hilltop; you lost it; you got it back. There was none of that excitement of being on the move. Men were kept going just by a crude feeling of 'To hell with it, those bastards aren't going to beat us.' ''[19]

Many men's service on the Naktong was painfully brief. Lieutenant David Bolté of the 2/8th Cavalry, son of the U.S. Army's Chief of Plans, arrived in Korea straight from West Point. Many of his men, he found, were slow to understand that here the penalty for failing to behave like a soldier was death. The shortages even of basic equipment were a constant source of frustration. Bolté found himself wrestling with a machine gun under heavy Communist fire, lacking the tool for removing a ruptured barrel. He had been compelled to take over the gun when he saw it standing abandoned. One of its crew had been wounded, and the others had seized the familiar excuse to take him to the rear. There were chronic problems with men drifting away out of the line in darkness: "They just didn't want to be up there at night." Bolté saw a man blow himself to pieces, clumsily dropping a primed grenade into his own foxhole. He himself lasted just ten days in Korea, before a bullet smashed into his shoulder as he peered at the Communist lines through his binoculars. In the days that followed, as he lay in a Japanese hospital where plaster was so short that they could not put a cast on his arm, he remembered his last night before embarkation watching three smart young paratroopers celebrating in the Top of the Mark at the Mark Hopkins Hotel in San Francisco. An excited woman said, "Oooh, it's just like World War II all over again." Bolté looked back from the perspective of a man who would never be fit to see a battlefield again: "One had this great romantic ideal, of an adventure in which people don't bleed." In that Japanese hospital where the halls were crowded with stretcher cases, where nurses were working twelve-hour shifts to cope with a thousand-patient overload, Bolté's youthful ideal died.

The difficulties of defending the Pusan Perimeter were caused, above all, by inadequacies of training and leadership in the American formations thrust into the line after five years' chronic national neglect of the armed forces. Some of Walker's formations were in desperate condition. After its terrible mauling in July, the 24th Division was scarcely battleworthy—"a completely defeated ragtag that had lost all will," in the words of Colonel Paul Freeman of the 23rd Infantry. Like most American officers, Freeman could also find little to say in favor of the ROK Army's contribution to the campaign: "It was pitiful. But it wasn't their fault. They lacked the training, the motivation, the equipment to do the job. Whenever their units were on our flanks, we found that they were liable to vanish without notice."[20] Nor were some of the American reinforcement units much better. The men of the 1st Cavalry Division were scornfully nicknamed "MacArthur's pets" for their supposedly decorative rather than active function in Japan. The 1st Cavalry suffered terribly in the autumn and winter of 1950 for their shortcomings of training and competence.

The line could not have been held at all without the ruthless professionalism of a handful of outstanding officers, among whom must rank Colonel John Michaelis of the 27th Infantry. "Iron Mike" was a thirty-seven-year-old "army brat" who graduated from West Point in 1936. By 1945 the tall, slim Californian had become one of America's outstanding combat soldiers, commanding the 502nd Airborne Regiment, a twice-wounded veteran of D day and Arnhem. Michaelis was posted to the Operations section of the Eighth Army in 1949, where he was dismayed to find so many of the best officers being diverted from regimental duty to administrative and staff jobs. He assumed command of the 27th "Wolfhounds" when its CO was abruptly relieved in the field. His second-in-command and two of his battalion commanders were likewise drafted in haste. With his ranks filled with so many green, frightened young soldiers, Michaelis resorted to drastic measures to raise their confidence. One of his master sergeants took post behind a wall while their own guns dropped 105-mm shells in front of it to demonstrate the effectiveness of cover. The 27th had lost many of its best NCOs because these were sent to stiffen the 24th Division when it was first committed to Korea. Michaelis was acutely conscious of the shortcomings of leadership at platoon level. He was ruthlessly frank about the difficulties of taking into battle men with pitifully little tactical or weapons training. At the height of the battle in August 1950, when many heroic myths were being circulated about the fighting qualities of the Eighth Army, Michaelis told an interviewer from *The Saturday Evening Post:*

"In peacetime training, we've gone for too damn much falderal. We've put too much stress on Information and Education and not enough stress on rifle marksmanship and scouting and patrolling and the organization of a defensive position. These kids of mine have all the guts in the world and I can count on them to fight. But when they started out, they couldn't shoot. They didn't know their weapons. They have not had enough training in plain, old-fashioned musketry. They'd spent a lot of time listening to lectures on the difference between communism and Americanism and not enough time crawling on their bellies on maneuvers with live ammunition singing over them. They'd been nursed and coddled, told to drive safely, to buy War Bonds, to give to the Red Cross, to avoid VD, to write home to mother—when somebody ought to have been telling them how to clear a machine gun when it jams. . . . The U.S. Army is so damn roadbound that the soldiers have almost lost the use of their legs. Send out a patrol on a scouting mission and they load up in a three-quarter-ton truck and start riding down the highway."[21]

If it sometimes appears, in the course of this narrative, that a British author is adopting too critical an attitude toward the professional conduct of the U.S. Army in Korea, it is worth recalling the brutal professional strictures of Michaelis, echoed by other objectively minded observers. In September 1950, even as the colonel talked to his interviewer at his command post in the chemistry laboratory of a Korean middle school, there was a shot outside, followed by a report that a man had killed himself cleaning his pistol. "See what I mean?" said the colonel. "They still don't know how to handle their weapons without blowing their own brains out. They've had to learn in combat, in a matter of days, the basic things they should have known before they ever faced an enemy. And some of them don't learn fast enough."[22] The colonel's comments on the shortcomings of the Eighth Army remained equally vigorous thirty-five years later.

The 27th Infantry became a vital ingredient in Walker's defensive operations, the Perimeter's "fire brigade," held in reserve to be rushed from point to point as enemy attacks developed. Again and again under Michaelis's ruthless leadership, the Wolfhounds proved the force that stemmed the tide. Their morale soared from this knowledge. It was a Korean officer, Paek Sun Yup, who remembered watching Michaelis lose his temper after a neighboring ROK unit broke off an action and withdrew without informing the Americans. "If we lose this battle, we may not have a Korea," the furious colonel of the 27th told the hapless ROK battalion commander. "We have nowhere else to go. We must stand and fight."

Throughout the struggle for the Perimeter, Syngman Rhee's army was being reinforced by the most ruthless means. Each day police combed the city and the countryside for any male capable of bearing arms: boys, teenagers, grandfathers were relentlessly rounded up, given a few hours' rudimentary weapon training, and herded into the line to join a unit. "It was never at any time possible to obtain a firm or official figure for the number of South Korean troops in the field," wrote a British correspondent.[23] "They were at most times heavily outnumbered, and their casualties were enormous. The intake was vast, the training almost unbelievably cursory. The man was drafted at the age of eighteen. On the Sunday he might be at work in the paddies or the shop; by the following Sunday he was in the line; in next to no time he was either a veteran or a corpse."

Lee Chien Ho, the young Seoul chemical engineering student who had sought
to defend his campus with a broomstick in the dying days of June, reached Pusan
on August 4 after an endless, painful journey by train, oxcart, and shoe power. He
went to the temporary Ministry of Education building and asked where he might
go to continue his schooling. An official looked at him in astonishment: ''Your
country is at war.'' Then he learned that Lee spoke a little English: ''The
Americans need interpreters.'' He was sent to the 1st Marine Brigade, and soon
felt relieved to be fed, clothed—to belong somewhere. He remained with them
through all the battles of the six months that followed.

As the struggle continued, American and South Korean units began to
learn—or, rather, relearn from history—painful tactical lessons. It was fatal to
seek to defend a sector by spreading men in penny packets along its length: defend
everything, and you defend nothing. Units must concentrate on key positions. If
the enemy outflanked a position, the defenders must hold their ground while
reserves were brought forward to counterattack. Every battalion, every company,
every platoon must site its foxholes for all-round defense. These were principles
essential to survival. Some units had still failed to learn them by November 1950,
with tragic consequences. But there were enough—just enough—men of the
Eighth Army who did so in August and September to hold the Pusan Perimeter.

In the last ten days of August, there came a lull in the fighting along the entire
Pusan front. The Communists were reorganizing and regrouping their shattered
formations. They acknowledged the mistake they had made by attacking succes-
sively at different points, enabling the Americans to rush reserves to meet each
thrust in turn. This time it would be different. They would mount a coordinated
assault. The North Korean 6th and 7th Divisions would attack in the south, by
Masan, on the U.S. 25th Division front. The 2nd, 4th, 9th and 10th would strike
at the Naktong Bulge, against the U.S. 2nd Division. The 8th and 15th Divisions,
in the north, would seek to cut off Pohang-dong and the ROK units covering the
line of communications from Taegu. The 5th and 12th Divisions would strike
directly at Pohang-dong. Underwater bridges were constructed across the Naktong, log and sandbag constructions intensely difficult to detect in the muddy water
even from the air. Each night there was intense activity on the Communist front:
guns and ammunition being moved forward, such tanks as remained being
concentrated, small armies of men laboring with shovel and mattock. Walker
knew for certain that the Communists were coming. He was in doubt only as to
when.

The onslaught, the last great North Korean effort of the battle, was unleashed
on the night of August 31. In the south the attackers broke through the defenses
of the 25th Division to threaten Masan. Further north the 2nd Division was almost
cut in two by KPA troops overrunning some of its forward positions, sweeping on

to leave others completely isolated. Around Taegu, the U.S. 1st Cavalry lost Waegwan, and Walker was compelled to transfer his own main headquarters to Pusan, so imminent seemed the threat to EUSAK HQ at Taegu. Pohang-dong fell once more. By September 5, Walker was obliged to consider a general withdrawal. Almost everywhere along the line the will and ability of his army to sustain their positions seemed in serious doubt.

Yet over the next hours and days reports reaching Eighth Army first hinted, then confirmed, that the Communist advance had run out of steam. On every sector of the front the fighting was withering away. Desultory North Korean movements were checked with little difficulty by the defenders and their air and artillery support. The Communists had reached the limits of men, guns, supplies, ammunition. The Pusan Perimeter held, and more than a few of its defenders had now heard the astonishing rumors of a great operation for their relief already being mounted from Japan. The spirits of the Eighth Army rose perceptibly, and with it their respect and gratitude to Walker, the fiercely energetic little Texan who had made their survival possible. Walker would not go down in history as a military intellectual, a man of ideas. But he would be remembered for bringing to the battle for the Pusan Perimeter the qualities that made its survival possible: ruthless dynamism, speed of response, dogged determination. He was leading one of the least professional, least motivated armies America had ever put into the field. Even many of its higher commanders seemed afflicted by bugout fever, a chronic yearning to escape from Korea and leave the thankless peninsula to its inhabitants. Walker kept his men at their business by sheer relentless hounding, goading, driving, with the support of a handful of exceptional officers and units whose competence decided the day. The Eighth Army's performance at Pusan narrowly maintained the United Nations' presence in Korea. It remained to be seen whether the achievement of survival on the battlefield could now be translated into outright victory over the Communists.

5

INCHON

For all its undisputed Korean provenance, the name of Inchon possesses a wonderfully resonant American quality. It summons a vision of military genius undulled by time, undiminished by more recent memories of Asian defeat. Inchon remains a monument to "can do," to improvisation and risk-taking on a magnificent scale, above all to the spirit of Douglas MacArthur. So much must be said elsewhere in these pages about American misfortunes in Korea, about grievous command misjudgments and soldierly shortcomings, that there is little danger here of overblowing the trumpet. The amphibious landings of September 15, 1950, were MacArthur's masterstroke. In a world in which nursery justice decided military affairs, Operation Chromite would have won the war for the United States.

From the early stages of the war, as the Eighth Army struggled to maintain fighting room in the southeast of Korea, MacArthur's thoughts had been fixed with almost mystic conviction upon a possible landing at Inchon. In July he told General Lemuel Shepherd, Fleet Marine commander, as they pored over the map in his office, "If I had the 1st Marine Division, I would make a landing here at Inchon, and reverse the war."[1] By all manner of improvisations and expedients, the 1st Marine Division was indeed being assembled and hastened across the Pacific. But six weeks of acrimonious, passionate debate preceded Inchon. On one side were ranged the Joint Chiefs of Staff, all the key naval officers in the Far East, and an overwhelming proportion of the Army, Marine, and amphibious specialists. For this, it must be recalled, was still the immediate postwar period, when the middle and upper ranks of America's armed forces were still thickly populated with officers who had planned and carried out opposed landings from end to end of the Pacific. These men understood from experience every subtlety of tides, beach gradients, unloading capacity, fire support plans. They examined Mac-Arthur's concept with acute professional care and, almost unanimously, declared against it.

When the G-3 of 1st Marine Division, Colonel Alpha Bowser, first arrived in Tokyo in the first days of September, he was greatly dismayed by the uncertain mood he encountered: "It seemed very 'iffy' to me. The feeling about whether we could go on holding at Pusan fluctuated from day to day. They appeared to be in a dreamworld at MacArthur's headquarters. I could not understand how they could be so sanguine about what was happening to them. It scared the hell out of me."[2] Lieutenant Colonel Ellis Williamson, G-3 of X Corps, also found the atmosphere "pretty dismal" when he arrived in Tokyo from California. When first he heard talk of Inchon, he was among those staff officers who feared that the landing was being conducted on the wrong side of Korea. But MacArthur said to them, "It will be like an electric fan. You go to the wall and pull the plug out, and the fan will stop. When we get well ashore at Inchon, the North Koreans will have no choice but to pull out, or surrender."[3]

Inchon was the only plausible target for an amphibious envelopment. Kunsan was so close to the besieged Pusan Perimeter that to make a landing there would be meaningless. Chinnampo, Pyongyang's port, was too far north. Posung-Myon, below Inchon on the west coast, offered inadequate scope for a breakout inland. Yet Inchon's thirty-two-foot tidal range was one of the greatest in the world. Only on three plausible dates—September 15 and 17 and October 11—would the tides be high enough to give the big landing craft three brief hours inshore before the coast became once more an impassable quagmire of mud. Beyond this problem, beyond the fierce current up the Flying Fish approach channel, there was no hope of achieving tactical surprise at the seawall where the main landing force must go ashore. Before the Americans could even assault Inchon, they must unmistakably signal their intentions eleven hours in advance by seizing the offshore island of Wolmi-Do, which commanded the approaches. Thereafter, the problems became worse: the limited cargo-handling facilities, the imminence of the typhoon season, the steep overlooking hills from which a competent enemy could pour a devastating fire onto the beachhead. Finally, the tide times dictated that the main landings must take place at evening, leaving the assault force just two hours of daylight in which to gain a secure perimeter ashore, amid a city of 250,000 people.

The memory of Anzio still bulked very large in military memory, when just such a grand envelopment as Inchon had landed—in Churchill's memorable phrases—not "a wild cat to tear out the heart of the Boche" but "a stranded whale," an invasion army besieged under heavy fire in a strangled perimeter. Why now take such vast risks when the commitment of the two available divisions to Eighth Army at Pusan should make possible a breakout by more conventional means? The Marines' General Shepherd opposed Inchon because he perceived the North Koreans as a fanatical enemy capable of mounting as fierce a resistance to the Americans as the Japanese on Iwo Jima six years earlier.

Arrayed against all these arguments, and their proponents glittering with brass, MacArthur stood alone. He, too, admitted a fear that Inchon was a long march from the Pusan Perimeter. Yet he also saw the deeply demoralized state of the UN forces in Walker's command. To commit the last readily available reinforcements at Pusan risked a disastrous strategic stalemate. MacArthur was determined upon a grand gesture, reaching out for strategic freedom, a war-winning thrust. Against all the reasoned arguments of admirals and generals and staff officers, he deployed only the rocklike, mystic certainty of his own instinct.

No man who was present ever forgot the conclusive August 23 meeting on the sixth floor of the Dai Ichi between MacArthur and America's foremost commanders in the Far East. Stratemeyer was there, and Radford, and Collins and Sherman from Washington; there was Shepherd, Fleet Marine commander; Struble and Doyle for the U.S. Navy. Collins spoke openly of the Army's fears about the consequences of withdrawing the Marine brigade from Pusan for the landing. Sherman advocated a safer landing at Kunsan. Then other naval officers, led by Admiral Turner Joy, outlined the overwhelming difficulties, as they saw them, of putting an amphibious force ashore at Inchon. It was Rear Admiral James H. Doyle who summarized the Navy's attitude, concluding bleakly, "The best I can say is that Inchon is not impossible." Then MacArthur stood, puffing on his corncob pipe.

"He spoke with that slow, deep resonance of an accomplished actor [recalled one of the officers who heard him]. 'Admiral, in all my years of military service, that is the finest briefing I have ever received. Commander, you have taught me all I had ever dreamed of knowing about tides. Do you know, in World War I they got our divisions to Europe through submarine-infested seas? I have a deep admiration for the Navy. From the humiliation of Bataan, the Navy brought us back.'

"Then—literally with a tear in his eye—he said, 'I never thought the day would come, that the Navy would be unable to support the Army in its operations.' "[4]

It was a great theatrical performance. MacArthur's peroration embraced the Communist threat to Korea: "It is plainly apparent that here in Asia is where the Communist conspirators have elected to make their play for global conquest. The test is not in Berlin or Vienna, in London, Paris, or Washington. It is here and now—it is along the Naktong River in South Korea. . . .'' He summoned up the ghost of his hero, General Wolfe, whose assault upon the heights of Quebec had also been opposed by his staff. He asserted the very implausibility of his own plan as its strongest argument for surprise, and thus success: ''The very arguments you have made as to the impracticabilities involved will tend to ensure for me the element of surprise. For the enemy commander will reason that no one would be so brash as to make such an attempt.'' Then, finally: ''I can almost hear the ticking of the second hand of destiny. We must act now or we will die. . . . We shall land at Inchon, and I shall crush them.'' The deep voice fell away to a whisper. After forty-five minutes of oratory such as the world seldom sees save from the orchestra seats of a theater, the Supreme Commander returned to his chair. The Chief of Naval Operations stood up and declared emotionally, ''General, the Navy will get you to Inchon.''

This was not the end of the debate, for many of the most senior officers present left the briefing room unconvinced. But it was the turning point. Shepherd and Sherman made one more vain private attempt to convert MacArthur to a landing at Posung-Myon. But in the absence of a flat rejection from Washington, MacArthur continued to make his plans. On August 28 he received the formal consent of the Joint Chiefs of Staff to the Inchon landing.

Yet even as the plans for the landing were finalized, the doubts persisted. The Chiefs of Staff in Washington gained the written sanction of the President for the operation, a step that was militarily quite unnecessary but reflected their anxiety to ensure that they were not saddled with sole responsibility for disaster. Faced with the new Communist drive against the Pusan Perimeter early in September, General Walker showed deep unhappiness about releasing forces from his front for Inchon. It was decided that the Marine Brigade would be taken out of the line and sent to sea only at the last possible moment, and that a regiment of the 7th Division would be kept in Pusan Harbor as a floating reserve to deal with a possible Eighth Army crisis until it became essential for them to sail for Inchon.

The planners were irked to discover that, throughout the three-year American occupation of Korea, nothing had been done to assemble raw information about the geography of the country. Even the dimensions of the Inchon tidal basin were unknown. In haste, Tokyo set about remedying the yawning deficiencies in SCAP's knowledge. Agents put into the Inchon area reported that there were only some 500 North Korean troops on Wolmi-do and a further 1,500 around Inchon. But only a few hours' warning would be necessary for the North Koreans to move major reinforcements from the southeast. In an effort to keep the enemy in confusion until the last possible moment, a British naval task force was committed to carrying out a deception bombardment against Chinnampo, while a British frigate landed a raiding party at Kunsan. A courageous U.S. naval officer, Lieutenant Eugene Clark, was put ashore at Yonghung-do, fifteen miles south of

Inchon, with similar coastal conditions. He returned to confirm the Navy's worst fears about the waist-deep mud, the shallow water extending three miles offshore, the high harbor wall against which the Marines must land.

Lieutenant Colonel Robert Taplett, a tall, steady South Dakotan commanding the 3/5th Marines, was more worried about the prospect of the landing than most of his officers, "because I knew more about it. I thought it would be a very rough affair. I received an extraordinary message stating that once we were committed to the landing, we would continue with the operation until we had suffered 82.3 percent casualties. I thought, 'God, what kind of idiot would write an order putting in a decimal point like that?' "[5]

Yet, against the background of such fears, it has been a mistake by some historians to presume that Inchon represented a great triumph for the underdog of the Korean campaign, against all odds. Rather, the mood of apprehension and outright dismay in which the landing was prepared showed how low had sunk the morale of the UN armies in Korea, and how great was the psychological dominance the enemy had achieved over their commanders, with the critical exception of MacArthur. The strength of the North Koreans' continuing thrusts against the Pusan Perimeter masked the enormity of their losses since the war began. Allied intelligence was seriously overestimating the size of the forces facing Walker's divisions. The staff continued to believe that the North Koreans possessed numerical superiority. Yet, in reality, Kim Il Sung's ruined regiments besieging Pusan could now muster only some 70,000 men, against a total of 140,000 in Walker's command. The Allies possessed absolute command of the air and sea and overwhelming superiority of firepower. The ferocity and effectiveness of the enemy's assault troops should not be permitted to mask the immense handicaps under which the Communists labored, lacking sophisticated logistic and technical support. Their intelligence gathering, for instance, was as lamentable as the American Army's security. The intention to land at Inchon was one of the worst-kept secrets of the war, the subject of open discussion among thousands of men in Japan and Korea. Yet, miraculously, no word leaked through to Pyongyang. Not a man was moved to strengthen the Communist defenses in the last critical days before the armada sailed.

At Walker's headquarters in Korea, pessimism continued to prevail, not only about Eighth Army's predicament, but about the western landing. It was MacArthur's knowledge of this spirit, or lack of it, that must have contributed significantly to his decision to appoint his own Chief of Staff, Lieutenant General Edward M. Almond, to command the Inchon landing force, designated X Corps. So much criticism was subsequently heaped upon MacArthur for his decision to divide military authority between two separate commands in Korea, which would have important and unhappy consequences later, that it is worth examining his motives for doing so. The most obvious, and the least admirable, was that Almond was the Supreme Commander's protégé, a ferociously ambitious soldier who had played a somewhat undistinguished role as a divisional commander in Italy in World War II and now hungered for a more promising battlefield command. Almond was not a man who inspired much affection among his subordinates. O. P. Smith, the 1st Marine Division commander whose poor relations with his Corps superior would become a serious blight upon the campaign, was antagonized by their first meeting before Inchon, when Almond dismissed the difficulties of amphibious operations: "This amphibious stuff is just a mechanical option." Smith then "tried to tell him a few of the facts of life. But he was rather supercilious and called me 'son,' which kind of annoyed me."[6]

Yet there was an entirely legitimate case for placing the conduct of the Inchon landing in hands other than those of General Walton Walker. MacArthur well knew the low morale that existed in Eighth Army headquarters, and it presented him with a difficult dilemma. Walker had conducted a stubborn defense of Pusan. But there was grave reason to doubt his ability now to lead the sort of imaginative and dynamic operation MacArthur planned. MacArthur considered, and rejected, the possibility of relieving him of his command. But this would have been a most unpalatable step to the American public. As is often the case in desperate situations, the figure of "Bulldog" Walker had been exalted by publicity to heroic proportions. MacArthur's compromise was to entrust the amphibious operation to Almond. Whatever his Chief of Staff's vices, he was an undoubted driver of men. MacArthur was supremely confident that this one great effort would be decisive. Once it had succeeded, issues of command would no longer be important. He told O. P. Smith, "I know that this operation will be sort of helter-skelter. But the 1st Marine Division is going to win the war by landing at Inchon."[7]

Among the senior officers of the Marine Division there was never a moment's doubt of the importance of the landing, not only for the cause of the United Nations, but for their Corps' survival. Since the end of World War II they had been compelled to watch its remorseless shrinkage to a shadow of its wartime might. Many naval officers made plain their belief that the Marines should be confined to a role providing token shipboard contingents with the fleet. No less a figure than General Omar Bradley had declared his conviction, at the 1949 congressional hearings on the B-36 bomber, that in the nuclear age there would never again be large-scale amphibious operations. "The Marine Corps was fighting for its very existence," said General Lem Shepherd.[8] In Korea, and above all at Inchon, he and his fellow Marines perceived a supreme opportunity to show their nation what the Corps could still do.

The 1st Marine Division's commander, O. P. Smith, was in many ways the least likely of Marine heroes. A slim, white-haired Texan of fifty-seven, of professorial manner, unfailing courtesy—even diffidence—Smith was a cautious commander who believed that "you do it slow, but you do it right." But many of his subordinates in this big, heavy division of some 20,000 men were cast in more exotic molds. Ray Murray of the 5th Marines was perhaps the outstanding regimental commander, who would become one of the critical figures of the campaign. Colonel Homer Litzenburg of the 7th Marines was slower and less impressive. Colonel Lewis B. "Chesty" Puller of the 1st Marines was already a legend of his Corps, a bombastic officer who led from the front, beloved of his men—perhaps less so of his seniors, who were sometimes exasperated by his tactical carelessness. All these men, and many of their subordinates, possessed immense combat experience in World War II.

The first slow convoy of Admiral Struble's armada of 260 ships sailed from Yokohama on September 5. It was a makeshift transport fleet that carried the Americans to Inchon. Of the bigger ships, thirty-seven LSTs were World War II veterans that had been transferred to the Japanese merchant service. They were now recalled to duty with their Japanese officers supplemented by American personnel flown in from the United States. Some ships smelled vividly of fish. There was much wisecracking speculation about the personal histories of their inscrutable deck officers. "Everybody believed," in the words of a Marine, "that he was being ferried to Inchon by a Japanese who had been an admiral at Midway." There were constant breakdowns of aged machinery: "The whole thing was a rusty travesty of World War II amphibious operations."

Few men found the voyage to Inchon agreeable, crammed aboard old ships devoid of creature comforts. Many were violently seasick as the convoy plunged and heaved amid Typhoon Kezia, whose 125-mph winds wreaked havoc with the nerves of the naval commanders and the stomachs of 70,000 hapless Americans below decks. On some ships, tanks and vehicles broke loose, demanding desperate struggles to resecure them as they smashed hither and thither on the cargo decks. The men lay in their bunks or played cards incessantly. There was little left to prepare. The plans were all made. The command ship, *Mount McKinley,* sailed from Sasebo in the small hours of September 13, the anniversary of Wolfe's triumph at Quebec. The ship's captain gave up his own cabin to MacArthur and had a shed built for himself on the bridge wing. The convoy was maintaining radio silence, but Almond demanded that dispatches should be air-dropped to him each day. To the glee of his enemies on the staff, the first day's attempt ended with the bag falling into the sea, and X Corps commander in a rage.

Lieutenant Jim Sheldon of the 17th Infantry, 7th Division, felt desperately anxious for the invasion and the war to be over, because Korea smelled so awful and he found his own platoon so dismaying. Sheldon was a rebellious twenty-year-old who had been dismissed from the U.S. Navy for misconduct, then enlisted in the Army and was commissioned from the ranks the day the Korean War broke out.

He arrived in Japan as an officer replacement and was abruptly given a fifty-four-man platoon composed partly of Koreans, of whom some were wholly untrained civilians, ranging in age from the mid-teens to mid-sixties: "They were a pretty unhappy group of people for a twenty-year-old lieutenant to have to cope with, with their strange eating and sanitation habits. I couldn't do anything to stop them sneaking out after dark and crapping in the middle of the compound." In four weeks, with the aid of a handful of experienced American NCOs, he had instilled the rudiments of tactical training in them. Then they were shipped to Pusan, where as part of the deception plan they were required to disembark from their ships, march out into the country, and reembark three times in succession. At last, to their astonishment, they were told that they were on their way to take part in an amphibious landing. Sheldon and his platoon were not impressed.[9]

Just before dawn on September 15, the *Mount McKinley* and the transport convoy attained the Inchon Narrows. It was the fifth day of air and naval bombardment of Wolmi-do Island. The commanders had gambled heavily upon the success of the diversionary operations to blind the defenders to the real significance of the barrage. At 6:33 A.M., after a final storm of rockets and napalm from the carrier strike aircraft, a last deluge of shellfire from the cruisers offshore, the first Marines hit Wolmi-do.

Throughout the voyage from Japan the Supreme Commander had remained invisible in his cabin. Only now, as the first men clambered down into the landing craft amid the rolling thunder of the naval bombardment, did MacArthur betake himself to the bridge of the *Mount McKinley* in his grandeur. This was his creation, his hour, his last great moment of martial glory before the worm of disappointment, disillusionment, defeat began to gnaw into that enormous ego and reputation. He took the captain's high seat on the bridge, to sit flanked by his reverential courtiers in all the stage properties of majesty: the corncob pipe; the massive peaked cap laden with brass; the proud chin and protective sunglasses. And there the photographers caught him for posterity, the master of ceremonies sitting high above the sea, watching the unfolding of his last triumph.

Ellis Williamson, G-3 of X Corps, did not trouble to beg a place in a landing craft, as had some staff officers. He remembered the British officer who said to him before D day in 1944, when he was still an impatient young lieutenant, "When you get over there, you'll find there's enough war for everybody." Williamson had been wounded five times in northwest Europe: "By Inchon, I was no longer overly curious."[10]

Until a late stage of planning, Almond had opposed the sacrifice of surprise for the seizure of Wolmi-do Island. But the Marines insisted that they could not assault the main beaches with the approaches unsecured. Their will prevailed. Now, Litzenburg's 5th Marines swept ashore at "Green Beach" on Wolmi-do with almost contemptuous ease. Two Marine tanks smashed through a feebly defended North Korean roadblock on the causeway to the mainland. The Stars and Stripes was raised 300 feet up on Radio Hill, dominating Inchon Harbor, at 6:55 A.M. The entire position was secure an hour later. Marine bulldozers wrote a macabre footnote by entombing a handful of defenders who declined to surrender alive in the caves in which they had taken refuge. From the bridge of *Mount McKinley,* MacArthur signaled Struble: "The Navy and Marines have never shone more brightly than this morning."

At noon, with half of the Chromite operational plan successfully completed and only desultory firing coming from the shore, the long, wretched interval began before the next act. As the tide swept back to reveal miles of dull, flat mud between the invasion fleet and the shore, the men in the ships waited, impotently, for the sea to return. The Marines on Wolmi-do, entirely isolated from the fleet, lay over their weapons, willing the enemy to maintain his silence. They requested, and were refused, permission at once to continue their advance across the causeway. They contented themselves by firing mortars and machine guns at the shore whenever they observed activity. Fighter-bombers roamed the roads for miles behind the coast, ready to strike at any Communist attempt to reinforce their coastal positions. Yet, astonishingly, none came. At 2:30 P.M. the cruisers resumed their fire upon the main waterfront.

"The guns began erratically [wrote the British war correspondent James Cameron]: a few heavy thuds from the cruisers, an occasional bark of five-inch fire, a tuning-up among the harsh orchestra. At what point the playing of the guns merged into the final and awful barrage I do not know; so many things began to take place, a scattered pattern of related happenings gradually coalescing and building up for the blow.

"All around among the fleet the landing-craft multiplied imperceptibly, took to the water from one could not see exactly where, because the light was failing now—circled and wheeled and marked time and milled about, filling the air with engines. There seemed to be no special hurry. We could not go in until the tide was right; meanwhile we lay offshore in a strange, insolent, businesslike serenity, under whatever guns the North Koreans had, building up the force item by item, squaring the sledge-hammer. The big ships swung gently in the tideway, from time to time coughing heaving gusts of iron towards the town. It began to burn, quite gently at first. What seemed to be a tank or a self-propelled gun sent back some quick, resentful fire, but it soon stopped. Later we found that one ship had thrown a hundred and sixty-five rounds of five-inch ammunition at the one gun: the economics of plenty."[11]

At 4:45 P.M. the first landing craft pushed off from the transports, laden with Marines, headed toward the smoke-hung skyline of the city of Inchon. At 5:31 the first Americans sprang up the ladders onto the seawall, covered by grenades from the men who followed. After a brief scamper, the British Consulate was taken and

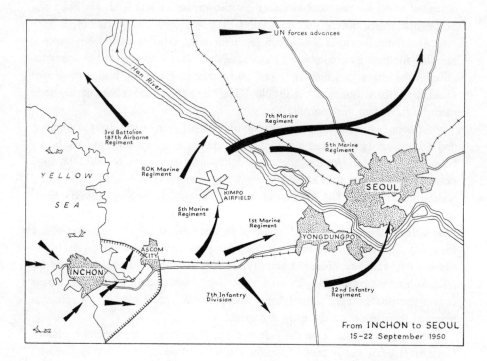

UN forces advances

Han River

3rd Battalion
187th Airborne
Regiment

7th Marine
Regiment

5th Marine
Regiment

ROK Marine
Regiment

YELLOW

SEA

KIMPO
AIRFIELD

5th Marine
Regiment

1st Marine
Regiment

SEOUL

YONGDUNGPO

ASCOM
CITY

INCHON

7th Infantry
Division

32nd Infantry
Regiment

From INCHON to SEOUL
15–22 September 1950

a platoon reached the foot of Observatory Hill, overlooking the harbor. Amid the sharp firefights with pockets of defenders, it became rapidly apparent that most of the surviving Communists were still stunned and dazed by the bombardment. In the industrial suburbs south of the city, where the 1st Marines were landing on Blue Beach, the regiment overcame difficulties with mud and natural obstacles to establish themselves securely ashore in the first hours of the darkness.

The makeshift manner of the operation persisted even as the Marines descended into the landing craft. Major Ed Simmonds, commanding the weapons company of the 3/1st Marines, was a twenty-nine-year-old from New Jersey who had seen action in the Pacific as an engineer, where every landing had been intensely rehearsed and meticulously timed. Now he found himself clambering aboard an amphibious tractor as a young naval lieutenant pointed toward the shore and shouted almost hysterically through a bullhorn, "There's your beach! Go find it!" A landing craft loaded with Koreans pulled alongside and somebody called, "Here's your interpreters!" Two Koreans climbed on Simmonds's tractor as it got under way. Neither proved to speak English. The Marine asked the driver where the compass was. The man shrugged. "Search me. Two weeks ago I was driving a bus in San Francisco." Simmonds, aided by his own compass, set off toward the point on the shoreline where the smoke seemed thickest.[12] The carefully planned landings by waves of craft were forgotten. They merely headed in columns for the beach, where they found a modest firefight in progress. Visibility was very poor amid the smoke and drizzle. Most men's clearest memory of Inchon was of struggling ashore in soggy clothing, which still hung clammily about them as the light began to fail. Officers and men hastened hither and thither, searching for headquarters and company positions in the darkness, broken by occasional gun flashes and the flames of burning buildings. As the sounds of battle died away, they were replaced by the insistent patter of operators murmuring into radio handsets, struggling to gain contact with straggling units. But already the vital moves of the day were complete. The seal was set upon the American triumph when eight LSTs grounded side by side against the seawall on Red Beach. As the tide fell, they remained there, "dried out," and from their cavernous holds poured forth a stream of tanks, trucks, jeeps, stores, laying vital flesh upon the bones of the beachhead.

Through the hours of darkness the Marines dozed over their weapons, apprehensive of a counterattack that never came. Astoundingly, two regiments were established ashore in Inchon at a cost of just twenty killed among a total of less than 200 casualties. If the landing on the west coast of Korea was a makeshift, amateurish affair by the standards of 1944 or 1945, it had proved formidablee- nough to overcome the primitive legions of Kim Il Sung. In the days that followed, as the men of 7th Division and the 7th Marines followed the vanguard ashore, MacArthur and his officers exulted. The gamble had triumphantly succeeded. All the Supreme Commander's instincts about the conduct of the North Koreans had been justified. He had driven his spear deep into the flank of the enemy, who now reeled stricken before him.

First light on September 16 revealed Korean civilians picking their way among the shattered debris of the Inchon waterfront, among the fallen power lines and flickering fires and broken walls.

"There was quite a lot of Inchon still standing [wrote James Cameron]. One wondered how. There were quite a number of citizens still alive. They came stumbling from the ruins—some of them sound, some of them smashed—numbers of them quite clearly driven into a sort of numbed dementia by the night of destruction. They ran about, capering crazily or shambling blankly, with a repeated automatic gesture of surrender. Some of them called out as we passed their one English phrase, as a kind of password: 'Sank you!' 'Sank you!¡ and the irony of that transcended the grotesque into the macabre."[13]

The 1st and 5th Marines linked up ashore early on the morning of September 16. They began at once to drive eastward, toward the capital, leaving the ROK Marines to mop up Inchon in characteristically ruthless fashion. Belatedly, a column of North Korean armor and infantry appeared, to be swept aside by air

strikes and ground fire. The 5th Marines now led the advance on the north side of
the Inchon-Seoul road while the 1st took the southern side. Smashing through
sporadic Communist resistance, by the night of September 17 they held much of
the big Kimpo airfield complex. By the evening of the nineteenth the 5th had
cleared the entire south bank of the Han River on their front. The 1st Marines had
meanwhile seen some heavy fighting in more difficult country, meeting a regiment
of the North Korean 18th Division deployed in their path. But on the nineteenth
they were on the outskirts of Yongdungpo, the suburb of Seoul on the south bank
of the Han.

The raw relations between the Army and the Marines became increasingly
apparent on the road to Seoul. O. P. Smith's men displayed a lasting bitterness
about the haste urged upon them by Almond, obsessed with fulfilling a promise to
MacArthur that he would liberate the capital by September 25. This would be three
months to the day since the Communist invasion. "He wanted that communique,"
said the disgusted Smith. "I said I couldn't guarantee anything—that's up to the
enemy."[14] But some army officers, in their turn, declared their dismay at the
headlong tactics of the Marines. "The Marines were always too keen on frontal
attacks," argued Colonel John Michaelis of the 27th Infantry.[15]

"The Marines are a product of their history [said Colonel Ellis Williamson].
They are trained, indoctrinated, to go from ship to shore, then to keep running
forward until they have taken the pressure off the beachhead. The thought of
outflanking a position would horrify a man like 'Chesty' Puller. We used to call
the Marines 'the nursery rhyme soldiers' because their motto was: 'Hey diddle
diddle, right up the middle.' On that march to Seoul, I saw Marines doing things
no army outfit would think of. I watched them crossing that great sweep of wide
open ground in front of Kimpo airfield, hundreds of young men rising up and
starting across the flats in open order. They took far more casualties than we
considered appropriate."[16]

It is interesting that Williamson's perception of the U.S. Marines, as a
soldier, is that shared by most army officers around the world about their
amphibious brethren. It is probably true that the Marine Corps places greater
emphasis upon headlong courage than upon tactical subtlety. Even their own
General Shepherd afterward challenged the sluggishness of O. P. Smith's move
into Seoul: "If a man who is in command of a pursuit is someone who likes to
have his ranks dressed all the time, you might just as well not pursue."[17] It was
agreed by most senior marines that "Chesty" Puller had been overpromoted to
regimental command and was saved from making disastrous mistakes only by the
professional competence of Major Robert Lorigan, his Operations officer. Yet in
Korea the courage and determination of the Marines remained unchallenged
through three years of war, while many army units proved disturbingly lacking in
morale and professional skill. If the senior officers of the 1st Marine Division

could not be described as intellectual warriors, between Inchon and Panmunjom, O. P. Smith and his men would earn great gratitude from their country.

Twenty-year-old Corporal Selwyn Handler of the Weapons Company, 2/1st Marines, found the advance from Inchon to Seoul an intoxicating experience. In checks and starts, the long files of men moved forward, jeeps carrying the heavy equipment, ahead the sound of spasmodic artillery and small-arms fire as the point companies cleared the road. The local Korean civilians seemed delighted to see them. They scurried hither and thither across the battlefield, looting rice stores and abandoned equipment, hastily removing their families and possessions from the immediate line of fire. Once they found some North Korean stragglers hiding in a cave. Two men were detailed to escort them to the rear, but they soon returned. They said, "Prisoners are too much of a bother, right now." Like most men on most battlefields, Handler retained brief snapshot glimpses of those days: leaping into a foxhole under shellfire, to be cursed by a man already sheltering in it whom he had last seen in high school in California; watching a child scuttling past, bent under the burden of a rice sack larger than himself; Marines filling themselves with beer in a brewery they occupied in Yongdungpo; watching a Corsair hit overhead, diving into the ground and blowing up. Korean children swarmed around them, even as they fought. One said incessantly, "North Korean! North Korean!" as he tugged at the American's leg and pointed. Exploratively, Handler tossed a grenade into the rubble. Nothing moved, but still the child gestured furiously. The Americans threw two more grenades, and were rewarded with the bodies of two Communist soldiers.

As Almond's X Corps drove east, on September 16 in driving rain Walker's Eighth Army launched its long-awaited breakout. It began sluggishly. The Americans were not across the Naktong in strength until the nineteenth. MacArthur suffered a period of serious concern that even now the North Koreans could hold in the southeast. For four days the weather severely hampered the Air Force's ability to support the UN advance. But as the weather cleared sufficiently to enable the bombers to operate, once the Communist front had been broken open, it collapsed with extraordinary speed.

The British contingent suffered a wretched little tragedy, indicative of the indifferent air-ground liaison of the period. On September 23 the Argyll & Sutherland Highlanders had just fought their way up Hill 282, on the left flank of the push across the Naktong. They called for air support and laid out their recognition panels. A flight of Mustangs swung in to attack with cannon and napalm, which they laid with terrible accuracy on the Scots' positions. The survivors retreated in confusion from the summit. But Major Kenneth Muir, second-in-command, determined that they must retake it. He led thirty men toward the crest and reached his objective with fourteen. "The gooks will never drive the

Argylls off this hill,'' he said as he fell mortally wounded by automatic fire. Muir won a posthumous Victoria Cross. The Argylls lost seventeen killed and seventy-six wounded.

But this was the bitter small change of war. All along the front, the enemy was collapsing. North Korean units began to melt away, thousands of fugitives throwing away weapons, equipment, clothing. On the twenty-sixth at Osan, men of the 1st Cavalry driving north from the Perimeter met the 7th Infantry pushing south from Inchon. ROK units advanced up the east coast from Pusan, meeting negligible resistance. Everywhere, the North Koreans were breaking in flight, surrendering in hundreds, or taking to the mountains to maintain guerrilla war.

Farther north, the 1st Marines were obliged to fight hard for three days for Yongdungpo. Meanwhile, after a setback to their first attempt on the night of the nineteenth, on September 20 Puller's 5th made a successful assault crossing of the Han River. By September 25 both Marine regiments were committed to the bitter, desperate street battle for possession of Seoul, which devastated great areas of the capital and continued for three days. Even as air reconnaissance revealed the main body of Kim Il Sung's army fleeing northward, Communist rearguards fought on to delay the advance of Smith's regiments, extracting their price yard by yard at each rice-bag barricade.

The battle for Seoul became a source of lasting controversy, and deep revulsion to some of those who witnessed it. It provided an example of a form of carnage that would become wretchedly familiar in Indochina a generation later— allegedly essential destruction in the cause of liberation. It was passionately argued by some correspondents and not a few soldiers that the civilian casualties and wholesale destruction could have been avoided by an effective enveloping movement rather than a direct assault supported by overwhelming air and artillery support. But MacArthur and Almond wanted Seoul fast. In their path stood some 20,000 still resolute Communist troops. ''The slightest resistance brought down a deluge of destruction blotting out the area,'' wrote an eyewitness, R. W. Thompson of the *Daily Telegraph*.[18] In the words of the historian David Rees, ''At the heart of the West's military thought lies the belief that machines must be used to save its men's lives; Korea would progressively become a horrific illustration of the effects of a limited war where one side possessed the firepower and the other the manpower.''[19]

The Marines advanced into the capital from north, south, and west, while a regiment of 7th Division and the 187th Airborne RCT covered their flanks. Some men were appalled by the evidence of atrocities they encountered. Selwyn Handler was among those who entered a jail compound in which they found several headless bodies, and the sword that had obviously been used for the executions. Ed Simmonds of the 3/1st saw a group of Marines clustered around a trench. A lieutenant waved him over. The trench was filled with dead Koreans—men, women, children, hundreds of them: "It was a ghastly sight. The stench was unbearable. For days civilians were coming out from the center of Seoul in the hope of identifying them."[20] Colonel Taplett of the 3/5th was less troubled by the evidence of the Communist occupation. "That's the way these people treat each other," he said, shrugging. It was a view that would be repeated through foreign UN contingents again and again in the years to come.

Darkness in the streets, still possessed of so many unknown perils, brought hours of acute tension to the Marines in the forward positions. On the night of September 25 the 5th Marines were appalled to receive a sudden order to launch an attack at 2 A.M. It was made clear that this was the direct consequence of General Almond's obsessive determination to control all Seoul within the deadline he had promised MacArthur. Major Simmonds had assumed temporary command of a rifle company in place of its commander, who was hiding in a cellar. "I can't do it! I can't do it!" the officer cried amid the stress of battle. "Take my bars! Take my bars!" Simmonds was horrified to discover that a supporting artillery bombardment would be put down in the area to which he had just dispatched an eight-man patrol. But the American attack was preempted. Long before H hour, the Marines heard the grinding clatter of armor advancing toward their own positions. The North Koreans had launched their own movement. All night the artillery poured fire in front of Puller's men, breaking up the Communist infantry concentrations. An immobilized Communist tank stood stalled in front of Simmonds's company position. The major feared what it might still do to them with its gun when daylight came. He ordered up a 75-mm recoilless rifle and told its gunner to fire as soon as he had enough light to aim. At last, in the first glimmerings of dawn, he said, "I can see it!" and fired. The Marines were so absorbed in the enemy that they forgot the backblast of their own weapon, which bounced off a house behind, blowing them off their feet and showering them in mud and debris. But the Communist impetus was spent. American tanks moved up, and they began to advance again. The Marines found their own patrol intact, having taken refuge in a culvert all night, their fatigues concealed beneath civilian clothing stolen from a washing line.

The 5th Marines reached the Capitol Building only on September 27, two days after Tokyo had announced the liberation, in relentless accordance with the Supreme Commander's schedule. To the chagrin of the victors, soon after they had hoisted the Stars and Stripes, they were diplomatically ordered to lower their nation's colors and raise the blue flag of the United Nations. Two days later, MacArthur himself presided over the solemn ceremony in the shattered Capitol Building, marking the liberation of Seoul and the return of the government of Syngman Rhee. The Joint Chiefs in Washington sought in vain to prevent the ceremony, because of their reluctance to identify the United States so closely with the controversial South Korean President. They were unsuccessful. MacArthur was determined to savor his moment of ceremony, indifferent to the cynicism of his own troops, who had made it possible. "If the Inchon landing had been as carefully planned as that ceremony, it would have been marvelous," said Ed Simmonds acidly. Immense labor and resources had been diverted from the battle to build a pontoon bridge across the Han that would enable MacArthur and his cavalcade to drive direct from Kimpo airport into Seoul.

In the midst of the ruined capital, the Supreme Commander unleashed a characteristic flood of rhetoric for the throng of soldiers, naval officers, and correspondents gathered around himself and Rhee: "By the grace of merciful Providence, our forces fighting under the standard of that greatest hope and inspiration of mankind, the United Nations, have liberated this ancient capital city of Korea. . . ." The Lord's Prayer was interrupted by the crash of glass and masonry from the damaged dome a hundred feet above. MacArthur appeared not to notice. He turned to address Rhee: "Mr. President, my officers and I will now resume our military duties and leave you and your government to the discharge of the civil responsibility." The two men shook hands. Rhee seemed overtaken by the emotion of the moment: "We admire you," he murmured to the general. "We love you as the savior of our race." The Supreme Commander flew home to Tokyo mantled in his own serene sense of destiny fulfilled, imbued with an aura of invincibility that awed even his nation's leaders. He was confident that the war for Korea had been won, and that his armies were victorious. Now it was just a matter of cleaning up.

6

TO THE BRINK: MACARTHUR CROSSES THE PARALLEL

When MacArthur came out onto the deck of the *Mount McKinley* the morning after the Inchon landing, his first question to the Marines' General Shepherd was, "Have we seen or heard anything of the Russians or the Chinese?"[1] It was an inquiry he repeated, insistently, each day thereafter as his army drove deep inland. The Supreme Commander was perfectly aware of the political embarrassments and military implications of killing, capturing, or even encountering Chinese or Russian advisers or troops. Yet as each day passed with no word of their presence, MacArthur's assurance grew. Peking and Moscow had backed off. This was a struggle between the United Nations and the crumbling divisions of Kim Il Sung. The Communists had reached out for their easy victory in South Korea, and come within a hairbreadth of achieving it. Yet when the will of the United States—the will, indeed, of the nation's supreme representative in Asia, Douglas MacArthur—was tested and shown to be strong, that of the enemy had crumpled. In MacArthur's perception, strengthened by each day of triumph after September 15, the crisis had passed.

Since June 25, 1950, the key figures in Tokyo, Washington, London, and indeed throughout the Western world, had explored a remarkable range of emotions. The shock of Kim Il Sung's invasion was succeeded by alarm about its global implications. Truman and his allies and generals overcame these fears, in their determination that the Communist onslaught must be resisted. Then, through

115

July and August, as defeat followed defeat upon the battlefield, it appeared that the only fruit of their efforts would be a massive humiliation for Western arms. Yet now, after the miracle of Inchon, the great burden had been lifted from their shoulders. From the brink of defeat, MacArthur's genius had brought them to the verge of overwhelming military triumph. Fears that the North Korean invasion signaled a worldwide Communist offensive had proved unfounded. The Russians, perceived as prime movers in Kim Il Sung's invasion, now appeared anxious to distance themselves from the Korean adventure, and certainly unwilling to commit their military power to Kim's support. The balance of advantage in Korea lay firmly with the UN, with the Western powers. The wider dangers had receded. The leaders of the Truman Administration, who had been so sensitive to the global risks of the original Communist invasion, were overtaken by something close to euphoria. Firmness had paid off. The Communists were in full retreat. No new world war would start in Korea.

The chief problem that now exercised Truman and Acheson, their allies and military commanders, was that of how the utmost political and strategic advantage could be extracted from military victory. The starting point for the debate was the view, held instinctively by many citizens of the Western Powers, that it would be intolerable if Kim Il Sung proved to have been able to launch and retreat from the failure of his monstrous adventure without cost to his own regime. Beyond his unprovoked invasion of a neighboring state, the atrocities his forces had inflicted upon the people of South Korea compounded the original outrage. If the North Koreans were now permitted to withdraw behind their original frontier, the 38th Parallel, and remain there unmolested, the huge efforts and sacrifices of the United Nations—and of the South Korean people—would seem hollow indeed. It would be absurd, said Acheson, "to march up to a surveyor's line and stop." It seemed equally inappropriate for MacArthur's army to pursue the North Koreans into their own land merely to complete the destruction of the enemy's forces, then withdraw, leaving Kim Il Sung's regime in place.

The United Nations' mandate for war was based upon the General Assembly vote of June 27 calling on members to "furnish such assistance to the Republic of Korea as may be necessary to repel the armed attack and to restore international peace and security in the area." The Soviet Union, which returned to its seat on the Security Council on August 3, argued in vain that the conflict did not come under the definition of aggression since it was a war, not between two states, but between two parts of the Korean people temporarily split into two camps under two separate authorities. Once the Russians were back at the UN, the possibility of directing the war through the forum of the Security Council, rather than at the behest of Washington, finally vanished. But weeks before Inchon there had been intense private debate in Washington as to whether the occupation of North Korea was a legitimate United Nations or, more frankly, American war aim. The

Defense Department believed that it was perfectly justifiable. So did some senior officials in the State Department, led by Dean Rusk and John Allison of the Far Eastern Division. The Policy Planning Staff raised serious doubts as to whether it was possible to invade North Korea without precipitating a wider war with China or the Soviet Union, and expressed doubts whether other UN members would support such a move. But even the PPS concluded in late July that a decision about invading North Korea or integrating it with the South could be postponed until these became more immediate military options.

Characteristically, while others havered, MacArthur alone harbored no doubts. In mid-July in Tokyo, he told Collins and Vandenburg that his war aim was not merely the repulse of Kim Il Sung's invasion, but the destruction of his army, for which the occupation of North Korea might prove necessary. There is no evidence that the two Chiefs of Staff disputed MacArthur's view, though they were perfectly aware that he had no authority to make such a decision for himself. When Collins returned to Tokyo in mid-August, he told the Commander in Chief that he personally favored crossing the 38th Parallel, but warned that Truman had not yet reached a decision on the issue. From the outset, while the State Department expressed serious reservations about the feasibility or desirability of sustaining Syngman Rhee as ruler of all Korea, MacArthur made it plain that he strongly supported this course. On September 1 the National Security Council circulated a frankly inconclusive working paper, NSC 81, which rehearsed the arguments for and against taking the Korean War to the enemy's homeland. It took note of the danger that the Russians would intervene to prevent the loss of their suzerainty over North Korea, but contrarily suggested that Moscow was unlikely to risk the wider war that could result from intervention. Finally, NSC 81 proposed a compromise: any crossing of the Parallel should be conducted only by ROK forces, and solely in pursuit of tactical objectives. It proposed that MacArthur should be required to "request new instructions before continuing operations north of the 38th Parallel with major forces for the purpose of occupying North Korea."

The Joint Chiefs of Staff condemned the "unrealistic" approach of NSC 81. They were determined that the military should have the flexibility they needed to complete the destruction of the North Korean People's Army, wherever its elements took refuge. An amended version—NSC 81/1—was agreed between Acheson and the Joint Chiefs at an NSC meeting on September 9, almost a week before Inchon. The passage in the original specifying that UN forces "should not be permitted to extend into areas close to the Manchurian and U.S.S.R. borders of Korea" was redrafted. Now it was agreed merely that they should not cross those borders. NSC 81 decreed flatly that only ROK troops should operate near the Russian and Chinese borders. NSC 81/1 declared only that it should be "the policy" not to deploy other UN forces in these sensitive areas. The paper restated Washington's determination that the U.S. "should not permit itself to become engaged in a general war" with China. But it also affirmed the position consistently adopted by the Administration since the war began—that if Chinese forces intervened in Korea, the U.S. would defend itself by whatever means it possessed, not excluding the bombardment of targets on the Chinese mainland. The political future of North Korea was not discussed in NSC 81/1, perhaps chiefly because the Administration regarded this as a matter of detail rather than new national policy. On September 1, Truman had publicly declared the right of all Korea to be "free, independent and united," and committed the United States to do its part to see that all Koreans gain that right "under the guidance of the United Nations."

There was an interval of almost three weeks between the drafting of NSC 81/1 and the promulgation of a formal JCS directive to MacArthur based upon its conclusions. A measure of confusion overtook the Pentagon during this period. The Defense Secretary, Louis Johnson, was sacked by Truman and replaced by General George Marshall. Meanwhile, in Korea, the distant military hopes that underpinned Washington's discussions in early September had been translated into triumphant reality. The victorious UN forces were streaming northward, the broken remains of Kim Il Sung's army in full retreat before them.

Now, the JCS told MacArthur:

"Your military objective is the destruction of the North Korean armed forces. In attaining this objective, you are authorized to conduct military operations, including amphibious and airborne landings or ground operations north of the 38th Parallel in Korea, provided that at the time of such operations there has been no entry into North Korea by major Soviet or Chinese Communist Forces, no announcement of intended entry, nor a threat to counter our operations militarily in North Korea. Under no circumstances, however, will your forces cross the Manchurian or U.S.S.R. borders of Korea and, as a matter of policy, no non-Korean ground forces will be used in the northeast provinces bordering the Soviet Union or in the area along the Manchurian border. Furthermore, support of your operations north or south of the 38th Parallel will not include air or naval action against Manchuria or against U.S.S.R. territory."

Although the directive cautioned MacArthur that changing military and political circumstances might make modification of these instructions necessary, a secret "eyes only" signal from Marshall to MacArthur on September 29 explicitly declared Washington's commitment to an advance into North Korea, but explained the desirability of avoiding public advance announcements of the crossing of the 38th Parallel, which might precipitate a new vote in the United Nations.

America's allies, Britain prominent among them, had publicly expressed their support for a move into North Korea. They were overtaken by the same euphoria that gripped Washington, the same belief that with the war almost over, it remained only to ensure that the maximum advantage was extracted from victory. But the Soviet Union was back at the Security Council. If there was a UN vote about crossing the 38th Parallel, the Russians would certainly veto it. There might then be serious questions about the legitimacy of the actions of MacArthur's army. On September 30 the general responded from Tokyo to Marshall's message. He would take care, he said, to caution General Walker against saying anything too specific about operations around or north of the Parallel. He made it clear that the only delay in ordering his forces to advance beyond it was not political but logistical. The Army would drive north as soon as it was ready: "My overall strategic plan is known to you. Unless and until the enemy capitulates, I regard all of Korea open for our military operations." On October 2, MacArthur made a broadcast to North Korea, calling upon the Communist forces to lay down their arms. He neither expected, nor received, any response. He continued his preparations for the drive north across the 38th Parallel.

MacArthur's strategy was guided by two principal considerations. First, he wanted forces moving fast northeastward up North Korea to cut off Communist forces retreating toward the Manchurian border. Second, the Taebaek Mountain Range, running up the spine of North Korea, made west-east movement across the country intensely difficult. The principal road and rail routes up Korea are determined almost entirely by the lines of the north-south river valleys. MacArthur was one of the great twentieth-century exponents of amphibious operations. At Inchon he had exploited the flexibility and resources of American sea power to cut short a land campaign across difficult terrain. Now he proposed to do the same again. He would withdraw Almond's X Corps from South Korea through Inchon, load it aboard his shipping, and transport it direct to North Korea's east coast port of Wonsan, whence the Marines and the Army's 7th Division could strike north toward the Manchurian border. Meanwhile, Walker's Eighth Army would drive directly north from Seoul, for Pyongyang and the west of Kim Il Sung's dominions.

MacArthur's plan roused immediate opposition from Eighth Army. First, Walker considered it absurd to subject X Corps to the immense upheaval of withdrawal from Seoul, and sea movement to Wonsan, when the ROK Army was already driving up the east coast in the face of negligible opposition. Second, Eighth Army's commander was disgusted by MacArthur's determination to maintain a divided command, with Almond continuing to report directly to the Commander in Chief. It seemed a deliberate insult to Walker, the defender of the Pusan Perimeter, the savior of American arms in the first desperate weeks of war, to withhold X Corps from his command, when all military logic demanded a unified ground authority.

Here were the seeds of serious difficulties ahead. Many of those in Korea believed that MacArthur was once again exercising his notorious weakness for favorites—granting his own Chief of Staff, Ned Almond, a privileged opportunity to gain independent glory. Yet, in MacArthur's defense, there were good reasons to doubt the ability of Walton Walker and his staff to conduct a vigorous major offensive on their own. The doubts about Walker's fitness for high command that were raised before Inchon persisted at the 38th Parallel. Visitors to his headquarters were often unimpressed by the confusion and lack of direction that they found there. MacArthur felt ill disposed to increase Walker's authority in the field. But there was no incentive to remove Eighth Army's commander when the war was almost won, the spine of Communist resistance broken. The detailed administration of the drive into North Korea against a foe in utter disarray scarcely seemed momentous. After the event, MacArthur's critics heaped devastating criticism upon the casualness, the military unsoundness, of the command arrangements for the drive into North Korea. It is difficult to dispute these charges. Yet the critics, in their turn, ignored the real grounds for doubt about the capabilities of Walton Walker. They also discounted the mood of the time. If MacArthur was guilty of allowing himself to lapse into complacency about the imminence of undisputed victory, he succumbed to a failing from which a host of his most distinguished contemporaries were not immune.

On September 28, ROK troops advanced north of the Parallel. American units waited impatiently for the signal to follow them, to complete the wretched task upon which they were embarked and go home before winter. Yet still the political and diplomatic maneuverings in Washington continued. Abroad, America's allies were growing ever more uneasy. The British were alarmed by the signals now emerging from Peking, though their Foreign Secretary had earlier been a prominent supporter of reunifying Korea. How was the British government to explain to its own people the new situation? "It would . . . be necessary," Attlee told his Cabinet on September 26, "to present clearly to public opinion the reasons justifying a military occupation of the whole of Korea, its temporary character and limited objectives."[2] The British government would dearly have liked to hold back its own contingent in Korea from crossing the 38th Parallel, but recognized that this was impracticable if the rest of the Eighth Army was moving into the North. Bevin, the ever-robust Foreign Secretary, "felt there was insufficient foundation for their apprehension that China or Russia might thereby be provoked into active intervention," but he suggested that the President or the UN General Assembly might make one more appeal to the North Koreans to lay down their arms before Walker's army entered their country. The British Chiefs of Staff recommended holding back MacArthur's army for a week or so, while offering the North Korean Army one further chance to surrender. This uneasy message, drafted amid much private wringing of hands, the British communicated to the Americans.

In reply, Bradley told Tedder, Britain's senior military representative in Washington, that UN forces on the Parallel were already making just such a final appeal to reason to the Communists. The British, their fears a little abated, sought to strengthen the American diplomatic position by securing the passage through the UN General Assembly, on October 7, of a resolution calling for "all appropriate steps . . . to ensure conditions of stability throughout Korea" and the formation of a unified government elected under UN auspices. This passed by 47 to 5, with 7 abstentions. Its purpose was to provide a cloak of UN support for military operations in North Korea, while preserving some vagueness about what form these operations would take. A growing body of moderate opinion in the West believed that action by Syngman Rhee's army in the North, restricted to battle between rival bodies of Koreans, presented a much lesser threat of Chinese or Russian intervention than a major foreign presence. In this they probably deluded themselves. Given the doubtful military abilities of the ROK Army, the Communists could almost certainly have driven Rhee's unaided forces out of the North, with or without Chinese intervention. The dilemma for Washington and its allies would then have been unresolved.

But to Acheson's dismay, MacArthur now declared openly and directly to the North Koreans that unless they laid down their arms, he would take "such military action as may be necessary to enforce the decrees of the United Nations." Yet again, the general had swept aside diplomatic niceties, ignored critical political sensitivities, overridden fundamental constitutional limitations upon his own powers. And yet again, however unhappily, the Administration in Washington muffled its own doubts and fears. The insuperable difficulty of containing or controlling MacArthur remained the same as ever: the general commanded in Tokyo upon his own terms, as he always had. Either MacArthur was endured or dismissed. Yet how could he be removed without devastating damage to the image and authority, not only of the Truman Administration, but of the United States? He was not merely the Pacific victor of World War II, but the sole begetter of triumph at Inchon, heroic arbiter of the destinies of a free Korea. It is not only with hindsight that it is apparent that MacArthur's gigantic hubris could lead only to tragedy. Many men in Washington and Tokyo also perceived this in the fall of 1950. But they could see no realistic means of ridding themselves of this old man of the sea. The play must be acted out to the end.

Washington continued to share with Tokyo the most fundamental misconceptions about the enemy's behavior and intentions. The Administration based its policy now, as from the outbreak of war, upon the conviction that the Communist powers were acting in concert. Available intelligence about Chinese thinking was negligible. It was much more plentiful, both from covert and diplomatic sources, about Moscow's frame of mind. By the winter of 1950 it was apparent that the Russians greatly regretted the North Korean adventure, were eager to distance themselves from it, and to prevent any widening of the war. Soviet signals to this effect were received, and understood, in Washington. Yet these entirely blinded the Administration to the danger of unilateral action by Peking. For the first, but by no means the last time in Korea, a preoccupation with ideological confrontation blinded the leaders of the United States to the nationalistic considerations at play. They simply did not entertain the prospect that the Chinese might act in Korea for their own reasons, quite heedless of Soviet wishes or policy.

On October 9 the Eighth Army at last advanced in full force across the 38th Parallel. For almost a week they encountered serious resistance. Then the North Koreans broke and fled north in full retreat. The 1st Cavalry and 24th Infantry began a headlong pursuit, the long convoys' road race interrupted only for spasmodic small-unit actions against isolated enemy rearguards.

At this moment, with military victory imminent and the Eighth Army heavily committed, MacArthur was astonished to receive a message from Washington informing him that the President sought his presence at a personal meeting on Wake Island, in mid-Pacific between Tokyo and the west coast of the United States. On the morning of October 15, nursing acute disgust for what he regarded as a piece of political grandstanding by Truman, the general and his staff took off from Haneda aboard his Constellation.

Truman wrote simply in his memoirs that a moment had come at which he considered his lack of personal contact with MacArthur a handicap: "I thought that he ought to know his Commander in Chief, and that I ought to know the senior field commander in the Far East." Yet there is little doubt that for once, MacArthur's skepticism about Washington's motives was justified. Truman was politically beleaguered at home, under fire from the Right for supposed softness toward the Communists. There were indeed good reasons for President and Supreme Commander to meet. But the timing was such that it remains difficult to doubt Truman's desire to associate himself in the public mind with victory in Korea, and with the victor.

MacArthur was anyway the least tractable of men. The consequence of this apparently blatantly political act by the President was to cause him to approach the meeting in a mood of cynicism bordering upon contempt. He flew to Wake Island on October 15, 1950, entirely unreceptive to open discussion of serious issues. When Truman stepped down onto the tarmac the following morning to be greeted by his theater commander, the general did not salute. He shook hands, as an equal. "I've been a long time meeting you," said Truman. "I hope it won't be so long next time," said MacArthur with historic triteness. They talked alone for an hour in a Quonset hut on the edge of the airstrip. Both Acheson and Marshall had declined to join Truman on the trip. Acheson afterward shook his head about the folly of private talks, "the sort of lethal things which chiefs of state get into" that lead to disastrous misunderstandings about points of view and decisions. On this occasion, according to Truman's subsequent account, MacArthur assured him that the Chinese would not attack, that victory was imminent, that he himself had no political ambitions. Then the two men emerged into the mounting Pacific heat and drove across to an airport office building for a full-dress meeting with their entourages.

Even at this, no formal record was taken. MacArthur told the gathering that "formal resistance will end throughout North and South Korea by Thanksgiving." He planned to withdraw the Eighth Army to Japan by Christmas, leaving X Corps as an occupation force. He reiterated his view that even in the unlikely event that the Chinese intervened, "now that we have bases for our air force in Korea, if the Chinese tried to get down to Pyongyang there would be the greatest slaughter." If the Russians provided the Chinese with air support, their competence was so limited "that I believe the Russian air would bomb the Chinese as often as they would bomb us." There was some desultory discussion about the political future of Korea, in which MacArthur warmly supported Syngman Rhee's claims to primacy. Truman agreed, "We must make it plain that we are supporting the Rhee government, and propaganda can go to hell." An hour and a half after it began, the meeting broke up. Truman invited MacArthur to stay for lunch, but the general demurred. Urgent military business called him to Tokyo. To his surprise, he found himself facing a brief awards ceremony, at which Truman presented him with his fifth Distinguished Service Medal. Amid eager public protestations of goodwill toward his commander in the field, Truman took off from the airstrip, declaring to reporters, "I've never had a more satisfactory conference since I've been President."

MacArthur left for Tokyo in a rage. He considered himself diminished by the summons to be cross-questioned by a group of political hacks for whom he felt only contempt. "Who was that young whippersnapper who was asking questions?" he demanded insistently, until his staff divined that he referred to Dean Rusk, the Assistant Secretary of State. "That conference," wrote MacArthur later, "made me realize that a curious, and sinister, change was taking place in Washington. The defiant, rallying figure that had been Franklin Roosevelt was gone. Instead, there was a tendency towards temporizing rather than fighting it through."[3]

With hindsight, the Wake Island conference can be seen as a disastrous landmark in the Korean conflict, as fatal to the interests of the Truman Administration as to those of the tenant of the Dai Ichi. Before Wake, Washington had been given ample grounds to doubt the tractability and judgment of MacArthur. Having summoned the general to meet the President, however, the Washington delegation signally failed to use the opportunity to drive home to MacArthur his absolute responsibility to accept instructions from his government. Instead, they allowed themselves to be impressed by his charisma, his sublime assurance, his omniscience about unfolding events in the Far East. They went home reassured that Chinese or Soviet intervention in Korea was not a significant danger. MacArthur, meanwhile, returned to Tokyo with all his antipathy to the leaders of the Administration confirmed. Whatever Truman and his party had done at Wake, this would have been unlikely to deflect the victorious MacArthur from his chosen course. Yet, by failing to use the opportunity to pursue a serious, prearranged agenda, by causing the Supreme Commander to fly 2,000 miles from his headquarters in the midst of a campaign merely to exchange banalities, Truman and his associates diminished, rather than reasserted, their authority over the general. It is difficult to regard Truman's initiation of the Wake meeting as other than a serious error of judgment by the President, prompted by uncharacteristically frivolous political considerations. Its cost to his stature in dealing with MacArthur, his weakening of his own position in the months that followed, are hard to overestimate.

On October 19, Pyongyang fell. General Paek Sun Yup led the 1st ROK Division into the city, the infantry clinging to the hulls of American armor. They swept aside the flimsy Communist barricades and clattered through almost empty streets. Most of the civilians had fled or were in hiding. Paek felt "utterly exhilarated. I had left five years earlier as a refugee. Now I was back with 10,000 men, 100 guns, and a battalion of M-46 tanks."[4] Kim Il Sung and his government had fled into the northern fastnesses. Fascinated, the South Korean and American officers poked among the chaos of his abandoned office in the old Japanese provincial governor's residence. There was an orgy of mutual souvenir photograph-taking, for this was the first war in which every soldier—among the UN at least—carried a camera in his pack. An American civil affairs officer, Colonel Archibald Melchior, chose a council of "representative non-Communist citizens" to run the enemy's capital from North Koreans plucked almost arbitrarily from the streets. "We thought the war was over," said General Paek. "The North Koreans were now completely wiped out, throwing away their weapons as we met them." On October 20, from MacArthur's headquarters, Colonel Charles Willoughby circulated an intelligence summary throughout Far East Command:

"Organized resistance on any large scale has ceased to be an enemy capability. Indications are that the North Korean military and political headquarters may have fled into Manchuria. Communications with, and consequent control of, the enemy's field units have dissipated to a point of ineffectiveness. In spite of these indications of disorganization, there are no signs, at the moment, that the enemy intends to surrender. He continues to retain the capability of fighting small-scale delaying actions against UN pressure. . . ."

While the Eighth Army pushed north from Seoul, X Corps was in motion in the east. The 1st Marine Division had embarked at Inchon. Alongside the Marines, the

7th Division was assigned to move south to Pusan to embark for Wonsan. Spirits in the formation were not high. The 7th's limited experience of combat during the advance from Inchon had done little to convince them of their own effectiveness. Lieutenant Jim Sheldon and his platoon of the 17th Infantry were sent on a motor patrol to secure an ammunition factory, which they found deserted. But a few hours after their arrival they were dismayed to encounter a column of North Koreans arriving to replenish their stocks, which provoked a little firefight in which the Americans lost four wounded. There was much wild firing at shadows in the darkness that night. In the days that followed, a succession of successful minor skirmishes with Communist stragglers began to persuade them that they were quite competent soldiers. Their commanders thought otherwise, and embarked upon a hasty field-training program. This ended abruptly when sixteen men were killed and eighty wounded by white phosphorus bombs from their own 4.2-inch mortar company during a demonstration exercise before spectators. It was in the aftermath of this grim fiasco that they were ordered to move to Pusan: "Morale in the regiment was pretty low," said Sheldon.

On the LSTs, plowing north toward Wonsan, the Marines cleaned their weapons and equipment, talked and slept with little sense of stress. O. P. Smith was exultant about the showing of his men in the battle for Seoul, optimistic that even when the war was over, the division had staked a formidable claim to be retained under arms. Smith's Operations officer, Al Bowser, nursing a bad cold, was chiefly preoccupied with the problem of where the formation might spend the winter. He had no thought for the far northern mountains or the Yalu, but merely for some coastal location where conditions might be made endurable if they had to remain. But with luck, they would not. With the North Koreans in headlong retreat, the war could be over in a matter of weeks. If that was the case, the Marines had already been told that two regiments would return at once to the United States, leaving only one regiment for garrison duty in Japan.

The Marine landing at Wonsan was seriously delayed by Communist mines blocking the harbor entrance. On October 12 two minesweepers were lost, impacting on Russian-built mines. It took two weeks, and cost three more minesweepers, before the field was cleared. To the intense irritation and discomfort of Smith and his men, they wallowed offshore in the transports while the Navy bustled hither and thither. Then, to their embarrassment, the Americans learned that the South Koreans were there before them. The ROK 3rd and Capital Divisions had entered Wonsan on October 10, after a dramatic two-week dash from the 38th Parallel. The Capital Division was already fifty miles north and still going. The 1st Marine Division staged its amphibious landing at Wonsan on October 25, twelve days after its own advance and technical parties had arrived by land and air. Even Bob Hope was there before them. To their profound chagrin, by a stroke which entered Marine legend, the entertainer staged a USO show in Wonsan the night before the division stormed ashore to take possession. The 7th Division suffered even more acute delays and counterorders before being put ashore at Iwon in the last days of October and the first days of November. X Corps was at last deployed, in time for MacArthur's last act. Men's thoughts were chiefly addressed to going home.

As the Eighth Army's drive north continued, MacArthur made plain his contempt for the carefully drawn niceties of Washington and the UN about restricting movement near the Chinese border to South Korean forces. He responded witheringly when he heard of a British proposal for the establishment of a buffer zone south of the Yalu, jointly policed by China and the UN: "The widely reported British desire to appease the Chinese Communists by giving them a strip of North Korea finds its historic precedent in the action taken at Munich on September 29, 1938. . . . To give up any portion of North Korea to the aggression of the Chinese Communists would be the greatest defeat of the free world in recent times. Indeed, to yield to so immoral a proposition would bankrupt our leadership and influence in Asia, and render untenable our position both politically and morally."[5]

When he issued orders, on October 20, for "all concerned" within his command to prepare for a "maximum effort" to advance rapidly to the border of North Korea, the Joint Chiefs made no attempt to interfere. Fear of Chinese intervention had sunk so low that on October 23, at a joint meeting in Washington of the British and American Chiefs of Staff, Bradley declared soothingly, "We all agree that, if the Chinese Communists come into Korea, we get out." On October 24, MacArthur's new directive removed all remaining restrictions on the movement of American troops toward the Yalu. Walker and Almond were "authorized to use any and all ground forces as necessary, to secure all of North Korea." The Joint Chiefs in Washington queried this order, which was "a matter of some concern here." MacArthur brushed them aside. General Collins and his colleagues were in no doubt that they were being flatly disobeyed by the commander in the field. In the same week they requested MacArthur to issue a statement setting at rest fears in the UN Security Council that the Chinese might move across the Yalu to protect their vital Suiho electrical generating plant unless this was declared safe from UN military action. MacArthur declined to give such an assurance unless he was sure the plant was not powering Communist munitions production. Yet again, with the war almost over, the Joint Chiefs showed their unwillingness to precipitate a confrontation. Washington resigned itself to playing the hand against the Communists MacArthur's way.

"We are going to go ahead and force the issue now," a Department of State spokesman told a correspondent in Washington.[6] The decision to advance north across the 38th Parallel was a classic example of military opportunity becoming the engine of action at the expense of political desirability. No rigorous debate was carried to a conclusion about UN, or U.S., objectives in occupying the North. The very great political and diplomatic hazards were submerged by the public perception of the prospect of outright military victory. At the root of American action lay a contempt, conscious or unconscious, for the capabilities of Mao Tse Tung's nation and armed forces. The Chinese Communists were perceived as a sinister ideological force in Asia, but not a formidable military one. Far greater courage and determination would have been required from the Truman Administration for a decision to halt the Eighth Army at the 38th Parallel than was demanded for acquiescence in MacArthur's drive to victory. If there remained a measure of apprehension within the Administration about entering North Korea, there was also the powerful scent of triumphalism among many prominent Americans. Harold Stassen declared in a speech in support of Republican candidates on November 5 that the war in Korea was ''the direct result of five years of building up Chinese Communist strength through the blinded, blundering American-Asiatic policy of the present national administration . . . five years of coddling Chinese Communists, five years of undermining General MacArthur, five years of snubbing friendly freedom-loving Asiatics, and five years of appeasing the arch-Communist, Mao Tse Tung.'' Now Mao was to be appeased no longer. American arms were being carried to the very frontier of his vast land.

7

THE COMING OF THE CHINESE

On the evening of November 1, 1950, Private Carl Simon of G Company, 8th Cavalry, lay in the company position with his comrades speculating nervously about the fate of a patrol of F Company, which had reported itself in trouble, "under attack by unidentified troops." As the darkness closed in, they heard firing, bugles, and shouting. Their accompanying Koreans could not identify the language, but said that it must be Chinese. When a wave of yelling enemy charged the Americans out of the gloom, firing and grenading as they came, no effective resistance was offered. "There was just mass hysteria on the position," said Simon. "It was every man for himself. The shooting was terrific, there were Chinese shouting everywhere, I didn't know which way to go. In the end, I just ran with the crowd. We just ran and ran until the bugles grew fainter."[1] The war diaries of the 1st Cavalry Division, of which the 8th Cavalry was a part, present the events at Ansung in a somewhat more coherent, less Armageddonist spirit than Private First Class Simon. But since his uncomplicated perception—of a thunderbolt from the night that brought the entire ordered pattern of his army life down about his head—was to become common to thousands of other young Americans in Korea in the weeks that followed, it seems no less valid than that of his superiors.

The twenty-year-old New York baker's son had joined the Army to see the world. He was in transit to Japan when the war began and had to look on a map

128

to discover where Korea was. When he saw the place for himself, he liked it not at all. His unit had been uneasy, unhappy, and uncomfortable since it crossed the 38th Parallel. Simon had been slightly wounded in a skirmish soon after entering North Korea. The only moment of the war he had enjoyed was the Bob Hope Show in Pyongyang, though he was so short that he had to keep jumping up and down among the vast audience of soldiers to catch a glimpse of the distant stage. Simon was one of many thousands of men vastly relieved to find the war almost over, impatient to get home.

Yet now he found himself among thirty-five frightened fugitives, in the midst of Korea without a compass. The officers among them showed no urge to exercise any leadership. The group merely began to shuffle southward. Most threw away their weapons. They walked for fourteen days, eating berries, waving their yellow scarves desperately but vainly to observation planes. Once, in a village, they got rice and potatoes at gunpoint from a papa-san. At night they gazed at the curious beauty of the hills, on fire from strafing. For a time they lay up in the house of a frightened civilian, who eventually drove them out with his warnings of Communists in the area. They were close to physical collapse, and to surrender, when one morning they thought they glimpsed a tank bearing a "red carpet" identification panel. They ran forward and found on the ground a London newspaper. Then they saw British ration packs and, at last, far below them in the valley, a tracked vehicle moving. They determined to make for it, whatever the nationality of its occupants. To their overwhelming relief, they found themselves in the hands of the British 27 Brigade.

Private First Class Simon and his companions were a small part of the flotsam from the disaster that befell the U.S. 1st Cavalry Division between November 1 and 3, which also inflicted desperate damage upon the ROK II Corps. The South Koreans were the first to be heavily attacked. The Chinese 116th Division struck against the 15th ROK. Then, on November 1 near Ansung, about midway across the Korean peninsula, it was the turn of the Americans. Strong forces hit them with great determination, separating their units, then attacking them piecemeal. Batteries in transit on the roads, rifle companies on positions, found themselves under devastating fire from small arms, mortars, and katyusha rockets. The 3rd Battalion of the 8th Cavalry was effectively destroyed. The regiment's other battalions were severely mauled, and elements of the 5th Cavalry damaged. Yet when the 1st Cavalry Division's action ended, activity across the Korean battle front once again dwindled into local skirmishes.

Herein lies one of the greatest, most persistent enigmas of the Korean War. More than three weeks before the main Chinese onslaught was delivered with full force, Peking delivered a ferocious warning by fire: we are here, said the Chinese, in the unmistakable language of rifle and grenade, in the mountains of Korea that you cannot penetrate. We can strike at will against your forces, and they are ill equipped in mind and body—above all, in mind—to meet us. We are willing to accept heavy casualties to achieve tactical success. The armies of Syngman Rhee are entirely incapable of resisting our assaults.

Yet this message, this warning, MacArthur and his subordinates absolutely declined to receive. They persisted in their conviction that their armies could drive with impunity to the Yalu. They continued to believe that the Chinese were either unwilling or unable to intervene effectively. They showed no signs of alarm at the evidence that not only the ROK divisions, but their own, were at something less than peak fighting efficiency. They had created a fantasy world for themselves, in which events would march in accordance with a divine providence directed from the Dai Ichi building. The conduct of the drive to the Yalu reflected a contempt for intelligence, for the cardinal principles of military prudence, seldom matched in twentieth-century warfare.

The first ROK forces reached the Yalu on October 25 and sent back a bottle of its intoxicating waters to Syngman Rhee. Some soldiers, like their American counterparts, equally symbolically chose to urinate from its banks. On the same day the ROK II Corps, driving north on the western axis of the UN advance, was strongly attacked and, in the action that followed, almost destroyed. The ROKs reported that the agents of their disaster were Chinese and sent some Chinese prisoners to the Americans. General Paek Sun Yup, probably the ablest South Korean commander, was at this time transferred to temporary command of II Corps, and demanded to see the POWs personally at his command post. He spoke fluent Chinese, and immediately established that the prisoners were indeed from the mainland, with southern accents. They wore Chinese reversible smocks. Paek asked them, "Are there many of you here?" They nodded. "Many many." Paek reported the conversation directly to I Corps' commander, "Shrimp" Milburn. But Milburn was no more impressed by the Korean than by his own intelligence officer, Colonel Percy Thomas, who was also convinced that there was now a serious Chinese threat. General Walker himself sought to explain away the presence of some Chinese among the North Koreans as insignificant: "After all, a lot of Mexicans live in Texas. . . ." II Corps fell back as the enemy advanced under cover of vast makeshift smoke screens, created by setting fire to the forests through which they marched. When the U.S. 1st Cavalry passed through the ROKs to take up the attack, the division was savaged. Meanwhile, in the east, ROK I Corps, moving north from Hamnung, was stopped in its tracks on the road to the hydroelectric plants of the Chosin Reservoir. As early as October 25 the ROK 1st Division found itself heavily engaged and captured a soldier who admitted that he was Chinese. The next day more prisoners were taken. They were identified as members of the 124th Division of the Chinese 42nd Army. By

October 31 twenty-five Chinese prisoners had been taken, and the strength of the Communist force at the foot of the Chosin Reservoir was apparent.

The Argyll & Sutherland Highlanders, of the British 27 Brigade, found themselves engaged in a skirmish near the Chongchong River which cost them five killed and six wounded. They advanced cautiously forward to examine the scattered bodies of the Communists on the hillside. "They were unlike any enemy I had seen before," wrote Lieutenant Colin Mitchell. "They wore thick padded clothing, which made them look like little Michelin men. I turned one body over with my foot, and saw that he wore a peaked cap with a red-star badge. These soldiers were Chinese. I then turned over another and, as I looked down at him, he opened one eye and looked up at me. I shot him with my luger, shouting to the platoon, 'They're alive!' It was quickly over, and all the enemy lay dead."[2] Yet still the UN Command could not bring itself to recognize the simple truth—that the Chinese had entered the Korean War in force.

Bradley, in Washington, speculated uncertainly as to whether Peking was merely seeking to make a face-saving gesture in support of its defeated North Korean allies. There was renewed debate about the merits of bombing the Yalu bridges. On November 13 the State Department sought opinions from London, Canberra, Ottawa, Delhi, Wellington, Moscow, and The Hague about possible overflights of Manchuria by UN aircraft in "hot pursuit." U.S. ambassadors in each capital reported that reaction to such an initiative would be highly unfavorable. CIA reports continued to give uncertain guidance: on November 8 the Agency estimated that there were 30,000 to 40,000 Chinese already in Korea, with 700,000 more poised across the border in Manchuria. The reports suggested that Peking had full freedom of action and might move in strength. But opinion in Washington remained obsessed with the belief that the Communist world acted in concert to a prearranged plan, that Peking would not or could not operate independently of Moscow, and that the assumed unwillingness of Moscow to see the war extended would preclude Chinese action. Bedell Smith, the CIA's director, urged the National Security Council on November 9 that MacArthur should be given a freer hand in North Korea because "the Kremlin's basic decision for or against war would hardly be influenced by this local provocation in this area."[3]

At a joint State-Defense meeting on November 21, Vandenburg and Forrest urged that, if MacArthur's advance to the Yalu was checked by the Chinese, Peking should be told to "quit, or we would have to hit them in Manchuria."[4] No evidence of dissent from this view by Marshall or any others present is recorded. Washington interpreted Chinese warnings and probes in October as evidence of weakness and reluctance to fight. The Administration's instinct was to call the Chinese bluff. Although Washington had some reason to be exasperated by MacArthur's public declarations and threats, the private mood in the capital, the confidence in imminent victory, and lack of apprehension about Chinese intentions mirrored that in Tokyo. And if the American assessment of Peking subsequently proved bitterly mistaken, the circumstantial evidence indeed supports the view that the Chinese moved with caution and circumspection into Korea, and committed themselves to all-out war only when it became apparent, first, that the UN forces were not entirely formidable foes; and, second, that unless they were defeated on the battlefield, they were committed to an advance to the Yalu. Some of the Chinese soldiers who took part in the first actions against the ROKs and the 1st Cavalry described how, afterward, they were marched back across the Yalu and moved eastward to cross the river into North Korea once more for the main offensive that followed. For an army as scantily provided with transport as that of China, this was scarcely an economical approach to deployment. It can be most readily explained by a measure of caution and indecision in Peking, as the Chinese leadership measured the military capability of the UN forces. In November 1950, General MacArthur thundered to the United Nations that the Chinese intervention was "one of the most offensive acts of international lawlessness of historical record." This was absurd. It may never be possible to piece together the precise decision-making process in Peking that led to the order to enter Korea. Almost all the key participants are dead, and among the living there is no reliable body of records to enable even those who wish to establish the objective truth about recent Chinese political history to do so. But the evidence is overwhelming that in 1950, Mao Tse Tung and his colleagues were deeply reluctant to engage the United Nations—or, more precisely, the forces of the United States—in Korea.

China had scarcely begun to recover from her civil war. In 1949 an estimated 40 million of her population were affected by natural disasters. To famine was added the new problem of local guerrilla war: the traditional phrase *"kung fei"*— "Communist bandits"—was now transferred to the Kuomintang. Over a million were rounded up or killed between May 1949 and May 1951, most of them south of the Yangtse. In the country, secret societies had grown up to resist land reform. There was widespread dissent in the cities. China was still seeking to secure what she considered to be her own borders. In October 1950 the People's Liberation Army moved into Tibet and completed its occupation of the country only the following year. Meanwhile, in the east, Peking's attentions were overwhelmingly focused upon eliminating Formosa as the base of Nationalist opposition. Through-out the summer of 1950 invasion barges were being built, some 5,000 junks assembled, airfields prepared to support the assault on Chiang's stronghold, which the Third Field Army's deputy commander, Su Yu, declared would be "an extremely big problem, and will involve the biggest campaign in the history of modern Chinese warfare." Yet amid all this, Mao was seeking to demobilize vast masses of his unwieldy army, to return soldiers to the factories and fields and workshops where they were so desperately needed. It was a problem that Peking had failed to resolve by the autumn of 1950, when China still possessed some five million men under arms.

Peking must have been well aware of Kim Il Sung's invasion plans—the railway system of northeast China played an important part in moving Soviet supplies and equipment into North Korea. But there is no evidence that China played a significant role in the North Korean decision to go to war. The Sino-Soviet Treaty of Friendship, signed in Moscow on February 15, 1950, had gone some way to heal the long-standing rift between Mao and Stalin. But it provided China with disappointingly little material assistance. It was rumored that Stalin had demanded, and Mao rejected, the wholesale appointment of Soviet advisers as a condition of major equipment aid. The People's Liberation Army was still equipped entirely with arms captured from the Japanese or supplied by the Americans to the Kuomintang. Despite considerable skill in fieldcraft, it lacked the communications or the training to operate cohesively much beyond regimental level. The PLA remained, in large measure, a guerrilla army, lacking the advantage of the heavy weapons—and the handicap of the impedimenta—of a modern Western army. Both for reasons of domestic political stability and military preparedness, in the autumn of 1950 it appears that many key figures among China's leadership were most reluctant to see their country exposed to war with the West.

But Washington's linkage of the invasion of South Korea with the threat to Formosa in June 1950 had an immediate influence on China. Truman's statement on June 27, declaring that "the occupation of Formosa by Communist forces would be a direct threat to the security of the Pacific area and to U.S. forces performing their lawful and necessary functions in that area," created—incidentally and almost casually—an entirely new and firm commitment to keeping Formosa out of the hands of Peking's Communist rulers. This was a much greater blow to China's perceived national interest than Washington seemed to recognize at the time. Premier Chou En Lai adopted a far tougher public attitude toward the American blockade of the Taiwan Strait than toward American intervention in Korea. Henceforward, as a leading historian of the PLA has written, "The struggle to liberate Taiwan began to be linked to the struggle against U.S. imperialism as such, and the achievement of the former was now seen in the more long-term context of the latter."[5] After years in which Chiang Kai Shek had been perceived as the foremost enemy of Communist China, with astonishing rapidity the United States took on this role. "The American imperialists fondly hope that their armed aggression against Taiwan will prevent us from liberating it," Kuo Mo-Jo wrote in the *People's Daily* in August. "Around China in particular, their designs for a blockade are taking shape in the pattern of a stretched-out snake. Starting from South Korea, it stretches to Japan, the Ryuku Islands, Taiwan and the Philippines and then turns up at Vietnam."[6] Westerners, and Americans in particular, sometimes made the mistake of allowing their scorn for propagandist rhetoric such as this to blind them to the very real Chinese fear of encirclement. Throughout the Korean War, Washington persistently sought the communist ideological logic behind Chinese actions. It might have been more profitable to consider instead historic Chinese nationalist logic. Korea had provided the springboard for the Japanese invasion of Manchuria only a generation before. As the Americans drove north after smashing Kim Il Sung's armies in September 1950, Peking was appalled by the imminent prospect of an American imperialist army on the Yalu.

Chinese alarm was intensified by the visibly strengthening relationship between the United States and Chiang. The warm words spoken by both sides during MacArthur's July visit to Formosa were widely publicized, as were Chiang's offers of Nationalist troops to fight alongside the United Nations in Korea. The Communists would have been even more disturbed had they known how close Truman came to accepting Chiang's offer of 33,000 men when MacArthur's armies were desperate for reinforcements.

In late September and early October, the Chinese issued increasingly forceful warnings, both in public statements and in private remarks to the Indian Ambassador in Peking, about their attitude to the American presence in North Korea. In the first weeks of fighting in Korea, the Chinese press scarcely reported the war. Yet now a growing crescendo of anti-American propaganda was printed and broadcast: "Resist America, Aid Korea"; "Preserve Our Homes, Defend the Nation." Massed meetings denounced the "bloodstained bandits," "murderers," "savages." The People's Republic did not intend, General Nieh Jung-Chen, China's Acting Chief of Staff, told Sardar K. Pannikkar, "to sit back with folded hands and let the Americans come to their border. . . . We know what we are in for, but at all costs American aggression has got to be stopped. The Americans can bomb us, they can destroy our industries, but they cannot defeat us on land." On the danger of American nuclear reaction, Nieh said, "We have calculated all that. . . . They may even drop atom bombs on us. What then? They may kill a few million people. Without sacrifice, a nation's independence cannot be upheld. . . . After all, China lives on the farms. What can atom bombs do there?"[7]

At the State Department in Washington, a handful of officials took heed and sounded a note of caution. John Paton Davies warned that a combination of "irredentism, expansionism, Soviet pressure and inducements, strategic anxieties, ideological zeal, domestic pressures, and emotional anti-Americanism" might lead China to intervene. Edmund Chubb, director of the Office of Chinese Affairs, expressed the conviction that China would fight. But his persistent pessimism on this issue had undermined his credibility. As late as October 12 the CIA argued that "despite statements by Chou En Lai, troop movements to Manchuria, and propaganda charges of atrocities and border violations, there are no convincing indications of an actual Chinese Communist intention to resort to full-scale intervention in Korea.'' Dean Acheson found the logic against Chinese intervention irresistible: they would lose all hope of their coveted UN seat; they would need to become clients of the Russians, dependent upon Moscow for air and naval support to be able to wage war at all; the PLA was too poorly equipped to compete convincingly with MacArthur's armies; the Chinese government must be daunted by the expectation of devastating American reprisals if Chinese forces were committed against those of the UN. The United States was convinced that its policies in the Far East presented no threat to any legitimate Chinese interest. Washington therefore persuaded itself that Peking would reach the same conclusion.

Peking did not. On October 2, Premier Chou En Lai summoned Pannikkar, the Indian Ambassador, and directly informed him that if the United Nations crossed the 38th Parallel, China would intervene in the war. Truman, when he learned of Chou's message, dismissed it as ''a bald attempt to blackmail the UN. . . . The problem that arose in connection with these reports was that Mr. Pannikkar had in the past played the game of the Chinese Communists fairly regularly, so that his statement could not be taken as that of an impartial observer.'' The absence of any direct link between Washington and Peking was a significant force in preventing the Americans from achieving even the level of understanding they possessed with Moscow. The lack of diplomatic relations together with the absolute ignorance of the Peking regime about how these might profitably be conducted ensured that Washington never received the sort of signals from Peking which, if believed, could have averted a confrontation on the battlefield. On October 8, the day after American troops crossed the 38th Parallel, Mao issued the order for ''Chinese People's Volunteers'' to ''resist the attacks of United States imperialism.''

For many years it was believed that the reinforced Fourth Field Army, which entered North Korea a week later, was under the command of Mao's close associate, Lin Piao. The Chinese today assert most firmly that this was not so. And while Lin's political disgrace might provide a motive for deceit on this issue, there is sufficient corroborative evidence to take the modern Chinese claim about Lin most seriously. Military sources in Peking say that, in the autumn of 1950, Lin was indeed urged by Mao and the Central Committee to accept command of a Chinese army to fight in Korea, and was their first choice to do so. Yet he himself argued strongly against immediate military intervention. He believed that the PLA was not yet ready to take on the army of the United States. He urged delay, if necessary for a year or more, until the army could be retrained and re-equipped. He was especially concerned about the impact of U.S. air power on an unprotected Chinese Army. Marshal Peng Te'Huai, on the other hand, argued that he could not see that China would be any better placed to fight in 1951, or for that matter in

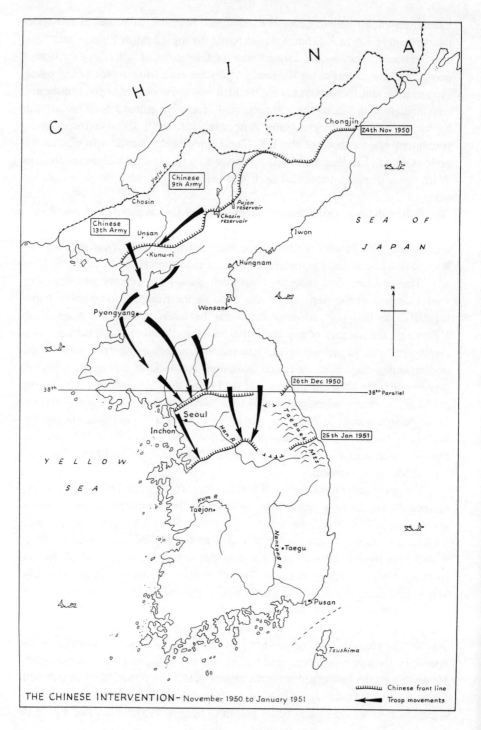

THE CHINESE INTERVENTION – November 1950 to January 1951

‾‾ʌ‾‾ʌ‾‾ Chinese front line
◄━━━ Troop movements

1952, than in 1950. He believed—to resort to contemporary cliché—that "imperialists could be shown to be paper tigers." A big, forceful, talkative man, Peng told his staff robustly that will and motivation could compensate for any shortcomings of equipment. One of his former officers says that Peng, from beginning to end, treated the struggle in Korea merely as an extension of the Liberation war against the Kuomintang.[8] According to a memoir published under Peng's name in 1981, on October 4 he found himself suddenly summoned from his headquarters, as commander in chief in northwest China, to fly to Peking for a conference and arrived to discover the Central Committee already in session, debating the dispatch of troops to Korea. At the next session the following day, he was appointed to command them. The simple fiction of describing the Chinese forces in Korea as "volunteers" was designed to prevent all-out war with the United States, above all to diminish the danger of massive American retaliation against the mainland.

China's initial force in Korea was organized as XIII Army Group and comprised four armies, each of three 10,000-man infantry divisions, a regiment of cavalry, and five regiments of artillery. They crossed the Yalu bridges by night. Their first essential task was to establish a wide-enough bridgehead on the south bank to give themselves room to deploy. Had they permitted the United Nations to close up to the Yalu border along its length, they would have been confronted by the intolerable initial task of conducting an opposed river crossing before they could join battle. The Forty-second Army came first, to block the road running northwest from the Chosin Reservoir. The Thirty-eighth Army was to deploy across the road north from Huichon. The Fortieth Army advanced from Sinuiju toward Pukchin. The Fiftieth and Sixty-sixth Armies followed.

It was an extraordinary achievement of modern warfare. Between October 13 and 25 the intelligence staffs of MacArthur's armies failed to discern the slightest evidence of the movement of 130,000 soldiers and porters. A combination of superb fieldcraft and camouflage by the Chinese, with their lack of use of any of the conventional means of detecting modern military movement—wireless traffic, mechanized activity, supply dumps—blinded the UN Command to what was taking place on its front. Above all, perhaps, the generals were not looking for anything of this sort. They had persuaded themselves that the war was all but over. Their senses were deadened to any fresh perception.

On the night of November 5-6, after the disaster to the 8th Cavalry and the crumbling of so many major ROK units, the UN Command was briefly sufficiently disturbed by the situation to consider a major withdrawal. Yet on the morning of November 6 Walker's staff found that it was the Communists who were disengaging all along the front. After ten days in which they had dramatically seized the initiative and forced back UN forces in a succession of battles, they chose to break off the action. Once more, their motives and intentions are not entirely clear. Military sources in Peking today declare that there were problems of supply and coordination, that having thus warned the Americans of their will and capability to intervene, the Chinese were prepared to linger for a time, to discover whether their message was heeded. Both these assertions seem at least plausible. The Chinese also claimed that their purpose in withdrawing was "to encourage the enemy's arrogance."[9] But it became immediately apparent that MacArthur, far from being deterred by the first Chinese offensive, considered that the Communists had striven their hardest to overcome his forces . . . and failed. Peking, he believed, had shot its bolt, and most unfrightening this had proved. The UN offensive, the drive for the Yalu, would resume forthwith. The Chinese, in their turn, prepared to meet it.

So who were they, the men of these "fanatical hordes" who were about to force upon the United States Army one of the most humiliating retreats in its history? It is sometimes forgotten that after twenty years of war, many Chinese soldiers were men of exceptional military experience. "My first memories as a child were of the Japanese burning and destroying," said Li Hebei, a twenty-two-year-old infantry platoon commander who crossed the Yalu with the 587th regiment on October 25. Li had served first with local guerrillas, armed only with a homemade rifle, then graduated to the PLA and a captured Japanese weapon when a unit passed through his devastated village when he was sixteen. Like thousands of politically aware young Chinese, he called the PLA "the big university," for it was in its ranks that he learned to read and write. Between 1943 and 1947 he saw his family just once. He learned to march . . . forever. Mile upon mile he and his unit could walk or even trot, in their quilted cotton uniforms and tennis shoes, up mountain tracks hauling all that they possessed in the world: personal weapon, grenade, eighty rounds, spare foot rags, sewing kit, chopsticks, and perhaps a week's rations—tea, rice, a little sugar, perhaps a tin of fish or meat. Thirty-five years later, Hebei said, grinning at the memory, "We had a saying—red army's two legs better than Kuomintang's four wheels. Life was very hard, but the atmosphere was very good, because we were full of hope."[10] A Chinese soldier required just eight to ten pounds of supplies a day, against sixty for his UN counterpart. Thus, to sustain fifty divisions in combat, Peking needed to move only 2,500 tons of supplies a day south across the Yalu. This compared with 600 tons for a single U.S. Army division, 700 tons for the 1st Marine Division. Each of the tens of thousands of porters supporting the Chinese drive into Korea could carry eighty to one hundred pounds on his shoulder pole or A-frame. Thus did the impossible become possible.

Yu Xiu was one of the men who stormed the 8th Cavalry's positions on November 1, exulting to discover the success of their techniques of hard-hitting night assault. Yu was a twenty-nine-year-old from Chungsu Province, brought up in the French sector of Shanghai, who joined the Fourth Field Army when his father was killed by a Japanese bomb in 1937. A deputy political commissar of his regiment, he said that the overwhelming lesson the PLA learned from its first brushes with the Americans was of the need for speed. "In the Liberation War, one might take days to surround a Kuomintang division, then slowly close the circle around it. With the Americans, if we took more than a few hours, they would bring up reinforcements, aircraft, artillery."[11]

Li Hua was twenty-three, from Shandung Province, a veteran of the Eighth Route Army since he was sixteen, a peasant's son who had been trained at one of the PLA's officer schools. On the train south to the Yalu in October, he and his comrades were told nothing of their destination, "but everybody guessed—we were going to support the Koreans against their invaders. We felt pretty confident, because we had just beaten the Kuomintang, with all their support from the Americans. We expected to do the same to Syngman Rhee's people. We weren't very wrong. They were a pushover compared with the Japanese." They walked across the Yalu bridge by night in their long files, then fifty miles onward to their initial contact near the Chosin Reservoir. Li, the propaganda officer of his company, examined his unit's first American prisoner at much the same time, and with much the same curiosity, as the Eighth Army was studying its captives from the PLA: "This young American, he fell on his knees and begged for mercy. We felt sorry for him. He obviously didn't want to fight."[12]

Americans who found North Korea an alien land might have reflected that it was almost equally so to the Chinese. The men of the PLA found the Korean peasants at first cold and unfriendly, the weather and the mountains unyielding and vicious. They were guided across country only by a few old Japanese maps—one to a regiment. Yet this initial wave of PLA veterans, in the months before massive casualties caused their replacement by less promising material, possessed some notable advantages over the Americans. For all their lack of equipment and sophistication, these Chinese soldiers were among the hardiest in the world. Many had known no other life but that of war since their teens. Most were genuinely enthused by the spirit of revolution, the sense of participation in a new China that seemed to offer brighter promise than the old land of tyrannical landlordism and official corruption. In Korea, in the months to come, the PLA would suffer its own difficulties with shaken morale and growing disillusionment in its ranks, matching those of its enemies. But in the winter of 1950 the spur of early success outweighed the impact of high casualties in Peng's divisions.

On November 15 the *Korea Times* described life in liberated Seoul as "returning to normal." Food queues were said to be fading. The government had just declared "Epidemic Prevention Week." A statement from ROK Army headquarters declared, "Our army is continuing its exterminating drive against the enemy,

who are taking refuge (remnants) in the mountains.'' Over 135,000 Communist
POWs were said to be in UN hands. Total North Korean casualties were estimated
at 335,000.

November 24 was Thanksgiving Day—bleak and blustery. Immense logistic
efforts had been made to ensure that the men of the Eighth Army enjoyed their
turkey dinner. By truck and even by airdrop, the traditional Thanksgiving
trimmings were shipped to the army that was still assured by its commanders that
it was victorious. The British and other allies mocked the idea of bringing
domestic comforts into the forward areas. ''I could not stop asking myself what on
earth it had all cost,'' said one British soldier,[13] faintly ashamed of his own
small-mindedness. Yet he and his compatriots were also secretly impressed by a
nation capable of such a feat in the midst of a campaign. The enemy were nowhere
much in evidence. In the forward areas the troops were uneasy, yet they clung to
MacArthur's promise: home by Christmas. In some units work had begun to clean
up vehicles and equipment, to crate surplus stores for shipment to Japan or
Stateside. The cold was already intense, though not as bitter as it would become.
In a thousand positions among the barren valleys and hillsides of North Korea,
American soldiers huddled around flickering fires fueled from the wreckage of
local huts and imported packing cases, and made what seasonal cheer they could.
Afterward, they looked back on that day as a hollow echo of a celebration, when
they had seen what was to come. The clothes that Colonel John Michaelis of the
27th Infantry was wearing on Thanksgiving Day, he did not take off until February
16.

On November 25, Walker's Eighth Army and Almond's X Corps began to move
forward once more. The men of B Company of the 1/9th Infantry, 2nd Division,
were approaching the crest of yet another faceless, meaningless geographical
feature—Hill 219, on the east bank of the Chongchon River on the road to
Kanggye—when they were hit with fierce grenade and small-arms fire. By
nightfall, fighting was in progress throughout the area. The 9th Infantry was in no
doubt that they were engaged against the Chinese. But poor communications and
extraordinary command lethargy hampered the 2nd Division in rousing itself to
meet a major new threat. In camps and vehicle concentrations along the length of
the Chongchon Valley, Americans found themselves wakened in their sleeping
bags by a terrifying cacophony of bugles, drums, rattles, whistles—and gunfire.
Again and again, Chinese assault groups smashed through ill-prepared perimeters,
overrunning infantry positions, gun lines, rear areas. By the night of November
26, 2nd Division had been driven back two miles southwest down the Chongchon.
The command posts of the 9th Infantry's 1st and 3rd Battalions were overrun.
Shortly before midnight the 2nd Battalion was heavily attacked and forced back,
losing most of its equipment. Some men waded the Chongchon in their flight, to

find their clothes and boots turning to ice as they climbed the southern bank. Not that the Chinese possessed any magical means of walking upon water. That first night the 23rd RCT captured a hundred Communist soldiers, stripped as they forded the river. On the 2nd Division's left, the 25th Division was also under pressure. Amid individual acts of great bravery, the collective American response was feeble. From Army Command to the meanest hilltop foxhole, men seemed too shocked and appalled by the surprise that had overtaken them to respond effectively.

Eighteen-year-old Private Mario Scarselleta and other men of the Mortar Company, 35th Infantry, had been less than happy for some days—the cold, the shortcomings of their shoepacs, the jamming of their weapons, and the rumors of the Chinese had already eaten deep into their morale. When the shooting began around them on the night of November 26, their first thought was to pull back. Their somewhat elderly lieutenant declared doggedly, "I'm not leaving until I get the word from battalion," which upset his men greatly. Then the shooting closed in around them, and somebody shouted, "Every man for himself!" "Then there was really chaos. Everybody just bugged out," said Scarselleta. They ran a few yards along the hillside, met a Chinese with a bugle, whom they killed, then dashed for their trucks and began to drive away. To their astonishment, they found that the Chinese appeared to be seeking to capture rather than to kill them. There were some extraordinary hand-to-hand fights. Scarselleta saw a friend laid out by a blow on the jaw from a Chinese. The man rejoined the unit a month later. They abandoned the hopeless effort to load the vehicles and started walking. They walked for four days, among a great throng of ill-assorted Turks, Koreans, fellow Americans. "There was a complete loss of leadership," said Scarselleta. "It was a nightmare, really. Many times, I felt that we'd never make it out of there, that to survive this would be a miracle. Those Chinese were just fanatics—they didn't place the value on the life that we did. To this day, I still think about it—the bodies blown up, the Americans run over with tanks, the panic and shooting in the nights."[14] He and his comrades did not reorganize as a unit until they were a few miles north of Seoul.

Yet the setbacks to IX Corps were insignificant compared with the absolute disaster taking place on the right of the Eighth Army: the whole ROK II Corps, three divisions in strength, had collapsed almost literally overnight and was falling back in chaos, abandoning guns, vehicles, equipment. Not a gap but a chasm eighty miles wide had thus been opened in the Allied line—if the United Nations deployments before the Chinese attack could be dignified as such—between the Eighth Army in the west of the country and the X Corps in the east. An attempt by the Turkish Brigade to move to the support of the ROKs was halted abruptly at a Chinese roadblock at Wawon, well behind the American flank. Eighteen

Communist divisions of the Chinese XIII Army Group were now committed. The Eighth Army faced a desperate danger of being cut off from the south. Walker ordered his forces' immediate retreat. But while they moved as best they could down the western side of the country, the 2nd Division around Kunu-ri, just south of the Chongchon, must hold open its own line of withdrawal and prevent the Chinese from bisecting Korea to the south.

General Keiser, 2nd Division's commander, only began his move back to Kunu-ri early on the twenty-eighth. By the next morning Chinese troops were already attacking road movements south of the formation, between Kunu-ri and Sunchon. Yet still there was a reluctance in the higher command to grasp the deadliness of the threat, to understand that the retreating units faced not roadblocks but enemy forces in strength. This, although as early as November 24, POWs had been reporting massive Chinese concentrations in the area. When "Shrimp" Milburn of I Corps telephoned Keiser that morning of the twenty-ninth to ask how things were going, Keiser replied, "Bad. Right now, I'm getting hit in my CP." Milburn promptly urged Keiser to bring his men out westward, via Anju. But the 2nd Division commander was unwilling to undertake such an extended diversion. He preferred the short road—directly south—to Sunchon. As Keiser's men were falling back in disarray around Kunu-ri, infantry were struggling to sweep the enemy out of range of the Kunu-ri to Sunchon road—and failing. Yet even this did not convince their commanders of the seriousness of the threat on their line of retreat.

In the first two days of the Chinese offensive, there was the bizarre kid-glove quality of a drawing-room game about their behavior. Though the men in the line might detect nothing frivolous about the Communists' assault, how could they rationally explain the repeated episodes when Americans who might easily have been killed were taken prisoner, then turned loose to return to their own lines? American officers returning to command posts that had been overrun discovered to their astonishment that nothing had been touched by the enemy. Colonel Paul Freeman was one of many commanders who were later convinced that the first days had been a test of American strength and will: "They came tongue in cheek at first, to see what we would do. Then they found what a thin line we had, how easily the South Koreans cracked. They saw what a pushover we were—that we would not even bomb across the Yalu. Then they became very aggressive, very bold—and stayed that way." The most savage American experience of the Korean War now began.

Major John Willoughby of the 1st Middlesex of the British 27 Brigade had spent the afternoon of November 26 soaking ecstatically in his first bath for weeks. The brigade was in reserve. He was still in the bath when an orderly brought in a signal reporting that four unidentified horsemen had been spotted near brigade headquarters who galloped off when challenged. They were Chinese, of course. Later, when they grasped their symbolic importance, they called them "the four horsemen of the Apocalypse." That night they were warned to be ready to move, and the next morning they were moved north in a piercing wind—still lacking winter clothing—to Kunu-ri. They could see the icefloes forming on the rivers they crossed as they drove.

Willoughby accompanied Brigadier Coad to IX Corps headquarters, where they found an atmosphere close to panic. The positions of several American formations were marked on the big Perspex map overlay with an enigmatic "?" following their numbers. In the center, pointing south, a great red arrow had been chinagraphed in, marked "2 MILLION?" The British were uncertain whether this was satirical. The 27 Brigade was directed to take up position north of Sunchon, on the road from Kunu-ri. There was no available transport to move them, so the men began to march the twenty-two miles back to the positions. It was a long, exhausting hike in the icy wind, and they heard unexplained bursts of firing from time to time up the valleys around them. The young soldiers were tiring. Willoughby found himself carrying five rifles for a time. After ten miles, to their enormous relief, trucks arrived to carry them the last stretch. At 4 a.m. they lay down to sleep for an hour in a frozen paddy.

The next morning they were ordered to move north once more, toward the pass through which they had marched unscathed the previous night. There was talk of an ambush. A few miles up the road, they met an American jeep coming the other way, a colonel hanging dead over the side of the vehicle, two other corpses lying in the back. The British dismounted and began to deploy. Suddenly, at the far edge of the paddy, they saw a cluster of white-clad figures leap up and begin running into the hills. There was absolute silence around them. Yard by yard, expecting a volley at any moment, the Middlesex advanced toward the southern end of the pass in front of them. At last, inevitably, the Chinese opened fire. The Middlesex began a battle which continued all day of November 30 and cost them some thirty casualties. And as they fought, they watched a great tragedy unfold in the pass before them.

At 1:30 p.m. on November 30, with his shrinking perimeter around Kunu-ri under violent pressure, General Keiser ordered his men to run the road south, whatever was in their way. The leading elements of 2nd Division's great nose-to-tail vehicle convoy drove south from Kunu-ri into a storm of mortar and machine-gun fire. The horrified British onlookers to the south watched trucks keel over and catch fire, men mown down as they ran for their lives from the Communist machine-gunning, occasional jeeps slewing crazily into the 27 Brigade positions laden with survivors, dead, and wounded. The Middlesex suffered several casualties from the fire of shattered Americans, driving forward, unable to understand that they had passed into safety. The "death ride" of the 2nd Division through the pass below Kunu-ri became one of the grimmest sagas of the Korean War. Through six miles of enemy fire vehicles sought to smash their way past the blazing wreckage of those that had gone before. Infantrymen ran among them, seeking their own salvation, and rarely finding it. A dreadful paralysis of command and discipline overtook the division. Major Walt Killalie, commanding the division's mobile antiaircraft battalion, saw men sitting motionless in their vehicles, incapable even of rousing themselves to return the hail of Chinese fire, merely waiting for death. Clusters of soldiers struggled to push wrecked vehicles off the road, falling as they did so. Others screamed and shouted in pain or fear. And the unemotional Communist mortaring continued. Nightfall brought infantry attacks from the Chinese, ending in desperate close-quarter fighting among the shambles of vehicles and casualties on the road. Only a handful of men like Colonel James Skeldon, commanding the 2/38th Infantry, kept their heads and maintained their units' cohesion sufficiently to maintain an effective defense and lead their survivors to safety.

Bill Shirk, a young gunner with the 15th Artillery, was newly returned to duty after a month in an Osaka hospital recovering from a bullet wound he had received on the Pusan Perimeter, where he found himself in a convoy that was ambushed and almost wiped out. After that experience he was reluctant to return to Korea. He hated the country. When the word came in late November to begin cleaning up the guns to return home, "like everybody else—I felt really happy to be getting out of this stinking place." But Korea had hardly started on the nineteen-year-old Ohioan. In the pass at Kunu-ri "the order came—'Every man for himself.' We dropped phosphorus grenades down the gun barrels, then we set about getting out." Shirk started off with a group of eighteen men, hastily shedding his gaiters to move faster. By dawn he was running clumsily in his overcoat, alone with an unknown major. They were trying to hide in a cluster of stacks of cornstalks when the Chinese reached them, and they were herded away into a large cave where they found some 200 other American prisoners already assembled. A bitterness about the war, a sense of betrayal by his own superiors, was born in Shirk which remained undiminished by the ensuing two and a half years of captivity.[15]

Some men escaped in small groups by taking to the hills. A few vehicles and even gun teams got through that night, or early the next morning, when American fighter-bomber support belatedly made some impact upon the enemy positions in the hills. The division's rearguard, the 23rd RCT, commanded by Colonel Paul Freeman, was successfully diverted to the Anju road. But in that one afternoon the 2nd Division lost 3,000 men and almost all its transport and equipment on the road from Kunu-ri. The division's history speaks of "a magnificent stand. . . . Even in defeat, the 'Indianhead' division proved to be a rock which held fast, giving other units an opportunity for survival.'' The truth was sadder, and more bitter. Much of the 2nd Division fell apart in those days. It was months before the formation was considered capable of fighting effectively again in Korea. "In general, to achieve quick decision," wrote Mao Tse Tung, "we should attack a moving and not a stationary enemy."[16] At Kunu-ri the PLA ruthlessly implemented his dictum.

At last, quiet fell on the pass, and 27 Brigade understood that no more Americans would be coming that way. They left the great graveyard of MacArthur's hopes and pressed on southward, under increasing fire. American air strikes sought to blast the hills around the road into silence, but still the shooting went on. Major Willoughby remembered an insanely irrational moment when he saw machine-gun fire striking the road around his vehicle and opened the door to let it pass through. Yet it was somewhere on that road that they heard a news broadcast in which it was reported that the British Prime Minister, Clement Attlee, had declared that Britain "has no quarrel with the Chinese."

On the road to Pyongyang, a growing element of panic was overtaking the whole of the Eighth Army. Rumors multiplied—of 20,000 Chinese straddling the line of retreat, of a Communist regiment at a ford where a patrol discovered only two dead farmers and three dead horses. A British officer was shocked to attend a briefing at which his American regimental counterpart warned his subordinates, "Remember—if you see a red Verey light, just get everybody you can together and head south." Private David Fortune of the 2/35th Infantry felt "numbed, stunned by the situation. We had believed that it was all over. Yet now we knew the war would be over no time soon." Fortune was captured on January 2 when his company was cut off. "You guys better get out while you can," a fugitive shouted to his platoon as he "bugged out." "There's no end to them—the more you kill, the more they come."[17] Fortune spent two and a half years in captivity.

Private James Waters of the 1/35th Infantry, 25th Division, had joined the Army "because I felt I had to get out of Joplin, Missouri." On the morning of November 26 his unit was marching in long files up a road some forty miles south of the Yalu when the company commander was called to a battalion O Group. He returned two hours later. The word was passed from man to man as they sat stunned and disbelieving by the roadside: "The Chinese are in the war, and they're behind us." There was no firing that day, but when they made camp on a hilltop, they lay awake, jumpy and watchful. An elderly NCO, Sergeant Jennings, confided sadly to Waters in the darkness, "I don't think I'm going to make it. I've just about had it—I'm not young anymore." Many men were taking counsel of their fears that night. The next morning they began to walk south before dawn. Each soldier seemed to be trying to tiptoe, fearful that a rash sound would bring the Communist hordes upon his head. At last, the stillness was broken. They heard the quad .50-caliber machine guns on a half-track firing, heard the shouts and screams of Chinese attackers. But still Waters's company marched on in darkness, past an abandoned field hospital, with a jeep full of dead medics lying beside it. Daylight brought Chinese mortaring . . . and casualties. Most were left behind. They quickened their pace, shedding sleeping bags, tents, heavy equipment to ease their burden. There were occasional brief scuffles with the enemy.

That day, and each day and night that followed, the sense of fear and desperate danger grew. They had no resupply, until one morning a jeep halted by the column to disgorge cooks bearing hot chow. They had abandoned even their mess kits, and held out their helmets to be filled with a mess of cereal and powdered eggs. The cooks' impatience to be gone—shouting, "Hurry up! Hurry up!" as the men queued before them—heightened their own fear. As they neared Pyongyang, Waters and his companions found themselves marching among a growing host of retreating Americans: "Somewhere along that road, an orderly withdrawal became a disorderly withdrawal."[18] A glimpse of Oriental faces became sufficient to cause a local panic, until the men were confirmed as ROK troops. Their feet were lacerated and bleeding, young officers hobbling like old men. Men lost their units and grew frightened in their loneliness amid a mob of soldiers and refugees harboring so much fright.

The men of the Eighth Army plodding south were awed by the great pillars of flame and smoke from the supply dumps of Pyongyang, fired to keep them from the hands of the enemy. Private Waters met a tanker by his ditched monster who told them sardonically, "This vehicle requires a new part that costs five dollars. We do not have one. Therefore we must blow up this vehicle." Pyongyang was abandoned on December 5, leaving behind vast quantities of stores and equipment. Having lost 11,000 casualties dead, wounded, and missing in the first days of the Chinese offensive, the Eighth Army was now in full retreat by land, sea, and air, its men fleeing from North Korea by every means available. It was fortunate for the reputation of United States arms that, while Walker's army hastened southward in disarray, almost incapable of organized resistance, farther east other Americans were salvaging at least a portion of honor from one of the most inglorious moments in their nation's military history.

Liberation: American forces enter Korea in the fall of 1945, greeted by the cheers of children overjoyed at the departure of the Japanese. *(UPI/Bettmann)*

President Harry S. Truman, who took the decision that the United States should intervene in the Korean War. *(UPI/Bettmann)*

Louis Johnson, Secretary for Defense at the outbreak of the Korean War, visits the White House with Stephen T. Early, his Deputy Secretary. *(UPI/Bettmann)*

Key players in the diplomatic drama: John Foster Dulles, chief U.S. delegate Warren Austin, together with Secretary of State Dean Acheson at a meeting of the UN General Assembly. *(UPI/Bettmann)*

The arch-accuser: Senator Joseph McCarthy, who charged the leaders of the Truman Administration and State Department officials with complicity in the "plot" to betray Asia to the Communists. *(UPI/Bettmann)*

Dean Rusk, one of the architects of the 1945 Korean divide at the 38th Parallel, and Assistant Secretary of State when the 1950 crisis broke out. *(UPI/Bettmann)*

The Joint Chiefs confront the Korean crisis: Chairman General Omar Bradley; Admiral Forrest Sherman, Chief of Naval Operations; and General Lawton J. Collins, Army Chief, arrive at a National Security Council meeting. *(UPI/Bettmann)*

The Supreme Commander: Douglas MacArthur. *(UPI/Bettmann)*

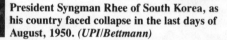

President Syngman Rhee of South Korea, as his country faced collapse in the last days of August, 1950. *(UPI/Bettmann)*

British Foreign Secretary Ernest Bevin. *(BBC Hulton Picture Library)*

British Prime Minister Clement Attlee. *(BBC Hulton Picture Library)*

One of the first American casualties of the war is laid to rest in a Korean grave. *(UPI/Bettmann)*

The face of defeat: Men of the American 24th Division who lost even their boots in the headlong flight from the Communists. *(National Archives)*

In the first weeks of the war the world was shocked by revelations of North Korean ruthlessness, above all the treatment of prisoners. This was one of the first photographs to be released, of a captured American soldier whose body was later found, bound and shot. *(National Archives)*

A picture that shocked the world: bound South Korean prisoners lying in the grave into which they were herded for execution during the Communist occupation of Taejon. *(UPI/Bettmann)*

American infantry on the march in the first weeks of war, passing a burning North Korean tank. *(U.S. National Archives)*

The face of fear: Political prisoners in the hands of the South Koreans mustered at Pusan. *(BBC Hulton Picture Library)*

The face of tragedy: From the beginning it was the civilian population of Korea that paid the heaviest price in the struggle. *(BBC Hulton Picture Library)*

A classic image of Korea: U.S. soldiers advance towards the battlefront, against the flow of civilian refugees fleeing from it. *(UPI/Bettmann)*

The hero of the Pusan Perimeter: General Walton H. "Bulldog" Walker with one of his divisional commanders. *(National Archives)*

A large portion of the port of Pusan lies in ruins after a fire swept through the overcrowded city. By 1953, most of the urban centers of both North and South Korea were similarly destroyed. *(UPI/ Bettmann)*

Amid the debris of their world, Korean civilians go about their business, clawing an existence from the ruins as they did from beginning to end of the Korean war. *(UPI/ Bettmann)*

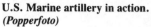

U.S. Marine artillery in action.
(Popperfoto)

The battle for Seoul: in the last days of September, 1950, U.S. Marines batter a path through the streets of Syngman Rhee's capital. *(UPI/ Bettmann)*

Chinese infantry enter the ruins of Seoul. *(Chinese National Army Museum)*

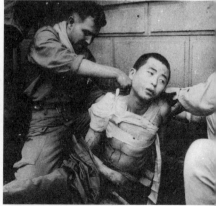

An American doctor tends a Korean civilian casualty of the bombardment. *(BBC Hulton Picture Library)*

Inchon: The 1st Marine Division make a surprise landing *(UPI/Bettmann)*

Inchon: Men of the 1st Marine Division grapple the seawall. *(BBC Hulton Picture Library)*

An LST, deliberately beached against a pier at Inchon, waits to be refloated by the tide. *(UPI/Bettmann)*

MacArthur savours his last triumph: Flanked by Vice-Admiral Arthur D. Struble (left) and Marine General Oliver P. Smith (right), the Supreme Commander inspects liberated Inchon. *(UPI/Bettmann)*

Major-General Edward M. Almond (left), controversial commander of X Corps through the Chosin campaign, rides a launch ashore at Inchon with Fleet Marine commander General Lemuel C. Shepherd (right). *(UPI/Bettmann)*

Gratitude: Syngman Rhee expresses his thanks to Douglas MacArthur for the liberation of Seoul, September, 1950. *(UPI/Bettmann)*

Walter Bedell Smith, Eisenhower's wartime Chief of Staff who became the principal architect of the massive expansion of
the Central Intelligence Agency as its Director for most of the Korean War. (UPI/
Bettmann)

Refugees under questioning by South Korean and American military police. (Popperfoto)

The road north: A British jeep surrounded by the
customary crowd of curious and importunate villagers and children. (Imperial War Museum)

The five-year-old frontier between North and
South Korea becomes a mere military attraction.
(Imperial War Museum)

The supply route across the frozen Yalu. *(Chinese National Army Museum)*

Marshal Peng Te Huai, commander of the Chinese People's "Volunteers" in Korea, with North Korea's leader Kim Il Sung. *(Chinese National Army Museum)*

The coming of the Chinese: The bugle that signaled so many Communist assaults. *(Chinese National Army Museum)*

Chinese "volunteers" in Korea. *(Chinese National Army Museum)*

Americans surrender to Chinese infantry. This seems almost certainly a posed propaganda picture, but its reality became grimly familiar in the winter of 1950. *(Chinese National Army Museum)*

Chosin: U.S. Marines look down from Hagaru upon the reservoir, graveyard of so many American hopes, yet monument to so much heroism, in November, 1950. *(UPI/Bettmann)*

Back from the reservoir: U.S. Marines rest in the midst of their desperate march down the thin thread of frozen road between Chosin and the sea. *(Topham)*

A column of porters wind their way up a Korean hillside. The porters, all conscripted civilians, provided vital assistance for the UN forces. *(Imperial War Museum)*

U.S. infantry amid a characteristic Korean winter landscape. *(Popperfoto)*

Frustration at Kaesong: Leaders of the UN delegation headed by Admiral Turner C. Joy (left) stand alongside a North Korean guard as they announce the breakdown of cease-fire talks on August 22, 1951. *(UPI/Bettmann)*

General Matthew Ridgway with one of his divisional commanders. Note the grenade on his webbing, which became a personal hallmark. *(National Archives)*

Chinese infantry laying Russian-made box mines and making a night advance. *(Chinese National Army Museum)*

The air war: Communist pilots being briefed for a mission over Korea. *(Chinese National Army Museum)*

The MIG 15, the first Communist jet fighter, whose intervention in Korea in November, 1950 sent ripples of alarm throughout the West. *(Jane's Defense Weekly)*

The Sabre, the outstanding fighter of the Korean War, that made a succession of U.S. pilot aces. *(UPI/Bettmann)*

A flight-deck mishap on HMS *Ocean* off Korea. The victim is a Sea Fury. Accidents remained almost as great a peril as enemy action throughout the war's intensive carrier operations. *(Imperial War Museum)*

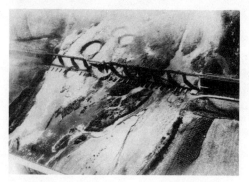

One of the North Korean bridges, which remained critical targets of UN air attacks throughout the conflict. *(Imperial War Museum)*

Chinese soldiers in one of the great network of tunnels that honeycombed the Communist line from 1951 until the armistice. *(Chinese National Army Museum)*

ROK and American troops on the move. Notice the age of the young Korean in the center. He was not atypical. *(Imperial War Museum)*

Artillery in action: Chinese and UN. *(Camera Press)*

Change of command: In Seoul, General James Van Fleet (left) greets his successor as commander of 8th Army, Lt. General Maxwell D. Taylor (second from right), on June 2, 1953. On the right stands Supreme Commander General Mark Clark; second from left is General Paek Sun Yup, ROK army Chief of Staff. *(UPI/Bettmann)*

LEFT: A much relieved Brigadier Francis T. Dodd, greeted by a fellow officer after his release from captivity in the hands of communist POWs whose stockades he supposedly commanded. The fiasco cost the jobs not only of Dodd, but of his successor who made concessions to gain his release. *(UPI/Bettmann)*

ABOVE: Crisis at Koje-do: In the summer of 1952, an aerial photograph of the vast UN camp reveals communist prisoners performing drills under their own compound commanders. *(UPI/Bettmann)*

RIGHT: The tough new commanding officer of Koje-do, Brigadier Haydon L. Boatner, harangues Canadian troops under his command about what is expected of them. *(UPI/Bettmann)*

Pork Chop: One among hundreds of U.S. casualties of the 1953 battle is carried down from the hill. *(UPI/Bettmann)*

One of the shuttle helicopters that carried the UN delegation to and from the peace talks at Panmunjom interrupts a Korean farmer's ploughing as it makes a forced landing beside his field. *(UPI/Bettmann)*

Helicopter casevac: This was the first "war of the whirlybirds" which saved the lives of so many wounded men and shot-down aircrews. *(Imperial War Museum)*

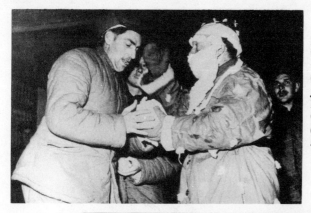

Propaganda: A Chinese picture designed to show the world that UN prisoners in Communist hands were enjoying good treatment. A POW in homemade Santa Claus outfit distributes gifts. *(Chinese National Army Museum)*

Repatriation: The last, grotesque act of thousands of Communist prisoners being shipped to Panmunjom for return to China and North Korea was to hurl away the clothing and boots with which they had been supplied by their UN captors. *(National Archives)*

"I Shall Go To Korea": President-elect Dwight D. Eisenhower meets an embittered Syngman Rhee in December, 1952. *(UPI/Bettmann)*

A grudging peace: UN and Communist delegates at their respective tables sign the Korean armistice at Panmunjom on July 29, 1953. *(UPI/Bettmann)*

ABOVE: Major-General William K. Harrison, senior UN delegate, and North Korea's General Nam Il, who led the negotiating teams that concluded the Korean war. *(UPI/Bettmann)*

Freedom: Major-General William Dean, commander of the U.S. 24th Division captured in August, 1950, was the most celebrated UN prisoner to be released at Panmunjom. He was taken across the armistice line by a communist jeep and driver. *(UPI/Bettmann)*

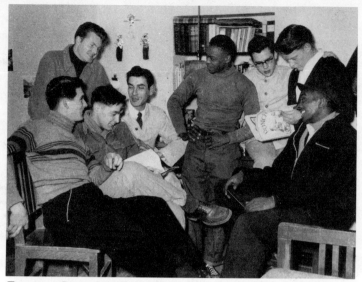

Turncoats: Some of the 22 Americans who shocked their country by refusing repatriation, along with a single British Marine, when released from communist captivity in August, 1953. From left to right: Harold Webb of Fort Pierce, Florida; Marine Andrew Condron of West Lothian, Scotland; Morris Wills of Fort Ann, New York; Richard Corden of Providence, Rhode Island; Clarence Adams of Memphis, Tennessee; Jack Dunn of Baltimore, Maryland; Andrew Fortuna of Detroit, Michigan; Bill White of Plumerville, Arkansas. In 1956, when this picture was taken at Peking University, 16 of the original 23 remained in China. *(UPI/Bettmann)*

Resurrection: In 1953, Korea was a nation of ruins. Yet within a generation, the people of the South had transformed their country into one of the most dynamic and successful industrial societies in Asia. Here, the Kumsong textiles mill outside Seoul is seen as it was by the end of the war, and as it was rebuilt a few years later. *(UPI/Bettmann)*

8

CHOSIN: THE ROAD FROM THE RESERVOIR

On the drive north of the 38th Parallel, MacArthur had deliberately separated the Eighth Army, under Walker, from the operations of X Corps, under his own Chief of Staff, General Edward Almond. The two divisions of X Corps—7th and 1st Marine—landed on the east coast and moved north, miles out of ground contact with the Eighth Army. Thus it was that, when disaster struck, Almond's and Walker's formations endured entirely separate nightmares, divided by the central spine of North Korean mountains. All that they possessed in common were the horrors of weather, isolation, Chinese attack—and the threat of absolute disaster overtaking American arms.

Relations between General Almond and O. P. Smith of the 1st Marine Division had been frigid since they came ashore at Inchon. Smith was thoroughly unhappy about the dispersal of X Corps strength on the advance north: "I told Almond we couldn't make two big efforts. I said, 'Either we go to the Yalu by Chosin, or by the northwest route, but not both.' " Almond, whatever his shortcomings, an undisputed driver of men, was exasperated by the sluggishness—even obstructionism—that he perceived in the Marines. Smith, in his turn, profoundly suspicious of Almond's lust for glory, feared that sooner or later the Corps commander's impatience would inflict a disaster upon his men: "What I was trying to do was to slow down the advance and stall until I could pull up the 1st Marines behind us, and get our outfit together."[1] The Marines' advance to the

Chosin Reservoir, and up its western arm, had indeed been slow because Smith insisted that at every stage reserves of ammunition and supplies should be brought forward and stockpiled. Meanwhile, Almond urged haste to prevent the Chinese from encompassing the destruction of the vast dams at the reservoir, which intelligence believed to be the Communist intention.

By November 25 two of Smith's three regiments—the 5th and 7th—had reached Yudam-ni, at the eastern extremity of the reservoir, and were scheduled to jump off on the twenty-seventh toward a link-up with the Eighth Army's northern movement at Mupyong. Thereafter, they would strike for Kanggye and Manpojin on the Chinese border. The 1st Marines were deployed along the main supply route between Hagaru and Koto-ri, alongside some army elements. The Corps' rear coastal area was the responsibility of the 3rd Division. On the Marines' right, three battalions of the 7th Division were moving up the east side of the reservoir. The bulk of the 7th Division was more than sixty miles northward, the most advanced American formation, behind the very banks of the Yalu.

Residual Communist strength in North Korea was reported by GHQ to be around 100,000 men—about the same as the UN's front-line numbers—while some 40,000 Communist guerrillas and stragglers were believed to remain behind the front. In reality, over 100,000 Chinese troops were already deployed on X Corps front alone. Whatever delusions persisted in the rear, the Marines who visited North Korean villages raiding for food, who talked to villagers about the masses of men that had passed through, were in little doubt about the scale of enemy activity. When Lieutenant Colonel Robert Taplett, commanding the 3/5th Marines, flew forward in a helicopter, he could see a maze of tracks and foxholes in the mountain snow. "Those damn holes are just crawling with people," said his pilot wonderingly.

The 1st Marine Division began to move forward on the morning of November 27. That night the Chinese launched violent assaults, not merely upon its leading elements, but for thirty miles down its main—indeed, only—supply route to the coast, seventy-eight miles to the south. To Marine officers in command posts among the positions at Yudam-ni, it seemed that every unit in the two regiments was reporting itself under attack that night. A Chinese grenade knocked out the switchboard of the 3/5th Battalion CP. One of its company commanders "froze" in his position, and his men could not be moved until another officer was hastily dispatched to take his place. All through the hours of darkness the Chinese hurled themselves again and again upon the company positions of the two Marine regiments. It is a remarkable tribute to the quality of units reconstituted only three months earlier, heavily manned by reservists, that they mounted so dogged a defense under the most appalling conditions. Almost every man who returned from the hills above the Chosin Reservoir brought with him an epic story of close-quarter combat amid the flares, mortaring, grenade and small-arms duels. Although the Chinese broke into a succession of positions and inflicted severe casualties, nowhere did they succeed in breaking the Marine companies.

By morning the Marines were holding three isolated perimeters: at Yudam-ni, farthest north; at Hagaru, on the base of the reservoir, and at Koto-ri, another ten miles south. There was brief discussion among the Americans about continuing their own offensive. "But I told Ray Murray, 'Stop,' " said General Smith. "It was manifest we were up against a massive force out there."[2] It was apparent to the Marines that their predicament was precarious. They were facing very large Chinese forces: some ten enemy divisions, it later emerged, were deployed in X Corps' area of operations. Hagaru, with its airstrip and supply dumps, at the junction of the only escape route south, was defended only by one Marine battalion and such local army elements as could be scraped together to man a perimeter on the surrounding hills. The formations of X Corps were dispersed among hundreds of square miles of barren mountains. Many of the American positions were accessible only by a single track or road, appallingly vulnerable to isolation by an enemy who moved at will among the mountains. As soon as the scale of the Chinese offensive became apparent, there was only one prudent option open to Almond's forces: withdrawal to the coast. Yet for this to be possible, it was necessary for the main supply route, the MSR, to be held open. And in those last days of November, the lonely track through the passes from Hungnam to Yudam-ni was a snowbound thread liable to snap at any moment. The X Corps commander was always ready to find reason to attack O. P. Smith. Almond believed that he had ample cause for anger with the Marine general in the weakness of the Hungnam garrison. X Corps had correctly perceived that the junction at the base of the Chosin Reservoir was a vital position which must be held in strength. Now, Almond raged, why had Smith left so few men to defend it? The Marine answered that he could never have pursued Almond's cherished advance from Yudam-ni with less than two regiments. Smith was furious that, even now, Almond was unwilling to recognize the urgency of their plight and call off his offensive. It was two days before the Marines at Yudam-ni received orders—or rather, consent—to withdraw. Meanwhile, Smith labored by any means to strengthen the garrison at Hagaru.

The 235 men of 41 Independent Commando, Royal Marines, had arrived at Koto-ri on November 28 to operate under X Corps. When transport and equipment had been found for the British unit, it was intended that it should act as a reconnaissance group. But it now became a matter of urgency to reinforce the Hagaru perimeter with every available man. On the morning of November 29 the Royal Marines, together with a company of U.S. Marines and another of infantry, 922 men and 141 vehicles in all, were ordered north under the command of

Lieutenant Colonel Drysdale. There was no time even to feed the men before they marched. The British had just time to remove a section of 81-mm mortars and .30-caliber Brownings from the crates in which they had been brought up from Hamnung before "Task Force Drysdale" moved north.

They met resistance almost immediately. The British and American Marines deployed from their vehicles and began painfully to clear the high ground overlooking the road. Yard by yard, under constant fire, they pushed forward, aided by a company of tanks which had arrived to support them. By 4:15 P.M., with darkness falling, they were only four miles north of Koto-ri. Drysdale radioed Hagaru to ask General Smith whether he was to keep coming. Smith answered that he needed every man he could get into the perimeter. After a delay while the tanks refueled, the column pressed on into the darkness. To Drysdale's fury, the armored company commander—"an opinionated young man"—flatly rejected his request to distribute his seventeen tanks along the length of the convoy and insisted that they should punch through in a body at the front. As a result, when Task Force Drysdale was ambushed by the Chinese in a defile known as "Hellfire Valley," above the Changjin River some five miles from their starting point, the soft-skinned vehicles were unprotected. When the Chinese hit trucks in the midst of the convoy around 10 P.M., those in the rear were cut off. Some of the U.S. Army company in the rear retired to Koto-ri without displaying much enthusiasm for a night battle against powerful enemy forces. Pockets of British and American Marines fought all night beside the road.

A mortar bomb hit the truck ahead of that carrying Marine Andrew Condron, a twenty-two-year-old radio operator from West Lothian. He and the others in his vehicle jumped down and lay in the monsoon ditch beside the road, watching the dim shapes of Chinese soldiers flitting to and fro in the darkness. His carbine jammed at his first attempt to fire it, and he picked up an M-1 rifle from a dead American lying nearby. They exchanged desultory fire with the enemy around them until, about 1 A.M., an officer ran up and urged them to join him in an effort to break out. They collected some ammunition and grenades and began to work their way across open ground. Condron was appalled to pass an American in agony by the roadside, on fire from burning phosphorus, screaming for someone to shoot him. The Marine lost track of his officer early on and found himself, with two other British rankers, wading an icy stream. There was a sudden shot, and the leading man fell. They heard American voices, at whom the outraged Marine with Condron shouted, "You've killed my mate!" When the emotional temperature had cooled, the little group of British and Americans lay together in silence, listening to the firing and explosions among the convoy, now some half mile distant. Condron hung his socks in a tree to dry, where they promptly froze. He put a beret on one foot, a camouflage net on the other under his boots. Condron was dressing the wound of a comatose Marine shot in the hip when he glanced up to see a South Korean standing above him, wearing a snow cape and carrying a Thompson gun. The man grunted aggressively. "Bugger off," Condron grunted back. An American shouted hastily to the Scot, "Hey, buddy, you'd better drop that rifle fast—we've surrendered." The "South Korean" was a Chinese soldier.

Condron's brother had been a Japanese prisoner of war in World War II and he told the young Marine to ensure that he always carried the vital essentials of life, in case he himself was captured. Condron took heed, and had stowed in his pack an emergency kit of razor blades, waterproof matches, vitamin pills, and two books of poetry—Burns and Fitzgerald. But all these things still lay in the distant truck. Like most of those who suffered the same fate in Korea, Condron passed into captivity with only the clothes on his back.[3]

Around fifty British and American soldiers and Marines, in all, surrendered at first light. Some others escaped back to Koto-ri. A few, like the British heavy-weapon section, eventually got through to Hagaru in desperate straits from frostbite. Captain Pat Ovens also made good his escape on foot to the Marine lines. The leading elements of the survivors pressed on in their vehicles until, within sight of the American engineers working under floodlights to improve the runway inside the Hagaru perimeter, they were hit again. An abandoned tank blocked the road, and Chinese mortaring ignited a succession of vehicles. After another fierce firefight, the tank company and the surviving infantry struggled into Hagaru around midnight. The armor came first, smashing headlong through the defending American roadblock, crushing a jeep. The British, according to one of the Marines manning the road position, appeared looking more like a raiding party than a military unit: "Don't shoot, Yank!" Colonel Drysdale himself was slightly wounded by a grenade fragment in the arm, and less than a hundred of his Royal Marines were still behind him. "I never thought I should be so glad to see an American," said Lieutenant Peter Thomas wryly. Thomas brought in the last two vehicles of the convoy, both loaded with wounded. Sixty-one British Marines had been lost on the road from Koto-ri, out of Task Force Drysdale's 321 casualties and 71 vehicles destroyed. 41 Commando became garrison reserve, under the command of Ray Murray of the 5th Marines.

The little town of Hagaru lay in a cleft in the mountains that otherwise appeared to the Marines to occupy the entire surface of North Korea. For those brief winter weeks of 1950, when it was occupied by the Americans, Hagaru resembled a nineteenth-century Arctic mining camp. Snow coated the peasant houses, the Marines' tents, the tanks and trucks, the supply dumps and artillery pieces and command vehicles. The local sawmill was kept in perpetual motion by the engineers, cutting timber to strengthen positions and assist in the vital labor of airfield construction. Thin plumes of smoke from a hundred fires and stoves curled into the air on the rare days when the air was still. More often, they were whipped aside by the driving wind that stung every inch of exposed human flesh. At first, men marveled at the depths to which the thermometer could sink: −10, −14, −20 at night. Then they became as numb to the misery of the cold as to everything else. Many said that it was not only their capacity for physical activity that diminished, but even their speed of thought. General Smith himself found it increasingly difficult even to move his jaw to speak. The simplest action—loading a weapon, unbolting a steel section, rigging an aerial—became a laborious, agonizing marathon. The jeeps were kept running continually. In some cases their headlights were run on cables into key positions such as the sick-bay and operations tents to supplement the feeble Coleman lanterns. To start an engine required hours of work—thawing its moving parts, persuading its frozen oil to liquefy. Blood plasma froze. Medical orderlies were obliged to carry morphine Syrettes in their mouths to maintain their fluidity. For the men, the miraculously effective space heaters in the tents became the very focus of life. All this, before the enemy had even begun to take a hand.

The battle for Hagaru was a strange affair, like so many of the actions of that first Korean winter. By day there was little enemy activity, and the Americans could move with almost complete freedom, while their own air strikes hammered the Communists' presumed positions. Then, with the coming of night, the struggle began in earnest. All through the hours of darkness the defenders fought back the Chinese attacks, glimpsing their enemy briefly by the light of flares and gun flashes, perceiving him above all by the eerie sounds he brought with him—the bugles, the whistles, the banshee yells. For many men the greatest fear was that when the moment came, when the Communist wave broke upon their positions, the cold would have jammed their life-saving weapons. After the first November battles, rumors swept the UN armies that some men—allegedly of 1st Cavalry Division—had been surprised by the Chinese in their sleeping bags and bayoneted where they lay, unable to extricate themselves in time. Thereafter, most men on the line were either themselves unwilling, or were forbidden by their officers, to zip up their bags to sleep.

On the forward positions the cold was so appalling that an extraordinary improvisation, perhaps unique to this campaign, became necessary: the introduction of "warming tents," a few hundred yards behind the front, where every two or three hours men retreated to thaw themselves a few degrees, to restore circulation to their deadened limbs, in order that they might be capable of resistance when the Chinese came again. How the Chinese themselves coped, lacking any such refinements yet presumably at the same extremities of human tolerance, men marveled to speculate. When the garrison received an occasional night air strike in support, they marked the pilots' aiming points by firing solid tracer. The optical effects of battle below zero were astonishing: mortar bombs flew through the sky like rockets, leaving fiery trails in the ice-cold air.

The garrison was a hotchpotch. There were two companies of the 1st Marines; some gunners conscripted as infantry; an army engineer company sent to build a command post for General Almond, but now pushed into the line; a ragtag of American and South Korean line-of-communication personnel, deployed on the hills as reluctant riflemen. It was a matter of pride to a platoon of army signalers that, during one Chinese attack, they successfully held their positions while the engineers broke. One night East Hill was lost, overlooking the vital airstrip. A scratch force of 200 cooks, drivers, and stragglers was ruthlessly rounded up from all over the perimeter and herded forward to counterattack at dawn, protected by an air strike. Only some seventy-five were still present when they mustered at the start line—the remainder had simply drifted away into the darkness. But they regained part of the hill, and G Company of the 3/1st Marines completed the job. One night a company clerk standing in as a heavy machine gunner was appalled to see a file of Chinese advancing upon his roadblock. Ignorant even of how to elevate the barrel of his gun, he could only lift the legs of the gun's tripod to bring fire to bear upon them. Fortunately, the company runner then woke up and took over, to more effect.

The Americans seemed to enjoy the company of their little British party from 41 Commando. They found Colonel Drysdale himself somewhat reserved, although the effects of exhaustion and his wound undoubtedly influenced his demeanor. The two nations set about reconciling their military inconsistencies— the British habit of calling a mortar round a bomb, while the Americans called it a shell; the instinctive British parsimony with ammunition, when the Americans believed in intensive bombardment if the rounds were there. A Marine rifle company commander sought to illustrate his approach to fire support to Drysdale: "Suppose we were going up that hill over there—we'd expect to put in 200 rounds before we left the start line." The British officer ruminated for a moment, then remarked dryly, "We wouldn't go up the hill at all. We'd go around it." The British insisted upon shaving each morning, in the interests of morale and discipline. Most Marines preferred to cultivate a stubble. The Commandos found the Americans' carelessness about showing lights at night almost incomprehensible. Their formidable regimental sergeant major, Jim Baines, tore a ferocious strip off a dim figure whose cigarette he saw glowing in a nearby foxhole and was embarrassed to find an American officer hastily stubbing out his butt. But if the Commandos and Marines found some of each other's habits incomprehensible, they also formed a deep admiration for the tenacity and determination common to both corps. "I felt entirely comfortable fighting alongside the Marines," said Colonel Drysdale.

Each day, as the men on the hills watched the C-47s taxi along the frozen airstrip to collect their loads of wounded, it was impossible not to feel a deep pang of envy for those who would be safe in warm beds, far out of range of enemy fire, within a few hours. It was too much to expect, in those circumstances, that they should count their blessings. While the Chinese deployed immense numbers of infantry, well supported by mortars, they possessed virtually no artillery. The center of the perimeter was thus almost immune to direct fire. The predicament of the X Corps would have been incomparably worse had their enemies possessed the normal support weapons of a modern army.

Among a host of tragic spectacles that MacArthur's forces were to behold that Korean winter, the arrival of the survivors of the 7th Division's "Task Force Faith" at Hagaru remained one of the most vivid. Across the great sweep of ice covering the reservoir, the Marines on the perimeter saw handfuls of men stumbling, limping, even crawling. Some were without weapons. Most had lost their equipment. Many were at the extremities of frostbite. "Some of these men were dragging themselves on the ice," wrote a Marine officer, "some had gone crazy and were walking in circles. It was pitiful."[4] The Marines hauled sledges out onto the reservoir, and brought in all the soldiers they could find. But only 385 of the thousand survivors from a force of 2,500 were considered sufficiently fit to take their place in the line at Hagaru.

Yet as late as November 27, the day that the elements of the 7th Division east of the reservoir at Sihung-ni first met the Chinese, General Almond had flown in by helicopter personally to emphasize his determination that the American offensive should not be deflected. "We're still attacking and we're going all the way to the Yalu," he said. "Don't let a bunch of Chinese laundrymen stop you." In the days that followed, X Corps only slowly began to understand the disaster that was unfolding east of the reservoir. "We didn't see it as a tragedy, because we had no idea at all how terrible their losses were, until they came out," said one of Almond's staff. Yet from the night of November 27 until their withdrawal in ruins three days later, the men of Task Force Faith—as 32nd RCT became when their original commander was killed—found themselves under constant attack from the Chinese, who drove them back down the east bank of the Chosin Reservoir, bleeding terribly as they marched.

Private Don McAlister was the son of a Kansas farming family who had spent his teens trying any job that would earn a buck: dishwashing, sawmilling, farmwork. It was a grindingly hard life. After spending the winter of 1949 clearing a hedgerow, he and his cousin decided to join the Army and try to get training in the engineers. McAlister was still in basic training in June 1950. He found himself abruptly shipped to the 1/32nd Infantry, 7th Division. He felt an instinctive sympathy for the South Korean farmers, whose poverty seemed only a degree or two worse than that from which he had come. He greatly admired his battalion commander, Don Faith, who walked every battlefield with a cane rather than a weapon. He had much less confidence in some of the other officers, and sometimes suspected that the battalion commander did too. On the night of November 27, McAlister was on an outpost position when the Chinese attacked in overwhelming strength. The BAR team and Browning gunners fired for as long as they could, but at last the Chinese swept over the position. The American survivors ran back to their own company front as fast as they could go. They fought all night. McAlister at one point found himself physically wrestling with two Chinese soldiers for possession of his BAR. His company commander was killed, the hillside littered with the bodies of dead Chinese and Americans. At dawn, when the attacks stopped, he and his section were sent back to their outpost. To their astonishment, lying in the bottom of a foxhole they found two of their own men, alive and unharmed. They had successfully played dead when the position was lost.

All that day Marine and Navy aircraft flew strikes against enemy concentrations in front of the Americans. But that night the Chinese came again. Their second assault pushed back McAlister's A company halfway down their hill line. They hung on only with urgent support from their neighbors of B Company. As they fought from foxhole to foxhole, American fortunes seesawing through the night, McAlister lost his pack, his sleeping bag, and extra rations. The bag had been important not merely for sleeping, but to stand in through the long hours in freezing holes. About 4 A.M. the battalion began to withdraw. Many of the machine gunners covering their departure were lost as the Chinese raced forward in pursuit. The 1st Battalion reached the positions of their own gunners and other infantry to find that they too had been attacked and surrounded. It was now that Colonel Faith assumed command of all the survivors.

That day, like its predecessor, the Americans spent stamping their feet in the desperate cold, trying to improve their positions for the night and watching the air strikes. The Chinese harassed and sniped at them. That night they lost their positions in one attack, and were compelled to counterattack to retake them, all the time losing men. The following morning, November 30, supplies and ammunition were air-dropped to the perimeter.

"Retrieving them was difficult [wrote McAlister], because the Chinese wanted them as much as we did, and some were dropped far out of reach. Of what we got, we found that a lot of the belts and clips were damaged, and we had to work in the cold refilling the BAR magazines. That night my BAR assistant got hit by rifle fire in the eye and had blood all over his face. He was still alive and in a lot of pain. I called the medic and pushed him down in the hole, because I had to keep firing as the enemy was almost on top of us. After a while the medic came and took him to the rear, and I never saw him after that. Later I ran out of ammo, and reached for the rifle that my buddy had left. There was no ammo in it either. I was reaching for my .45 when a grenade was thrown into the hole. The next thing that I remember, I was back in the center by the artillery, but all I could see around me was men that had been wounded or killed.

"I left the area on a truck with the rest of the wounded. We were being fired on constantly by enemy machine guns. Our planes were trying to help by dropping napalm between our troops and theirs. As a result some of our men got burned pretty bad and were put aboard the trucks with us wounded. I will never forget the smell of human flesh after that. A lot of them died before too long.''

McAlister himself was hit shortly afterward by a stray bullet which rendered his right arm useless. Then the trucks were halted by a Chinese roadblock. Their captors ordered the occupants out. When those who could walk had climbed down, to their sick horror they watched North Korean soldiers run along the line setting fire to the vehicles, together with those who remained aboard them. For several days that followed, McAlister and his comrades were held captive close to the road. Then, numb and at the limits of exhaustion, they were gathered together to be marched north. McAlister sat down on the running board of a burned-out American truck. He could not bring himself to move when a Korean guard ordered him to his feet. He was hit twice, hard, on the head, and passed out.

"When I came to, I was alone. I guess they figured I was dead. I stumbled around for what seemed to be hours, and finally got back to the lake. I could only walk for a few minutes before falling down. My feet were frozen and I couldn't use my hands much. Somehow I got started towards Hagaru-ri. At last I met a 'big ole Marine colonel' who carried me to a truck, and onto an aid station from which I was flown to Japan. I had frostbite in both feet and hands, shrapnel in the head, and my right wrist was almost severed. I was in hospital until May 31, 1952.''[5]

When the predicament of Task Force Faith became apparent, General Almond blamed O. P. Smith for the Marines' failure to leave a force at Hagaru strong enough to be able now to send a relief force to 7th Division's aid. At Almond's insistence, an attempt was made to cut a path up the east side of the reservoir to link up with the retreating units. But this rapidly encountered heavy opposition. It was abandoned. Colonel Faith spoke to Hagaru for the last time through a Marine air liaison officer's radio link: "Unless someone can help us, I don't have much hope that anybody's going to get out of this." He was told, "We are bringing in an awful lot of air support, but that's all we can give you. We just don't have enough people here to risk losing our hold on the foot of the reservoir."

"I understand," said Faith.

This was his last contact with Hagaru. Air support could do nothing by night, when the fate of Task Force Faith was sealed and its courageous commanding officer killed. "Whenever I hear the words 'task force,' I shudder," said a distinguished Marine veteran later.[6] In Korea, all too often, the phrase became an apology for a makeshift collection of vehicles and men committed to disaster.

A staff officer who entered the general officers' mess at Hungnam the evening of the arrival of the news of the destruction of Task Force Faith found inside it, alone by the stove, General David Barr, the 7th Division's commander. He was sobbing quietly. "Barr was a nice man," said the officer later, "but he had no personal magnetism, and should never have been permitted to command a division at war. He was too old, and too soft. The Chosin campaign finished him." Barr was relieved of his command and sent home.

If General Almond's chief preoccupation in mid-November had been to seize North Korean real estate, at whatever cost to the dispersal of his corps, by the end of that month he had become as hasty in his anxiety to get his command back to the coast. As the weight of Chinese forces confronting the X Corps and threatening its main supply route became apparent, those privy to the intelligence reports felt a growing, gnawing fear that they were close to the brink of a great disaster for American arms. "I really thought we'd had it," said Colonel Al Bowser, G-3 of 1st Marine Division. "We did not know the details of what was happening to Eighth Army, but we knew that there was only eighty miles of open flank on our left. We knew the size of the Chinese forces against us—and we didn't at that time understand their shortcomings. I would not have given a nickel for our chances of making it. Fortunately, a lot of people down the line could not see the overall position as I could see it, and continued to conduct themselves as if they were going to get out."[7]

Fresh argument now broke out between the Army and the Marines, precipitated by the newly acute sense of crisis: the soldiers favored abandoning all heavy equipment and artillery and pulling back south as fast as 1st Marine Division could march and ride. O. P. Smith, however, was determined to conduct what he termed "an orderly and honorable withdrawal." He would bring out all his vehicles and guns. "Don't worry about your equipment," Almond told Smith impatiently one morning at Hagaru. "Once you get back, we'll replace it all." Smith said, "I'm not going to do that. This is the equipment we fight with."

"Okay," said Almond wearily. "I just wanted you to know that we would replace it." When the two men parted Smith turned to Colonel Bowser: "This guy is a maniac. He's nuts. I can't believe he's saying these things."[8]

On this occasion it was Smith's will which prevailed, that formed the basis for the legend of the retreat from Chosin, perhaps the only really creditable American military performance of that winter campaign of 1950. On December 1 the 10,000 men of the 5th and 7th Marines began their epic fourteen-mile fighting retreat from Yudam-ni to Hagaru, battalions leapfrogging each other southward, pressed at each pass by the Chinese, machine-gunning and mortaring every point upon the road upon which their weapons would bear. The Marines could move forward only by clearing the ground commanding the road in front of them, yard by bitterly contested yard. The 3/7th, leading the assault, became bogged down, and Taplett's 3/5th was ordered to pass through them and take up the lead. When night came, with the men utterly exhausted by wading in snow up to their hips on the hillside, Taplett asked if his battalion might halt, at least for long enough to

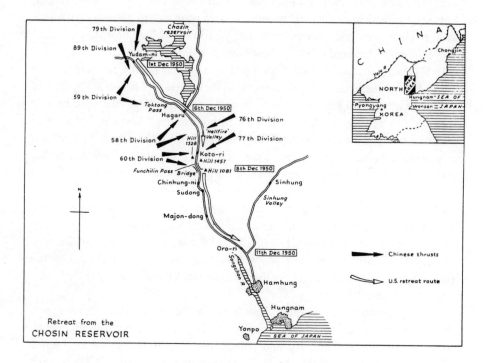

Retreat from the
CHOSIN RESERVOIR

establish its own precise location. Permission was refused. "Attack, keep attacking," he was told. Item Company of Taplett's battalion was almost wiped out on the first day. Taplett himself lost four runners attempting to pass messages to its commander. A single tank led the column, followed by Taplett's command jeep, directing the infantry on the shoulders above the road. Ray Murray appeared at Taplett's jeep and demanded to know why the attack was stalled.

"We can't even get artillery support," said Taplett.

"We've got trouble behind us, too," explained Murray.

"If you want to get out of here," said Taplett flatly, "you'll give the guys at the front the support."[9]

In a sea of mountains reaching to the horizon, it was impossible for the infantry to reach and command the higher ground. They could seek only to hold the shoulders and suppress the Chinese small-arms fire while the great regimental train crawled along the road below. It was fortunate for the Americans that the Chinese now appeared to have outrun the artillery they had brought down on the Marines at Yudam-ni. The Marines could see Communist troops swarming on the hills around them. Without the dedicated support of the Marine Air Wings, few men believed they would ever have made it. Even Marine pilots who were tasked to fly interdiction missions against targets farther north kept a bomb, a rack of rockets, or a few seconds of cannon ammunition to expend in close support of their own people on the way home. Men marveled at the great gushers of snow, the black impact on the hillside, as a Skyraider unloaded its ordnance. It reminded Major Ed Simmonds "of a giant bird taking a crap."[10]

On the one day when blustering snow and low clouds made air support impossible, the column scarcely moved. Every few hours a group of Chinese would succeed in breaking through to the road, disabling a vehicle, blocking the route. Then the Americans were compelled to counterattack, to shift the wreckage, before they could get movement started again. Even without the intervention of the enemy, mechanical failure or a moment's carelessness by a driver would block the road with a stranded or ditched vehicle. There were difficult decisions: whether to keep the artillery moving or suffer the delays of causing guns to unlimber on the road to provide urgent support for the infantry. It was an agonizingly slow business, by day and by night, for men crippled by exhaustion and the weather, the inescapable elements. The cold seemed to gnaw into their bodies, sapping reserves of strength, making every movement painfully slow and clumsy.

The first units of 1st Marine Division entered the perimeter at Hagaru on the afternoon of the third, the last men on the evening of the following day. Taplett's battalion was reduced to 326 effectives out of some 2,000 whom he had commanded at Yudam-ni. Many of the casualties were suffering only from frostbite, but the serious cases still required evacuation from the overworked airstrip. It was also found necessary to introduce rigorous security on the runway to prevent stragglers from sneaking aboard one of the C–47 casevac aircraft, which could offer them a priceless passage to safety. The aircraft that flew out wounded brought in supplies and some replacements, many of them men wounded on the Naktong or in Seoul. "The feeling now was—'Let's get the hell out of this,' " said Taplett. " 'This is too much for us with our resources.' It was hard to take, for men who had been told that the war was won, who were looking forward to that big parade we had been promised in San Francisco."

The performance of the 1st Marine Division in desperate circumstances had begun to command the attention of America, so hungry for heroic news at a moment when there was so little to be had. O. P. Smith captured headlines all over the country when he told correspondents who flew into Hagaru on December 4, "Gentlemen, we are not retreating. We are merely advancing in another direction." His remark was interpreted as a magnificent defiance of reality. Yet, as he said afterward, it was also tactically accurate, as the great military historian S. L. A. Marshall perceived: "Slam was the only one who understood that what we were doing really was attacking in another direction, because you couldn't withdraw when you were completely surrounded," said Smith.

The feud—for it was nothing less—between Smith and Almond became a focal point of controversy both during the campaign and in the recriminations after it ended. At times the Marines almost seemed to relish the X Corps commander's misjudgments. During the desperate struggle to hold the Hagaru Perimeter, Smith took bleak pleasure in the discovery of a group of big treadway trucks with winches, which Almond had dispatched to prepare his Corps command post when he believed that he was presiding over an administrative advance to the Chinese border. Officers who flew down to Hamnung returned with scornful tales of the china, napkins, fresh fruit, and meat flown in from Japan for Almond's table.

Almond seemed to lack any instinct for identifying himself with the men of his command in their brutal predicament. One morning he flew into Hagaru from his headquarters and sought to make himself agreeable to some of the Marines on the perimeter. "Well, men, and how are you today? Pretty cold, isn't it?" The bearded, mufflered scarecrows peered out at him from the inch or two of exposed flesh around their eyes. "Do you know I wear a plate?" persisted Almond conversationally. "When I got up this morning, there was a film of ice on the glass by my bed." "That's too f**king bad, General," said one of these men who could not dare to dream of ever seeing a bed again. Almond strolled on, still oblivious of the impression he had made. It was a soldier, a member of Almond's staff, and not a Marine, who recounted witnessing that incident.[11]

Yet some able officers retained great respect for the X Corps commander's abilities: "I consider Almond was an excellent Corps commander," said General Lemuel Shepherd, commanding the Fleet Marines. "He was energetic, forceful, brave, and in many ways did a good job under most difficult conditions. He and O.P. just didn't get along."[12] Ed Rowney and Al Haig, both officers who served on Almond's staff in Korea and rose to high rank in the U.S. Army, retained a lifelong respect for their old commander. Lieutenant Colonel Ellis Williamson, Almond's G-3, took an ambivalent view: "O. P. Smith wasn't a team player at all. He just wanted to do what he wanted. Ned Almond was one of the most energetic, dedicated officers I have ever known. He was so energetic, that at times he was tactically careless. He could not visualize himself being wrong. He was almost as bad as MacArthur in this. Once he had made up his mind that something was so, he was just not listening anymore."[13] The evidence is overwhelming that O. P. Smith was indeed a slow and cautious commander. Likewise, his habit of lapsing into sturdy silence when confronted with Almond's tantrums precluded any possibility of understanding between the two men. Smith was disgusted by Almond's undoubted obsession with achieving a personal triumph on the battle-field. If fortune had fallen otherwise, if Almond had been granted his opportunity to lead a Patton-like pursuit, a dash for victory, he might indeed have earned his place in military history, while Smith would have been remembered as a plodding encumbrance. Instead, however, on the road back from Chosin, Smith's dogged, imperturbable leadership not only saved the honor of the 1st Marine Division but the reputation of American arms in Korea. Almond, on the other hand, was branded by many as the commander whose impatience and overweening personal ambition came within a hairbreadth of creating a catastrophe.

Although the first great danger to the 1st Marine Division had been overcome by the successful withdrawal to Hagaru, there were no delusions about the difficulties of the next stage. At Koto-ri, when officers of the 1st Marines were briefed about the plan for the movement of the 5th and 7th, there was obvious concern about its feasibility. But "Chesty" Puller, whose capacity for histrionics had markedly not been diminished by circumstances, climbed on a ration box beside the space heater in the briefing tent and harangued his team, "I don't give a good goddamn how many Chinese laundrymen there are between us and Hungnam. There aren't enough in the world to stop a Marine regiment going where it wants to go! Christ in His mercy will see us through."

On December 6, the 1st Marine Division set out on the eleven-mile journey from Hagaru to Koto-ri. It was intended that the entire formation should be clear of the base of the reservoir by nightfall, but the slow progress of the vanguard caused the rear elements to linger at Hagaru into the darkness, fighting off the Chinese, who began to descend from the hills and bring down fierce fire on the road. Finally, sluggishly, the last Americans pulled out. They left behind vast dumps of stores, burned or destroyed to keep them from the Chinese. Yet one cargo the Marines insisted upon taking with them, to the renewed exasperation of X Corps staff: their own dead. Some British Marines found it macabre to advance alongside trucks from which the frozen limbs of the corpses protruded, uncovered. Smith's men were merely determined that dead or alive, the entire division should make it back. "We were grateful for what the cold had done to those bodies," said Robert Tyack, a British Marine. "You were looking at a chunk of frozen meat, rather than a messy, stinking corpse."[14] The march took thirty-eight hours through the snow, under constant harassment from the Chinese. Not every Marine was a hero. When the Chinese broke through close to the road, it proved essential for American officers to stay close to their men, to drive them to respond. Lacking immediate leadership, some exhausted men were prone to lapse into a ditch and lie huddled together, too numb to trouble to fire back. Robert Tyack remembered vividly a moment when his mate fell asleep on a hillside as they scraped a position with their bayonets and furiously shook off every attempt to rouse him: "Leave me! If I don't wake, what the hell?" Stragglers had to be kicked, pushed, cajoled. Those who stopped never started again.

When they were not under direct fire, men plodded wearily beneath the ice-laden telegraph poles, their helmets and weapons and clothing decked in crusts of snow. It was better to feel the pain in their feet. The thousands of men who no longer possessed any sensation in their boots were suffering from various extremes of frostbite. Once again, as on the withdrawal from Yudam-ni, while the thousand-vehicle convoy crawled along the road, leapfrogging battalions cleared the high ground above. When they passed the dozens of burned-out vehicles from Task Force Drysdale's battleground, they gathered up the frozen dead, and to their utter astonishment, found one wounded man in a hut by the road still alive.

Clearing the road from Hagaru to Koto-ri cost the Marines another 103 killed and 506 wounded; also, the loss of all but thirteen of 160 Chinese POWs they were marching south. When the POW contingent came under fire from the hills, they broke and ran from the road, causing the Marines to shoot them down. Their arrival at Koto-ri, the reunion with the garrison on its perimeter, was another emotional landmark, celebrated with bearhugs between men clumsy in their layers of clothing, rejoicing to have survived another desperate stage of their journey. Men who had been fighting at Koto-ri searched the ranks of those from Hagaru for friends and even relations. Corporal Selwyn Handler of the 2/1st looked for his brother Irwin among the men of B Company, 5th Marines. For hours he stood hunched by the road as the gaunt files marched in, peering between raised collars and lowered helmets for the familiar face he had last seen at Wonsan. Irwin was eighteen and planned to be an optometrist. He was one of those who never made it down the road from Yudam-ni.

Among the few scrubby trees and the forest of tents in the overcrowded perimeter at Koto-ri, the dead were at last buried in a grave blasted from the iron-frozen earth. There was an old-fashioned little squabble when General Smith insisted that the indomitable *Herald Tribune* correspondent Marguerite Higgins should be evacuated by air, despite her enraged protests of sexual discrimination: "There are a lot of good Marines who are getting frostbite," said O.P., "and if you march down with these Marines, you will probably get frostbite, and then somebody is going to have to take care of you. I am sure these Marines will see that you are taken care of, and we haven't got men for that kind of business." Smith's chivalrous concern almost misfired when the aircraft carrying Higgins and General Lem Shepherd came under heavy Chinese fire as it took off. "My God, Maggie," said Shepherd as they sat hunched together watching the tracer pass beneath them, "won't it be an awful scandal if the two of us are found crashed together?"

With 15,000 men and almost 1,500 vehicles crowded into the perimeter at Koto-ri, there was precious little room for movement. The new arrivals blasted themselves foxholes with C-3 demolition sticks and stripped every house in the little town to provide roofing and firewood. There was a moment of raw comedy when the "recreation packs" air-dropped to the division were discovered to include contraceptives: "What the ——— do they think we are doing with those Chinese?" If the pressure of enemy attack had diminished, that of the cold never did so. Men carried C-ration tins under their armpits, wore one of their two canteens under their clothing, to keep it usable.

A new and serious difficulty developed when it was learned that the bridge over the gorge in the Funchilin Pass, a few miles south of Koto-ri, had been destroyed by the Chinese for the third time in the battle, this time irreparably. The only conceivable means of getting Smith's marines through was to air-drop and lay a new treadway bridge. Could it be done? Lieutenant Colonel John Partridge, the divisional engineer officer, overflew the gap, making notes about the equipment that would be needed to bridge the thirty-foot culvert: "I got you across the Han River," he told Smith reassuringly. "I got you the airfield here. I'll get you a bridge." In the South a young engineer captain experimented with parachuting a bridge section, which smashed on impact. "It's okay—we'll use bigger parachutes and the next rehearsal will go fine," he reassured the Marine headquarters. "We don't have time for a 'next rehearsal.' Next time is for real," he was told bleakly. Eight bridge sections were parachuted into the perimeter at Koto-ri. Six were recovered intact. The culvert was bridged.

The routine—if such a word does not diminish the nature of the ordeal—for the march from Koto-ri to Hamnung was identical with that from Hagaru. Some men trudged along the road, among the vehicles, while others took their turn "ridge-running," sweeping the shoulders of the high ground above the column. When the snow squalls came, it was sometimes impossible even to see the man a few yards in front. And still, every few hours, parties of Chinese managed to work close enough to put in fire somewhere on the column. "Aw, quit horsing around," said Corporal Handler of the 2/1st in some exasperation when his buddy, "a kid named Freudenberg," began to pull wounded men out of a truck that suddenly came under fire, only to topple over sideways into the snow. But Freudenberg was suddenly dead.

Not all the memories of that march were heroic. Colonel Taplett of the 3/5th had a ferocious argument on the road with an army officer who suddenly sought to get his men into the column in front of Taplett's battalion. The Marine was disgusted, since he knew that the army officer had been instructed to bring up the rear, behind the 5th. At the rear of the great snake of Marines and their 1,400 vehicles, some 3,000 refugees struggled with their carts and pitiful possessions. It was critical for the American rearguard to maintain a clear field of fire between themselves and the Koreans. Desperate measures became necessary in order to achieve this. Finally, the divisional engineers blew a bridge behind the Marines. The Koreans were left on the other side, gazing hopelessly into the chasm.

On December 10 the first men of the great Marine column began to trickle into the port of Hamnung. The first ships of a vast amphibious armada awaited them. Many Marines, including their most senior officers, believed that they could easily have held a perimeter around the port through the winter, a formidable enclave deep in North Korean territory. But by now the Dai Ichi had no stomach for such dangerous gestures. Rather than a stronghold, a perimeter at Hamnung could become a vast beleaguered fortress. Unit by unit, 100,000 men of the U.S. Army, the Marines, the ROKs boarded the ships and sailed away for Pusan. Behind them an orgy of looting and destruction was taking place, as one of the greatest supply dumps in Korea was stripped by civilians or blown up by engineers. Pillars of black smoke plumed along the horizon behind the waterfront. As the last Marines departed, thousands of civilian refugees boarded the ships behind them, taking a last chance to escape the return of Kim Il Sung. On December 24, with the evacuation completed, the U.S. Navy unleashed a huge bombardment on the abandoned port, blasting its facilities and remaining dumps into wreckage. It was much more a gesture of frustration, of embittered anger and disappointment, than of military utility. The Marines' performance had been heroic. They had retired from the Chosin Reservoir in column of units, with virtually all their heavy equipment and transport intact, maintaining the cohesion of the division to the end. But X Corps' battle was lost. The Marines alone had suffered 4,418 battle and 7,313 nonbattle casualties, the latter mostly minor cases of frostbite. From subsequent POW interrogations and captured documents, the Chinese were estimated to have suffered some 37,500 losses in the Chosin campaign, many of these from the cold.

The Communist army endured privations more dreadful than those of the Americans. In the last stages of the American march to the coast, and through the evacuation, X Corps suffered scarcely at all from Chinese intervention. The enemy, too, was spent. He had outrun such supply lines as he possessed, and his men were at the extremities of misery from hunger and cold. But the formations of the People's Liberation Army who inherited the wreckage of Hamnung in the last days of 1950 could at least exult in the certainty of strategic achievement. They had driven the U.S. X Corps headlong out of North Korea.

9

THE WINTER OF CRISIS

The Big Bugout

As Walker's Eighth Army reeled before the Chinese offensive in the first days of December, one morning Colonel Paul Freeman of the 23rd Infantry turned bitterly to his executive officer. "Look around here," he said. "This is a sight that hasn't been seen for hundreds of years—the men of a whole United States Army fleeing from a battlefield, abandoning their wounded, running for their lives."[1] Freeman was among those few senior soldiers in Korea who never lost their grip, who remained bewildered to the end of their lives about the fashion in which their commanders and their comrades allowed the collapse of the American Army in North Korea in the winter of 1950. Freeman watched with pride his own 1st Battalion, holding the Chinese on the Chongchon for thirty hours, his regiment undertaking thirteen successive redeployments without losing a man. Suddenly he received an air-dropped message from 2nd Division "to extricate ourselves as best we could" and retired under cover of a powerful artillery barrage. Only then did he begin to discover what was happening to the rest of the Army: in the 25th Division, only the 27th Infantry held together effectively. In the 2nd Division, Freeman's regiment remained the only combat-effective unit by the turn of the year.

Private Pete Schultz, a platoon runner in A Company of the 1/23rd, had been feeling somewhat dejected about the promise of MacArthur's "home for Christmas'': "Here I was, full of life, eighteen years old, fresh out of basic training, and about as green as they come. I wanted to see some action."[2] He spent the night of November 25 crouching in a foxhole listening to the intense firing all around him, without the remotest idea what was going on. A small-town boy from Kansas, Schultz found the action that he wanted in the next few days. The memories merged into a blur: picking among abandoned supply dumps as they retreated; manning a .30-caliber machine gun, watching the tracer arch toward a cluster of Chinese on the next ridgeline; running to clamber up on the hulls of their supporting tanks when they heard the engines rev up, a sure sign that they were about to move. They feared above all being left behind, finding themselves last out. "A lot of men convinced themselves that each was the last man left in the Eighth Army," said Lieutenant Carl Bernard of the 21st Infantry.[3]

Lieutenant Karl Morton of the 5th RCT found the first reports of the retreat incomprehensible, for his unit had scarcely been engaged. The first symptom of defeat was the absence of transport to carry them back. They began to walk. And as they walked, day after day their morale sank. They did not fight, but they heard rumors. Faster, faster, they were constantly warned, lest you be cut off by the Chinese. Morton's thighs became raw, agonizing, with the constant slapping of wet fatigue cloth against them. One of his corporals walked with a toilet roll on his rifle barrel, in permanent misery from diarrhea until they somewhere found him a packet of cornstarch to solve the problem. One day they watched from a roadblock as men of the 2nd Division moved past "in awful disarray." Only one black battalion, led by a ramrod-straight white-haired colonel, still appeared to possess all its equipment. As they marched on, and on, they discarded gear to lighten their burdens: rocket launchers went first, then spare clothing, ammunition, even sleeping bags. One evening at dusk they saw a solitary soldier pedaling maniacally past them on a bicycle. They tried to stop him: "Hey, what's going on up there?" The cyclist did not check, but shouted back over his shoulder, "Hell of a lot of Chinamen!" As the supply system cracked, men grew desperate in their hunger. Morton saw two soldiers discover an abandoned, half-empty can of peas coated in days of dust. They simply scraped off the dust with a bayonet and wolfed the remains. The young lieutenant found this spectacle, of thousands of men on the margins of panic, very frightening.[4]

As Captain Fred Ladd drove north to a divisional headquarters, against the endless stream of traffic fleeing southward, to his astonishment he saw among the files of marching men a leathery NCO whose face was instantly familiar. Sergeant Davis had served with his father, half a lifetime ago, in the 15th Infantry. Davis faced Ladd with tears in his eyes: "This just isn't the goddamn American Army—running away. We ought to be taking up positions." Ladd could find no words of comfort for the old NCO: "I know, I know." He nodded helplessly. Then he drove away, and Davis trudged on, shrunken, southward.[5]

In ten days the men of the Eighth Army retreated 120 miles. By December 15 they had crossed the 38th Parallel and the Imjin River, and still they were moving south. Since the destruction of the 2nd Division south of Kunu-ri, they had scarcely even been in contact with the Chinese. Yet while the Marines conducted their measured, orderly retreat from Chosin despite acute difficulties of terrain, in the west Walker's army astoundingly collapsed.

Few men ever forgot the sights of those days. They looted what they could carry from the vast supply dumps in Pyongyang—alcohol, tobacco, sugar—but acre upon acre of equipment was put to the torch. The great pillars of smoke from the fires were visible for miles to the retreating army. "The march out of Pyongyang will be remembered mainly for the intense cold, the dust, and the disappointment," recorded an officer of the 8th Royal Irish Hussars, a British Centurion tank regiment. "Nothing appeared to have been attempted, let alone achieved. Millions of dollars' worth of valuable equipment had been destroyed without a shot being fired or any attempt made to consider its possible evacuation. Seldom has a more demoralizing picture been witnessed than the abandonment of this, the American forward base, before an unknown threat of Chinese soldiers— as it transpired, ill-armed and on their feet or horses."[6] Yet everywhere they expected the Chinese to catch up with them. It was almost as if they were tiptoeing away. As the British armor clattered noisily across the bridge south of Pyongyang, Captain James Majury of the Ulsters found himself desperately wishing that the tanks would make less noise. A young troop commander's tank knocked over an ROK soldier in the long files trudging alongside the roadside. A track ran over the man's leg. The horrified young officer jumped down to aid the Korean. But even as he knelt the man's platoon officer pulled the Englishman's pistol from his holster and put a bullet in the mangled man's head.

On the road south of the North Korean capital, General Paek Sun Yup of the ROK 1st Division met the 27th Infantry's commander, Colonel John Michaelis, whom he greatly admired. The Korean was deeply depressed by the loss of Pyongyang, his home city, which he had entered in such triumph a few weeks earlier. Now he asked the American what was happening. "I don't know," said Michaelis. "I'm just a regimental commander. But we may not be able to stay in the peninsula."[7]

The Korean people were, of course, the principal victims of the Chinese winter offensive, as they were of every phase of the war. As the Eighth Army straggled south in disarray, everywhere around them a great human tide of refugees surged and stumbled. When the army monopolized the road, the civilians fled along the railway line. Many scarcely knew where they were going or why—only that they had lost whatever they had owned behind them and sought to attain something fresh in front, if it was only shelter from the battle. But Moon Yun Seung and his

family knew why they were on the railway embankment south from Pyongyang—
to escape the Communists. Moon was eighteen, and until 1945 his family had
owned a silk mill in the north. When they lost that, they moved to Pyongyang and
became silk traders. But in the autumn of 1950, as the Communists fled from their
own capital, they left behind them an epidemic of grim rumors. Moon was assured
that the Americans proposed to drop an atomic bomb on Pyongyang. He and his
family moved hastily back to the village where once they had owned their mill,
and it was there that they saw their first Americans, advancing north at the height
of their triumph. Then, when the Chinese came and the retreat began, Moon and
his family began walking. "There were too many people," he said. "We could
not keep together. When the American fighters came, machine-gunning the roads,
everyone scattered like bean shoots." He never saw his family again. For eighteen
days he walked toward Seoul, scavenging scraps of food from abandoned houses,
pathetically waving a South Korean flag when the F-86s strafed the refugee
columns, as he saw them do repeatedly. In Seoul, Moon had expected to find
refuge with a friend of his father. But this man, like three quarters of the
population after their dreadful experience the previous summer, had fled. Moon
kept walking south. He was picked up in one of the ROK Army's periodic
roundups of conscripts, but after three months was rejected as unfit—this despite
the bleak United Nations' joke that an ROK medical examination merely involved
holding a mirror to a man's mouth to check that he breathed. Moon was a
scavenger in Pusan when he was run over and his leg broken by an American army
truck. A Scandinavian medical team rescued him. He spent six months in a
Swedish hospital, a year on crutches. Finally, he got a job as a longshoreman at
the docks. He was merely another stray scrap of flotsam amid a great sea of such
private tragedies in the winter of 1950.[8]

Lieutenant Bill Cooper and a couple of brother officers of the 5th Northumberland
Fusiliers left their positions guarding the Han bridges to drive into Seoul on
Christmas Eve. It seemed fantastic to leave the snow and the refugees, the sense
of imminent disaster outside, and walk into the brightly lit Chosan Hotel, where
a ferociously drunken party was in progress. Men of all ranks lurched around the
corridors clutching their Korean bar girls. If there was no food to be had,
everybody was helping themselves to drink. At last the British walked out once
more to their jeeps in the darkness, to the reality of Korean figures scuttling
urgently through the snow, of acute desolation and apprehension. Cooper had
spent much of the voyage out from England attempting to diminish the bloody-
mindedness of his platoon, largely recalled reservists, about their commitment to
Korea. He told them, "It's going to be no good sitting on top of some mountain
saying 'I shouldn't be here' while some bugger blows the top of your head off."
For all his efforts, he felt that throughout their time in Korea "there was still that

undercurrent of resentment.'' Yet now, Cooper's men, like the rest of the British 29 Brigade, were warned to be ready to move.[9]

When the North Koreans held Seoul in the summer of 1950, thirteen-year-old Suk Bun Yoon's father had a miraculous escape. Denounced as an anti-Communist, he was taken to a hillside outside the city, along with a group of others, and shot. But the wound was not fatal. He crawled away and eventually found his family and convalesced with them through the winter. His son became the most important male in the household, which did not cost his education much, since by the end of the year almost all his teachers had been recruited or taken prisoner by one side or the other. But his father was still a sick man on January 3, 1951, when the family determined that they must flee Seoul. That evening they made their way among thousands of Koreans on a similar mission, toward the frozen Han River. It was a terrible spectacle, a terrible night. Shellfire broke the ice in some places, and the boy watched struggling refugees sink helpless into the river, while thousands more ran hysterically past them. Somewhere in the darkness and the hysterical crowds, their grandfather disappeared: ''We simply lost him. We never saw him again. Maybe he froze to death.'' In the days that followed, the family crawled south with their possessions. They had gone only twenty-five miles when they were overtaken by the Chinese. That night, in an abandoned house, they held a family conference. It was decided that as they were, they stood no hope of breaking through to the UN lines. They left their grandmother and Suk's three younger brothers and sisters, aged ten, seven, and three, in the village, reliant upon the charity of the peasants. Suk and his parents struggled on through the darkness, amid the gun flashes and refugees and wailing infants, until at last they crossed into the ROK lines.

To a Westerner, the decision to abandon the very old and the very young seems almost fantastic. But as the UN armies so often observed, the people of Korea seem to draw their character from the harsh environment in which they live. This was the kind of parting, the kind of decision that was commonplace in hundreds of thousands of Korean families that created the legions of starving orphans and infant beggars that hung like flies around every UN camp, supply dump, refuse heap. Behind the UN lines, for the next two months Suk and his parents lived with an aunt deep in the countryside. Only when the Eighth Army at last moved forward again did the boy return to the village in search of the rest of the family. They found the children. Their hair was dropping out. They were in rags; their bodies were lice-ridden; they could not readily digest food. But they were narrowly alive. Thanks to canned food begged and stolen from the armies, they survived. Their grandmother was dead. The surviving family was ruined, destitute, homeless. But like millions of other Koreans that winter, they clung tenaciously to the margins of existence and waited for better times.

*   *   *

Among the Eighth Army, mile by mile and day by day on the road southward, as men abandoned equipment and lost their officers, allowed themselves to be washed with the great tide of American and Korean humanity flowing south away from the Communists, the withdrawal became "the big bugout." The impulse to escape not only from the enemy but from the terrible cold, the mountains, from Korea itself became overwhelming for many men. In December 1950 most of the Eighth Army fell apart as a fighting force in a fashion resembling the collapse of the French in 1940, the British at Singapore in 1942. The men of 45 Field Regiment RA were reduced to hysterical laughter by an American intelligence report announcing that the Chinese were employing large numbers of monkeys as porters. Rumor of every kind, the more dramatic the better, held sway over the minds of thousands of men. "Everything the Chinese were showing they could do, their aggressiveness, was strange to us," said Major Floyd Martain. "What we knew of the Chinese in America was so different—they were so submissive."[10] Most Americans expected Chinamen to be dwarves, but they found themselves assaulted by units which included men six feet and over. Yet the enemy wreaking such havoc with the Eighth Army was still, essentially, fighting a large-scale guerrilla war, devoid of all the heavy firepower every Western army considered essential. It was a triumph not merely for the prestige of communism, but for that of an Asian army.

From Walker's headquarters to Tokyo and on to the Joint Chiefs' offices in the Pentagon, there was bewilderment and deep dismay about the collapse of the Eighth Army. For public consumption, the sheer surprise and weight of the Chinese offensive were emphasized. But professional soldiers knew that these were not enough to explain the headlong rout of an army that still possessed absolute command of sea and air, and firepower on a scale the Communists could not dream of. The Chinese victories were being gained by infantry bearing small arms and regimental support weapons—above all, mortars. The Americans had been subjected to very little artillery fire, and no air attack whatever. The mobility of the Chinese, moving across mountain ranges without regard for the road network, was achieved at the cost of carrying very limited supplies of arms and ammunition—of behaving, indeed, like a large guerrilla army. Chinese peasants might be somewhat better attuned to hardship than Western soldiers, but they were not superhuman. The men of the UN complained of the difficulty of fighting the ferocious cold as well as the enemy. But the winter was neutral. The Chinese were far less well-equipped to face the conditions than their opponents, possessing only canvas shoes and lacking such indulgences as sleeping bags. Marshal Peng's casualties from frostbite dwarfed those of the Americans. And the Chinese could expect no ready evacuation or medical care. UN soldiers told terrible stories of taking prisoners with whole limbs blackened and dead in the cold. Chinese veterans later declared that 90 percent of the "Volunteers" in Korea suffered from some degree of frostbite in the winter of 1950. Their Twenty-seventh Army suffered 10,000 noncombat casualties: "A shortage of transportation and escort personnel makes it impossible to accomplish the mission of supplying the troops," declared a Twenty-sixth Army document of November 1950, later captured by the UN. "As a result, our soldiers frequently starve. . . . They ate cold food, and some had only a few potatoes in two days. They were unable to maintain their physical strength for combat; the wounded could not be evacuated. . . . The firepower of our entire army was basically inadequate. When we used our guns, there were often no shells, or the shells were duds."[11]

The Chinese could achieve great shock power, but they possessed only the most limited ability to sustain an attack, whether at company or army level. They missed dazzling opportunities to annihilate rather than merely drive back MacArthur's army in Korea in the winter of 1950 because they could move only as fast as their feet could carry them, and their radio communications were so poor that they could not coordinate large-scale movements effectively. Some PLA units were out of contact with their higher formations for days on end. The key to tactical success against the Chinese was to create all-round defensive perimeters, and not to allow panic to set in when it was discovered, as it so frequently was, that the Communists had turned a unit's flank. If UN firepower could be brought to bear in support of a counterattack, this was almost invariably successful. But in those weeks of November and December, Peking's armies achieved psychological dominance not only over UN units at the front, but over their commanders in the rear. After the first battles of November, the flimsiest rumor of the men in quilted jackets being observed on a main supply route behind the front was enough to spark fears of encirclement, and often outright panic. The undoubted Chinese skills as tacticians, night fighters, navigators, masters of fieldcraft and camouflage caused even many senior officers to forget the enemy's huge disadvantages in resources and firepower. Worse, the leaders of the UN forces in Korea found themselves facing the stark fact that, man for man, most of their troops were proving nowhere near as hardy, skillful, and determined upon the battlefield as their Communist opponents. It is difficult to overestimate the psychological effects of this conclusion upon strategic and tactical decision-making.

Yet even at this phase the struggle was not entirely one-sided. The Chinese were learning bitter lessons about the potential of air power. They discovered that their truck drivers could not move by day because they could not hear the sound of enemy aircraft. Every infantry movement had to be completed before dawn, the men deeply covered by the snow into which they dug themselves, before the prowling Mustangs, Corsairs, Panthers found them. A nationwide system of air-raid precautions was created, sentries stationed at intervals of two hundred yards along every mile of the Chinese supply routes, ready by whistle and rifle shot to warn of impending air attack the moment engines were heard.

Hung She Te, the Chinese officer responsible for all logistics inside Korea, performed miracles with his legions of porters and oxcarts. But throughout that winter campaign of 1950, the overwhelming limitation upon the Chinese was not manpower, of which their reserves were almost unbounded, but supply. Chou En Lai exhorted every family in China to fry flour for the "Volunteers." Great columns of men and trucks moved south across the Yalu each night, backs bent and springs groaning under their burdens. They learned to place wide brooms on the front of vehicles to sweep aside the puncture nails dropped on the roads by U.S. aircraft. They organized emergency-repair parties to replace broken bridges and ruined roads within hours. But the Chinese were never able, in that first campaign, effectively to deploy artillery in support of their advance. Probably the most critical contribution of American air power in the Korean War was the interdiction of supply routes during the winter battles of 1950. This alone, it may be argued, prevented the Chinese from converting the defeat of the UN forces into their destruction.

How could Marshal Peng and his staff organize their own intelligence about UN movements effectively when they lacked equipment to intercept American communications or aircraft to conduct effective reconnaissance? Thirty-five years later, the face of Hu Seng, one of Peng's secretaries, cracked into a craggy grin at the memory: "It was very easy to get intelligence, in the beginning. There was no censorship in the West at that time about troop movements. We gained much vital information from Western press and radio."[12] Daily from July, from the agency wires in Seoul clattered details of the landings of the Marines, the arrival of new foreign contingents, the assault on Inchon (ten hours before this took place), the deployment of the first F-86 Sabre fighters. At the end of December censorship was introduced of all disclosures concerning the UN Order of Battle. Western correspondents introduced private codes to evade this. The Eighth Army asked for a press blackout on the UN evacuation of Seoul until this was completed. The story was broken in the United States within hours by a correspondent who simply did not submit his copy for censorship. Restrictions on reporting were never, of course, enforced on the media outside the Korean peninsula.

The impetus of the Chinese advance could be sustained only into the new year of 1951 by the vast captures of arms and supplies on the drive south. Thousands of Chinese picked up new American weapons, learned to eat C rations, and handle some American heavy weapons. "We quickly got used to American biscuits and rice," said Li Xiu, a regimental propaganda officer with the 27th Corps, "but we never cared for tomato juice. We were particularly glad to get carbines, because we found rifles so heavy to carry. Without the American sleeping bags and overcoats that we captured, I am not sure we could have gone on. Two thirds of our casualties were from the cold that winter, against one third from combat. The main problems were always—how to avoid American planes and artillery, and how to catch up with the Americans in their trucks."[13]

"The chief problem was to gather all the prisoners," said Li Hebei of the 587th Regiment. "On New Year's Day, an order was issued for our troops to compete to see which unit could collect most prisoners as a New Year gift for Chairman Mao. American prisoners at first didn't understand the 'lenient policy' of our volunteers toward them. But after a period of contact, they began to believe it. We gave them whatever we could offer to eat. One or two were very stubborn, and would not admit that their action was aggression. Because of our poor weapons and equipment, they didn't take us seriously. So we did some work to persuade them. We told them, 'The U.S. is far from Korea, but the Yalu River is the border between Korea and China. If you cannot accept this, let us settle it on the battlefield.' Always the problem was, how to win the battle with less advanced weapons than the enemy."[14]

For all the shame and humiliation of the precipitous American flight from North Korea in the winter of 1950, the simple truth remains that the very speed of the retreat saved many units from annihilation, and left the Eighth Army with forces that could be rebuilt to fight another day. It was bitterly apparent that where the Chinese could catch American troops at that time, they could almost invariably defeat them. But American mobility was not entirely useless. It enabled many thousands of men, who would not otherwise have done so, to outrun their pursuers and escape to fight better another day.

Yet nothing could diminish the dismay both in Korea, and in the capitals of the West, about the performance of the Eighth Army in the retreat from the Yalu. After the winter battles, the British General Leslie Mansergh visited Korea and delivered a devastating secret report to the British Chiefs of Staff upon the situation that he discovered there.

"I doubt whether any British really think that the war in Korea will be brought to a successful conclusion. The reason for this is primarily because of the American lack of determination and their inability, up to the time of my visit, to stand and fight. Most Americans sooner or later bring the conversation around to an expression of the view that the United Nations forces ought to quit Korea. The British troops, although sympathetic to the South Koreans in their adversity, despise them and are not interested in this civil war. . . . I would judge the American morale as low, and in some units thoroughly bad. They appear to think that the terrain is unfavourable for American equipment and methods. . . . It must be remembered that many thousands of the Americans joined the Army for the purpose of getting a cheap education after their service and that they, at no time, expected to fight. Their training is quite unsuited to that type of country or war and, in spite of lessons learnt, they will not get clear of their vehicles. . . . Their rations, supplies, and welfare stores are on such a scale as to be comic if they were not such a serious handicap to battle. . . . Regular American officers have been a high proportion of those lost. As a result, the problem of replacement of men with experience is becoming very difficult. . . .

"They have never studied or been taught defense. They appear only to have studied mechanised and mechanical advances at great speed. They do not understand locality defence in depth or all-round defence. They do not like holding defensive positions. They have been trained for very rapid withdrawals. Americans do not understand infiltration and feel very naked when anybody threatens their flank or rear."[15]

Mansergh expressed respect for American artillery, whose gunners the British had also found more courageous than the infantry, and for the performance of the U.S. Marines. But he was highly critical of the staff work within the Eighth Army:

"They do not understand the importance of reconnoitring ground. Units in action almost invariably overestimate the enemy against them, the casualties inflicted, and the reasons for their rapid withdrawal; this I have known in our own units in war, but it appears worse here and more frequent. At night, main headquarters blazed like gin palaces. . . . Roadblocks, car parks, dumps etc. were as crowded as Hampstead Heath on a bank holiday."[16]

Mansergh summarized his conclusions about the problems of the U.S. Army in Korea: "a) training on wrong lines b) bad staff organisation c) low quality infantry d) disinterest in the war in general e) weak and inexperienced commanders at all levels." The general's views must certainly have been influenced by those of Brigadier Basil Coad, commanding the British 27 Brigade in Korea since September. Coad at about this time submitted an unhappy report of his own, citing the lack of liaison with American higher commanders and the general inadequacy of direction: "Since the withdrawals started, the behaviour of some senior staff officers and Formation HQs was, at times, quite hysterical and resulted in the issues of impossible orders which, if obeyed without question, would have resulted in unnecessary loss of life. American commanders frankly tell me that they have never taught defence in any of their military schools. The American soldier does not like being attacked, especially at night, and with exceptions will not stand and fight. I think their [the British contingent's] attitude to the American infantry is largely one of contempt."[17]

"Standards of discipline in the U.S. Army in Korea, never very high, are now lower than I have ever known them," wrote the military assistant to the British Ambassador that December. "Officers told me quite openly that it is useless ordering their troops to attack, because they simply won't go. The U.S. Army is still roadbound, and it is very difficult to describe their tactics, since it seems that tactics in the normal sense of the word do not exist. In an advance, motorised columns headed by a few tanks are sent up the roads making use of what is described as 'prophylactic fire.' This seems to consist of everyone who has a weapon blazing away on either side of the column into the blue."[18]

In assessing the justice of these British opinions, it is necessary to make some discount for the chronic skepticism of one nation toward another's methods of making war. Throughout the twentieth century there has been a measure of jealousy in the British Army, traditionally accustomed to fight with scanty means, toward the vast weight of resources available to the Americans. Yet the evidence of such able American professionals as John Michaelis and Paul Freeman supports the British view of U.S. performance in the winter of 1950. Matthew Ridgway himself, on his arrival, wrote of the remarkable difference between the demeanor of the American and British troops under his command. A problem that was already familiar from World War II reasserted itself in Korea, as it would again in Vietnam: the disproportionately low percentage of the nation's best manhood that served the infantry regiments of the United States.* Because the American instinct for war favors a technological, managerial approach, far too many of the ablest men are diverted to technical and managerial functions. At the time of Korea, indeed, overwhelmingly the most talented section of America's young manhood remained in colleges at home, as a result of the workings of the Selective Service Act. Yet in this war as in every war, it was upon the infantry that the greatest burden of battle, and of casualties, fell. As in America's other major Asian war a generation later, terrain and the circumstances of the enemy made it difficult to employ technology and firepower anywhere near as effectively as upon a European battlefield against a European enemy. From beginning to end in Korea, the United States Army labored under grave disadvantages in fitting itself to meet the enemy on favorable terms.

"It is well-nigh impossible for any man to retain a vision of United Nations action in Korea as a great and essential experiment in international relations [wrote a British correspondent on December 27 in a private report to the War Office in London] should he be subjected for long to the atmosphere of Korea. Inefficiency and squalor among the civil population make some contribution to the overall feeling of disillusionment. But the major fault lies with the morale of the armed forces. Men of the United States Army so completely dominate the scene, numerically, that their attitude is all-important. It can be very simply expressed: 'How soon can we get t'hell out of this goddamn country?' That is the one question in the minds of every GI and almost every officer up to the rank of colonel encountered in Korea. Half has no thought beyond the single objective of escape. Of the remainder, a few felt that crossing the 38th Parallel was a mistake, either

---

* This problem is discussed at more length in the author's *Overlord: D-Day and The Battle for Normandy* (London and New York, 1984).

tactical or moral. But far more took the view that the United States should stop consulting anybody, and should use the atomic bomb. They did not wish it employed against the North Koreans, or even, to any great extent, against the Chinese Communists. Their emotional reaction to the whole problem was that the Russian is solely responsible, and that therefore the logical thing to do is to atom bomb Moscow. . . . Offensive thinking amongst junior officers and men was confined almost entirely to the Marines. It was prompted mostly by a drive for revenge for the losses inflicted on them at the Chosin Reservoir, and was accompanied by a distrust and contempt for higher leadership almost more frightening than the lack of fibre of their army compatriots. There can be few occasions in history when officers and men of a fighting force have expressed themselves so freely and violently, in public, on the subject of their commanding officers."[19]

"Dear Folks," Private First Class James Cardinal of the 3/5th Cavalry wrote home to his parents in the Bronx on January 7, 1950, "We are now about 60 miles NW of Taegu, holding a mountain pass thru which the entire 8th Army is moving headed south. It looks like the beginning of the end. The Chinese are kicking hell out of the U.S. Army, and I think we are getting out, at least I hope so. I think they are going to evacuate all UN troops from Korea soon, as it's impossible to stop these Chinese hordes. Theres just too many of them for us to fight in Korea. If the big wheels in Washington decide to fight here it will be the biggest mistake they ever made, as I don't think we can hold the Chinks. Anyway, lets hope they decide to evacuate us.

"When you get complaining and bitching letters from me, remember every soldier over here feels that way. The troops over here are mad, mad at America, Americans and America's leaders. We all feel we've been let down, by our incompetent blundering leadership, from the White House down. It seems to me to be—to hell with the troops in Korea. If we must fight communism, let's do it in Europe which is the cradle of western culture and our own civilization. It seems to me that's more worth fighting for than some barren oriental wasteland, with uncountable hordes of savage warriors. It's about time that all of you back home awakened to the truth of the matter, and let your voices be heard thru letters to your congressmen. That's the only way to get direct action. Well, folks, that's all for now. I'm in the best of health and spirits and hope that you all and the rest of the family are too. Love, Jimmy."[20]

The American Army had reached its lowest point of the Korean War. Corporal Robert Fountain, late of Task Force Smith, gazed around the schoolhouse at Chonan in which he found himself sheltering in the depths of the retreat, and recognized the very same building in which he had taken shelter in July, in the midst of the first traumas of the war. It was too much to bear: "We had fought all the way south, and all the way north. I thought—'Look what we have suffered, and we are back where we began. I have nothing in this country, and I never will.'"[21] Corporal Fountain was not alone in his dismay. Defeat on the battlefield had also provoked a crisis of confidence among statesmen and politicians at home which now threatened, for a time, to escalate the Korean War into a nuclear conflict.

Washington and Tokyo

On the morning of November 28, Truman told his personal staff in his office at the White House, "General Bradley called me at 6:15 this morning. He told me a terrible message had come in from General MacArthur. . . . The Chinese have come in with both feet." This was the day, he wrote later, "when the bad news from Korea had changed from rumors of resistance into certainty of defeat."[22]

At a meeting of the National Security Council later that day, the President, Marshall, and the Joint Chiefs agreed that all-out war with China must be avoided. Acheson said he believed that if the United States bombed China's airfields in Manchuria, the Russians would come into the war. Yet none of this caution prevented Acheson from denouncing Peking's action the following day as "an act of brazen aggression . . . the second such act in five months. . . . This is not merely another phase of the Korean campaign. This is a fresh and unprovoked aggressive act, even more immoral than the first." Dean Rusk declared, at the November 28 meeting of the National Security Council, that the Chinese intervention "should not be on our conscience, since these events are merely the result of well-laid plans, and were not provoked by our actions." To a remarkable extent, Washington still failed to consider exclusively Chinese motives for intervention and focused upon Russian reasons for inciting Chinese action and the new interpretation that must be placed upon Moscow thinking. The CIA predicted that the Russians would give the Chinese maximum support. Bedell Smith said there was now "a much better case than they previously thought for believing Russia plans for war soon. . . . They probably do not plan on war now, but are willing to have it if they can bog us down in Asia."[23]

MacArthur now issued a desperate plea for reinforcements. But Frank Pace, the Army Secretary, said that the only available unit was the 82nd Airborne Division. MacArthur again demanded to be allowed to use men of Chiang Kai Shek's Nationalist Army. His request was again refused. He also wanted more air and sea power, and some additional forces were dispatched. All the senior soldiers were now increasingly bitter about the political restriction upon bombing beyond the Yalu. Bradley wrote on December 3: "We used to say that an attack on a platoon of United States troops meant war. Would anyone believe that now if we don't react to the Chinese attack?"[24] No one wanted war with China, he said, but if the Eighth Army was driven out of Korea, the United States should retaliate by hitting China's cities.

In Tokyo, from the first moment of the Chinese intervention, MacArthur issued a flood of bulletins and statements which drifted further and further from reality as each day went by. First, he declared that his own drive to the Yalu had forced the Chinese hand, interrupting plans for a grand Communist offensive which would have been disastrous for the United Nations. He rejected utterly the suggestion that his forces were engaged in a retreat. He castigated "ignorant" correspondents for their inability to distinguish between a planned withdrawal and a "full flight." His flights of Olympian rhetoric contrasted ever more grotesquely with the reality of what was taking place within his command: "Never before has the patience of man been more sorely tried nor high standards of human behavior been more patiently tried and firmly upheld than during the course of the Korean campaigns." He cast direct blame upon the Administration in Washington for imposing restrictions upon bombing and military operations beyond the Yalu— "an enormous handicap, without precedent in military history."[25] Harry Truman wrote, "Now, no one is blaming General MacArthur, and certainly I never did, for the failure of the November offensive. . . . But . . . I do blame General MacArthur for the manner in which he tried to excuse his failure."[26]

When the British General Leslie Mansergh met MacArthur in Tokyo at this period, he found him intensely emotional:

"At these times, he appeared to be much older than his seventy years. . . . Signs of nerves and strain were apparent. . . . When he emphasised the combined efforts and successes of all front-line troops in standing shoulder to shoulder, and dying if necessary in their fight against communism, it occurred to me that he could not have been fully in the picture. I cannot believe he would have made these comments in such a way if he had been in full possession of facts which I would inevitably learn later, facts that some Americans had been far from staunch. It occurred to me then, and was emphasised later, that the war in Korea is reproduced in Tokyo with certain omissions of the more unpalatable facts."[27]

And if MacArthur was prey to powerful private delusions about what was taking place within his command, he was also entering the most perilous political waters with his public statements about the course of things to come. His enigmatic comments, when questioned by a magazine interviewer about the desirability of employing the atomic bomb, left nothing to the imagination:

"Question: Can anything be said as to the effectiveness or ineffectiveness of the bomb in the type of operations in which you are now engaged?

"Answer: My comment at this time would be inappropriate.

"Question: In the type of warfare now going on in Korea, are there large enough concentrations of enemy troops to make the bomb effective?

"Answer: My comment at this time would be inappropriate."[28]

But if MacArthur was alone in reflecting aloud about the possibilities of employing atomic weapons, he stood among a large company within the military who were privately thinking furiously about the possibilities. On November 20, J. Lawton Collins told colleagues that it was conceivable that the JCS would be called upon to present views about the possible use of atomic weapons.

Then, at a press conference on November 30, President Truman allowed himself to be trapped into making a statement on the atomic bomb which reverberated around the world, caused consternation among America's allies, and whose repercussions were never entirely stilled for the remainder of the Korean War. Truman declared that the United States would take "whatever steps are necessary to meet the military situation." A reporter inquired, "Will that include the atomic bomb?"

Truman said, "That includes every weapon we have."

"Mr. President, you said, 'every weapon we have.' Does that mean that there has been active consideration of the use of the atomic bomb?"

"There has always been active consideration of its use. . . ."

Among America's allies, above all in Europe, unease had been mounting for many months about developments across the Atlantic. The stridency of conservative Cold War rhetoric, the rise of McCarthy, increasing fears in government circles, prompted by diplomatic reports from Tokyo, about the extravagances of MacArthur, coupled with the Administration's inability to control him, had combined to create the gravest unease about the course on which the United States might be headed. For the most part, real fear of what the Russians might attempt, coupled with nervousness about any statement that might encourage American isolationism—above all a possible American retreat from Europe—encouraged discretion in Allied public statements about Washington policy. The British had never been enthusiastic about the commitment to Korea. Henceforward, they were the most reluctant partners in the war. As early as November 13 the Cabinet's OS Committee reported its view "that it was no longer practicable, without risking a major war, to attain the original objective of occupying the whole of North Korea and placing it under a UN regimen. They were doubtful whether the UN forces could reach the northern frontier without making air attacks on targets in Manchuria, and even if the frontier could be reached, it would be a difficult task to hold it along a line of about 450 miles in mountainous country. Korea was of no strategic importance to the democratic powers; and further operations there should now be conducted with a view to preventing any extension of the conflict and avoiding any lasting commitment in the area. The Chiefs of Staff favour shorter lines along the 40th Parallel."[29]

Truman's statement of November 30, publicly declining to exclude the nuclear option in Korea, provoked the British to new ecstasies of uncertainty. In a debate that evening in the House of Commons, Foreign Secretary Ernest Bevin made it apparent that he had no clear idea of American intentions toward China, or indeed of any change in American policy in the Far East. The Tory front bencher R. A. Butler said, "I want to come immediately to some circumstances which have arisen this evening, and which have caused many of us great concern and anxiety. . . . I want to express, at any rate on my own behalf, and I believe on behalf of a great many other Honorable Members, my very great disquiet . . . the horror that many of us would feel at the use of this weapon in circumstances which were not such that our own moral conscience was satisfied that there was no alternative."

Attlee, the Prime Minister, expressed his wholehearted sympathy and agreement with Butler. Even Churchill, whom no one had accused of lack of zeal in the confrontation with communism, declared in the House of Commons, "The United Nations should avoid by every means in their power becoming entangled inextricably in a war with China. . . . The sooner the Far Eastern diversion . . . can be brought into something like a static condition and stabilised, the better it will be. . . . For it is in Europe that the world cause will be decided. . . . It is there that the mortal danger lies." Attlee concluded the debate by announcing that he proposed himself to fly to Washington to meet the President.

If Britain was always the most junior of partners with the United States in the struggle to defend South Korea, in 1950 she also remained indisputably the second non-Communist power on earth, the most important ally of the United States. Attlee's meeting with Truman in December 1950 provided both sides with an important opportunity to articulate their private convictions about the state of the global confrontation. As had been the case since the Korean War began, British views were deeply colored by fear that American strategic attentions were being diverted from Europe toward the Far East. The British were also profoundly opposed to direct confrontation with China, with their own vital trade interests in the Far East. Attlee came to Washington as "more than the spokesman of the United Kingdom and even the U.S.A.'s allies in NATO." He also represented "the fears and doubts of all the states which had supported the original decision by the UN to resist the North Korean attack."[30] Truman, meanwhile, came to the conference table as leader of an Administration which was even now suffering humiliating defeat upon the battlefield, and which stood beleaguered by its political critics at home. Senator McCarthy was demanding the resignations of Acheson and Marshall and threatening impeachment proceedings against the President. Attlee's very coming provided new ammunition for Truman's Republican critics, for it provided new evidence of the unwelcome influence of enfeebled Europeans upon American policy, the very force that they alleged had done so much to "lose" China for the United States. Even had Washington been immersed in torrential downpours, the British were wise to arrive with no umbrellas at the airport.

The discussions that began on December 5, and included both British and

American Chiefs of Staff, were held under the shadow of real fear that the United Nations might be compelled to evacuate the Korean peninsula. One of Field Marshal Sir William Slim's first questions to the American delegation was whether MacArthur had been ordered to withdraw. Marshall told him that no such order had been given, but that the Supreme Commander had been told that "the security of his command is his first consideration." Probably the chief significance of the discussions was the reassurance that Attlee gained from Truman, that the United States was *not* actively considering the employment of nuclear weapons in Asia. Much discussion also centered upon British economic and financial difficulties in sustaining their program of rearmament, which Washington strongly supported. At this time the United States possessed an extraordinary proportion of the world's stockpile of vital metals and other strategic materials. The British made it clear that, without greater access to this, their defense buildup could not continue.

Sir Oliver Franks, the British Ambassador in Washington whose close friendship with Acheson made him a key participant in the talks, believed that the Administration never seriously considered the use of nuclear weapons in Korea. In this he may have underestimated the pressures that would have closed in upon Truman had the Americans been driven out of Korea with heavy loss. And even Franks, like Attlee, acknowledged fears about what the Americans might do "if their backs were to the wall. There was a fear of the consequences of hot pursuit into China, or bombing across the Yalu. There was a fear that War, with a capital W, might break out in the Far East. The last thing that we wanted to see was the United States getting bogged down with China, because we saw no end to it."[31]

The most interesting feature of the discussions was the clarity with which they emphasized the differing British and American attitudes to Communist China. The British pressed their view that all-out war with China must be avoided at all costs. They remained convinced that Communist access to China's UN seat must be held out as a possible negotiating card with Peking. This the Americans strenuously resisted. Acheson asserted that "in his view, the central moving factor in this situation was not China but Russia. Some promise of support must certainly have been given by them before the Chinese intervened. There would not be many who would advise the President to embark upon an all-out war with China on land, sea, and air. But on the possibility of negotiations, they were far less optimistic. . . . This was the very worst moment at which we could seek to negotiate with the Communist forces in the world." Acheson, traditionally the Europeanist, sharply reminded the British at the Washington meetings of the United States' global responsibilities, and made plain his belief that the British position toward China was founded upon self-centered political and commercial considerations. If the U.S. gave up now in the Far East, "we are through. The Russians and the Chinese are coming in, and other Far Eastern peoples would make their best terms with them."

The Americans agreed that it was doubtful whether MacArthur's army could hold on in Korea. They would willingly settle for a cease-fire based upon the restoration of the prewar position, but saw no real prospect of attaining this. Truman said that he wished it to be on record that he could not agree to voluntary withdrawal from Korea: "We must fight it out. If we failed, we should at least fail honorably."

Attlee replied sturdily that the British would stand shoulder to shoulder with the Americans in the bridgehead. But he then turned to the much more contentious issue of China. He believed that Britain and the United States had different appreciations of the new China. It was a mistake to think Peking the pawn of Moscow. Western policy should be to detach the Chinese from the Russians. The West could look with considerable satisfaction upon other societies whose nationalist aspirations had been indulged—India, Pakistan, Burma. Acheson declared that he agreed with Attlee's overview, but could not see how it helped to determine an immediate policy. When the British expressed their concern for the risk to their interests in Hong Kong, Malaya, and Singapore if the Chinese mainland was attacked, Bradley inquired sarcastically whether a Chinese attack on Hong Kong would mean war when it was not considered war for the Chinese to attack American troops in Korea. Field Marshal Slim asked whether a limited war against China would be likely to provoke the invocation of the Sino-Soviet Friendship Treaty. Marshall said that it would, and Truman acknowledged his concern about this possibility. Slim remarked that if the Soviet Air Force intervened in the war, "we should have to say good-bye."

At a session following dinner at the British Embassy on December 7, the vexed question of MacArthur was raised, and Attlee voiced British anxieties. Truman agreed that some of the Supreme Commander's statements had been unfortunate. Acheson said there were two questions: "First, whether any Government had any control over General MacArthur, a point on which he desired to express no view; and secondly, the question of what arrangements should be made for consultation in future." Marshall declared that wars cannot be run by committee. Yet the British were determined to emphasize their misgivings about direct military action against China. Their greatest cause for concern when they left Washington after the summit was that they seemed "not to have convinced the Americans of the need to make a serious effort to reach a political settlement with the Chinese, and not to have shaken them in their intention to undertake some form of 'limited war' against China."[32]

As from the beginning of the war, the chief British motive for supporting America in Korea continued to be fear that if she did not do so, America's sense of betrayal by her Western allies might have disastrous political and strategic consequences for Europe. It was not that the British did not sincerely share Washington's dismay at North Korean aggression—merely that they feared that the political and military costs of preserving Syngman Rhee's shoddy dictatorship in South Korea were in danger of exceeding any possible gains. This apprehension would persist to the end of the war.

On the American side, President Truman and his advisers clearly perceived, as much of the American public did not, that the legitimacy of U.S. policy in the Far East rested heavily upon maintaining the concept that a wider cause and greater principles than mere U.S. national interest were being contested in Korea, and were being upheld by a family of nations. If Attlee and his delegation failed to gain many explicit assurances in Washington, certain implicit understandings were achieved: above all, that Britain and other major allies would be consulted before any major step was taken to expand the war. This concession to British sensitivities, as it became known in the upper reaches of the U.S. military, caused disgust at the Dai Ichi and among higher commanders who believed the moment had come for a showdown with communism. It was knowledge or suspicion of what had been said between the British and American governments in Washington in December 1950 that sowed the seeds of belief in an Anglo-American conspiracy against MacArthur in the MacArthur camp during the crisis of the following spring.

The British delegation might have returned to London in less tranquil spirits had they been aware that, even if the President had not lied to them, he had certainly not disclosed the extent of American nuclear contingency planning. Since mid-November the Army Plans and Operations Division and the Joint Strategic Survey Committee had been conducting studies about the possible use of nuclear weapons in Korea. On November 28, Plans and Ops recommended that the armed forces should ensure their readiness to make "prompt use of the atomic bomb . . . as, if and when, directed by the President." On December 7, Acheson correctly predicted that the British would demand consultation on any planned American use of nuclear weapons. He recorded that he would promise to move "in step with the British . . . but will agree [to] nothing that will restrict his freedom of action."[33] As the Chinese entered Pyongyang, the Joint Chiefs dispatched a memorandum to all commands giving their view "that the current situation in Korea has greatly increased the possibility of general war. Commanders addressed should take such action as is feasible to increase readiness, without creating an atmosphere of panic."[34] Throughout December and into the New Year, a ground swell of opinion within the United States demanded that the country's armed forces should no longer be compelled to endure punishment at the hands of the Communists if this could be prevented by the ultimate expression of American technology, the atomic bomb. The national commanders of the four largest veterans' organizations petitioned the President to use "such means as may be necessary" to check the Communists.[35] On December 24, MacArthur submitted a list of "retaliation targets" in China and North Korea, requiring twenty-six atomic bombs in all. He requested four bombs for use against

Communist forces in North Korea, and four on "critical concentrations of enemy air power." The remainder were destined for enemy installations and industrial concentrations.[36] Such politicians as Senator Owen Brewster and Congressman Mendel Rivers pointed out publicly how effectively the atomic bomb had been used against the Japanese.

Yet if Truman and his advisers had talked very toughly to the British about their refusal to concede defeat as the price of a cease-fire with the Chinese, they had also underlined the extraordinary change in American objectives in Korea brought about overnight by the Chinese intervention. In a few short days of battle and retreat, Washington had tacitly renounced any prospect of presiding over a unified, non-Communist Korean state. The Administration was now willing to consider a peace proposal based upon restoring the prewar status of Korea, divided at the 38th Parallel. This was a momentous change of heart, and one which proved entirely unwelcome when it became known at the Dai Ichi.

And if the Americans were often impatient of what they perceived as crude displays of self-interest by the British, in the aftermath of Attlee's visit, they brooded to considerable effect about what the British delegation had said. First, the British had cast some penetrating doubts upon the likely effectiveness of limited war with China. Nothing could be worse for the United States than to launch a blockade of the Chinese coast, or even a bombing offensive against industrial targets, only to find that these made no impact upon Peking's behavior. Acheson also declared at the National Security Council meeting of December 12 that the Anglo-American talks had emphasized how important a close relationship with Britain remained, "since we can bring U.S. power into play only with the cooperation of the British."

In the weeks following the departure of the British delegation, the domestic debate about policy in Korea raged with increasing bitterness in the United States, in both public and private forums. The Administration's standing with the electorate fell to unprecedented depths. A December 8 Gallup poll found 49 percent of respondents disapproving of Truman's leadership, and only 20 percent of those who had heard of Acheson thinking well of him. It was a paradox of the period that right-wing Republicans alternated between demands for all-out war with China and immediate withdrawal from Korea. A January opinion poll found 49 percent of Americans believed that the U.S. entry into Korea had been a mistake, and 66 percent considered that the U.S. should now abandon the peninsula. These confused responses would become wretchedly familiar a generation later in the midst of another Asian war. In 1950 they represented the impotent political thrashings of a public opinion unaccustomed to frustration of its will at home or abroad, to military defeat—least of all at the hands of a primitive people, or to the exercise of patience. Grass-roots America had only the dimmest perception of what was taking place in Korea, but it understood with disagreeable clarity that little glory or happiness was being won there. It was incomparably easier to understand the rhetoric of Republicanism, demanding that America's full might should be employed to bring the Asians to heel, than the uncertain pleading for restraint from the Administration. Why should the United States be called upon to exercise restraint, when the enemy was apparently displaying none?

It was in the hope of focusing public understanding on the importance and seriousness of what was taking place in Korea that Truman declared a state of national emergency on December 16. The Administration now believed that Korea could be held—following the return of General Collins, the Army Chief of Staff, from a fresh visit on December 8—and should be held. Kennan and Rusk recalled the defiant example of the British in 1940: to abandon South Korea now "would set a poor example of what it means to be a friend of the United States." Truman and his advisers had determined to resist the calls of the allies for an immediate cease-fire, and to resist any such resolution in the United Nations. They were determined that MacArthur's army must improve its military position, regain some lost ground, to be able to negotiate from reasonable strength. To appease world opinion, Washington felt obliged to take a desperate diplomatic gamble, supporting a United Nations resolution calling for an immediate cease-fire in Korea proposed by a clutch of Asian states on December 11. The Americans, who wanted no such thing, counted upon the Chinese rejecting it.

Fortunately for the Administration's hopes, the Chinese indeed dismissed the resolution, since it included no call for the removal of all foreign troops or for the withdrawal of the Seventh Fleet from Taiwan, or for the recognition of Peking at the UN. Washington now forced through its own resolution, against the deepest misgivings of Britain and the other allies, branding China an aggressor. Even such a moderate man as Bradley believed that, if the United States suffered the humiliation of military expulsion from Korea, she should retaliate with air attacks upon the Chinese mainland.

As the military position in Korea continued to deteriorate into the New Year, a growing divide became apparent between America's political and military leaders about possible responses. Admiral Sherman, consistently the most bellicose of the Joint Chiefs, demanded early in the New Year that America should stop equivocating and recognize a full state of war with China. On January 12 the Joint Chiefs recommended hitting China with "damaging naval and air attacks" if the Communists attacked American forces outside the Korean peninsula. They also favored sponsoring guerrilla action in China, allowing the Nationalists to invade the mainland, and "aerial reconnaissance" of Manchuria and the Chinese coast. If the UN did not agree, said Admiral Sherman, "the time had come for unilateral action by the United States." When Acheson and the National Security Council proved unenthusiastic, Bradley emphasized that the JCS were not advocating a large-scale invasion of the Chinese mainland. But he remarked that there was "heavy popular pressure for the United States to do something," unilaterally if necessary. Marshall took the point, but suggested that the United Nations would deteriorate into a mere forum for debate if the United States acted alone in Korea. Truman postponed any decision by referring back the whole subject of direct action against China for further study.

Then, through the last days of January and early into February, imperceptibly the mood began to shift in Washington. As it became evident that military disaster was no longer imminent in Korea, as the choices before the Administration became less stark, so passions cooled and the more dramatic options receded. State Department analysts argued strongly against the view that the Chinese intervention in Korea represented a Soviet buildup to a new world war. Washington was at last beginning to look much more closely at narrower, more nationalistic reasons for Chinese behavior. In the eyes of the "hawks," MacArthur notable among them, the change of mood in Washington represented a weakening of the American position, influenced by the feeble fears of the allies and, above all, the British. Yet the British might legitimately claim that events increasingly supported their interpretation of Chinese behavior. Acheson told Bradley, "We are fighting the wrong nation. We are fighting the second team, whereas the real enemy is the Soviet Union."[37] Increasingly, senior members of the Truman Administration and the State Department began to develop the view that would grow increasingly dominant in the months that followed: that the United States was fighting the wrong war against the wrong Communist power in Korea. On January 30, Peking attempted to get a letter through to the U.S. government, a gesture Marshall declared should be treated with "the utmost seriousness." CIA estimates of Chinese casualties suggested cause for growing concern in Peking. Washington began to adopt a more attentive attitude to straws in the wind that suggested possible Chinese interest in a cease-fire. On February 12, C. B. Marshall of the Policy Planning Staff suggested to Paul Nitze that stabilization in Korea would save "two sets of faces."[38] Acheson, more than any other man, may claim credit for having discouraged the President's most bellicose advisers, arguing constantly for further discussion and delay. A February 23 paper from the State Department summarized his arguments against any escalation or change of policy in the Far East:

"a) the capability of the Moscow-Peiping axis to inflict a decisive defeat upon United Nations forces if they make the decision to do so; b) the risk of extending the Korean conflict to other areas and even into the general war at a time when [the United States] was not ready to risk general war; c) the heavy additional drain on American manpower and resources without a clearly seen outcome of the effort; d) loss of unity among [America's] allies and in the United Nations in support of the Korean effort, and e) the diversion of additional United States effort from other vital requirements."[39]

*   *   *

It is easy to focus attention upon Washington and London's misjudgments in the winter of 1950–51 and to forget those of the other side. If, at the end of 1950, Peking had shown itself ready to negotiate a cease-fire based upon the *status quo ante* in Korea, Mao Tse Tung's government would have been in an overwhelmingly strong position to gain its seat at the UN and to divide America from its allies if Washington proved reluctant to negotiate. MacArthur was not alone in his hubris. Peking deluded itself that absolute military victory, the reunification of Korea under Communist rule, lay within its grasp. Between December and May, when repeated defeats at the hands of the UN gradually convinced the Chinese that total victory was not attainable, they showed themselves entirely intractable until their moment had passed and threw away a commanding political advantage. In December, as the first Communist power to inflict a great defeat upon the West, their worldwide prestige was at its zenith. Had they accepted a negotiated end to the struggle with their own armies victorious, China's military standing for a generation to come would have been immense. Instead, however, by continuing the war, they gave time for the West to reassert its own military might, to demonstrate that even the greatest peasant army could be repulsed and defeated. If Washington had made a devastating miscalculation in the autumn of 1950, by driving for the Yalu, Peking's error that winter was equally great, in reaching out for a victory beyond its powers.

Pragmatic considerations almost certainly weighed far more heavily than moral ones in bringing about America's decision against extending the war to China in the winter of 1950. There were grounds for overwhelming doubt as to whether bombing China, unleashing Chiang's Nationalists upon the mainland, or enforcing a blockade would have a decisive impact upon China's capacity to continue the war in Korea or upon the stability of Mao Tse Tung's regime in Peking. However, the exercise of any of these options would have created a real danger of Soviet intervention. If this took place, the Pentagon was doubtful whether American forces in the Far East could hold their ground, or even whether a third world war could be avoided. Any major initiative against China by the United States would cost Washington the support of the United Nations—more serious, that of the Western allies. President Truman and his advisers were scarcely enthusiastic about, or even satisfied with, the policy of waging a limited war for limited objectives, to which they became tacitly committed in the winter of 1950, after seeing imminent victory slip from their grasp. But their debate, and its conclusion, had a decisive influence upon the struggle with General Douglas MacArthur, which reached its climax three months later. For MacArthur attempted to pursue an argument about the war, and about its extension to China, which had been effectively concluded in Washington before the Supreme Commander made his belated play.

How close did the United States come, in the winter of 1950, to employing atomic bombs against the Chinese? Much closer, the answer must be, than its allies cared to believe at the time. If Truman and the fellow members of his Administration recoiled from bearing the responsibility for so terrible an act, America's leading military men, from the Joint Chiefs downward, were far more equivocal and seemed far less disturbed by the prospect. All those at the seat of power in Washington drew back from discussion of the nuclear option as the military situation in Korea improved. But had the Chinese proved able to convert the defeat of the UN forces into their destruction, had the Eighth Army been unable to check its retreat, and been driven headlong for the coastal ports with massive casualties, it is impossible to declare with certainty that Truman could have resisted the demands for an atomic demonstration against China. The pressure upon the politicians from the military leaders of America might well have become irresistible in the face of military disaster. The men who turned the tide on the battlefield in Korea in the first weeks of 1951 may also have saved the world from the nightmare of a new Hiroshima in Asia.

The Arrival of Ridgway

On the Korean battlefield, the United Nations entered the New Year of 1951 still losing ground, still in desperate straits. Yet more than a week earlier an event had taken place which was to have an overwhelming influence upon the transformation of the war in Korea. On the morning of December 23, General Walton Walker was driving from his headquarters to that of 27 Commonwealth Brigade. Walker, the doughty little hero of the Pusan Perimeter, was a weary, almost broken man. His quarrels with Almond, the collapse of his army, the knowledge that MacArthur was considering his replacement had reduced the morale of the Eighth Army commander and his staff to an ebb as low as that of their troops. At Eighth Army headquarters, officers spoke openly of evacuation as the only course and talked without shame of the need for every unit to have its "bugout route." Walker was indisputably a brave man. But he was not a clever one. He had given all that he could offer to the cause of the United Nations. Now an ROK truck turned across the road in front of his jeep. The general was thrown out in the collision and suffered head injuries from which he died on the way to the hospital.

General Matthew Ridgway was sipping an after-dinner highball at the home of a friend when he was summoned to receive a telephone call from the Army Chief of Staff, Lawton Collins. Walker was dead. MacArthur had asked for Ridgway to succeed him. To lull his companions' curiosity, Ridgway lingered drinking for a few minutes before driving home with his wife. The next morning, Saturday, he paid a brief call at the Pentagon to collect his papers, chat briefly with Sherman, Chief of Naval Operations, and left that night for Tokyo without an opportunity to see his family again. He arrived at Haneda airport just before midnight on Christmas Day. The next morning at 9:30 he called on MacArthur at the Dai Ichi. The Supreme Commander had no hesitation in expressing his enthusiasm for an attack on mainland China by the Nationalist Chinese as a means of relieving the pressure upon South Korea. He showed his acute concern at the "mission vacuum" in which he considered that the Army was operating while the politicians decided where they wanted to go. He painted a bleak picture of the military situation before assuring Ridgway of his support in whatever he decided to do: "The Eighth Army is yours, Matt. Do what you think best." At 4 P.M. that afternoon of December 26, Ridgway was shivering on the apron at Taegu, being met by the Eighth Army's Chief of Staff, General Leven Allen.

Matthew Bunker Ridgway was fifty-six. At the beginning of the Second World War he had been a lieutenant colonel in the Plans Division of the War Department, where he remained until 1942. He then became first assistant commander, soon commander of 82nd Airborne Division, which he led with distinction in the Sicilian and Normandy landings. In August 1944 he took over the XVIII Airborne Corps, which he commanded in the Ardennes campaign. He was regarded not only by his fellow countrymen but by their British allies as one of the outstanding American soldiers of the war. Had he, rather than Browning, commanded at Arnhem, the outcome of that operation might have been astonishingly different—or certainly less disastrous. He possessed almost all the military virtues—courage, brains, ruthlessness, decision. He made the grenade and field dressing on his shoulder straps familiar symbols, as much his own trademarks as Montgomery's beret or Patton's pistols. It has been cruelly but appositely remarked that Walton Walker's death, making possible the coming of Ridgway, was the salvation of the Eighth Army. It is difficult to overstate the importance of the contribution that Ridgway made to the United Nations' cause in Korea, and to the achievement of a tolerable outcome of the war.

Ridgway arrived on December 26 full of hope that with the Chinese impetus temporarily spent, he might be able to organize a rapid counteroffensive. But within a few hours, visiting his formations, "I had discovered that our forces were simply not mentally and spiritually ready for the sort of action I had been planning. . . . The men I met along the road, those I stopped to talk to and to solicit gripes from—they too all conveyed to me a conviction that this was a bewildered army, not sure of itself or its leaders, not sure what they were doing there, wondering when they would hear the whistle of that homebound transport."[40]

The new commander was dismayed to discover the lack of essential winter clothing and equipment, the poor food and lack of comforts available to the troops. "The leadership I found in many instances sadly lacking, and I said so out loud." Ridgway was unimpressed, to put it politely, by "the unwillingness of the army to forgo certain creature comforts, its timidity about getting off the scanty roads, its reluctance to move without radio and telephone contact, and its lack of imagination in dealing with a foe whom they soon outmatched in firepower and dominated in the air and on the surrounding seas."[41] He met the British General Leslie Mansergh and told him that "training was needed, and touched on the problem of pampered troops. I [Mansergh] said that all ranks felt the absence of information and were in a vacuum. He said he could tell me nothing, because he knew nothing except 'Stand And Fight.' "[42]

The transformation of the Eighth Army after the coming of its new commander astonished and profoundly impressed all those who witnessed it. "It was incredible, the change that came over the Americans and their discipline," said a British gunnery officer.[43] "They started to wash their vehicles, and things like that." Colonel John Michaelis of the 27th Infantry called it "magic, the way Ridgway took that defeated army and turned it around. He was a breath of fresh air, a showman, what the army desperately needed."[44] From the outset, Ridgway demanded a new attention to terrain, and the assessment of key features that must be defended. There would be a fresh focus upon defense—and attack—in depth, with unit flanks secured against infiltration. Above all, the army must get off the roads, must be willing to reach for and hold high ground—some British officers had been bewildered to see American units digging in to defend roadside positions at the base of prominent hills, where they were totally exposed to incoming fire. Ridgway was unimpressed by the performance of the corps and divisional commanders. He wrote to Collins in Washington, urging the need to awaken Americans both in government and across the land to what was taking place in Korea, the demand for "a toughness of soul as well as body." He had no patience with the preoccupation among the Eighth Army—and at the Dai Ichi—with evacuation of the peninsula. Ridgway did not believe this should be remotely necessary. The only contingency for which he was willing to prepare was withdrawal to a new Pusan Perimeter—but this one would be dug and prepared on an unprecedented scale. A senior engineer officer and thousands of Korean laborers were soon working day and night, creating a powerful defensive line in the southeast.

Ridgway—and soon MacArthur also—perceived the immense advantage of his own shortening supply lines, while those of the Chinese were now extended to the limits of their fragile logistics system. MacArthur told the British Brigadier Basil Coad on January 26 that on the Yalu the Chinese might be able to support a million men under arms, but at a line through Pyongyang this figure fell to 600,000; at the 38th Parallel, it became 300,000; forty miles south of Seoul, it became only 200,000. This was one of the Supreme Commander's less fanciful judgments. Prisoners were reporting that as much as 50 percent of the Chinese front-line length was afflicted by frostbite. "While we wished to continue to push the enemy, we could not open our mouth too wide," said Hu Seng of Marshal

Peng's staff. "China was unprepared for the new military situation created by the deep advance. We were now in a position where we could not continue to reinforce our army in Korea, because we could not supply more men." The Chinese offensive had exhausted its momentum. After inflicting a devastating shock upon the UN Command and the nations from which it was drawn, the initiative in the Korean War was once more about to change hands.

10

NEMESIS: THE DISMISSAL OF MACARTHUR

In December 1950, by a remarkable paradox, it became General Douglas MacArthur's purpose to persuade his political masters in Washington, not only that the war in Korea could not be won, but that the absolute defeat of the United Nations was imminent. To this end his headquarters launched a propaganda campaign of doom-laden pessimism. They exaggerated the numbers of Chinese troops now believed to be in Korea, or capable of being committed. They proclaimed their insistent doubts as to whether the UN armies could confront the Communists successfully. The Supreme Commander's belief that the war against the Communists in Korea should be extended across the border into China had become an obsession. In a long series of letters and cables, he pursued his argument with the Chiefs of Staff about the bombing of the Yalu bridges and beyond.

It will never be certain how far MacArthur's affronted personal hubris influenced his attitude to the Chinese, how far he became instilled with a yearning for crude revenge upon the people who had brought all his hopes and triumphs in Korea to nothing. But there can be no doubt that in the winter of 1950, the sense of destiny which had guided MacArthur from Corregidor, back across the Pacific, to the reconstruction of Japan, the salvation of South Korea and the landing at Inchon, now persuaded him that he should confront the power of Communist China. It seems probable that he did not consider it beyond his own powers to reinstate Chiang Kai Shek's Nationalist regime in Peking. Certainly, his enthusiasm for committing Nationalist troops in Korea in the largest possible numbers seemed to go beyond any direct military considerations in the peninsula. If Nationalist divisions were deployed in Korea in strength, if they could drive Mao Tse Tung's legions back to the Yalu, would not the momentum to allow them to go farther become irresistible? Given the strength of militant anti-Communist feeling in the United States, if the Chinese Nationalists got as far as the border of their own country, would not the pressure upon the Administration be irresistible, to allow them to reverse the "loss" of China, which had caused so many prominent Americans so much grief? "Brave, brilliant, and majestic," one of MacArthur's biographers, William Manchester, has written, "he was a colossus bestriding Korea until the nemesis of his hubris overtook him. He simply could not bear to end his career in checkmate."[1]

In an attempt to curb the extravagant statements emerging from the Dai Ichi, on December 6 Truman had issued his presidential order to all U.S. theater commanders warning them to exercise "extreme caution" in their public pronouncements and to clear all of these with the State or Defense Departments. But MacArthur continued his propaganda campaign, merely issuing his threats and demands "off the record" to correspondents. There was a real danger, he warned, that if he was compelled to continue the war under the present restrictions imposed by Washington, the evacuation of the entire peninsula would become necessary.

His play was called. On December 29 a new directive from the Joint Chiefs of Staff confirmed that he could expect no further major reinforcements, and that Washington remained convinced that Korea was the wrong place to precipitate a major war. MacArthur was called upon to maintain a front as best he could in "successive positions." If his armies were forced back to the Kum River, then the United States would indeed be obliged to preside over an evacuation. But the JCS reminded SCAP, somewhat limply, that "a successful resistance to Chinese–North Korean aggression at some position in Korea, and a deflation of the military and political prestige of the Chinese Communists would be of great importance to our national interest. . . ." In other words, MacArthur must continue to do his best with what he had, upon existing terms.

The general disagreed. On December 30 he dispatched a reply to Washington, bitterly protesting the flagging will for victory that he perceived in the Administration and the attempt to make himself a scapegoat for disaster. He made four demands of his own. First, for a blockade of the Chinese coast; second, for an onslaught on China's industrial capability for making war, by air and naval bombardment; third, for the reinforcement of the UN forces in Korea by Chinese Nationalist forces; fourth, for all restrictions imposed upon Chiang Kai Shek's forces to be removed, enabling them to launch direct attacks upon the Chinese mainland. This program, MacArthur declared, would not only save Korea but inflict "such a destructive blow upon Red China's capacity to wage aggressive war that it would remove her as a further threat to peace in Asia for generations to come."

Once again, amid acute dismay in Washington, MacArthur's proposals were rejected. The stakes in Korea, he was informed, had risen as high as the Administration intended that they should go. If the peninsula could not be held within the existing framework of UN operations, then it must be conceded to the Communists. MacArthur's tone toward Washington now became increasingly distraught. He accused the Joint Chiefs of crippling his authority and suggested that the morale of his men was suffering acute damage from "shameful propaganda which has falsely condemned their fighting qualities." This assertion alone suggested a disturbing measure of ignorance, or wilful fantasy, about events during "the big bugout." He spoke of "extraordinary limitations and conditions" imposed upon his own command, and ended with an Armageddonistic flourish: Eighth Army could hold, he said, "if overriding political considerations so dictate for any length of time up to its complete destruction."

Many years later, General Charles Bolté, Chief of Plans at the Pentagon, freely conceded the nervousness even the Joint Chiefs suffered in dealing with MacArthur: "We were all rather scared of him. When you considered what he had been. . . ."[2] Yet if, in the past, the Administration and the Pentagon had sometimes havered in their handling of MacArthur, they did so no longer. His threats and bombast received a response of exemplary dignity. A new JCS directive on January 12 reasserted American policy. The following day, in a personal letter, Truman sought to restore some heart to MacArthur for continuing the struggle in Korea. Even if the mainland was lost, he urged, the struggle might continue from the offshore islands. Even if evacuation became necessary, it would be made clear to the world that this "is forced upon us by military necessity, and that we shall not accept the result militarily or politically until the aggression has been rectified." MacArthur's credibility suffered a serious blow a few days later when Collins, Vandenburg, and Bedell Smith reported back to Washington after a tour of the front. They discovered the change of mood that Ridgway was already creating, the growing optimism that the line could be held. If Ridgway lacked the status of MacArthur, he was a battlefield soldier of great distinction. The new commander of the Eighth Army offered Washington hopes and judgments incomparably more acceptable than those emerging from Tokyo.

In one respect, however, MacArthur correctly perceived an undeclared, radical change of policy by the Administration. There was no longer either hope or expectation of achieving a unified non-Communist Korea. Washington's hopes now centered upon achieving sufficient military leverage to cause Peking and Pyongyang to negotiate upon the basis of a return to the prewar division of Korea. The United Nations' objectives from the spring of 1951 to the end in 1953 were plainly limited. At an acceptable cost in casualties to the Eighth Army, Ridgway's forces sought to kill sufficient Communists and defend sufficient real estate to secure peace.

That was all, and for many soldiers it was not enough. In the two years that followed it became progressively more difficult to define the war aims of the UN in terms comprehensible, far less acceptable, to the men on the line. Even many higher commanders never entirely came to terms with the new, undeclared circumstances. Month after month through 1951, even after the peace talks began, Army and Corps planners devised elaborate schemes for airborne or amphibious envelopments, for full-blooded thrusts to the Yalu. None was ever to be implemented.

Ridgway's achievement in the first weeks of 1951 was that despite all this, despite the political congealment that disgusted and infuriated the chief inhabitant of the Dai Ichi, Eighth Army's commander successfully motivated his beaten and battered forces to make important gains, and decisively to demonstrate their ability to turn the tables on the Chinese. The enemy entered the New Year with the very problem that so afflicted the UN two months earlier—a long and vulnerable supply line. Communist casualties had been enormous, not least from the winter weather. There were still believed to be some 486,000 Chinese and North Korean troops in the country, against around 365,000 under the flag of the United Nations. But the raw figures masked the immense UN superiority of resources, above all air power. The balance of advantage had shifted sharply away from the Communists.

The Eighth Army now undertook a series of cautious probes to test the enemy's mood. In mid-January the 27th RCT pushed north to Suwon without meeting significant resistance. There were no major Chinese formations more than a few miles south of Wonju. A second reconnaissance by the IX Corps on the twenty-second also found itself treading empty space. On the twenty-fifth, Ridgway launched a more ambitious operation on a two-division front. The Chinese Thirty-fifth and Fiftieth Armies fell back, offering only sporadic resistance. By February 9 the ruins of Inchon and Suwon were back in UN hands, and a fine attack by the 25th Division had seized Hill 440, north of Suwon. Ridgway's men lost just 70 killed, while they counted over 4,000 dead Chinese on the battlefield. The I Corps pushed steadily onward to the line of the Han River.

Farther east, there were now two weeks of much heavier switchback fighting. An advance by X Corps was met by a counterattack against three ROK divisions on February 11. The Americans were forced to give ground in order to hold their line. In mid-February there was a fierce battle for the town of Chipyong-ni, where the 23rd Regiment of 2nd Division, under Colonel Paul Freeman, found itself encircled together with the French battalion. But they held on, sustained by air-dropped supplies. The Americans were vastly encouraged to see the effects of their firepower upon headlong night attacks by massed Chinese infantry, the awesome "human wave" technique. "We could see them tumbling down like bowling pins," wrote Corporal Pete Schultz, a machine gunner with the 1/23rd. "As long as the flares were up we never had trouble finding a target, and the flares also slowed the advance as the Chinese took what cover they could to avoid being seen. . . . As soon as it got light enough some Boxcars came flying in, and those beautiful parachutes with more supplies came falling down. I will never forget that sight. It was just beautiful. As it turned out, we did not need it. We had held, and tanks from 5th Cavalry Regiment broke through to our positions. The Chinese had left."[3]

The Chipyong-ni battle represented not only a fine performance by American units but also an important stage in the rehabilitation and revival of the morale of the 2nd Division, which had been so desperately mauled at Kunu-ri. After a week of hard fighting, in which North Korean forces broke through close to Chechon, exposing the X Corps flank, the Communist offensive ran out of steam. It was a decisive moment of the war, of incalculable importance to the spirits of the UN forces. They had confronted the strongest offensive that the Chinese could throw against them, and they had driven it back. Formations that only a few weeks earlier possessed no thought beyond escape from Korea on any terms now found renewed energy and will. The "gooks" could be beaten. Americans had done it once, they would do it again. A British observer, Air Vice-Marshal C. A. Bouchier, reported exultantly to London, "The myth of the magical millions of the Chinese in Korea has been exploded. In the last United Nations offensive, the Americans have learned how easy it is to kill the Chinese, and their morale has greatly increased thereby."

Ridgway's army jumped off on the next phase of his advance, Operation Killer, on February 21. By March 1 they had closed up the UN line south of the Han, driving back the Chinese with huge casualties, by the progressive, massive use of firepower. The advance of the seven American divisions now in the line was the twentieth-century successor to the Roman "tortoise": instead of long columns, exposed to surprise attack, Ridgway's units now deployed at every stage for all-around defense in depth, securing themselves against infiltration while they waited for the massed artillery and air strikes to do their work upon the Chinese positions. On March 7 Killer was succeeded by Ripper, a measured advance to a new phase line, Idaho, on the central front. Ridgway successfully dissuaded MacArthur from providing his customary signal to the enemy of an impending offensive by visiting the front to be photographed "firing the starting gun" with the formations involved. The envelopment of Seoul by the success of Ripper made the Communist evacuation of the capital inevitable. On March 14 the victors recovered a devastated city, a metropolis of ruins and corrugated iron in which, of the principal buildings, only the Capitol and the railway station survived. An attempted airborne envelopment of the retreating enemy by the 187th RCT at

Munsan—the only major operation of its kind during the war—was unsuccessful. Another disappointment was the extraordinary escape of the North Korean 10th Division, which had been fighting since January in the south of the country as guerrillas, far behind the UN lines. Now, perceiving the protracted shift in the strategic situation that was taking place, the 10th broke through the ROK lines near Kangnung to rejoin the Communist armies. The British General Sir Richard Gale reported to London, "The enemy has conducted his withdrawal methodically and with no little military skill. He knows how to make the best use of the terrain, both on large scale and on a minor tactical scale."[4]

In a shrewd letter to London on March 12, the British Military Attaché Brigadier A. K. Ferguson drew attention at a local level to difficulties which, at theater level, were precisely those which so irked General MacArthur:

"I foresee difficulties in maintaining morale indefinitely in present circumstances, in view of the ill-defined task set for the United Nations forces. You have no doubt heard of General MacArthur's remark of some months ago, when he said he was fighting 'in a political vacuum.' It seems to me that the reputed objective of UN forces in Korea which is 'to repel aggression and restore peace and security to the area' is much too vague under present circumstances to give the Supreme Commander in the field a military objective, the attainment of which would bring hostilities to a close. While it is outside my province to discuss the political issues, I consider the question of the maintenance of the morale of the troops to be a matter for serious consideration. For the past ten days, 'Operation Killer' has been conducted in Korea with the publicly pronounced intention of 'killing Communists.' While this no doubt gave the U.S. 8th Army a limited objective, it is neither a desirable nor lasting objective which will appeal to any educated individual. Already many British and American officers and other ranks have asked such questions as 'When will the war in Korea end?' 'When do you think the UN forces can be withdrawn from Korea?' 'What is our object in Korea?' Such questions tend to make me believe that, unless the British and American forces in Korea are given some definite goal at which to aim, the commander in the field will have the greatest difficulty in maintaining morale. I have only included British and American troops, because generally speaking the relatively small numbers of troops of other Western nations which are represented are adventurous mercenaries who are as content to serve as part of an international fighting brigade in Korea as elsewhere."[5]

But on March 27 another landmark was passed when the first UN troops—ROK I Corps—once more crossed the 38th Parallel. They took the town of Yangyang four days later. The Americans kept pace with them, driving north from Uijongbu. But this time there was to be no headlong race for the Yalu. Ridgway's objective was merely to reach the "Iron Triangle," south of Pyongyang, the heart of the

Communist supply and communications network. By April 9 the UN armies had reached line Kansas. Here, with their positions anchored upon the barriers of the Imjin River in the west and the Hwachon Reservoir in the center, they could pause and gather breath before embarking upon the next phase. The line from coast to coast had shortened to just 115 miles. In the days that followed, I and IX Corps pushed forward a few miles farther, and a new advance to line Wyoming was being planned. "We now had a tested, tough, and highly confident army," wrote Ridgway, "experienced in this sort of fighting, inured to the vicissitudes of the weather, and possessed of firepower far exceeding anything we had been able to use on the enemy heretofore. The only development that could possibly cause us to withdraw from the peninsula was, I felt sure, massive intervention by the Soviets. In the spring of 1951, such intervention was not altogether an impossibility."[6]

But the next move belonged not to Moscow, or the Eighth Army, but to Peking and Washington: Peking, where a massive spring offensive by nineteen Chinese armies was being prepared, in an attempt to undo all that Ridgway had accomplished in his astonishing four months in Korea, and Washington, where patience had at last expired with the dangerous military majesty of the Dai Ichi.

President Truman's dismissal of General Douglas MacArthur has been the subject of millions of words of narrative and analysis. It is unlikely that any important new evidence will emerge to alter historical perceptions of events in Washington and Tokyo in the spring of 1951. In a primarily military study of the war in Korea, it is redundant to rehearse once again much familiar detail. Here it is relevant only to summarize the arguments and the events that culminated in the Great Fall of April 11.

Ten months of crisis in Korea had exercised a powerful influence upon the domestic politics of the United States. They had witnessed the growing ascendancy of the right wing of the Republican Party, convinced that the United States faced a coordinated external and internal Communist conspiracy, of which North Korean aggression was merely one manifestation. Republicans found it intolerable to behold the spectacle of United States military power lurching ineffectually to maintain a tenuous grip in Korea against the Communist hordes. If their opposition to deep entanglement in European alliances was founded upon their dislike of the restraint that European liberals thereby sought to impose upon American foreign policy, their enthusiasm for a "forward policy" in the Pacific and the Far East assumed an American freedom of maneuver in the hemisphere which events in Korea seemed to deny. It was only five years since the United States had emerged from a war in which she triumphantly projected her huge power across five continents, and emerged with her primacy in world affairs apparently unchallenge-able. Yet now America seemed unable to impose her will upon a continent of tin-pot dictators and cotton-clad Communists. In the 1980s this frustration of power seems a commonplace. But in 1950–51 it was a repugnant revelation to much of the American people. It seemed intolerable that American boys should be suffering and dying in thousands in an odorous Asian wasteland, fighting a war with goalposts set by Pyongyang and Peking. Prominent Republicans such as Senator Taft demanded that America should fight for her interests in Asia upon terms that would enable her to use her vast technological superiority. Implicit if not explicit in much conservative rhetoric of this period was the conviction that American policy should not exclude the use of nuclear weapons, America's greatest technological advantage of all. The Republicans also exploited the charge that President Truman had acted unconstitutionally by sending American troops to Korea without the formal assent of the U.S. Congress.

The most conspicuous consequence of Senate pressure upon the Administration for a more vigorous brand of anticommunism was the commitment of hundreds of millions of dollars, and firm guarantees of American support, to Chiang Kai Shek's regime on Formosa. Dean Rusk declared, "We recognize the National Government of the Republic of China, even though the territory under its control is severely restricted. . . . We believe it more authentically represents the views of the great body of the people of China, particularly the historic demand for independence from foreign control. . . ." And matching the United States' new commitments to the anti-Communist cause in the Far East, four further divisions were dispatched to reinforce the U.S. Army in Europe.

But these developments of the Cold War were peripheral to the central debate, about what was to be done with America's hot war against communism in Korea. From Tokyo, MacArthur maintained constant pressure on the Administration to commit the United States to the defeat of communism in Asia. On February 13, MacArthur declared that "the concept advanced by some that we establish a line across Korea and enter into positional warfare is wholly unrealistic and illusory." He had now conceived a plan to cut off Korea from China by massive air attack. Even more ambitiously, he proposed to create an impassable boundary between the forces of communism and those of freedom by sowing a no-man's-land with radioactive waste. He discussed amphibious and airborne envelopments of enemy forces on a scale that would have dwarfed Inchon. "MacArthur believed even more deeply than before," wrote Courtney Whitney, one of those closest to his confidence, "that Red Chinese aggression in Asia could not be stopped by killing Chinese, no matter how many, in Korea, so long as her power to make war remained inviolate."[7] On March 7 at Suwon, MacArthur proclaimed loftily, "Vital decisions have yet to be made— decisions far beyond the scope of the authority vested in me as the military commander, but which must provide on the highest international level an answer to the obscurities which now becloud the unsolved problems raised by Red China's undeclared war in Korea."

Truman, in Washington, was making it clear both in public and in private that with the armies close to the line from which the war had begun, it was time to discuss a peace on these positions. MacArthur at once made clear his profound disagreement with the President's view by issuing his own statement. "The enemy," he said, "must by now be painfully aware that a decision of the United Nations to depart from its tolerant effort to contain the war to the area of Korea, through an expansion of our military operations to its coastal areas and interior bases, would doom Red China to the risk of imminent military collapse. . . . The Korean nation and people, which have been so cruelly ravaged, must not be sacrificed. This is a paramount concern. Apart from the military area of the problem where issues are resolved in the course of combat, the fundamental questions continue to be political in nature, and must find their answer in the diplomatic sphere. Within the area of my authority as the military commander, however, it would be needless to say that I stand ready at any time to confer in the field with the commander in chief of the enemy forces in the earnest effort to find any military means whereby realization of the political objectives of the United Nations in Korea, to which no nation may justly take exception, might be accomplished without further bloodshed."

A constant stream of propaganda now flowed out of the Dai Ichi, directed as much against the Administration in Washington as against the Communists. Above all, the general and his entourage were disgusted by the attitude of America's enfeebled and compromising allies. MacArthur's staff spread word of a conspiracy by the British to induce the United States to give Red China Chiang Kai Shek's seat at the UN. The constant refrain from Tokyo was that any truce, any botched-up compromise in Korea which left the Chinese militarily undefeated, would be a national disaster for the United States.

It was ironic that in this crisis between the civil and military power of the United States, President Truman and his close advisers found themselves in much closer accord with the governments of America's allies than with their own people. There is no evidence to support the view—later widely propagated in the Dai Ichi—that the British "conspired" with Truman—or, indeed, had a decisive influence upon his decision—to dispose of MacArthur. But they left no doubt of their fears about where his excesses might lead, and certainly strengthened the will of the Washington Administration to act. On April 9 that eminently sensible soldier Sir William Slim, Chief of the Imperial General Staff, presided over a meeting of the British Chiefs of Staff at which he said that "in his opinion, General MacArthur personally wanted war with China. . . . As he had proved in November and December last year, he had few scruples about colouring both intelligence and operational reports to suit his own ends. In present circumstances, it would be most inadvisable to delegate to the United States Joint Chiefs of Staff responsibility for deciding what constituted 'a massive air attack' [around the

Yalu]. They were scared of General MacArthur; his definition of the scope of air attack would be what they would work on, and this definition might well be coloured to suit his own wishes."[8]

In a long message about Anglo-American attitudes to Korea, the Foreign Secretary cabled to the British Ambassador in Washington, "Our principal difficulty is General MacArthur. His policy is different from the policy of the UN. He seems to want a war with China. We do not. It is no exaggeration to say that by his public utterances, he has weakened public confidence in this country and in Western Europe in the quality of American political judgement and leadership. Here we seem to have a case of a commander publicly suggesting that his policy is not the stated policy of his government, not subject to the control of his own government, and whom his own government is, nevertheless, unwilling and unable to discipline."[9]

No more. The fears and intense debates among the British and other allies about what was to be done about MacArthur were redundant when this cable was sent. Truman had already determined that MacArthur must be sacked: "I could no longer tolerate his insubordination." On April 5 a letter was read on the floor of the House of Representatives, from MacArthur to Representative Joe Martin, answering his request for the Supreme Commander's comments on Martin's demand that Chiang's Nationalists should be permitted to land on the mainland of China.

"It seems strangely difficult for some [wrote MacArthur] to realize that here in Asia is where the Communist conspirators have elected to make their play for global conquest, and that we have joined the issue thus raised on the battlefield; that here we fight Europe's war with arms while the diplomats there still fight it with words; that if we lose this war to Communism in Asia the fall of Europe is inevitable; win it and Europe most probably would avoid war and yet preserve freedom. As you have pointed out, we must win. There is no substitute for victory. . . ."

The yawning chasm between Washington and the Dai Ichi was now entirely apparent to the governments and peoples of the United States and her allies. Senator Wayne Morse remarked that the nation possessed two foreign policies, "that of General MacArthur and that of the President." There was open speculation in the American press about the general's possible recall, though Washington still doubted Truman's will to carry it through. "MacArthur Recall Ruled Out," headlined the *Washington Post*. "Reprimand Is Still Seen Possible." On Friday, April 6, Truman presided over a meeting of his closest advisers at the White House to discuss the future of General MacArthur. He did not tell them that he had already made the decision to dismiss his Supreme Commander. Averell Harriman said he believed that MacArthur had given ample grounds for his own removal two years ago by his high-handedness in opposing aspects of the Administration's occupation policy in Japan. Marshall opposed precipitate action and asked for time to consider. Bradley believed that MacArthur must go on the plain grounds of insubordination. Both he and Dean Acheson urged ensuring that the White House had the support of the Joint Chiefs of Staff before taking any action. But all the men in the room knew that the need for secrecy was paramount to prevent MacArthur's supporters, in Congress and the country, from mobilizing. At a second meeting later that morning, Truman asked Marshall to review all the messages that had passed between Washington and the Dai Ichi in the previous two years. The next day, Saturday, the five men met once more. Marshall declared that, having read the papers, he considered that he shared Harriman's view: that MacArthur should have been sacked two years earlier. Truman now asked Bradley to give him the recommendation of the Joint Chiefs on the issue by Monday.

At 2 P.M. on Sunday afternoon the Joint Chiefs met in Bradley's office at the Pentagon. After almost two hours' discussion, the Chiefs went up to the office of the Secretary for Defense. They gave Marshall their unanimous recommendation that MacArthur should be sacked ''on purely military considerations.'' It was Bradley who provided the simplest and best reason for MacArthur's sacking. SCAP had provided overwhelming evidence that he was ''not in sympathy with the decision to try to limit the conflict to Korea . . . it was necessary to have a commander more responsive to control from Washington.''

On the afternoon of Tuesday, April 10, the President and his advisers met once more to examine Bradley's draft of the order for MacArthur's removal and replacement by Ridgway, and to consider the press release by which the decision would be announced. It was decided that it should be broken to MacArthur at 10 A.M. on the twelfth, Tokyo time, 8 P.M. on the eleventh in Washington. But that evening of the eleventh, Bradley hastened to Blair House with disturbing tidings: there had been a leak. The Chicago *Tribune* would break the story of MacArthur's removal the following morning. It had become essential for the White House to rush its timetable. The order for MacArthur's relief went out on the Pentagon Teletype half an hour after midnight, Washington time, on April 11. The White House press corps was summoned to a press conference at 1 A.M. for a ''special announcement.'' On their arrival they were handed a copy of the President's order for MacArthur's relief, the announcement of Ridgway's promotion, and a statement from Truman:

''With deep regret I have concluded that General of the Army Douglas MacArthur is unable to give his wholehearted support to the policies of the United States government and of the United Nations in matters pertaining to his official duties. In view of the specific responsibility imposed on me by the Constitution of the United States, and of the added responsibility which has been entrusted to me by the United Nations, I have decided that I must make a change of command in the Far East. I have, therefore, relieved General MacArthur of his commands, and have designated Lieutenant General Matthew B. Ridgway as his successor.

"Full and vigorous debate on matters of national policy is a vital element in the constitutional system of our free democracy. It is fundamental, however, that military commanders must be governed by the policies and directives issued to them in the manner provided by our laws and Constitution. In time of crisis, this consideration is particularly compelling.

"General MacArthur's place in history is fully established. The Nation owes him a debt of gratitude for the distinguished and exceptional service which he has rendered his country in posts of great responsibility. For that reason I repeat my regret at the necessity for the action I feel compelled to take in his case."

From the perspective of thirty-five years later, respect for the political courage of Truman, Acheson, Marshall, and the others who perceived the need to limit the war in Korea and to sack MacArthur may make it hard to understand why so many Americans recoiled from the action of the Administration. Above all, perhaps, it can be difficult to grasp the lack of awe with which the atomic bomb was perceived by some Americans in those days. For a large part of the nation, it remained merely a weapon—a greater weapon than any other, perhaps, but nonetheless a legitimate instrument of American military power. Flight Lieutenant John Nicholls, a young RAF pilot who served in Korea with a U.S. Sabre squadron, was struck by the difference in attitude he perceived between that of his American comrades and that of Europeans toward the atomic bomb: "Americans seemed to take the view that it was a weapon which was there to be used, if necessary. Yet we had been brought up with the view that it was there not to be used."[10] It is striking to observe how many senior American veterans of Korea, looking back thirty-five years, still believe that nuclear weapons should have been used to inflict outright defeat upon the Chinese. Colonel Ellis Williamson, G-3 of X Corps, was one of the soldiers in Korea who supported the nuclear option: "I favored using one bomb in one unoccupied area—say, the Punchbowl. Pop it off. Say to the Communists, 'Come off of this stuff and get out.' The Korean War was our first real national vacillation, the first evidence of the great decline in our will as a nation to make a real hard decision."[11] Colonel Paul Freeman said, "We should have knocked the Chinese out, whatever it took. My senior officers were certainly in favor of using atomic weapons. But some of the European nations were scared we were going to start something."[12]

Yet if views such as this were widely expressed in the middle and even some of the upper reaches of the U.S. Army, it is surely significant that America's most distinguished soldiers—her outstanding commanders of the twentieth century— were at one in their conviction that MacArthur had to go. Beyond Marshall and Bradley, Ridgway had very quickly wearied of the Supreme Commander's posturing and egocentric fantasies. The Eighth Army's commander was far too big a man to allow his historical judgment on MacArthur to be clouded by the promotion that he gained by his superior's fall. After Ridgway planned Operation Ripper, he was compelled to endure the spectacle of MacArthur flying into Korea on February 20 and announcing to the press that the new offensive was entirely his own conception and decision. Ridgway later wrote of his deep regret at the undignified manner of MacArthur's sacking. But he minced no words in his judgment of the Supreme Commander's plan for extending the war to China: "[It] entailed the very considerable risk of igniting World War III and consequent overrunning of Western Europe, with the loss of our oldest and staunchest allies sure to follow. . . . It was an ambitious and dangerous program that would demand a major national effort. . . . It is clear that the nation's top civilian and military leaders, using a wider-angle lens, with deeper sources of information on the atomic situation in the Soviet Union, and with more comprehensive estimates of the possible consequences of general war in Europe, had a much clearer view of the realities and responsibilities of the day."[13]

The dignity of Truman's action was marred by the clumsy haste with which it proved necessary to inform MacArthur to forestall a press leak. Just after 3 P.M. on the afternoon of April 11, a messenger delivered a personal signal for MacArthur to the Blair House, from Bradley in Washington. It announced his relief from all his commands, minutes after the news had been broadcast to the world. Reporters were already gathering at the general's gates. The calls of sympathy quickly began to flow in. MacArthur did not conceal his hurt, the anger at being "publicly humiliated after fifty-two years in the army."[14] Early on the morning of April 16, 1951, MacArthur flew out of Tokyo in his Constellation, bound for the United States, amid scenes of deep emotion among his staff and many Japanese, who still regarded him as their savior.

The circumstances of his return to America have passed into national legend: the ticker-tape parades, the address to Congress, the Senate hearings at which he sought to establish once and for all the justice and constitutionality of his actions. Among the press, from the beginning the *Washington Post, The New York Times,* the *Herald Tribune* and other liberal organs sided decisively with the President. But among ordinary people it was not only conservatives who felt a wave of revulsion against Truman for his action. Many Americans, with their instinctive emotional enthusiasm for a man larger than life, a national symbol, a hero, were bitterly grieved to see him brought low. Yet MacArthur himself, exalted by the warmth of his reception in his own country, failed to grasp its ambivalence. He believed that his prestige and the case he sought to argue were inseparably entwined. In reality, even many of those who cheered his passing through their cities had no stomach for embarking upon another great war, such as he believed necessary. If Truman's personal popularity was deeply wounded by his sacking of

MacArthur, in the months that followed it became apparent that only a minority of Americans doubted its constitutionality. Many grieved that MacArthur the man had been humbled, but few in the end doubted that Truman, the elected President, had been obliged to curb MacArthur, the general.

The shock and emotion in the United States about MacArthur's dismissal was in marked contrast to attitudes in Korea. Many senior officers had long since lost faith in SCAP's judgment. Even among junior ranks, his standing had never recovered from the disasters of the winter, for which so many men held him personally responsible. One UN officer wrote, "MacArthur's departure made as much impact on the soldiery as would have, say, the replacement of Scipio Africanus on a Roman outpost in the wilds of Mauretania."[15] In the same mood, Lieutenant Jim Sheldon of the 17th Infantry said, "MacArthur was too distanced from us for his going to make much impact. The only sort of thing we noticed was the food getting better after Ridgway took over."[16] Colonel Paul Freeman echoed the ambivalent attitudes of some senior officers who could not forget MacArthur's past great deeds: "I thought his sacking was disgraceful. Sure, he had it coming. He should have been relieved. But it should have been done in a dignified way. He was an actor and an egoist, but he had been a very great man." Colonel Ellis Williamson thought MacArthur's removal "absolutely necessary. I think the world learned a lesson—when you leave a man in a position of authority too long, he stops looking for ideas different from his first thoughts." Williamson added, in a moment of compassion common to thousands of Americans in Korea, "He was a pompous old bastard, but a great soldier." Almond's aide, Captain Fred Ladd, said, "I think he went out like he would like to have gone. How would it have been if he stayed, and eventually gone like Admiral Rickover, just told to retire because he was too old? This way, he went in a blaze of glory."[17]

The surge of relief at MacArthur's dismissal among most of the world's democracies served, if anything, to enhance the anger and strengthen the isolationist impulses of right-wing Americans. The President was compelled to console himself for the abuse he received at home with the enthusiasm his action inspired abroad. The British Ambassador in Tokyo gave an acid description of MacArthur's departure, "after a brief ceremony that, possibly appropriately, was marked by all the traditional discourtesy and casualness to the Diplomatic Corps to which we have become so used. . . . To me personally, MacArthur's departure is a tremendous relief as it is, I think, to nearly all my colleagues."[18] Many Asian newspapers welcomed the news: "Truman has earned the gratitude of all peace-loving peoples everywhere, by eliminating the greatest single opposition to peaceful efforts and policies in the Far East," enthused the *Civil & Military Gazette* of Pakistan. The British Ambassador in Paris reported that Premier Schuman "referred at once to General MacArthur's dismissal in terms of heartfelt thankfulness. . . . He had the impression that the United States Administration had almost lost control of the situation.''[19] Outside the United States, many Western newspapers greeted MacArthur's fall with something close to exultation. The general had deeply frightened the allies of the United States. They saw in his pronouncements the threat of nuclear war. The impunity with which he spoke suggested that he was a military commander so powerful that he might be capable of action beyond the control of the civilian power. Whether or not these fears were fully justified, they were sincerely held in Europe. The relief of MacArthur's departure was matched by pleasure at the succession to the Supreme Command of Ridgway, whose abilities and judgment commanded immense respect. General James Van Fleet, a wartime divisional commander under Eisenhower in the European theater, was appointed to direct the Eighth Army in Ridgway's place.

MacArthur's memory faded with remarkable speed in Korea. Ridgway proved to be all that was hoped as Supreme Commander. He took with him to Tokyo the military skills he had already displayed in full measure in the peninsula, and showed in addition all the discretion and political judgment that had so conspicuously eluded MacArthur. If Ridgway proved no more able than his predecessor to produce a magic formula for extricating the United States, and the United Nations, from the Korean morass, he nevertheless ensured that throughout his tenure of command no new crisis of authority developed between his headquarters and Washington. Ridgway was unyielding in his opinion that only a display of firmness on the battlefield could force the Communists to make peace. But he shared the Administration's conviction that Korea was not the theater in which to embark upon a major war. Civilian authority to determine policy in Korea was never challenged again.

Thus far, history has supported Truman's view of the Asian battlefield in 1951 rather than that of MacArthur. Some conservative writers continue to argue that, had the West displayed the will to achieve decisive victory in Korea—with or without the use of nuclear weapons—there need have been no war in Vietnam and communism could have been driven back across Asia. This seems highly doubtful. In Korea as in Vietnam, the United States showed itself militarily at a loss about the conduct of a war amid a peasant society. The will simply did not exist, in the United States and far less among her allies, to treat Kim Il Sung's act of aggression in Korea as a pretext for all-out war against Asian communism. And had it done so, it remains doubtful whether MacArthur's policy was militarily practicable, even with the support of nuclear weapons. If MacArthur had had his way, the cost to the moral credibility of the United States around the world would almost certainly have been historically disastrous.

Truman's greatest difficulty was that his own political authority was too weak to explain to his own people the realities of the new world in which they lived, where immense military power could not always be translated into effective foreign influence. Perhaps more than any other conflict in history, the outcome of

World War II could be claimed as a simple triumph of good over evil. Yet in 1951, only six years later, such clear-cut decisions already seemed obsolete. Americans were learning to come to terms with a world of constant crises, of problems chronically resistant to solutions. The finest minds in the Administration understood all this. But it was a wholly unwelcome message to convey to Middle America—or to such a man as Douglas MacArthur. It was Truman's misfortune that MacArthur chanced to be commanding in Tokyo when the Korean conflict began. The accident was compounded by the hesitancy and weakness with which Washington handled this Olympian figure through the months that followed. Inchon was indeed a masterstroke, but it was a perverse tragedy for MacArthur and those around him because its success prevented them from confronting the fact that his judgment was gone. He was too remote, too old, too inflexible, too deeply imprisoned by a world vision that was obsolete to be a fit commander in such a war as Korea. It was fortunate that his removal was eventually achieved before he could inflict an historic military, moral, or political disaster upon the West's cause in Asia.

Acheson and Truman endured phlegmatically the emotional scenes that followed MacArthur's recall. The Secretary of State told a story of a family with a beautiful daughter living just outside an army camp. Her mother worried constantly about her daughter's virtue, and nagged her husband incessantly about the perils to which she was exposed. One day the daughter came home in tears and confessed that she was pregnant. The father mopped his brow and said, "Thank God that's over."[20]

11

THE STRUGGLE
ON THE IMJIN

On Sunday, April 22, 1951, the new commander of Eighth Army, General James Van Fleet, held his first press conference. "General," a correspondent demanded, "what is our goal in Korea?" Van Fleet replied memorably, "I don't know. The answer must come from higher authority." Yet the most obvious goal of the United Nations forces—survival in the face of enemy assault—required no definition. That same Sunday the Chinese launched their fifth offensive of the Korean War. Eighth Army was well advised of its coming, and anticipated that the enemy's main attack would fall upon the center of the front in the Pakyong-Chunchon area, against the IX Corps. For three weeks the United Nations had been pressing cautiously northward with the intention of securing a line of commanding ground around the 38th Parallel—the "Kansas" line. The Chinese proposed to arrest the UN advance and throw Van Fleet's army back southward. Chinese prisoners declared that their commissars were promising the celebration of May Day in Seoul.

The 1st Marine Division in the so-called Iron Triangle between Chorwon, Pyongyang, and Kumhwa received two hours' tactical warning of the Chinese assault, which fell most heavily in the west against the 7th Marines, who were engaged a few minutes into the darkness of April 22. Their position deteriorated rapidly when the ROK 6th Division, on their left, collapsed and began streaming to the rear, impeding the advance of American supplies and reinforcements. The

Marines were compelled to hinge back their line, to cover the open flank to the west. By the morning of April 24 they had been obliged to give substantial ground. But they had broken the impulse of the Chinese advance and inflicted the usual huge casualties on the enemy's massed frontal assaults.

The gunners of the 16th New Zealand Field Regiment, who had been supporting ROK 6th Division, found themselves in a desperate position when the South Korean infantry broke in front of them. IX Corps insisted that the New Zealanders must continue to support the ROKs. But they gained permission to take a British battalion, 1st Middlesex, to protect their positions. For a few perilous hours the two units held their ground. Then, when it became apparent that the ROK collapse was irreversible, they were allowed to pull back down the Kapyon River. Here they were joined by the rest of 27 Commonwealth Brigade, brought out of reserve to fill the gap opened by the Koreans' precipitate departure. Between the nights of April 23 and 25 the three British, Australian, and Canadian battalions fought a fine defensive battle against repeated attacks by the Chinese 118th Division. For almost twenty-four hours the men of Princess Patricia's Canadian Light Infantry were surrounded and cut off, dependent on air-dropped supplies and ammunition. Their achievement has been overshadowed by the bloodier and even more dramatic action that took place farther west at this time. But 27 Brigade won much professional admiration from their allies for the fashion in which they broke the Communist attack north of Chongchon-ni. It is a typical irony of history that, because their battle ended in success at small cost in Commonwealth lives, it is little remembered. There, at the center of the UN front, the line stabilized . . . and held. The surviving attackers withdrew. One arm of the Chinese offensive was shattered.

But even as the U.S. Marines were fighting their battle, twenty-five miles farther west on the I Corps front, another action was taking place that passed into the legend of Korea. The British 29 Brigade—three infantry battalions with a fourth, Belgian unit under command—was holding positions along the line of the Imjin River, just over thirty miles north of Seoul. Throughout the war the contribution of the lesser United Nations contingents was dwarfed by the dominant role of the Americans. But just once the British played a part that captured the imagination of the Western world: the battle of the Imjin River in April 1951.

To an inexpert eye the hill range south of the Imjin offers a defensive position of such overwhelming strength that it appears almost impregnable. The highest peak, Kamak-san, rises to 2,000 feet. The river bows north in front of the British line, almost every yard of its banks plainly visible from the high ground. The ROK 1st Division occupied positions to the west. The American 3rd Division stood to the east.

Yet the Imjin position was by no means as strong as at first appeared. The river at this point was shallow enough to be easily forded, and thus to offer little difficulty to an attacker. The brigade relied for fire support upon the twenty-five-pounders of the 45 Field Regiment, R.A., but lacked ready access to medium or heavy artillery, always in chronic short supply. Any position is only as strong as the force that defends it, and 29 Brigade possessed pitifully small numbers to cover almost seven and a half miles of front. If they were to do so, indeed, there was no possibility of holding a continuous line. Brigadier Tom Brodie determined to deploy his men in separate unit positions, centered upon key hill features. He placed the Belgian battalion on the far right, north of the river. On the south bank, the Northumberland Fusiliers took the right flank, with the Gloucesters on the left, the Royal Ulster Rifles in reserve. Up to two miles separated each of the Northumberlands' company areas from its neighbor. Their positions were neither deeply dug, nor wired, nor mined, because the British did not expect to hold them for long. They were merely a springboard from which the advance to the "Kansas" line would be continued. Though some work had been done to clear fields of fire, the thick scrub covering the hillsides throughout the area offered plenty of useful cover to an attacker. It is difficult to overstate the influence of the lack of defensive preparations upon the British difficulties that were to follow. Infantry with good overhead protection, and minefields and wire to impede assaults, can achieve miracles even against overwhelming enemy forces, especially when these lack artillery support. Infantry without these things are critically handicapped in their own defense.

Some officers were most unhappy about the scattered deployment of the small force, when 29 Brigade's position lay across the historic route southward to the Korean capital. They argued in favor of concentrating the battalions where they could provide effective mutual support, for instance on the dominant heights of Kamak-san, where there were superb natural defenses and ready access to water. Major Tony Younger, commanding the brigade's engineer squadron, was in Japan on leave when he saw speculation in the U.S. Army newspaper *Stars and Stripes* about a possible Chinese thrust toward the Imjin. He flew hastily back to Seoul and rejoined the brigade. He was dismayed to find that no special precautions were being taken: "We were not really in a defensive frame of mind. We had been crawling forward, probing forward for months. We didn't even really know exactly where on our front the Imjin was fordable."[1] Major Guy Ward of 45 Field Regiment, the gunner battery commander with the Gloucesters, found the atmosphere "relaxed. Too relaxed." Despite all the intelligence indications of an imminent Chinese offensive, the extraordinary absence of enemy activity in front of Brodie's men suggested that the blow would fall elsewhere. The Imjin position was deemed safe.

During the days following their arrival in the line on April 5, the British probed north in search of the enemy. On the fourteenth the Belgians and tanks of the 8th Hussars skirmished with a Chinese patrol four miles north of the river and took a prisoner. On the sixteenth the Northumberland Fusiliers and the British Centurions carried out a reconnaissance in force nine miles into no-man's-land. Again, they met only token Chinese fire. Their officers carried out laborious interrogations of local villagers through interpreters. "In a language which required eight minutes to say 'perhaps,' " wrote one of the participants irritably, "battleground interviews of this nature were often more exasperating than instructive." On April 20 yet another "armored swan" drove eighteen miles north. "Lowtherforce," led by the CO of the 8th Hussars, again skirmished with a small Chinese force which withdrew at once under pressure. Aerial reconnaissance reported no sign of significant enemy forces on the British front. All the evidence suggested that the Chinese possessed only a few observation posts, keeping a cautious eye upon 29 Brigade.

On the morning of April 22 patrols of the Gloucesters and the Northumberland Fusiliers north of the Imjin reported the astonishing news that major enemy forces were on the move on the British front. By afternoon the Gloucesters' CO was at "Gloucester Crossing" on the riverbank, personally directing mortar fire on Chinese parties moving on the north side. By 6 P.M. that evening the Belgian battalion also reported contact with the enemy. The brigade adopted a 50 percent stand-to for the night hours. But the Chinese were still expected to open the battle with their customary local probing attacks before committing themselves to a major assault. At 10 P.M., on Brodie's orders, the Ulsters' battle patrol was sent hastily forward in Oxford carriers to secure the bridges at "Ulster Crossing," the ford by which they had been passing the Imjin for three weeks, and to protect the Belgians' line of retreat.

Few young men had gone to as much trouble to arrange their own presence on the Imjin as Lieutenant P. J. Kavanagh, the battle patrol's twenty-year-old second-in-command. The son of a well-known comedy scriptwriter, Kavanagh found the tedium of National Service at the regimental depot intolerable and volunteered for Korea. Once in the country, he lobbied incessantly for a transfer from the rear areas to a fighting battalion. His wish had been granted a few days earlier. Now he stood with the patrol commander, Lieutenant Hedley Craig, peering warily into the darkness north of the river.

" 'Looks a bit fishy.'

" 'Yes.'

" 'Better push on a bit, though.'

" 'Right.'

"He screwed his eyes up so tight he saw stars, private semi-voluntary comment on fatuousness [Kavanagh wrote later]. Slowly they move off again, pressing into the tautening membrane of the night. Grind, whirr, whine go the tracks, the engines, a defined envelope of noise in the white moon-silence.

"Penetration! The membrane snaps. Flames, rockets, yells, a thousand Cup Final rattles, Guy Fawkes, one of the carriers in front goes up, whoosh! Christ! Fifty of us have run into a bloody army! Weapons, helmets, wireless sets, all go flying in the mad scramble to get out, back into the womb of the dark away from the red bee-swarms of the tracers.

" 'Come back,' he shouted. Not quite sure why, except that he didn't particularly fancy being left sitting there alone. Anyway it annoyed his schoolboy sense of order to see them running off into nowhere. Run home by all means, I'll come with you except the river's in the way, but not into the meaningless no-direction dark.

" 'Stop!'

"Some do uncertainly. A few run on, never to be seen again, ever. He dismounts gingerly from his lonely chariot.

" 'Lie down, face your front and return the fire.'

"Good notion that, keep us occupied for a bit. Irregular spiritless bangs begin around him.

" 'Get that bren gun going.'

" 'There's something wrong with it, Sorr.'

" 'Mend it.'

"Splendid stuff this. And will the First Cavalry, just in the nick, pennants a-flutter come riding riding. . . . No. He wished he wasn't there.

" 'I can find nothing wrong with this Bren, Sorr, known to God or to man.'

"Oh, the Irish, the irresistible cadence, unresisted."[2]

In the chaotic loneliness of the night, Kavanagh struggled to push a morphine Syrette into a wounded man, scrambled alongside Craig to restore some control to the ruin of the patrol after the Chinese ambush. They began to straggle back on foot toward the river, losing men as they went. A few hundred yards on, they paused for the survivors to regroup.

" 'Sir, Leary's got hurt on the way across. Can I go and get him, Sir?'

" 'No.'

" 'But he's my mukker, Sir!'

"Blank consternation. Greater love than this . . . Another face, contorted, is thrust into his—

" 'Sir, there's one of 'em moving about just down there. Shall I kill him? I'll throw this at him.'

"Brandishing a grenade, hopping up and down. You'd have his head in your knapsack, too, wouldn't you, you bloodcrazy little bastard. Takes people different ways, apparently.

" 'Shall I kill-kill-kill um, Sir?'

" 'No.' "[3]

*   *   *

The Ulsters' survivors were bewildered that they were allowed to withdraw, when the Chinese seemed to have the patrol utterly at their mercy. Communist infantry were moving all around them. Lieutenant Craig and ten men covered the withdrawal of Kavanagh, wounded in the shoulder, with the remainder. Craig himself was briefly taken prisoner, but escaped to find his way back to the British lines two days later. Kavanagh rejoined the battalion in the early hours of the morning with five men. That brief, ferocious glimpse of battle was the young officer's first and last. He was evacuated to a hospital in Japan. He was one of the lucky ones, the men who escaped the carnage that now overtook 29 Brigade.

Lieutenants Bill Cooper and Jimmy Yeo of the Fusiliers' W Company had taken a jeep down to Yongdungpo that Sunday to visit the 8th Hussars. For St. George's Day every Fusilier had already been issued with the regiment's traditional red and white roses, specially flown in from Japan. Yeo, a regular in the East Lancashires who had volunteered for Korea to get in some active service, met a friend from Sandhurst, with whom they shared a pleasant tea. They drove back to their own positions for evening stand-to, lying in silence in their slit trenches gazing out into the dusk. Nothing happened. Stand-down was called. Then, as they cooked the usual Sunday stew, they began to hear grenades and gunfire farther west, toward the Gloucesters' positions. Once more the word was whispered down from trench to trench by running NCOs: "Stand to!" They lay straining their ears, momentarily unnerved by the sound of many feet running near them. Yet even as they cocked their weapons, the alarm was dispelled: the feet were British. For two more hours they waited, passive. Flares erupted from time to time to their left, but strict standing orders specified that they should keep silent and remain in their slits.

Then brief bursts of fire opened in front of them, and shuffling movements began in the darkness. The Chinese were probing toward them. There was an explosion, then the muffled thud of a mortar illuminant bursting before them. Cooper and Yeo's neighboring platoons began to fire across each other's fronts, exactly as they had planned. But the Chinese did not throw their weight against W Company that night. They were fully occupied elsewhere. Throughout the hours of darkness, wave after wave of attackers threw themselves upon the Fusiliers' X and Z Companies and the Gloucesters' A and D. The absolute unsuitability of the brigade deployment for meeting an all-out attack by large forces now made itself clear. Each company was compelled to meet the Chinese alone. The Northumberlands' X Company, nearest the river on the left, was impossibly exposed and withdrew toward the battalion position before first light. To the alarm of the Fusiliers, however, at 6:10 A.M. on the twenty-third, the Chinese gained a key hill position overlooking a major road junction held by Z Company. The enemy had been able to bypass Y Company, nearer the river, and strike at the positions behind it. Major John Winn, Z Company's commander, won a DSO for his superbly courageous direction of the defense of his line that day. But the Northumberlands were compelled to fall back. Of all the actions at this period, that in which the Northumberlands lost vital ground so early in the battle had most serious consequences, and is most open to criticism. The British were dismayed to find Chinese infantry now firing upon their artillery positions and already establishing themselves upon the untenanted high ground of Kamak-san. Centurions of C Squadron, 8th Hussars, covered the retreat of the Fusiliers Y Company. The Ulsters, hastily moved forward from their reserve positions, were now committed to clearing and holding the high ground east of the vital road to the rear.

On the left flank, the battle began well for the Gloucesters. Their standing patrol on the riverbank, commanded by Lieutenant Guy Temple, poured devastating small-arms fire into the first Chinese attempting the night river crossing. "Guido" Temple, nicknamed for his swarthy Italian looks, had been considered a somewhat feckless young officer back in England, repeatedly in trouble for late return from nightclub outings. Yet now, in the words of a fellow officer, he proved "a good man in a difficult time," lying with his men over their weapons, looking down on the moonlit river. Four times the Chinese came, and on each occasion they were repulsed. Then, with their ammunition expended, Temple's platoon withdrew into C Company's perimeter on the hillside more than a mile to the rear.

The Chinese were now crossing the river in force at a dozen places. In the hours before dawn they launched repeated attacks on the Gloucesters' A and D Companies. Lieutenant Philip Curtis won a posthumous Victoria Cross for leading a counterattack to recover A Company's Castle Hill position. Although wounded early in the action, he struggled on to the summit, wiping out a Chinese machine-gun team with grenades seconds before he fell dead from the effects of their fire. The company commander, Pat Angier, spoke by radio to Colonel Fred Carne, the Gloucesters' CO: "I'm afraid we've lost Castle Site. I want to know whether I am to stay here indefinitely or not. If I am to stay, I must be reinforced as my numbers are getting very low." Flatly, Carne told him that the position must be held—at all costs. Angier signed off reassuringly: "Don't worry about us; we'll be all right." He was killed fifteen minutes later. By midmorning only one officer of A Company remained in action. All the others were dead or wounded. Yet still Carne was compelled to order the survivors to hold on. If A Company's ground was lost, the remaining battalion positions also became untenable. Again and again, with their customary indifference to casualties, the Chinese assault groups crawled to within yards of the British trenches under cover of withering long-range machine-gun fire, then threw themselves forward with their burp guns and grenades, their screams and bugle calls. Each party was eventually destroyed. But each assault knocked out a bren team here, killed the occupants of a slit trench there, removed an officer or NCO with grenade splinters. Major Pat Angier was one of the last Gloucester casualties whom a handful of his comrades and the padre

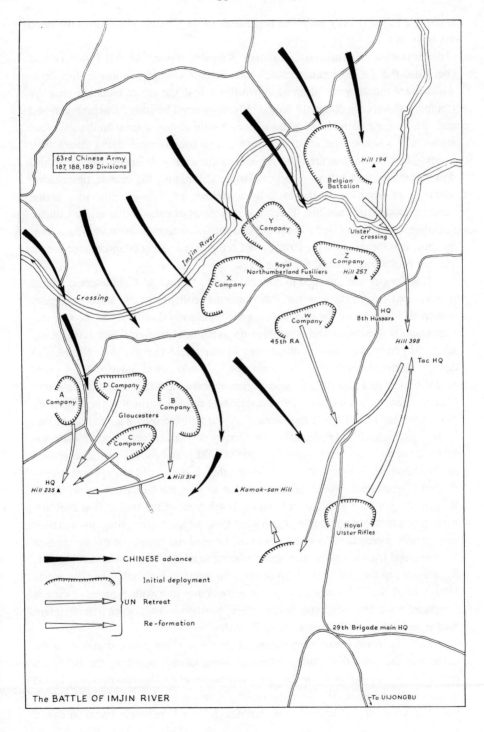

63rd Chinese Army
187, 188, 189 Divisions

Hill 194

Belgian Battalion

Imjin River

Y Company

Ulster crossing

Z Company
Hill 257

Royal Northumberland Fusiliers

X Company

Crossing

W Company

45th RA

HQ 8th Hussars

Hill 398

Tac HQ

A Company

D Company

B Company

Gloucesters

C Company

HQ
Hill 235 ▲

▲ Hill 314

▲ Kamok-san Hill

Royal Ulster Rifles

CHINESE advance

Initial deployment

UN Retreat

Re-formation

The BATTLE OF IMJIN RIVER

29th Brigade main HQ

To UIJONGBU

could spare time to bury with the hasty rituals of the Church. His orderly followed his body in tears.

Meanwhile, farther east, Colonel Kingsley Foster of the Fusiliers had concluded that he must counterattack to recover Z Company's lost hilltop, from which the Chinese were bringing down fire across the entire battalion area. W Company clambered doggedly up the hillside covered by heavy machine-gun and tank fire, taking pains to keep their line, hardly losing a man until they came within fifty yards of the crest, for the Chinese rounds were flying above their heads. Then, as they neared the objective, the enemy defenders began to hurl down grenades and satchel charges. Brian Millington, the mortar observation officer, was wounded in the back by a grenade exploding below him as the Fusiliers gained the crestline. There was a moment of exhilaration as the Chinese manning it turned and fled. Then, beyond them, another Chinese unit rose from the ground and charged at the British. W Company's assault collapsed, men turned and ran back down the hill for their lives.

Bill Cooper was shocked to hear clearly the "Thwack!" as bullets slammed into his own men. He saw his radio operator collapse to his knees, mortally wounded, as the set on his back disintegrated. Halfway down the hill, he saw that Millington was missing and scrambled up again until he found him lying in the scrub. Urgently, he asked if the young officer could move. "No, I think I'm dead," muttered Millington. "It's no good. You'd better leave me." Cooper picked him up in a fireman's lift and staggered down the hill, pursued by desultory Chinese fire. Back at the start line, the doctor examined Millington for a moment, then shook his head: "He's moribund." About half the men who had taken part in the counterattack had failed to return. Deeply despondent about their failure, the survivors of W Company trudged back to their old positions. Cooper became even angrier later, when somebody told him that they had never been expected to gain the hill. Their attack was chiefly a diversion to keep the Chinese busy while the Belgians began their withdrawal from the north bank of the Imjin. That evening, with the assistance of some American tank support, the Belgian battalion successfully disengaged from its positions, crossed the bridges at the junction of the Imjin and Hantan rivers, and began moving to take up new positions alongside Kamak-san, to the rear of the Gloucesters and Northumberlands. The British had always liked the Belgians, a tough, swashbuckling unit with a proud "Vive la Belgique!" banner displayed behind their positions. That week the Belgians fought as hard as any battalion in 29 Brigade.

That afternoon Padre Sam Davies of the Gloucesters listened grimly to the news over the radio that Chinese elements were already attacking the Brigade's rear echelon: "Standing in the sunny hollow where main Headquarters lay, I tried to realise the position. We were isolated by Chinese hordes intent on the kill. It was simply a matter of hours before darkness fell, and the lonely battalion would be assaulted on all sides in the nightmarish moonlight. Gloucester was 11,000 miles away. I longed to be able to say 'Stop' to the rushing minutes—to prolong this quiet, sunny afternoon indefinitely.''[4]

By evening on April 23 it was apparent that the forward battalions of 29 Brigade must concentrate or be wiped out piecemeal. Around 8:30 P.M. the survivors of the Gloucesters' A and D Companies withdrew from their positions and filed through the darkness into the battalion headquarters area to redeploy, Korean porters moving their heavy equipment. During a lull in the renewed Chinese attacks that night, Major Paul Mitchell's C Company was also pulled back. But it proved impossible to disengage Major Denis Harding's B. Between 11 P.M. that night and dawn the following morning, Harding's men faced seven major assaults.

The company commander was a thirty-six-year-old veteran with great experience in World War II. That morning one of his NCOs had led a patrol to explore the ground around the company positions and returned to report bleakly, "There's not just dozens of them down there—there's thousands." Yet Harding still felt confident of his company's ability to hold its ground. He had spent much of his day with his artillery observation officer, calling down fire on enemy concentrations whenever they could see them. Then he fell asleep for a time, and while he rested ammunition and food were brought up to the company area from the battalion echelon. The officer who brought them, Captain Bill Morris, should then have returned to the rear with the carrying party. But he was reluctant to wake Harding and stayed to cover for him. By evening it was too late for him to go anywhere. Morris remained, to share the fate of the battalion.

All that night, amid the cries and orders and bugles from the darkness, B Company grenaded and poured fire into the Chinese with rifle, bren, and sten. By dawn one platoon's positions had been entirely overrun. Sheer weight of numbers had driven in Harding's perimeter. At first light the survivors withdrew to join the rest of Carne's men on Hill 235—the height that was to become known to the British Army as Gloucester Hill. There were only Harding himself, his sergeant major, and fifteen others. Their ammunition was virtually exhausted. The remains of B and C were merged to form a single weak company. The Gloucesters had begun the battle with some 600 infantrymen holding a front of over 12,000 yards. Now both their numbers and their perimeter had shrunk dramatically. Yet one of Support Company, hearing from the colonel that they were to concentrate on the higher ride for the last round, declared cheerfully, "We shall be all right, sir, 'twill be like the Rock of Gibraltar up here."

The quality about the Gloucesters' stand upon which all the survivors focused in their later accounts was the confidence: the serene conviction of most of the officers and men that they could cope, even as their casualties mounted, their perimeter shrank, and their ammunition dwindled. Infantrymen are often impressed by the magical fashion in which a gunner battery commander can use his telephone to drop fire within yards of their own positions. Guy Ward and his officers from 70th Field Battery were acknowledged as supreme wizards. Ward was astonished to see Chinese cavalry in the valley below him. As a professional gunner, he said "they were magnificent targets," as 25-pounder shells poured down on them. The 4.2-inch heavy mortars of 170 Battery, R.A., compounded the Communists' dreadful losses. Chinese infantry concentrations were shattered again and again by devastating British artillery fire: "The slaughter we did was absolutely tremendous," said Ward, though like most of his companions, he was astounded by the fashion in which the enemy still kept coming.

That day of the twenty-fourth, efforts were made to pass a column of the 8th Hussars' Centurions down the narrow, winding valley road to the Gloucesters' positions. Infantry cover was provided by a Filipino battalion, who were responsible for sweeping the high ground on either side. The operation failed. One of the three Filipino light tanks leading the column was knocked out, blocking the road. It could not be dislodged by its successor. There is little doubt that the infantry advanced too close to the road, and did not climb high enough to have any chance of keeping the armored column out of range of the Chinese. But the track was anyway almost impassable by the big, heavy Centurions. And with the limited forces available, it is not unlikely that the relief column would itself have become trapped with the Gloucesters, even had it been successful in making contact.

Some of those most intimately concerned with 29 Brigade's battle believed that it revealed the fatal disadvantages of committing an independent national brigade group in a major war. Brigadier Tom Brodie found himself bearing the brunt of an assault by two Chinese divisions, with important implications for the safety of Seoul. Yet as a British officer under temporary American command, he could not be expected to achieve the clear understanding with higher formations that would have been possible with his own fellow countrymen. A British officer at brigade HQ believed that the Americans did not understand until much too late how desperate was the predicament of 29 Brigade: "When Tom told Corps that his position was 'a bit sticky,' they simply did not grasp that in British Army parlance, that meant 'critical.' " Brodie was twice told by American Corps headquarters that he could not withdraw his brigade and he felt that he had no choice but to obey. Those around the brigadier said that he found the strain almost intolerable, commanding a brigade that was being shattered beneath his eyes. The Imjin battle confirmed the urgency of bringing into being the planned Commonwealth Division, commanded by a major general with the rank and authority to safeguard the interests of his command.

It was not that Brodie blundered, but that his position was exceptionally difficult, as a British officer naturally anxious to "keep his end up" with the

Americans. Weeks earlier 29 Brigade had dug and wired rear positions. On Gloucester Hill the battalion adjutant, Captain Tony Farrar-Hockley, repeatedly asked himself why they had bothered to dig rear positions if not to fall back upon them in just such a situation as this. Knowing that his men were asking the same question, and demanding why they were receiving such limited air support, he told them that another big battle was being fought elsewhere. "Higher Sunray"— higher command—"have insisted we stay." There were other difficulties: although 45 Field Regiment's 25-pounders were fine guns, they possessed limited killing power. There was a desperate need for the support of heavier metal. Yet the Gloucesters' American artillery liaison officer had been withdrawn a few days before the battle, and they possessed no means of calling in 155-mm fire. The British battalions' establishment of automatic weapons was inadequate to face the sort of devastating attrition battle in which they were now engaged. Above all, perhaps, the brigade was able to call upon too little close air support too late. That first bloody day the Gloucesters received none whatever. Even in the days that followed it was apparent that 29 Brigade was not being given high priority.

Once the assessment had been made that the British faced a major Chinese assault, which they could not possibly hope to overcome in the dispersed positions they held, rapid disengagement and withdrawal were by far the most prudent military options. This was a classic case for "rolling with the punches." Like so many sacrificial actions which pass into military legend, that which was now unfolding on the Imjin should never have been allowed to take place.

The men in the British trenches, and even their officers, possessed astonishingly little notion of what was happening in the next twenty-four hours beyond the knowledge of wave after wave of Chinese attacking their positions. Rumors filtered through that the brigade would soon be fetched out. The Brigade-Major told the Gloucesters' adjutant on the radio that an American infantry-armor column in brigade strength would be moving to the battalion's relief later that day. Lieutenant Bill Cooper's company commander in the Northumberlands told him that "the idea is to make the Chinese deploy, then withdraw onto the Americans behind us, who need more time." The Fusiliers had received a hasty reinforcement of National Servicemen, thrown overnight from a transit camp in Japan into the midst of the battle. Cooper's quota of seven replacements were understandably appalled and bewildered by their new circumstances. In the darkness the platoon commander was exasperated to see one of the new arrivals yet again defying the order to stay in his trench. "Bloxham!" he called furiously. "Get back in your trench!" Then he saw that the man was a Chinese. Cooper was not holding a weapon, and found himself thrashing on the ground hand to hand with the Communist soldier, until an NCO ran forward and shot the man in the head.

By dawn, nervous and uncertain, the Northumberlands were ordered to withdraw and redeploy, some 800 yards to the rear. To their immense relief, the Chinese did not interfere. That day they lay in their positions, suffering little from the enemy but listening to the fierce struggle farther west, where the Gloucesters were under desperate pressure. They cursed the feebleness of their air support, the sluggishness of the reinforcements alleged to be preparing the blocking positions behind them. The tempo of battle was leavened by a moment of black comedy when inquiries were made about charges against a Fusilier who had stopped dead in the midst of an assault because he claimed that "the Lord Jesus had instructed him to take no part in the attack." He was sent for court-martial.

Men were constantly asking their officers, "What happens next, sir?" "When can we get out?" They received repeated bland reassurances about help on the way. Ammunition was running short, above all, grenades. The Fusiliers met one Chinese attack with a barrage of tins of compo cheese to deceive the enemy into putting their heads down. The incoming mortaring intensified. The weariness showed above all in men's eyes, red and raw and aching from their tiredness. Yet still they remained unaware of the huge risk that they would not get out at all.

During the night of April 24–25 orders at last reached 29 Brigade to withdraw from the Imjin to new positions north of Seoul. Infiltration parties were now deep behind the British flanks. Chinese snipers were firing on transport four miles behind 29 Brigade's front. Yet the Ulsters were bemused and dismayed by the order. Throughout the battle their acting CO, Major Gerald Rickord, a highly experienced officer who ended World War II in command of an airborne battalion, had felt less than happy with the level of information reaching him from brigade HQ. He knew nothing of the Belgian withdrawal, of the exposure of the brigade's right flank, of the increasingly desperate predicament of the Gloucesters. His men had thus far repulsed the Chinese wherever they met them, and had suffered very few casualties. Above all, Rickord was dismayed by the plan for the withdrawal, which called for his companies to leave their positions on high ground and descend to the valley road. The Ulsters would have vastly preferred to walk out along the ridges, keeping the enemy below them. But Brigadier Brodie decreed otherwise. While the OC 29 Brigade had been given an impossible task, holding a difficult area of front with a small force against overwhelming odds, there was considerable criticism after the battle of his tactics from some of those who survived.

At 8 A.M. on the twenty-fifth the retreat began in a thick ground mist, commanded by Colonel Kingsley Foster of the Fusiliers. There is no more difficult operation of war than disengagement when closely pressed by the enemy. Chinese infantry were now deployed on high ground from which they could overlook every stage of the British movement. As soon as they understood what was taking place, they hastened forward to exploit their success in forcing 29 Brigade back.

Most of the Northumberland Fusiliers got away intact down the road south, past a vital defile held by B Company of the Ulsters and a troop of 55 Squadron Royal Engineers. Their worst enemy was now their own exhaustion: "The infantry, after seventy-two hours of fighting, were in no state to do more than walk out, fate being willing, on their own feet," in the words of a Hussar officer.[5] The British began their descent from the high ground in textbook fashion, counting their men through checkpoints, moving by bounds. But as the Chinese swarmed forward in their wake, the Ulsters and the Belgians became engaged in a desperate piecemeal scramble for safety. In the words of Major Henry Huth of the 8th Hussars, it was "one long bloody ambush." After so many months in which the tanks had languished idle, without a role in impassable country, along the valley road from the Imjin to Uijongbu they found their moment. They fought in troops and half-troops, some tanks providing direct fire support for infantry defending stretches of hillside, others crashing down the road to safety laden with exhausted and wounded survivors, others again covering their departure. Their 20-pounders and Besa machine guns raked the hillsides. When Chinese infantry began to scramble onto the hulls, Captains Peter Ormrod and Gavin Murray resorted to machine-gunning each other's Centurions to sweep them off. Sergeant Jack Cadman drove his tank through a Korean house to dislodge a Chinese battering on his turret hatch. All that day the Centurions fought along the road with a continuous rain of small-arms fire splattering against their armor, driving off periodic rushes of Chinese seeking to dash near enough to ram pole charges through their track guards. Major Huth, C Squadron commander, won a DSO for his direction of the tank actions during the retreat and for the personal example he set, for his own was the last Centurion out of the valley.

A runner reached Bill Cooper's platoon of the Fusiliers around 11 A.M. with news of the withdrawal. They were told to "leave the heavy stuff, but bring all the ammunition you can." There were believed to be enemy across their line of retreat, and they must be prepared to cut their way through. The Gloucesters would be moving independently. Cooper and his weary men reached the pass held by the Ulsters and Engineers to see Colonel Foster standing among a clutch of Centurions and a half-track ambulance clustered by the roadside under increasingly heavy fire. Foster stopped him: "I can't order you to do this," he said, "but I would be very grateful if you would stay and see the wounded out on the half-track." Cooper's subsequent memories were a confused blur of grenades and mortaring, of a boy named Angus screaming after a tank ran over his legs, of a Chinese grenade that blew him off his feet and knocked him out. He awoke to find a Chinese searching his body. He sat up, causing the astounded enemy soldier to spring backward. It was dusk. His elbow was shattered, he had splinter wounds from his knee to the top of his thigh. He was led to join a group of fellow prisoners, lying and sitting by the roadside. Suddenly an American aircraft swung low past them, and a napalm tank fell away from its belly to land by the crippled Centurion it had been sent to destroy. For the watching British captives, this was the last glimpse of friendly forces for many months to come.

Colonel Foster followed his Fusiliers down the road in his jeep. At the pass held by the Ulsters, their company commander urged him to take to his feet—the route was under heavy fire and a jeep was instantly vulnerable. Foster declined and was killed a few moments later by a Chinese mortar bomb, which destroyed his vehicle. The commanding officer of the Belgian battalion was terribly burned by phosphorus pouring from a tank grenade discharger as he stood alongside it when it was hit by a chance Chinese bullet.

Private Albert Varley of the Ulsters had been slightly wounded by fragments in his eye early in the battle, when a bullet struck his bren. The regimental aid post sent him back to his company, as they lacked means to evacuate him. His platoon was one of those on the high ground, swarming with Chinese, which received the order "Every man for himself!" He and his "oppo," a National Serviceman from Bristol named Ronnie Robinson, stumbled down the hill toward the road. Robinson was supporting a man with a shattered arm who kept pleading to be allowed to stop and give himself up. Varley paused every few moments to turn and fire a brief burst toward their pursuers. He was convinced that they would never make it. But at last they staggered thankfully onto the road and clambered onto a Centurion, Varley casting away the pieces of his bren. They bucketed off down the road, Ulsters clinging desperately to every hull projection, the tankers firing their Besa continuously until its ammunition was exhausted, then bouncing high-explosive shells off the road in front of them. A clutch of Americans appeared from somewhere who also boarded the Centurion. One fired his bazooka at a hut surrounded by Chinese who were also overrunning a stranded Centurion by the roadside. The surrounding hillsides now seemed infested with running, standing, crouching Chinese, firing down upon the hapless British below.

Varley was one of the lucky escapers. Many of the wounded and survivors of the Ulsters who crowded onto the tank hulls for that last desperate ride out of the valley were shot off as the Centurions drove back through the Chinese. On the radio net the retiring tank crews heard their doctor, left behind them on the road with his charges, reporting bleakly, "I am about to be captured. . . . I have been captured." It was now a race between the retreating British, struggling along the road and over the hills, and a mass of thousands of Chinese, moving with astonishing speed across country, unmoved by the losses inflicted upon them at every turn by tank gunfire.

Private Henry O'Kane of D Company had scarcely fired a shot during the preceding days, which he remembered chiefly for the confusion of moving from position to position every few hours, apparently without reason. As the withdrawal lapsed into a chaotic struggle for personal survival amid the milling rush of

Chinese, he was hit in the leg by a mortar fragment. He collapsed into a ditch by the roadside for a moment. Then he unbuckled his equipment, threw it down, and limped along the road, until somebody pushed him up onto a tank already crowded with men. He lost consciousness, then woke to find himself once more in a ditch beside the Centurion, which was slewed, disabled, across the paddy. Chinese soldiers scuttled up and thrust pole charges through its track guards. Those of the British who could still move now ran. Those who could not, such as O'Kane, lay exhausted as the battle lapped past them. Another Ulsterman put a field dressing on his leg and gave him a swig of rum. The sound of gunfire receded, while Chinese infantry ran heedless past, still intent on pursuit. At last a Chinese officer wearing a wooden Mauser holster stopped, gazed down on the motionless huddle of men nursing their pain, and said in careful English, "I think it is a good fight." O'Kane and the other walking wounded were gathered and led away, hands on their heads. They never saw the stretcher cases again. They were given "safe-conduct passes," declaring that they had been "liberated by peace-loving peoples." Then they passed into the bleak cycle of marches, makeshift political lectures, weary pauses in peasant huts, and the diet of sorghum, peanuts, and bean flour that was their introduction to captivity.

The survivors of 29 Brigade reached safety behind the protection of a blocking position established by the U.S. 25th Regimental Combat Team. Word was passed from the 8th Hussars to brigade headquarters: "Everybody's come down who's coming." The road back from Imjin lay strewn with the wreckage of the British retreat: wrecked vehicles, abandoned equipment, bodies, and shell cases. Fire still flickered from the remains of one of the abandoned Centurions, demolished to prevent its use by the enemy. Tom Brodie seemed vastly relieved, even frankly surprised, to see Gerald Rickord and the Ulsters' B Company, who had provided the rearguard. They were told that they must expect to fight another battle, that they must begin to dig in again at once. "It was odd to hear that old clink of picks and shovels going again," said Rickord. But late that night new orders came. It was recognized that the brigade was exhausted. Sufficient American forces were now in the line to hold it against any new Chinese pressure. The exhausted men were coaxed and prodded a few miles farther down the track to a rendezvous with transport. Then they were driven away, overwhelmed with relief at their own survival, to recover from their ordeal.

For one group, of course, there was no escape from the ridge above the Imjin: the survivors of 1st Battalion, Gloucestershire Regiment. Attempts to resupply them by air had achieved little—most of the drops fell outside their perimeter. Since the first day, helicopters had been unable to reach them to evacuate wounded. Their contact with the outside world was fading as their last wireless batteries died. They knew at 6 A.M. that morning that they were doomed to death or captivity. At that hour 29 Brigade informed Colonel Carne's headquarters that the other battalions were withdrawing, that no further attempts to break through to their rescue were possible. Brodie could only tell Carne to stand his ground. "I understand the position quite clearly," said the colonel. "But I must make it clear to you that my command is no longer an effective fighting force. If it is required that we shall stay here, in spite of this, we shall continue to hold." Carne left the radio set to tell his adjutant:

"You know that armor/infantry column that's coming from 3 Div to relieve us?"

"Yes, sir."

"Well, it isn't coming."

"Right, sir."[6]

The natural comradeship of war is surpassed by the bond between men who find themselves doomed to share disaster. Colonel Fred Carne was a taciturn, indeed almost inarticulate, officer who had never in his army career been regarded as a "high flier," indeed had seen limited battlefield service. Yet Carne, with his pipe and unshakable calm in the face of tragedy, assumed heroic stature on Gloucester Hill. Early that morning his adjutant, Captain Anthony Farrar-Hockley, met Carne coming down the hill with two regimental police, a driver, his pipe, and a rifle after a brutal little firefight.

"What was all that about, sir?"

"Oh, just shooing away some Chinese."[7]

Farrar-Hockley himself was an exceptionally tough, clever, and ambitious officer who had enlisted underage in World War II and served as an airborne soldier. His ruthless single-mindedness and commitment to discipline did not make him universally beloved. Yet in the Imjin battle he was able to show what the same uncompromising purpose and stubbornness could do to the Chinese. Farrar-Hockley it was, in the early dark hours of the twenty-fifth, who responded to the nerve-stretching bugles of the Communists, gathering for yet another assault, by ordering Drum-Major Philip Buss to return their calls on his own bugle. The moment when Buss stood at attention on the position, playing in succession "Reveille," "Cookhouse," "Defaulters," and "Officers Dress for Dinner" passed into the legend of the Imjin battle.

There were others: Sergeant-Major Jack Hobbs; Padre Sam Davies; Denis Harding; Guy Ward of 45 Field Regiment; Captain Bob Hickey, the doctor; and a roll call of officers and other ranks whose names became familiar throughout the British Army. There are those who have claimed, since the war, that the ranks of the Gloucesters were filled with exceptionally keen and dutiful soldiers. This does the regiment no service. In reality, there were as many disgruntled reservists and jaded regulars on Gloucester Hill as in any other unit of 29 Brigade. It was this that made their fate and their performance the more moving. They were a typical, perhaps a little above average, county battalion who showed for the thousandth time in the history of the British Army what ordinary men, decently led, can achieve in a situation which demands, above all, a willingness for sacrifice.

Brodie left it to Carne's discretion whether his battalion should attempt to break out or whether, if this was impossible, they should surrender. Soon after 9:30 A.M. on April 25 the colonel was informed by 29 Brigade that within the hour he would lose all artillery support as 45 Field Regiment were compelled to pull out their guns. He gave the order to his company commanders to make for the British lines as best they could. Most of them had not eaten for forty-eight hours. When the men checked their ammunition, they found that each rifleman possessed just three rounds, the bren gunners a magazine and a half. They had begun the battle with more than fifty refills a magazine. "I'm afraid we shall have to leave the wounded behind," Carne told Bob Hickey. "Very well, sir," said the doctor. "I quite understand the position." Hickey and the chaplain, along with some of the medical staff, stayed with the eighty casualties on the position. "This looks like a holiday in Peking for some of us," remarked Padre Davies to the RAMC sergeant.[8] He and the others were taken prisoner soon after. Captain Mike Harvey led the survivors of D Company by a circuitous route, first north toward the river, then west and south again. They encountered only one group of Chinese, whom they killed. Thereafter, they survived intact until, two days later, they exposed themselves before a group of American tanks, which promptly opened fire, inflicting some casualties. When they had at last identified themselves, Harvey and his thirty-nine men were carried in safety into the UN lines. They, alone of their battalion, came safe home.

Some men, too weary to face a desperate march in doubtful pursuit of freedom, lay down on the battalion position to await capture. The men of A, B, and C Companies who set off directly southward immediately encountered heavy Chinese machine-gun fire. It fell to Farrar-Hockley, of all men, to call on them to lay down their arms and surrender. "Feeling as if I was betraying everything that I loved and believed in, I raised my voice and called, 'Stop!' "[9] This did not prevent him from making three escape attempts in the days that followed.

Like many men that week, throughout the battle Major Guy Ward had sustained a curious conviction that in the end "it would all be all right." Even after the order was given to make for the British lines independently, he did not lose this faith. Then, as he walked, "I suddenly saw hundreds and hundreds of Gloucesters in a corner surrounded by Chinese. I thought, 'Oh my God, here we go again.' " Guy Ward had been a prisoner of the Germans from 1941 to 1945. Colonel Carne, Sergeant Major Hobbs, and a handful of others evaded capture for twenty-four hours. Then they, too, joined the rest of the battalion "in the bag," where thirty more of them were yet to die. It was weeks before the survivors of 29 Brigade even knew that more than half the Gloucesters were alive and in enemy hands. A large part of Brigadier Brodie's personal trauma stemmed from the conviction of himself and his staff that all but Major Harvey's party had perished. "The Brigadier seemed shattered by the whole experience," said one of his officers.

The Imjin battle has been the subject of some controversy in the past thirty years. Men of the Ulsters and the Northumberland Fusiliers have been irked by the massive tide of publicity that flowed over the Gloucesters in the days and years after the destruction of Carne's battalion. They point out that the overwhelming majority of the Gloucesters' casualties were taken prisoner—the battalion also suffered sixty-three killed and perhaps thrice as many wounded. It is invariably the case that decorations and eulogies are heaped upon the survivors of military disasters to make both themselves and their nations better able to endure sadness and dismay, less likely to ask "the reason why." There is a quality about "last stands" that draws painters and poets. Intelligent soldiers are more inclined to demand, skeptically, whether it should have been necessary for any last stand to have taken place. In the cold accountancy of war and history there may be headlines to be extracted from defeat, but there is no virtue.

It is unlikely that 29 Brigade's battle will find a place in any manual of military instruction, except as an example of how not to hold a difficult position. If the brigade had been prepared for a big defensive action, its men had had ample time to surround themselves with obstacles covered by fire, the first resort of the infantryman in defense, they could have concentrated their forces to cover either the eastern or western passes through their sector. They had insufficient forces to do both. Yet the Communist attackers did not hold all the cards. They possessed ample mortars, which they used to great effect, but no air or artillery firepower. It is a remarkable tribute to the limitations of air support that, with the vast air forces at the disposal of the UN, tactical air strikes could not be used to more effect to break up the Chinese attacks. It was a tragedy—worse than that, it was a blunder somewhere in the UN chain of command—that the brigade was not pulled back from the Imjin positions as soon as the scale of the Chinese assault became clear. In the Korean campaign, from the beginning of 1951 to the end, there was no other instance of the UN Command permitting a substantial force to be isolated and destroyed piecemeal over a period of days. Campaign histories attribute losses of 10,000 killed and wounded to the Chinese, against 1,000 29 Brigade casualties in the battle, around a quarter of the British front-line strength. After the battle 169 of 850 Gloucesters mustered for roll call with the brigade. The estimated Communist loss figure is an arbitrary one, based upon the minimum that seemed credible to the British, given the weight of their own fire they had seen take effect upon their enemies.

Major Rickord, the Ulsters' acting CO, came away from the Imjin "feeling devastated. I believed that we had lost the battle, had suffered a disaster. But I was afterwards reassured that it was by no means a disaster. The morning after we came out, the soldiers were singing Irish songs, playing a banjo. I told the quartermaster to get them a bath and their green tropical uniforms. He said, 'It's much too cold for that.' But I said—'No, go on, do it. It'll make all the difference in the world to them to get a change of clothes.' And forty-eight hours later, they were fit to fight again, which was a wonderful feeling. I think they felt very proud of the fight they had put up. We felt no particular animosity towards the Chinese. Indeed, I think we felt great respect, even liking for them. But the regiment's old motto—*Quis Seperabit*—was something we felt very strongly about.''

The Northumberlands, the Belgians, the Gloucesters, the gunners and mortar crews would have said the same. If Rickord's words might sound to a cynic like the bromides of a professional soldier, the sentiments are none the less powerful and valid for that. When all the skeptical comment has been made, when all the exaggerations of time and regimental pride have been discounted, the British can still reflect with pride that they broke one arm of the Communist spring offensive in those three days on the Imjin. If it was always unlikely that the Chinese could have gotten through to Seoul, they could have expected at least to drive south farther and faster, and at much lower cost. There were repeated instances in Korea of UN units crumbling remarkably easily in the face of pressure, giving ground which had to be regained later in bloody and painful counterattack. On the Imjin, the Chinese discovered the price of meeting efficient, determined foot soldiers who cared little for the Cold War, for the glory of the United Nations, or the survival of Syngman Rhee, but to whom the regiment, the unit, a man's ''oppo'' in the next trench were everything. The most political army in the world encountered the least political—and was savagely mauled to gain its few sterile miles of rock and paddy. Across the breadth of the Korean front, Peking's spring offensive had failed. Never again in the war did the Communists mount an all-out assault which appeared to have the slightest prospect of strategic success.

12

THE STONY ROAD

Toward Stalemate

While the British 29 Brigade stood on the Imjin, Van Fleet hastened to create a reserve position north of Seoul—the "No Name" line—where the Eighth Army had no difficulty holding the Communists, the momentum of their offensive spent. Yet the Chinese continued to reinforce failure. On May 15, Marshal Peng launched a new assault with twenty-one Chinese and nine North Korean divisions. Once again, III ROK Corps collapsed, as it had done with monotonous regularity throughout the war. The Communists pushed forward as much as thirty miles in some places. The ROK 5th and 7th Divisions gave way. But on the right, the ROK I Corps held its ground. Despite sustaining some 900 casualties, the U.S. 2nd Division also stood firm. One of its batteries fired more than 12,000 rounds of 105-mm ammunition in a single twenty-four-hour period. The 38th Infantry stemmed repeated attacks on the night of May 16. "Artillery, crashing into the ground forward of the lines, took a terrific toll of the attackers," recorded the divisional history, "while other hundreds died in the minefields checkered with barbed wire. The groans of the wounded, screams of the attackers and the blast of bugles mingled with the clattering roar of battle as waves of Chinese pushed against the lines. . . . Searchlights were turned on to illuminate the battle area and aid the defenders in locating and slaughtering the onrushing Chinese."[1] The divisional commander, Major General Clark Ruffner, played a prominent front-line role in organizing the defense and concentrating his units for counterattacks, surviving a helicopter crash as he flew between positions.

The U.S. 3rd Division and the 187th Airborne RCT plugged the gap on the right of the 2nd Division opened by the ROK collapse. By May 20 the Chinese offensive was spent, and the UN was estimating that it had cost the Communists 90,000 casualties. Even if this figure was exaggerated, like so many "guessti-mates" on the battlefield, there was no doubt that the enemy had been decisively worsted. The U.S. Army, above all the 2nd "Indianhead" Division, had displayed heartening determination in holding the line. On May 22, Van Fleet opened his own counteroffensive, designed to exploit the exhaustion of the Chinese. The ROK I Corps moved up the coast against negligible opposition and gained the town of Kaesong. The 187th RCT and 1st Marine Division reached the Hwachon Reservoir. On the left, I Corps regained the old Imjin line, including the positions from which the British 29 Brigade had withdrawn in April.

There was little doubt that, had the political will existed, the Communist front now lay open. The morale of the Chinese armies in Korea was shattered. After all their exhilarating successes of the winter, they were now compelled to confront the new face of the UN armies, the careful deployment of men and firepower which the Communists could no longer break through. But Washington and its allies possessed no inclination to press the crumbling enemy northward, to extend the UN front and put at risk all that had been gained. The objective declared by the Joint Chiefs was to bring about "an end to the fighting, and a return to the status quo; the mission of Eighth Army was to inflict enough attrition on the foe to induce him to settle on these terms." In the words of a British gunnery officer, "Everybody could see that we had reached stalemate, unless someone started chucking atom bombs."[2] Ridgway wrote, "We stopped on what I believe to be the strongest line on our immediate front."[3] In the first half of June, Van Fleet mounted limited operations to consolidate his positions—an exact repeat of the movement Ridgway began in April but which was frustrated by the Chinese spring offensive. This time, "Operation Piledriver" successfully gained Chorwon and Kumwha, the base line of the "Iron Triangle." The X Corps cleared the "Punchbowl," another important Communist fortified zone. On the new front, give or take a few miles at various points, the United Nations would hold its ground for the remainder of the war.

The Chinese were compelled to concede stalemate. At vast cost in lives, they had demonstrated their inability to break through the revitalized divisions of the Eighth Army, whatever local gains they could still achieve against the vulnerable ROKs. However limited the war aims of the Chinese in November 1950, there is no doubt that their early triumphs opened up, in the eyes of Peking, illusory visions of absolute military victory in Korea, of an all-embracing Communist success. Now, once again, the prospect open to Mao Tse Tung had narrowed dramatically. Chinese hopes of unifying Korea had died. The economic cost of the war to China was proving crippling, with the Russians insisting upon payment for the arms and ammunition which they supplied to Marshal Peng's army. The West had convincingly demonstrated its determination to defend South Korea, at whatever cost in lives and treasure. Yet, from a Western perspective, the war had thus far proved an unhappy and divisive experience. America's relationship with her allies had been deeply strained by the behavior of MacArthur, the real fears in Europe that American desperation might provoke the use of nuclear weapons and even a third world war in defense of another "faraway country of which we know nothing." As a leading political historian of the period has written, "Alarm that Britain might be dragged into war sharpened anti-Americanism, always latent in the Labour Party, and as a study of the Press shows, soon began to undermine confidence in American leadership."[4] Many Westerners in Korea, above all many Europeans, were dismayed by the brutal injustice and corruption of Syngman Rhee's government, which they were being asked to uphold, and of which more will be said below. "We felt a great hatred of being there, of the country," said Captain St. Clair Tisdall of the 8th Hussars. "We seemed to be doing nothing very useful."[5] The cost of rearmament, above all for Britain, was proving almost insupportable. Even the modest British contingent in Korea was a very serious financial burden.

On June 1, 1950, the UN Secretary-General Trygve Lie declared his conviction that if a cease-fire could be achieved roughly along the 38th Parallel, the resolutions of the Security Council would have been fulfilled. The next day Dean Acheson made a speech in which he reaffirmed the objective of a free and independent Korea, but he spoke of the prospects for peace resting upon the defeat of Communist aggression and the creation of suitable guarantees to prevent a repetition of that aggression. On June 7 he told a U.S. Senate committee that UN forces in Korea would accept an armistice on the 38th Parallel. The world was learning to live with an acknowledgment of changed military and political realities in Asia. On June 23, when Jacob Malik, the Soviet delegate to the United Nations, proposed a cease-fire in Korea, his olive branch was received with overwhelming relief in the Western world. The Peking *People's Daily* endorsed the Russian initiative. At last the end seemed in sight. Some compromise could be agreed, and the armies could go home. "I . . . believe," Ridgway had concluded a report to the Joint Chiefs on May 20, "that for the next sixty days the United States government should be able to count with reasonable assurance upon a military situation offering optimum advantage in support of its diplomatic negotiations." On July 10, Communist and UN delegations met for the first time in the town of Kaesong to open cease-fire negotiations. It was fortunate for the peace of mind of the governments of the West that they had no inkling of the two years of struggle and bloodshed that still lay ahead. The Communists were about to teach the world yet another bitter lesson in Korea: that war can be waged as doggedly and painfully at a negotiating table as with arms upon the battlefield.

Panmunjom

From the outset Ridgway urged upon his government the toughest possible posture toward the Communists in negotiations: "To sit down with these men and deal with them as representatives of an enlightened and civilized people," he wrote to Washington, "is to deride one's own dignity and to invite the disaster their treachery will bring upon us."[6] If the UN Commander's remarks would have been considered embarrassingly bellicose had they been known to some of America's allies, they were bleakly justified by the events that began to unfold at Kaesong.

At the front, on the first day of talks with the Communists, sixteen men of the UN forces were killed, sixty-four wounded, fifteen missing. In Seoul, Western correspondents provoked a near riot because of the UN Command's initial refusal to allow them to attend the truce meetings. Ridgway himself had to leave his headquarters to pacify them. Floyd Park, the Pentagon's Chief of Information, issued a defensive statement: "Arranging for an armistice during the progress of actual fighting is one of the most delicate negotiations in human affairs and must necessarily be conducted in strictest secrecy. Moreover, ultimate success must depend in some measure upon the willingness of the public to await concrete results, and especially to refrain from violent reaction to incomplete or unfounded reports and rumors." Yet within weeks all these sensible considerations would be buried without a trace as the peace talks began their rapid deterioration into a public circus.

The UN Command perceived no special import about the Communists' proposed choice of a site for talks until these began on July 10. The UNC delegation was led by Vice Admiral Turner Joy of the U.S. Navy, the Communist group by the North Korean General Nam Il. The significance of the fact that Kaesong was firmly in Communist hands became rapidly apparent: the Chinese and North Koreans were not seeking the give-and-take of armistice negotiations. They had come to receive the UN's capitulation, or at least to score a major propaganda triumph. It had been agreed that the UN party should fly to the talks under a white flag, which the Westerners regarded as an emblem of truce. They quickly discovered that the Communists were presenting this symbol to the world as a token of surrender. Joy's delegation found that, across the conference table, they had been seated in lower chairs than their Communist counterparts. Every speech from the North Korean and Chinese team was punctuated with propaganda phrases about "the murderer Rhee," "your puppet on Formosa." Every exchange was delayed by interminable adjournments demanded by Nam Il's delegation. Every procedural detail, the most basic discussion of an agenda, was dragged down into a morass of ideological rhetoric and empty irrationality. One of the most urgent UN demands, for the Red Cross to have access to prisoners in Communist hands, was unhesitatingly brushed aside. A low point in negotiations was attained on August 10 when the two delegations stared across the table at each other in complete silence for two hours and eleven minutes, a Communist gesture intended to display their rejection of the preceding UN statement. An extraordinary catalog of ludicrous, indeed often fantastic, complaints was presented against the UN Command.

By August 22 the talks had gotten nowhere. The Communist delegation had wrung every conceivable propaganda advantage from the meetings, while talking for long enough to see that the UN delegation had not the slightest intention of yielding on acceptable terms. Nam Il therefore broke off the talks, claiming that UN forces had attempted to murder his delegation by air attack.

The Communists had gained an immensely useful breathing space. Ridgway's forces had passively held their positions during the five weeks of talks, and the Chinese were able to reinforce their formations strongly with artillery. The UN battle for its next important objective, the Hwachon Reservoir, which provided both water and electricity for Seoul, proved bitter and costly. The names of Heartbreak Ridge and Bloody Ridge, dominating the reservoir, entered the unlovely vocabulary of the campaign. These features changed hands again and again between August and October. But on October 14 they fell to the U.S. 2nd Division for the last time. Meanwhile, farther west, UN forces advanced up to nineteen miles north of the 38th Parallel. Chinese casualties were enormous. There was little doubt that the tide of war had turned once more against the Communists. On October 7 they proposed a resumption of negotiations. This time there seemed little doubt that the military pressure was forcing them to parley in earnest.

Talks began once more on October 25, 1951, at the genuinely neutral site of Panmunjom, in no-man's-land between the armies. On November 12, Van Fleet, Eighth Army's commander, was ordered to desist from major offensive action and restrict his forces to the defense of their existing front, to be known as the MLR—main line of resistance. Local attacks were still permissible, but no operation in greater than battalion strength could be mounted without authorization from Ridgway. This was the prelude to a striking negotiating bid by the UN delegation at Panmunjom: if the Communists signed an armistice within thirty days, Joy's group told the Chinese and North Koreans, the existing front could be frozen into the final demarcation line between the two sides.

This was a move designed to show the Communists, and the world, that the UN had no interest in further territorial gains in Korea. It was also intended, of course, to hasten Peking and Pyongyang toward a rapid ending of a war of which Western opinion was becoming increasingly weary. The Communist negotiators hastened to ratify the proposal on November 27. Then for thirty days they talked empty nothings at Panmunjom. And while they talked, immune from major UN military action, on the mountains their armies dug. Day by day, yard by yard, they sank their trenches and tunnels into the hillsides. For 155 miles from coast to coast of Korea, through December 1951, they created a front of defensive positions, manned by 855,000 men, almost impregnable to artillery fire and assault. Successive lines were interwoven into a fortified belt from fifteen to twenty-five miles in depth. By December 27, when it was amply apparent at Panmunjom that the Communist delegation had merely been playing for time, their armies were dug into the positions that, with only minor variations, would form the final armistice line nineteen months later. The Communists could feel entirely satisfied with their progress. They were well aware of the growing war-weariness with Korea among the Western democracies. Granted that they had been compelled to forgo the immediate prospect of a military takeover of South Korea, they could hold their existing positions confident that it was most unlikely that the governments providing the UN contingents would tolerate the casualties that would be necessary to break the Chinese line. Peking and Pyongyang, facing the real risk of complete defeat in June 1951, had now achieved a virtual no-lose position. They could settle down at Panmunjom with a sense of time on their side, to wear down the fragile patience of the democracies, with only occasional injections of offensive action on the front to keep up the drain of casualties and maintain pressure on the UN.

Yet if the December semi-truce had been an error by the UN, throughout this period their military commander remained undeceived by and unyielding toward the Communist strategy. The secret communications between Washington and Matthew Ridgway, which have now been released for historical scrutiny, underline the American general's qualities. Unlike MacArthur, Ridgway never allowed his rhetoric to descend into bombast. But he displayed a commitment and sense of purpose of the highest order at a moment when the public will in the United States was being visibly sapped by the frustration of stalemate.

"Already in the press and radio [he wrote to the Joint Chiefs in July 1951], such expressions as the following are beginning to appear: 'Let's Get the Boys Back Home' and 'The War-Weary Troops.' I can hardly imagine a greater tragedy for America and the free world than a repetition of the disgraceful debacle of our Armed Forces following their victorious effort in World War II. We can never efface that blot on the record of the American people on whom the responsibility squarely rests. Within my authority and in the light of common sense and my best judgement, I shall seek to the limit of my ability to eliminate among all U.S. military personnel in this theatre the type of thinking indicated by the use of such expressions. If this be 'Thought Control,' then I am for it, heart and soul. To condone it would be a cowardly surrender of everything for which we have fought and plan to fight. It would coincide completely with the line the Communists would wish us to take."[7]

But if Washington's patience and resolve were being tested by events at Panmunjom, in Tokyo Ridgway remained certain that there must be no indication of weakening will. "I have a strong inner conviction," he wrote in September, "admittedly based on the Korean as contrasted with the world situation, that more steel and less silk, more forthright American insistence on the unchallengeable logic of our position, will yield the objectives for which we honorably contend. . . . With all my conscience I urge that we stand firm."[8]

Yet between July and the end of November 1951, the United Nations Command had suffered almost 60,000 casualties, more than 22,000 of these American. Communist resistance in the air was strengthening, with the appearance of the first Tu-2 light bombers. The war in Korea had entered its longest and most frustrating period—of stalemate on the ground and sterile attrition at the negotiating table. The United Nations Command had renounced any military objective beyond the defense of the MLR and spasmodic local operations designed to sustain morale and demonstrate its army's continuing will to fight. For many months the airmen had been urging the Chiefs of Staff in Washington—as airmen so often urged commanders throughout the twentieth century—that they could pursue the allies' strategic objectives at far lower cost in lives by a sustained bombing campaign. From the last months of 1951 until the end of 1952, while the negotiations at Panmunjom dragged interminably on, the U.S.A.F. waged a massive campaign to bring pressure upon the Communists by bombing, of which more will be said below. Yet by December 1952 the Communists had been able to increase and supply forces in Korea that numbered 1,200,000 men of seven Chinese armies and two North Korean corps. And through all those weary months, on the mountains of Korea the UN armies alternately baked and froze, fought fierce little local actions, whiled away the weeks in their foxholes and bunkers— in the name of a cause whose meaning and purpose had long been forgotten by those "at the sharp end," if they had ever understood it.

The Cause

From beginning to end of the Korean conflict, most United Nations soldiers found considerable difficulty in reconciling the ideals that they were alleged to be fighting for with the unattractive conduct of the regime of Syngman Rhee. As early as July 18, 1950, the British Minister in Korea, Henry Sawbridge, wrote to the Foreign Office from Pusan:

"It appears from here that this war is being fought *inter alia* to make Korea safe for Syngman Rhee and his entourage. I had hoped that I might find it otherwise. I may be wrong, but I fancy that the inexperience, incompetence, and possibly corruption of the present regime are in some measure responsible for this crisis."[9]

"Nor is there any real soul to this war [the Australian Richard Hughes wrote in the London *Sunday Times* on September 5]. No powerful sympathy or even warm liking exists between the Americans and the South Koreans. The soldiers of the United States and Britain notoriously have little abstract opinion or articulate comment on why they are fighting, but they can usually detect in any war a menace to their country or their homes. They can perceive nothing of that sort in this war."

Through the months that followed, American and British soldiers constantly witnessed dreadful acts of brutality by the South Koreans toward their own people. One man, a Private Duncan, wrote to his MP: "40 emaciated and subdued Koreans were taken about a mile from where I was stationed and shot while their hands were tied, and also beaten unnecessarily by rifles. The executioners were South Korean military police. The whole incident has caused a great stir and ill-feeling among the men of my unit. We have heard of lots of other occasions of the same happening. I write to tell you this, as we are led to believe that we are fighting against such actions, and I sincerely believe that our troops are wondering which side in Korea is right or wrong."[10]

In the spring of 1951 a wave of outrage swept through the ranks of the British 29 Brigade following the publication in the London *Sunday Times* of a statement by Syngman Rhee denouncing the alleged British role in the dismissal of MacArthur and declaring, "The British troops have outlived their welcome in my country." This was one of Rhee's notorious tantrums. He told an Australian Embassy official, "They are not wanted here any longer. Tell that to your government. The Australian, Canadian, New Zealand and British troops all represent a government which is now sabotaging the brave American effort to liberate fully and unify my unhappy nation."[11]

British diplomats in Korea sighed, and sought to take refuge in an urbane view of Syngman Rhee's deficiencies. After the British Minister in Korea had seen the President, he wrote to London on June 16:

"The South Koreans—as is perhaps to be expected at their stage of national development—are going through one of the more acute stages of the 'awkward age.' It is their misfortune, and their allies', that this should coincide with the obligation to fight for the survival of their newly-acquired independence. When they show themselves, as they often do, uncomprehending and intolerant of other people's views, their extreme inexperience is an extenuating circumstance that has to be taken into account when evaluating the irresponsible statements made by people in prominent positions. Chief among these is the President himself."[12]

This line of reasoning, of course, offered little consolation to the men on the line. And even some UN officials took a far less sanguine view than the British Minister of the South Korean government's behavior. "At least many hundreds [of alleged Communists] have been shot," reported the Australian delegate to the UN Commission for Korea, John Plimsoll, on February 17, 1951. He described how the prisoners had been compelled to dig their own graves, then "rather clumsily and inexpertly shot before the eyes of others waiting their own turn." In fairness to the Seoul regime, Plimsoll pointed out the immense bitterness and yearning for revenge among South Koreans for the dreadful atrocities committed by the Communists during their occupation: "The members of the Korean government and the Korean police are literally fighting for their lives. Any one of them or of their families who fell into enemy hands would be killed. They therefore do not take quite the detached view of the situation that persons overseas can take. . . . Even allowing for all this, the executions remain shocking. The picture is not a pretty one, even when due weight is given to the special conditions of war and of a relatively primitive country."[13]

It was made even less pretty by such scandals as the creation of the so-called National Defense Corps by the South Korean government in December 1950. This was intended to act as a paramilitary militia. In the months that followed it became evident to foreigners in Korea that something was going wrong when they glimpsed bodies of starving beggars in the streets, and when it was learned that thousands of wretched members of the NDC were dying of cold and exposure, kept confined in barracks unfed and deprived of warmth. Even the Seoul government could not indefinitely resist demands for an investigation. It was discovered that the NDC commanding officer, Kim Yun Gun, had embezzled millions of dollars intended to clothe and feed the militia. He and five of his officers were shot outside Taegu on August 12, 1951. Yet every allied government knew that this case was only the tip of the iceberg of official corruption.

Throughout the war Rhee conducted his own dictatorship without reference to allied sensibilities, almost indeed as if the war did not exist. The National Assembly fought a long series of political battles with him . . . and lost all of them. The last, and most dramatic, came in May 1952, when the Assembly voted to overrule Rhee and lift martial law in the Pusan district. On May 27 the Assembly building was surrounded by military police. Some fifty assemblymen in shuttle buses were towed by army trucks to a military police station. Four were jailed, although their arrest in mid-session was blatantly illegal. Rhee then wielded power as if the legislature did not exist. "Spontaneous" demonstrations were organized in his support. Coercion of anti-Rhee assemblymen became outrageous. At midnight on July 4, eighty were dragged into the Assembly hall under police guard to prevent their escape. None were allowed to leave until constitutional amendments had been passed, placing all effective power in South Korea in Rhee's hands. Thus armed, he called a presidential election on August 5 at which he was declared elected with 72 percent of the vote. Thereafter, official corruption in Korea ran entirely unchecked, and meaningful political debate was at an end. The United States and her allies were deeply embarrassed. Rhee made it plain that he could not care less.

Captain Ves Kauffroth arrived in Korea in December 1950 from New Orleans to serve as an air traffic controller. Driving toward Kimpo, ''the truck was stopped by Korean police while a procession of Korean prisoners marched across the road directly in front of us. The procession was led by a long line of men wearing pointed, conical hats that even covered their faces. The long lines were four abreast and were followed by women who were also roped together. The women's heads were not covered, and several looked up to us in the truck in a most beseeching manner as they were dragged along. I asked the driver what was happening, and he said they were Communists being taken away for execution. He said that now the Chinese had entered the war, all Communists were being 'gotten rid of.' ''[14]

Here was a pattern that was to become bleakly familiar in Indochina: of two opposing authoritarian regimes, each waging war *à l'outrance,* each committing acts of extraordinary brutality by Western standards. In Seoul, as in Saigon later, it could be argued that the scale of atrocities committed by the anti-Communist forces was far less great than that attributable to the Communists. Yet nothing could change the fact that the process of law scarcely existed in Seoul, any more than in Pyongyang. The vengeance of Syngman Rhee and his officials upon their perceived enemies was quite as casual and ruthless as that of Kim Il Sung. The Communist guerrilla activity in South Korea, which remained a constant feature of life there until the end of the war, required unceasing military activity to contain it, and provided the Seoul regime with an alibi for all manner of brutalities to its own people, ''suspected of assisting the enemy.'' Western soldiers were struggling to believe that they were fighting in Korea to defend certain principles of justice and freedom, which they witnessed daily being flaunted, indeed trampled underfoot, all around them.

Throughout the first year of the war, Washington conducted a tireless diplomatic offensive to broaden to the utmost the participation of foreign contingents in the struggle. If the concept of the war as a United Nations crusade, rather than a narrow pursuit of American national interests, was to remain plausible, the member nations of the UN must be seen to contribute on the battlefield. Yet the very insistence of the Washington Administration that the Korean War must be regarded as one front in the worldwide struggle against communism made many nations reluctant to flock to the standard. It might have been easier to persuade them to fight against North Korean aggression than to participate in a confrontation in which, they were told, Pyongyang was merely acting as the tool of Moscow and

Peking. In the first year the towering shadow of MacArthur, together with his pronouncements, deterred some governments. It was embarrassing enough to be invited to send troops to fight as subordinate partners of the American Army. But when there was also serious doubt whether the Washington Administration could control its own theater commander, when the specter of a third world war hung heavy over the battlefield, even greater fears came into play. Many nations were still in deep economic difficulties in the aftermath of World War II. Their men in the field had to be clothed, armed, equipped, ammunitioned, even fed by the United States. Each country repaid the U.S. government $14.70 per man per day in the field—for some reason, in the case of the Canadians, it was $16.50. Individual nations also paid for some of their supplies. Once when a Filipino artillery battery was called upon to lay down a heavy barrage in support of the Turkish Brigade, it is claimed that the following morning the Filipino commander protested to his American divisional commander about the cost to his poor country of all that ammunition. Yet, for all the great and sincere efforts that were made by senior Americans to cloak their effort in Korea in the mantle of the United Nations, from beginning to end the conflict could never be other than Washington's war, to which other states provided token contributions chiefly for the diplomatic appeasement of the United States.

Among the most prominent contributors, the Turks sent a much-respected infantry brigade, whose men were evidently uninterested in higher tactics or sophisticated military skills, but possessed much rugged courage and willingness to endure. The Philippines, Thailand, Holland, Ethiopia, Colombia, Belgium, and Greece each contributed infantry battalions with some supporting elements. South Africa provided a fighter squadron. The more cautious Indians, Scandinavians, and Italians provided medical units. The French, whose military resources were strained to the utmost in Indochina and North Africa, provided a token infantry battalion which was exceptionally well regarded. The French unit, like those of all the other small nations, was incorporated into an American formation. But by far the most important non-American contribution was that of Canada and other nations of the British Commonwealth. The major Commonwealth countries all provided significant air and naval forces. Canada dispatched three destroyers and an air transport squadron soon after the outbreak of war and maintained a significant naval presence until the end. In addition, on the ground the British provided two infantry brigades, an armored regiment, and supporting artillery and engineers. The Canadians sent a reinforced infantry brigade. In June 1950 their armed forces totaled only 20,369 men of all ranks, and thus assembling a contingent posed great problems. Their initial unit, the 2nd Princess Patricia's Canadian Light Infantry, proved to include much unsatisfactory material, many men who had to be sent home. But after the initial shakeout, the "Princess Pats" were welded into a fine fighting unit. The Australians also sent two exceptionally good infantry battalions, the New Zealanders, an artillery regiment. In July 1951 all these elements were combined to form the Commonwealth Division, under the command of Major General James Cassels. In the two years that followed, the formation achieved an outstanding reputation in Korea. "There was enormous enthusiasm for the ideal," said the division's first artillery commander, Colonel William Pike. "There was tremendous competition between the units, because nobody wanted to be thought less good than the others." The genuine excitement within the division, about proving that the experiment of an integrated Commonwealth fighting force could work, gave its senior officers, if not its men, reasons for being in Korea that seemed to many more worthwhile than defending the regime of Syngman Rhee. "You must remember that at that period, we still assumed that the Empire would go on," said Pike.[15]

And among all the UN formations fighting in Korea, there were the Koreans themselves. The decision to provide a contingent of "Katousas," Korean Attached Troops, to every allied subunit was partly a desperate expedient to bring some UN formations up to strength and partly a reflection of the High Command's lack of confidence in the ROK troops' ability to fight in formations. Thus almost every American and Commonwealth platoon possessed its handful of Koreans. Some were adopted as much-beloved mascots, some were respected as memorable comrades. Others were treated with callous contempt. As a system of reinforcement, it left much to be desired, because few Koreans became sufficiently integrated into the units to which they were attached to be fully accepted and trusted. Meanwhile, the ROK Army's formations continued to cause chronic concern to the commanders of the Eighth Army. Faced by a Communist offensive, they collapsed with monotonous regularity. Knowing themselves to be untrusted by their foreign sponsors, the Koreans repeatedly showed themselves militarily untrustworthy. Until the end of the war the worst excesses of corruption were commonplace in the ROK Army. Officers neglected their men, sold their rations on the black market, paid phantom soldiers to line their own pockets, neglected even to give the men in their ranks the pittance of pay to which they were entitled. The only consolation for being a ROK soldier was that, for some men, life was marginally more endurable than for their civilian counterparts. The South Korean people, from beginning to end of the war, suffered an eternity of hardship and injustice, modified only by the efforts of foreign refugee organizations who did their best to feed and clothe the worst sufferers. "The whole country seemed to have become a quagmire," said Lieutenant Chris Snider of the Canadian Brigade. "Everything had been beaten down to the lowest level. There seemed no society but peasant society. The place was a huge armed camp, strewn with homeless children and devastation."[16] To foreigners, the poverty was almost unbelievable. President Rhee's official salary was $37.50 U.S. a month; that of a ROK army colonel, $10.75. The Bank of Korea claimed that the average salary of a Korean was $5.00, yet the average spending in a family of 4.6 adults was $32. The Koreans claimed, denying the vast influence of the black market, that the difference was made up by families selling odd valuables, putting children in street stalls, and "calling on Confucius for aid." The equation was distorted by foreign largesse: every Korean employee of EUSAK was paid $17.50, and the average houseboy received $30 to $60. It was a web of hardship interwoven with corruption and foreign free-spending, which was to wreak equal havoc with the moral fabric of Vietnamese society a decade later.

Suk Bun Yoon, the fourteen-year-old schoolboy who had twice escaped from Seoul under Communist occupation, was living with the remains of his family as suppliants upon the charity of a village south of the capital in the spring of 1951. A government mobilization decree was suddenly thrust upon the village: twenty able-bodied men were required for military service. Suk's family was offered a simple proposal by the villagers: if the boy would go to the army in place of one of their own, they would continue to feed his parents.

An American army truck bore him and the other bewildered young men first to Seoul and then on up the dusty road toward the front. They spent a night in an old station warehouse, where they were given chocolate and a can of corned beef. It was the first meat the boy had tasted for six months, and was impossibly rich. He was sick at once. Next morning, after five hours on the road, he and a cluster of others were deposited at the camp of the Royal Ulster Rifles. He was not to be a soldier, but a porter under military discipline. He found himself joining a unit of some forty porters attached to the battalion. His first job was to carry a coil of barbed wire up to the forward positions. It was hopeless. He was too young and too weak. The corporal in charge took pity on him. He was assigned to become a sweeper and odd-job boy at the rear echelon. Yet life remained desperately hard. Each night the porters were confined to their hut, yet they were sometimes awakened amid the sound of the gunfire to carry ammunition or equipment forward. One day they found themselves hastily ordered back to a new position. Suk scarcely understood what was happening, beyond the confusion of retreat. Gradually he and the others understood that there had been a battle and heavy casualties. Around half the porters had disappeared, been captured, or killed.

After the battle the porters' conditions seemed to improve. Suk became more accustomed to the life and determined to educate himself. As he learned a little English he questioned the soldiers incessantly: What was the longest river in the world? Which was the highest mountain? How was England governed? Since in later life he became a professor of economics, this experiment could not be considered a complete failure. The soldiers called him "Spaniard" because he had a reputation for a hot temper. Yet when the Ulsters were relieved and he found himself attached to the Royal Norfolks, conditions deteriorated again. He was caught scavenging for food, roughly handled, and sent for a spell to a barbed-wire cage. He was then sacked from his job as a porter at battalion headquarters and sent to the pioneer platoon, where he spent several more months.

"I was very homesick," he said. "By February 1952 I was on the verge of a mental breakdown. The only letter I had sent to my family was returned undelivered. I was missing them desperately." That month he was given leave to go to Seoul. He reached the capital determined not to go back to the front. He contacted some of his old schoolmates and in April was able to arrange to return to school—a school without books or desks. His only asset was a strong command of the English language he had acquired on the hills behind the Imjin.[17]

The men of the UN Army sometimes behaved with dreadful callousness toward South Koreans. Eighth Army was compelled to issue a forceful order of the day in the summer of 1951: "Many soldiers seem to take a perverse delight in frightening civilians by driving very close, and then suddenly blaring their horns at the unsuspecting. Others make repeated attempts to drive the Koreans off the roads and into ditches. Americans are notably impatient, and too often drivers direct vile and belittling profanity toward those who slow their progress. Swearing at the driver of an oxcart will not make the ox move faster. It will cause the owner of the cart to resent the impertinent discourtesy of the soldier who curses him. We are not in this country as conquerors. We are here as friends."[18]

Some of these "friends" were gentle and generous to Koreans, adopting and educating orphans, raising large sums for Korean charities, giving all the food and clothes they could spare from their units. Yet many never overcame their chronic suspicion of "the gooks" and carried this to savage limits in moments of stress. One morning in February 1951, Private Warren Avery of the 29th Infantry was out on "chicken patrol" with a handful of other men in a local town, searching for fowls for the platoon pot. They were stopped at a Korean military police checkpoint: "One of them said something to Gibson, and they all put a round in the chamber. We didn't know whether to believe they were South Korean or North Korean. When I heard a bolt snick, I just turned around with the BAR and wiped them off the f***ing crossroad."[19] There is no reason to doubt the truth of the story, for such episodes were commonplace. "Unless you were an anthropology student," said Marine Selwyn Handler, "Koreans were just a bunch of gooks. Who cared about the feelings of people like that? We were very smug Americans at that time."[20] Talking of the Eighth Army's treatment of refugees approaching the UN lines, Lieutenant Robert Sebilian of the 5th Marines said, "We probably shot some people who were innocent—but how could you know which side they were on? The military problem was simply: Do you let these people filter through?"[21] The answer, very often, was a ruthless negative.

UN soldiers' sense of alienation from the Koreans was intensified by observing their brutality toward each other. "One had a hard time thinking of them as civilized human beings," said Major Gordon Gayle, executive officer of the 7th Marines. "I was impressed by their absolute absence of Christian spirit. The ROKs thought it was funny to see some other guy over the hill being shelled."[22] Americans were told not to interfere when the ROK CIC were interrogating prisoners. "We found it hard to watch a man being beaten to death," said Major Ed Simmonds of the 1st Marines.[23] When Sergeant William Norris was sent to join the KMAG training mission, he was horrified by the Korean Army's discipline: "I saw a deserter shot; a kid who lost a rifle—an $87 rifle—was made to stand in a barrel of water all day in January. Men were beaten with pine saplings. Whole cities were roped off to collect people for the draft. And Americans could do nothing about it. You have to understand the Asian way."[24] The young Canadian, Chris Snider, complained about one of the Korean Katcoms (Korean Attached Troops with Commonwealth forces) in his platoon who persistently fell asleep on duty. The Korean liaison officer came down from battalion headquarters to deal with the matter. Snider was awakened to be told by one of his men that the visitor, along with a Korean senior NCO, had taken the offender out and ordered him to dig a grave. The man was shot before the Canadians could intervene. The liaison officer and NCO were replaced, but the episode had a traumatic effect on the whole platoon. The Canadians were astounded that men of any society could behave in such a fashion to each other. Yet almost every UN veteran of Korea saw South Koreans do such things to each other. Indeed, arbitrary execution appeared the foundation of ROK army discipline. The South Korean army officer, wrote a KMAG adviser—Lieutenant Colonel Leon Smith of I ROK Corps—in a scathing report to the Pentagon, "in almost all cases had no love or respect for his superiors—only homage—and no love, respect, nor sense of responsibility for his subordinates. He will browbeat his juniors, steal from all. He spends his time and effort on 'eyewash,' rather than the actual correction of conditions. He works hard at building his own ego to the point where he believes himself infallible, but when times really get rough, he comes back to his adviser for strength and decision."[25]

Upon such a foundation of mistrust and contempt for the nation in whose interests the war was being fought did the UN seek to make the ROK Army an effective instrument and South Korea a viable political entity.

13

THE INTELLIGENCE WAR

In the aftermath of World War II it was not merely America's uniformed armed forces that were abruptly run down and demobilized. William Donovan's intelligence organization, the Office of Strategic Services, built up almost from scratch over five years of intensive wartime activity, was reduced to a tiny bureaucracy in Washington, operating a handful of field agents. In the summer of 1950 this was the extent of the renamed Central Intelligence Agency and its resources. "The Company" maintained a small office in Tokyo, but its operations in the Far East were chronically crippled by the hostility of MacArthur. Ever since World War II, when he had refused to allow clandestine activities by any of the intelligence "private armies" in his theater, the general had cherished a distaste for such practices. Only in May 1950 was the CIA allowed to set up its first Tokyo station. And only later that summer, under the desperate pressure of war, was this expanded into an active operational network. William Duggan's Office of Special Operations was responsible for Far East intelligence gathering. George Aurell, with some difficulty, maintained liaison with SCAP's headquarters. An outlandish Danish-American named Hans Tofte, whose enthusiasm for behind-the-lines adventuring took him into the OSS in the last stages of World War II, set up a new unit named the Office of Policy Coordination to organize covert activity. Meanwhile, back in Washington, as the Administration became brutally aware of the consequences of attempting to conduct foreign policy with inadequate intelligence about enemies actual and potential, the director of the CIA, Admiral R. H. Hillenkoetter, was sacked. On the strong recommendation of General Marshall, Truman replaced him with General Walter Bedell Smith, Eisenhower's wartime chief of staff in northwest Europe. Bedell Smith's appointment gave the CIA almost overnight a credibility and claim upon resources in Washington that provided the motive power for the Agency's massive expansion in the next three years.

Yet throughout the war United Nations intelligence about Chinese and North Korean strategic intentions remained very poor. There is still no evidence to suggest that Washington possessed any high-placed agent in either Pyongyang or Peking. By far the most important and effective sources of operational intelligence, as in World War II, were decrypts of enemy wireless transmissions by the vast signals organization established outside Washington for the purpose. But the available quantity of "sigint"—Signals Intelligence—was restricted by the enemy's shortage of sophisticated communications equipment. From 1950 onward a variety of organizations were established in South Korea to provide "humint"— intelligence based upon agent observation behind the Communist lines—and to sponsor covert guerrilla operations. None were notably successful, and all paid a frightful toll in lives—most of them Korean. But their efforts have a place in any portrait of the war.

When America entered the Korean conflict, a CIA station was hastily established in the peninsula, initially at Pusan, under the direction of a veteran paratroop commander from World War II, Ben Vandervoort. But Vandervoort had little special operations experience and seemed unhappy in his role. He was replaced by a big, formidable ex-FBI man who had spent many years in South America, Al Haney. Jack Singlaub was an ex-World War II paratrooper who had served with the Office of Strategic Services in Indochina, and thereafter in OSS's successor organizations, the Special Services Unit, the Central Intelligence Group, and finally the newly created Central Intelligence Agency. Until the Nationalists were driven out of mainland China, Singlaub was CIA station chief in Mukden. When the Korean War began he was a lieutenant colonel, building a Ranger organization at Fort Benning. He volunteered for Korea in the hope of being given a battalion command. Instead, he was seconded to the CIA to serve as Haney's deputy station chief.

A complex chain of command was established to preside over intelligence gathering. At its summit stood JACK—Joint Advisory Commission, Korea, which was in turn part of CCRAK—Combined Command Research and Activities in Korea—controlled from Tokyo by Willoughby, MacArthur's G-2. They were primarily concerned with the parachute insertion of parties of locally trained Koreans to gather intelligence behind the lines. The accident rate was high. The recovery rate was low. Yet in the customary empire-building contest between service bureaucracies, a multiplicity of covert operations groups developed in Korea. The U.S. Navy was sponsoring coastal raiding parties of their own. The British were landing Royal Marine hit-and-run assault groups. There were outposts on the offshore islands running escape and evasion organizations for downed pilots or monitoring enemy movement. By a characteristic irony, the only interested body not known to be sponsoring intelligence operations in the North was the government of South Korea. Syngman Rhee's intelligence organization confined its attentions to keeping a close watch on its own society.

The CIA was determined to maintain its independence of CCRAK, and was largely successful in doing so. A strict edict was issued that no Americans were to be dispatched into the North. But the Seoul station, based in the Traymore Hotel, rapidly expanded to a strength of more than a hundred officers, training Koreans to land in enemy-held territory by small boat from the coast. In the first year of the war some 1,200 recruits were trained on the island of Yong-do, an island off the southern tip of Korea where a marine named Colonel "Dutch" Kraemer ran the program.

Initially, the purpose of putting agents into the North was to discover whether there was any basis upon which a local resistance movement might be built up. A few Koreans were set for long-term training. Most were merely given the most rudimentary instruction before being pitched ashore on a hostile coast with a radio set. Some, perhaps to their controller's surprise, sent back remarkably optimistic messages giving rendezvous at which more agents and supplies could be dropped. It was many months before the Americans began to perceive that almost all these operators had been captured, "turned," and were transmitting under Communist instruction. Slowly and reluctantly, the CIA recognized the ruthless efficiency of the Communists' control of their own countryside. North Korea was simply too small, too overcrowded with troops, militia, and police, to make covert movement readily possible.

But the lesson was learned the hard way, at tragic cost in lives. There were fewer stranger stories of behind-the-lines operations in Korea than that of Major William Ellery Anderson of the Royal Ulster Rifles. Anderson, an Englishman, played a major role in one of the early attempts to wage war behind the lines in Korea under the auspices of the U.S. Army. He was an architect's son, commissioned into the British Army in 1940. He saw considerable service as a paratrooper, was wounded in Sicily, and in 1944 survived for some weeks in Occupied France after being dropped after D day with a Special Air Service party to support the Resistance. When the war ended Anderson spent some months as a war crimes investigator, then accepted a regular commission in the Ulsters because he had a friend in the regiment. He found the routine of peacetime soldiering intolerable, and by 1950, when the battalion was sent to war, he was barely on speaking terms with his colonel. As soon as they arrived in Korea, Anderson was sent off to a "Battle Training Team" and it was made clear that the colonel hoped not to see him back.

Anderson was a natural adventurer, and he was bored. There was an exciting rumor that the SAS was to send a squadron to Korea, which he hoped to join. But then it was learned that MacArthur, with his intense dislike of special operations, above all foreign ones, had quashed the idea. One day early in 1951, Anderson was complaining to the correspondent René Cutforth about the lack of imagination of the high command in failing to organize guerrilla operations behind the Communist lines. Cutforth said he had heard something of that kind was in the wind. Anderson at once asked for an interview with General Van Fleet. He got as far as seeing the Eighth Army commander's G-1. He was then passed on to Colonel John Magee of Eighth Army's Operations staff. Magee welcomed Anderson's enthusiasm and invited the Englishman to join the embryo organization, Combined Command for Intelligence Operations, Far East. Indeed, Anderson found himself running his own little section of it. From a Quonset hut in a reinforcement depot, Anderson began to recruit Koreans. ROK officer cadets were invited to volunteer, with the promise of commissions if they survived. Within a few days Anderson had twenty recruits. One of them was Lee Chien Ho, the chemical engineering student who had escaped from Seoul as a refugee and become an interpreter with the 5th Marines. Jimmy Lee, as he now called himself, developed great respect for Anderson's skills as a special operations officer and indeed contrasted them favorably with those of some American officers with whom he subsequently served.[1] With the aid of an American Ranger officer, one British and two American NCOs, Anderson began to put the Koreans through classic commando training. At a simple ceremony Colonel Magee presented the Koreans with their parachute wings on completion of their jump training. In March 1951, Anderson felt ready to lead their first simple operation. They were to blow up a railway in a tunnel.

Anderson took four Koreans and two Americans. One of their Koreans had already acquired an American name, John. They rechristened the other three Matthew, Mark, and Luke. On the night of March 17 they parachuted uneventfully from a Dakota. All the next day they laid up in paddy fields some fifteen miles south of Wonsan. The next night they marched some eighteen miles to reach the Kyongwon railway line, between Osan-ni and Huchang-ni. On the night of March 19, covered by a heavy snowfall, they climbed down into the railway tunnel and laid their charges and pressure switches. Then they lay and dozed, waiting for the sound of a train.

It came in the early hours of the morning. In an agony of suspense they waited . . . and waited. Then there were two heavy explosions. The little group of men on the hillside leapt with glee like schoolboys. Their exhilaration faded somewhat an hour later when they made radio contact with their base to learn that the U.S. Navy could not pick them up from their intended rendezvous on the coast. A lot of walking lay ahead if they were to get home. They marched for three nights. "Each man was silent," wrote Anderson afterward, "lost in his own thought, plodding along mile after mile, wet, cold and hungry or, during the day, escaping reality in brief snatches of troubled sleep. The map meant nothing in this area, and many times I felt that we were heading for a hopeless wilderness. My compass showed that we were still moving in the right direction, but at times I doubted it. I sensed a feeling of resentment behind me as we walked mile after stumbling mile. Perhaps I should never have committed these men to such an ordeal. At times I even toyed with the idea of surrender. After all, perhaps we would never find the place we were looking for; perhaps we might wander for weeks about these hateful rain-soaked mountains without food or shelter. Perhaps the war would end and nobody would think of us again."[2]

Somehow, they survived. They evaded the North Korean troops whose paths they crossed. But they suffered another disaster when Matthew and Mark, two of the Koreans whom Anderson had dispatched to steal food from a peasant house, did not return. They were never seen again. Anderson himself was feverish, and his spirits were not improved by difficulty making radio contact with their base. But at last, when they had almost despaired of rescue, they were given a new rendezvous. Two helicopters closed in under powerful fighting cover. One by one, they were winched into the sky and away to safety. "We were over the moon— we felt as if we'd won the war," said Anderson.[3]

Anderson now began to plan his next operation. His American parent organization at Taegu was expanding fast. He was excited by the idea of creating long-term bases deep in the mountains of North Korea, from which his teams could sally forth to attack communications and dumps. Above all, they would seek to create an indigenous resistance movement in North Korea on the familiar lines of the French Maquis. This time, he would be more ambitious. He planned to take twenty men, to form a nucleus for a guerrilla army. In a mood of high excitement, he and his reinforced team prepared to drop once more into North Korea: "The very fact of belonging to a 'secret' operational unit is exciting in itself," Anderson wrote, with frank delight. "All active-minded men the world over are boys at heart, be they generals or privates, and there are few things more stimulating or conducive to high morale and self-confidence than the knowledge that you have been chosen to do something about which others know nothing and which calls for a high standard of efficiency, integrity and courage. Basically, I suppose, it is conceit—a buccaneer complex."[4]

That conceit was soon to be brutally shattered. But for the time being, they reveled in their fantasies. Anderson concocted one plan—to find and kidnap a Russian adviser. Colonel Magee was appalled: "My God, Bill, don't do that for heaven's sake!'' he said. ''I admit it seems quite feasible, but Washington would go mad if they suddenly found a Russian officer on their hands.'' To Anderson's consternation, only a few days before they planned to leave he received new orders from Eighth Army: no British or American personnel were to engage in operations behind enemy lines. In future, these would be conducted exclusively by Koreans. But Anderson drove to headquarters and persuaded them to allow himself and his British and American colleagues to go. There was another setback when the shortage of aircraft compelled Anderson to reduce his Korean contingent for the operation to fourteen men. The remaining six, desolated, signed a petition in their own blood demanding to be allowed to go. But the space problem was insoluble.

There was a momentary embarrassment at the airfield from which they departed when the guerrilla party queued at the Red Cross canteen for coffee and doughnuts. ''Say, are those Koreans in your party?'' asked the Red Cross helper behind the counter. ''Well, I'm sorry, we don't serve Koreans.'' The Koreans smiled sadly. The whole party took off without their coffee. They landed this time in the center of North Korea, near Isang-ni. One of the Koreans, John, a veteran of the earlier operation, was severely injured in the drop. Uneasily, Anderson watched a North Korean patrol moving across the valley near their position. Then a young, ragged Korean peasant walked into the midst of their group. He told them that the police had seen their parachutes the previous night. He said that he himself was hiding from conscription for the army. Anderson's party debated what to do with the boy. Eventually the Englishman let him go, with the promise of food if he brought some of his friends to help them. This, after all, was what they had come to do—to recruit North Korean sympathizers for a local guerrilla force.

The boy, named Lim, led Anderson to a nearby valley where he pointed out some hundreds of North Korean and Chinese soldiers bivouacked. Anderson thought the concentration big enough to justify an air strike. He radioed the coordinates of his position back to base. Sure enough, within a few hours aircraft strafed and rocketed the area. Then they let Lim go.

Now matters rapidly began to go wrong. The parachute landing of a reinforcement party was botched—they were landed two miles from their landing zone. A supply drop resulted only in smashed equipment and radios littered across the mountainside. Anderson requested a helicopter to take himself out, to return to base to grip the situation. The helicopter came under fire as they climbed away, but Anderson felt confident that his party's location would not be discovered. He returned to Taegu to find that a new draft of Korean recruits had arrived to be trained. Anderson personally checked the parachutes and cargo nets for that night's supply drop.

But three days later disastrous news came. In a garbled radio message from his British wireless operator in the field, Anderson learned that his party had been surprised by the Communists and was heavily engaged. That night Anderson overflew the area in an American aircraft and established voice contact with his party. They told him that the situation was hopeless. "It's no good, sir," said the voice of the Northumberland Fusilier on the ground. "They've got us—we'll try and make our way out as best we can. Over."

Anderson urged the wireless operator to light a fire or otherwise show his position to a helicopter. But the Englishman said finally, "There's just me and Sergeant Monks, sir. But he's hurt and I can't leave him. We'll be all right, sir, but there is no place a chopper can put down here and I think the place is lousy with the bastards. I'll stay here with the sergeant, we'll be all right. Out."

Neither the English Fusilier nor the American sergeant were ever heard from again. Wretched with the burden of responsibility and guilt, Anderson flew back.

Most of his party were killed. Ten days after Anderson lost contact with the group, two Koreans, his American Ranger officer, and an NCO walked into his office and saluted. They told a bitter story. In an act of criminal folly, a supply aircraft had arrived over their position in broad daylight and dropped a string of parachutes, which brought the Communists hastening down upon them. When the party scattered the four men had been able to make their escape. They walked south through the mountains, miraculously got through the Communist lines, and swam the Imjin River to reach the American lines.

In the months that followed a growing ruthlessness was evident in the American approach to covert operations in the North. No more Americans or British were to go, but there was an ample supply of Koreans. To his astonishment and dismay, Anderson found himself asked by a new American commanding officer to train Koreans to be parachuted into the North seven days after their induction.

"Seven days!" exclaimed Anderson. "Good God! I can't even train them to shoot straight in that time, let alone give them parachute training and practice jumps."

"There won't be any time for practice jumps, just ground training and weapons training. Sorry, but there it is—that's the assignment. The Air Force knows where to drop them."

Anderson was told that this was to be a new scheme—dropping Koreans in pairs some fifty miles behind the lines, with orders to make their way back with whatever information they could gather: "That way we can cover a hell of an area and get some really good information." He smiled at Anderson. "You don't seem too happy about it. What's worrying you?"

"How many do you think will get through, sir?"

"Maybe four or five. Hell, it's their war, too, isn't it?"

Bitterly unhappy, Anderson accompanied the first party of Koreans to their drop zone: "Never before had I taken unprepared men into battle and now I was about to do something far worse. I was sending untrained men into the most frightening and lonely of battles—a battle within a battle in which one's own mind becomes the field of conflict, where hope, discipline, and courage must fight against loneliness, fear, and panic."[5]

The British officer asked to be relieved of further involvement in the program. At the behest of a British intelligence officer serving under diplomatic cover at the Seoul Embassy, Anderson made some further attempts to run intelligence-gathering teams into North Korea from the island of Chodo. But after the loss of his surviving British officer and most trustworthy Korean during a Chinese raid on their base, he withdrew. Anderson was posted back to England, where for some months he worked in small-boat operations in the Adriatic for the A19 intelligence organization. They discussed and planned the setting up of a unit to aid prisoner escapes from North Korea, burying supplies and inflatable boats along the coast. But by now the talks at Panmunjom seemed likely to succeed. And by 1953 the heart had gone out of both American and British enthusiasm for covert operations in the North. There had been too many tragic accidents such as Anderson's "Operation Vixen."

The United Nations never established successful covert operations in North Korea. The Royal Marines' coastal raiding parties could inflict minor pinpricks on the enemy at small cost, with the heavy air and naval support they could call upon. But any operation that demanded the support of local North Koreans proved doomed to failure. The Communist control of the countryside was too ruthlessly effective. From the spring of 1951 even the peasants of North Korea understood how very unlikely it was that the UN forces would ever reoccupy their country. The realities of power, or, rather, of personal survival, demanded obedience to the regime of Kim Il Sung. It remains difficult today to believe that the information brought south by the small numbers of South Korean agents who survived justified the cynical squandering of so many lives by the various intelligence organizations in the South.

Yet as the Korean War progressed, like the Japanese economy and the regime of Chiang Kai Shek, the Central Intelligence Agency became one of its principal beneficiaries. Korea put the CIA on the map. Its principal officers were eager, ruthless, and ambitious for their organization. They acquired control of forty old C-47s with the markings of CAT—Civil Air Transport—a forerunner of Air America and Air Continental, which they sponsored in Vietnam. Their network of offices and bases extended throughout Japan and Korea. Hans Tofte even sponsored the shooting of a full-scale propaganda feature film in Japan about the experiences of Japanese prisoners in the hands of the Soviets, which became a local box-office success.

As the war progressed the CIA attempted ever more elaborate and ambitious operations. Hans Tofte claimed to have organized the interception of a Norwegian freighter loaded with medical supplies donated to the Chinese by the Indian government. Nationalist Chinese gunboats with CIA agents aboard boarded the ship north of Formosa, seized its cargo, and set the freighter adrift, apparently the victim of piracy. According to one historian of the operation, "the nurses, doctors, and other medical personnel were never heard of again, and he [Tofte] does not speculate as to their fate."[6] Yet such dubious adventures plainly impressed somebody. Resources continued to be lavished upon the Agency's Far East operation. A hydrofoil was built to the Agency's specifications in a Japanese yard, to which a junk upper deck was fitted to provide a high-speed covert-landing vessel. A succession of Korean teams were dispatched to try to contact American prisoners in the Yalu camps. All failed. A major base was established on one of the islands in Wonsan Harbor, from which to land parties on the mainland. A technique was developed for snatching men off the ground from a moving aircraft, which was employed to recover a handful of agents from North Korea. But the sum result from all these efforts was pathetically small.

The CIA operation, as its veterans readily admitted later, was disturbingly amateurish. They experimented with recruiting some ex-Rangers from Fort Benning. But they discovered—in another foretaste of Indochina—that by the time these men had grasped the job, they were due for rotation back to the United States. The CIA's first generation of direct recruits were young and green; many had volunteered in order to avoid being drafted into the Army. Perhaps most serious of all, the quality of the intake of Koreans was poor. CIA recruiters constantly trawled the refugee camps, searching out North Koreans sufficiently motivated to return to their country. But the dropout rate in training was very high. And the casualty rate among agents dispatched into North Korea was appalling, perhaps 80 percent. The Agency's officers also chafed under the difficulties of gaining access to the Navy's ships and the Air Force's planes for moving its men and supplies. This problem was increasingly solved by the creation of their own sea and air fleets.

In the view of Jack Singlaub, the greatest single cause of the Americans' difficulties in running effective operations in the North was that almost every anti-Communist in the country had long left it. When the Eighth Army retreated south in the winter of 1950, North Korean refugees followed in the hundreds of thousands: "The lesson was—'don't strip out all your friendlies.' We had made the mistake we repeated in Vietnam—offering everyone who wanted to leave, everyone with pro-Western sympathies, the chance to go. There was simply no one left in the North likely to help us."[7]

It was a lesson that was learned at bitter cost in Korean lives: several hundred infiltrators and agents were landed in the North between 1951 and 1953, and pitifully few of them returned. It is difficult to regard the manner in which they were recruited and dispatched as any more than cynical exploitation of a supply of manpower whose depletion no one would bother to question. But for the CIA's future, the Korean operation paid off handsomely. In 1949 its covert activities branch possessed a staff of 302, seven foreign stations, and a budget of $4.7 million. By 1952 the staff had swollen to 2,812, with a further 3,142 "overseas contract personnel" on the payroll, forty-seven stations, and a budget of $82 million.

The simple truth was that, at this moment of history when the Cold War seemed so close to becoming a hot one, Washington's craving for information about the Communists around the world was so great that it seemed necessary to seize upon any means by which to gain it. The crushing shocks of the North Korean invasion, the Chinese intervention, the sudden ruthless gambits of the Russians in Eastern Europe created a desperate need to know more, much more, about the enemy. An organization to achieve this had to be created from scratch. The wartime reputation of Bedell Smith, the Agency's director, did much to give the CIA credibility, and bankability, in Washington. Lower down the scale, among a number of distinguished and highly professional intelligence operatives, it is not surprising that the dramatic growth of the CIA made room for a small army of adventurers, charlatans, and men more temperamentally suited to becoming rodeo riders. Let loose around the world with astonishing freedom of action, it was these men who conceived the plans to poison Patrice Lumumba's toothbrush, to parachute a long succession of doomed agents into Eastern Europe to foment hopeless revolutionary programs, and to organize guerrilla operations in North Korea and China. To give the CIA its due, throughout the later war in Indochina its intelligence assessments were consistently more realistic and better informed than those of the Pentagon. But in Korea it is difficult to judge that its operations remotely justified the scale of resources it eventually deployed or the lives that were squandered in its name.

14

THE BATTLE IN THE AIR

Throughout the great conflicts of the twentieth century, professional airmen have asserted their claims to a unique status. They have argued that their ability to pass over the ground battlefield, to carry the campaign to targets miles behind the front lines, exempts them from the traditional precepts of warfare. In the First World War, until the last months, the technical limitations of aircraft restricted their role. Although they carried out some bombing operations, their principal importance was as scouts, reconnoitering and photographing the battlefield below. The seesaw struggle for air supremacy, waged between fighter aircraft, focused chiefly upon securing freedom for reconnaissance. The first generation of heavy bombers, the British Handley-Pages and German Gothas, inflicted some damage upon targets and civilian populations behind the lines in 1918. But it was the prophets of air power who were most excited by their achievements, who anticipated a future conflict in which great fleets of bombers could inflict fatal damage upon an enemy's industrial heartland while the armies were still contesting irrelevant strips of earth hundreds of miles behind them.

The Second World War confirmed the decisive importance of aircraft in tactical support of ground and naval operations. But the conflict's message was far less certain about the effectiveness of bombing either as a means of destroying an enemy's industrial capacity to wage war or in a long-range interdictory role, preventing an enemy from moving men and weapons to a battlefront. No one disputed that air attack had inflicted great damage upon lines of communications. Yet the fact remained that the Germans had been able to continue moving sufficient supplies to the front to fight with formidable effect for the last eleven months of the war, even in the face of absolute Allied command of the air. While vehicles moving in the open presented targets that could be attacked with devastating results, the impact of bombing upon foot soldiers in broken country— or well dug in—remained far less impressive. Japan's surrender was precipitated by the effects of two air-dropped atomic bombs, but these demonstrated the intolerable consequences to humanity of the use of nuclear weapons much more convincingly than they argued a new dimension for air power.

Objectively perceived, the experience of World War II suggested that air forces employing conventional weapons were subject to much the same constraints as ground and sea forces. The bomber possessed none of the mystic force with which it was endowed by the prophets of the 1930s, who believed that air attack could terrorize a civilian population, or cripple vital industries, regardless of the scale upon which it was employed. The successful employment of aircraft, like that of any other instrument of military power, depended upon the weight of force available, the skill with which it was employed, and the suitability of the targets that it was offered. The more closely air forces worked in harness with ground or naval forces, the more effective they were. Their pursuit of a strategy independent of the other services produced more questionable results.[1]

Yet while these conclusions were readily accepted by generals and admirals, and even by military historians and defense intellectuals, in the years following World War II they were less enthusiastically adopted by professional airmen. Throughout the brief history of their arm, the world's military airmen had striven for an independent role, divorced from the control of unsympathetic groundlings. Many senior airmen both in Britain and the United States simply declined to accept the unpalatable conclusion of the official postwar bombing surveys, which cast doubt on the achievements of bomber offensives against Germany. They continued to assert that bombing had been a decisive—indeed, in the view of some, *the* decisive—force in the defeat of Germany and Japan. They were also enthused by the vital role they gained in postwar strategy as a result of the invention of the atomic bomb. It was The Bomb, and the U.S.A.F.'s new stature as its carrier, that clinched the American Air Force argument for becoming a separate and equal service in 1947. In the postwar years of straitened service budgets, it was Strategic Air Command which absorbed the lion's share of funds for its big bombers. The Air Force sometimes gave the impression of wanting to forget all that it had learned with such pain during World War II about ground-air coordination and close-support techniques. It carried its obsession with arranging matters differently from the ground forces to remarkable lengths: airmen wore their name badges on the opposite breast of their uniforms to the Army, their officers even signed documents at the opposite corner of the paper. In 1948 a seminar was held at the Air University at Maxwell Field, Alabama, to discuss the theme "Is there any further need for a ground force?"

The air war over Korea gave birth to a new concept—combat between jet aircraft—and revived all the traditional arguments about air support for ground operations. From the first days of the war there was intense and often bad-tempered debate between the ground commanders and senior officers of Far East Air Force about the quality and quantity of close air support they received. This was heightened by Army jealousy of Navy and Marine organic air support, which the soldiers considered both more dedicated, and more professional, than that of the Air Force. "Whenever we received close support from the Marine Air Wings," said a skeptical army consumer, Colonel Paul Freeman of the 23rd Infantry, "it was better than anything we got from the Air Force."[2] It was not that the Army disputed the vital importance of close support—indeed, soldiers freely declared that the Army could not have stayed in Korea without it. The argument hinged upon the weight of Air Force effort that should be given directly to the ground forces, and at whose discretion this should be allotted. "There was a lack of cooperation between the Air Force and Army at all levels," said Group Captain "Johnnie" Johnson, a British World War II fighter ace who flew some B-26 missions in Korea with the U.S.A.F. "U.S. Air Force morale was very high, and they thought they were doing a vital job. But there were not the army officers present at briefings that we had in Europe in World War II. In the first months, forward air control seemed very limited."[3] The ground forces were constantly frustrated by the difficulty of getting air support when it was needed, rather than when aircraft chanced to reach position over the forward area. Battalion commanders were irked by the arbitrary arrival of a flight of fighter-bombers whose commanders would radio laconically, "I have twenty minutes on station. Use me or lose me."

There is little doubt that in the first months of the war, thousands of the interdiction missions flown by the Air Force were valueless because of inadequate targeting. "The Air Force bombed and bombed all the main routes during the winter retreat of 1950," said Major John Sloane, an officer on the ground with the Argyll & Sutherland Highlanders, "but they achieved very little because they didn't understand Chinese techniques. The Communists simply weren't on the main routes."[4] Attempts to identify and bomb Communist troops on the move, especially during the first weeks of the war when target intelligence was almost nonexistent, caused substantial casualties among friendly forces and refugee columns fleeing desperately from the battlefield.

From the first day of the Korean War, the importance of fighter-bombers in a close support role was beyond doubt. The Yak piston-engined fighters of the North Korean Air Force were cleared from the skies within a matter of weeks, and the U.S.A.F.'s Mustangs, together with carrier-based American Corsairs and British Seafires and Sea Furies, played a critical tactical bombing role. In the last months of 1950 land-based UN aircraft were flying almost 700 fighter-bomber sorties a day, matched by a further 300 from the offshore carriers. One of the most experienced and respected air commanders in the U.S.A.F., General O. P. Weyland, was dispatched to Tokyo to direct the Far East Air Force. But serious problems quickly became apparent in determining the effective employment of medium and heavy bombers. There were pitifully few targets in North Korea large enough to justify attack by bombers in the big formations they were trained and accustomed to fly. How could fast modern aircraft fly effective interdiction missions against an enemy who moved most of his supplies by porter and bullock cart? This was a problem that would become familiar a generation later in Indochina. In Korea the United States Air Force encountered the difficulty for the first time, after a decade in which its commanders and its pilots had focused overwhelmingly upon the problems of fighting industrialized nations that deployed vast mechanized power upon the battlefield. It would be absurd to dispute that the UN—or, rather, overwhelmingly the U.S.—air forces contributed greatly to the supply difficulties of the Communist armies. But the central reality remained, that the North Koreans and Chinese continued to be able to move tolerable quantities of food, arms, and ammunition to their front-line forces from beginning to end of the conflict. The Air Force commanders sought refuge for their disappointments and failures in incessant protest about the political limitations on their operations around and beyond the Yalu. But there remains no reason to suppose that, even had all political restrictions been lifted, strategic bombing could have decisively crippled the Communist ability to sustain the war any more than it was able to do so in the next decade in Vietnam.

Lieutenant Oliver Lewis had spent the last months of World War II in the Pacific ferrying B-17s and B-29s, for he was too young to fly combat missions. On June 26, 1950, he was flying F-80s when he was abruptly ordered to the Far East. He had just time to take his wife home to Salt Lake City before reporting to Travis Air Force Base. There he was issued with a .45 pistol, a mosquito net, and a water canteen before boarding a C-54, still coated in coal dust from its role in the Berlin Airlift, for the long haul to Japan. He expected to be posted to fighters, but with his heavy aircraft experience, he was sent to the 3rd Bombardment Wing, flying B-26 bombers out of Iwakuni. "The whole thing was pretty bad in Japan at that time," he said. "You can't believe the confusion. They were trying to get the dependents of the Australian Mustang squadron off the base and away home. They were trying to find some targets in Korea big enough for us to hit. They simply had not crystallized how to fight this type of war, when we had aircraft designed for large-scale formation operations."[5]

Lewis spent forty-five minutes being "checked out" on the B-26, flew two mail runs into Korea, and was then rostered for combat operations. At first they flew by day. Each pilot was allotted a stretch of road to patrol for a given period of time, with instructions to shoot up anything that moved upon it. Occasionally they were directed to a specific target, perhaps a warehouse "believed to contain war materials." They had standing orders to attack all trains or suspicious concentrations. "Trains were the best targets," said Lewis. "Hitting one made you feel like a king. But the Koreans got pretty good at blowing off steam from the engines to make themselves hard to see." Within a few weeks of the outbreak of war, the Communists had abandoned any attempt to make major movements by day. The bombers, too, were transferred to night operations. They carried a variety of ordnance: rockets, high-explosive and fragmentation bombs. Some aircraft carried a devastating battery of fourteen fixed .5-caliber machine guns in the nose. Even in the darkness, at low speed and low level, the pilots found that they could see reasonably well with the instrument lights extinguished. Above all, they could detect motorized movement. In the first weeks of the Chinese intervention, crews sometimes found and attacked great convoys of trucks moving with their headlights ablaze. The bombers would fly down the column, toggling a bomb every 500 yards, then swing back to machine-gun the blazing ruins. But as the enemy became more practiced at giving aircraft warning, as the extraordinary Chinese network of road sentries developed, halting every vehicle when a bomber was heard, it became far more difficult to spot targets. Novice crews preferred to fly in moonlight. The more proficient found that it was easier to identify enemy movement on clear dark nights, when the mountains were stripped of the haze that hung around them under the moon.

For the crews, a tour of operations consisted of fifty missions. Most wanted to get it over as speedily as possible and go home. Thus they would seek to fly every night, and some did. As winter came the reflection from the snow made it possible to see more in darkness. But the lack of heating and deicing gear in the aircraft began to cause serious problems. There were shortages of everything, in the air and on the ground. The weather became as dangerous a killer as the enemy. Every pilot had to make his own decision about the trade-off between layers of clothing to fight the cold, which caused some to climb into their cockpits looking like overstuffed teddy bears, and the clumsiness this created, hampering their ability to respond to the controls.

As the months went by and the problems of fighting a primitive enemy became more apparent, new equipment and new techniques were introduced: PQ-13 bombing radar, terrain radar to defeat the chronic bad weather. At the other extremity of the technological scale, some aircraft were fitted with troughs into which the crews laboriously loaded the contents of keg upon keg of roofing nails. Over a North Korean road the engineer would shovel these, with the aid of a paddle, in a long stream out of a funnel at the rear of the aircraft. Later the nails were replaced by purpose-designed tetrahedrons, designed to cripple the bare feet of men and beasts.

The more thoughtful pilots were far more conscious than some of their commanders in Tokyo of the uncertainty of assessing what they were achieving. "We were very aware of how imprecise was our ability to judge what was being done," said Lieutenant Lewis. "But of course the intelligence people are always eager to have you say that you've done well."

The first MIG-15 jet fighters appeared in the skies over Korea in November 1950, sending a shockwave through the West comparable to that of the launch of the Sputnik satellite a few years later. Some fifty MIGs, flown by Chinese and Soviet pilots, were initially deployed. The Communists revealed their advance to the frontiers of technology. Within six months there were 445 MIGs operating from the political sanctuary of air bases beyond the Yalu. By 1953 there were 830, mostly flown by Chinese pilots, though a Russian air corps also participated. The Soviets, like America's allies, used Korea as a proving ground where their pilots could be rotated in and out, to gain experience of the new shape of air warfare. The American B-29 bombers began to suffer a steady drain of losses to fighter attack, coupled with the impact of radar-controlled antiaircraft guns. A struggle for air superiority began over North Korea, which continued until the end of the war. For the first few weeks after the MIGs' arrival, the available American fighters in the theater, notably the F-80 Shooting Stars, were disturbingly outclassed. But then came the Sabre, the F-86 which became the principal weapon of the UN. The first wing was deployed in December 1950, reinforced by a second a year later. Sabres were in chronically short supply to maintain U.S. air strength worldwide, and there were never more than 150 deployed in Korea, against the much greater number of MIGs. But the West, and the United States in particular, has always produced pilots of exceptional quality. From beginning to end, they proved able to maintain air superiority over North Korea, despite all that the Communist air forces could throw against them. More than that, the Korean War and the shock of discovering the Communists' possession of the MIG stimulated the United States to an extraordinary program of technical innovation and aircraft development which continued long after the conflict had ended.

In Korea, as in every war, the fighter pilots considered themselves the elite, despite the irony that their prospects of survival were significantly better than those of the ground-attack pilots. Three squadrons of Sabres were based on the huge airfield at Kimpo, a few miles west of Seoul, where they shared the strip with a squadron of Australian Meteors and another of B-26s. Each night the squadrons' "fragmentary orders" clattered down the Teletypes from headquarters decreeing the number of aircraft that would be required the following day. The pilots slept in Quonset huts, little less cold or uncomfortable than those of army rear elements. Each morning the rostered officers mustered for briefing to be allotted their respective roles: high cover and close cover for daylight bomber missions or routine combat patrols.

They took off one by one at three-second intervals, then climbed into formation, spreading out across the sky to cross the bomb line above the confronting armies. They patrolled at around 40,000 feet, or as low as 20,000 if they were escorting fighter bombers. At those heights the Communist flak presented a negligible threat. They flew in fours—the famous "finger four" created by Hitler's Luftwaffe and the basis of all fighter tactics ever since. Larger formations were too difficult to control or maneuver. Number three commanded the flight, but the essential combat unit was the pair, each of the two leaders being protected by his wingman. They cruised steadily, for there was no purpose in exhausting their fuel at .9 mach if there was no enemy in sight. Pilots liked the Sabre—"a very honest airplane," in the words of Lieutenant Jim Low, one of the Korean aces, "it was a beautiful plane that sort of wrapped around you."[6] Men who had trained or fought on the old propeller-driven fighters found the jets simpler to fly, without the problem of countering torque, and far less prone to technical failure—the lack of vibration placed less strain upon every mechanical element. At first, for a pilot trained to fly with the constant roar of a piston engine in front of him, the muted vacuum-cleaner whine of the jet was almost unnerving. A careful pilot could extend his patrol endurance to as much as ninety minutes. A less skilled one—or a man feeling the strain of combat flying, eager for an excuse to return to the ground as fast as possible—might need to land after forty-five. In winter their endurance was extended by the strong prevailing northwest jet streams that pushed them home. It was also easier to spot the enemy in those months, when the cold, damp air created a prominent condensation trail behind an aircraft. In summer they could only look for the glint of silver in the sun.

Throughout the war the Sabres achieved almost undisputed dominance of the skies over Korea, North and South. Senior American airmen became exasperated by the manner in which the military took it for granted that they could conduct ground operations without the slightest threat of enemy interference in the air. "It's a terrible thing to say," remarked General William Momyer thirty years later, "but I think we would be in a much stronger position today with regard to the importance of air superiority if the enemy had been able to penetrate and bomb some of our airfields and had been able to bomb the front lines periodically. It would have brought home to our ground forces and other people the importance of air superiority. The Army has never had to operate in an environment where it had to consider: 'Do we dare make this move at twelve o'clock noon because that road is under the surveillance of enemy aircraft, or can we move that division from here to here during this period of time?' Those considerations are absent in all of the planning by virtue of this experience: they have never had to fight without air superiority."[7]

Some American fighter pilots in Korea went weeks, even months, without glimpsing an enemy aircraft. Others, in inexplicable fashion, seemed to possess some magnetic force that drew the MIGs into the corner of the sky through which they flew. Jim Low, a twenty-six-year-old Californian, shot down an enemy aircraft on his first mission in Korea. Low was widely recognized as a natural hunter—indeed, a killer. It was a pilot in his squadron, James Horowitz, who later wrote the popular novel about the Korean air war, *The Hunters*. The picture that the book painted, of a group of men among whom a few were ruthlessly, competitively dedicated to "making a score," was readily acknowledged by some of the survivors. Low himself suggested that there were three identifiable groups of fliers within his squadron, within most of the Korean squadrons. There were the average pilots, who merely did the job. There were the veterans of World War II, some of them highly skilled pilots, among whom were the foremost aces of the war—68 percent of pilots who destroyed MIGs in Korea were twenty-eight or over and had flown an average of eighteen missions in World War II. But more than a few of the veterans had lost something of their cutting, killing edge with the passage of time. They wanted to stay alive. There were reservists among them, "the retreads," men recalled from civilian life to fight again, who resented their presence in Korea. And finally there were the young gladiators, the men like Low who had joined the Air Force not merely to fly but to fight. "I think wars are designed for twenty-three-year-olds," said Flight Lieutenant Roy Watson, a British pilot flying F-84 Thunderjets. "I enjoyed it very much—it was the time of my life."[8] Their enthusiasm, their hard-living, hard-dying, high poker-playing life-style repelled some of their comrades. But in the air, few could dispute that they were good. When the priceless radar stations out on the islands off North Korea reported a "bandit train"—perhaps eight successive elements of two MIGs—making for their sky, the hunger of their response could not be gainsaid. A flight leader once ran his entire flight out of fuel to reach a MIG and get a kill. Despite the strict rules against crossing into Chinese air space, many Sabres in hot pursuit did so; some claimed to have shot down aircraft on the traffic pattern at Mukden.

They cast off their wingtip tanks and swung toward an estimated rendezvous with the enemy, clawing height out of the sky, for the MIG's greatest advantage was its superior ceiling—that and its tighter turning circle. The tactics of fighter combat in Korea were identical with those of World War II, save only that at higher speeds the aircraft maneuvered across greater spaces. The flight leader might radio to his second pair "You take the bounce!" indicating that he would watch the higher sky, cover the rear, while the other men dived, at a speed of perhaps 500 knots. Sometimes they would push their aircraft to its limits, frighten themselves considerably, shattering the sound barrier in their dive. If the MIGs saw them as they came, the enemy pilots would break sideways. Then, for the most part, there was merely a chase as the Communist aircraft fled for home. On the rare occasions when the MIGs stayed to dogfight, the Americans knew that their opponents were uncommonly determined and were likely to prove unusually skilled. Optimum killing range was around 200 yards, and to gain an accurate shot a man might be flying as slow as 200 knots.

The MIGs' cannon could be deadlier killers than the six .5-caliber machine guns in the nose of the Sabres—if they could be brought to bear. But the Sabre was a more stable fighting machine at high speeds than the MIG, and the American pilots were of higher quality than the Chinese, or even the Russians when the Soviets sent a "volunteer" air corps to fly some aircraft over North Korea. Each encounter came and went so fast: after weeks of boredom, one June morning on patrol Low's flight spotted two MIGs crossing the Yalu at low level. The Sabres rolled over, diving from 30,000 feet to 2,000 to intercept. Then Low channeled— made a fast climbing turn to the right—and fired a burst into a MIG's belly, momentarily glimpsing its pilot in a red silk scarf. The Communist fighter exploded, its debris smashing the Sabre's windscreen. The Americans went home.

If an American aircraft was hit, in winter the pilot would try to bale out overland, for the sea was too cold to offer much prospect of survival. A pilot who ditched in the winter months could last three minutes in the water before reaching his dinghy, and seven minutes thereafter before his saturated flying suit froze. But in summer he would always opt for the sea if he could, where the huge and efficient rescue organization might reach him, even under the Communist guns. On the ships and the offshore islands, helicopters waited at constant readiness—for this, too, was the first war in which the "whirlybirds" played a significant role and became lifesavers for so many wounded soldiers and downed airmen. If a wingman could mark his companion's ditching position, a rotating procession of fighters would fly cover above him until he was rescued. Gillies, a Marine pilot in the 4th Fighter Wing, was retrieved from the very mouth of the Yalu after the first helicopter sent to rescue him itself ditched. Sometimes the overhead fighters would be called in to drive off Chinese patrol boats. Over North Korean territory, F-80s often attacked Communist ground troops again and again to keep them away from a downed pilot waiting desperately for a chopper. Scores of pilots were rescued successfully from the coastal areas of North Korea in the course of the war, an immense boost to the confidence of UN aircrews and a tribute to the extraordinary UN command of air and sea, even close inshore.

Kimpo was a dreary place, surrounded by rice paddies. There was little to do when off duty except play poker or gin rummy, or pay an occasional call on the nearby nurses' compound. The pilots were relatively rich, with their $60 a month combat pay and two-bottles-a-month ration of Old Methusalem whiskey, which most gave away, for few fliers cared to drink seriously. It was mostly the older men who drank, and cured their hangovers by flying on 100 percent oxygen the next morning.

The Australian Meteor squadron, also based there, had a fine reputation, but the Australian pilots were chronically jealous of the Sabre. The Meteor was considered to be an aircraft that could take punishment, but it also possessed a highly vulnerable hydraulic system that could be crippled by a single small-arms round through a leading edge. Heavy on the ailerons, it was hard work to fly from its cramped cockpit. The pressure on the pilots was intense: one British officer flew 114 Meteor sorties in six months, on one occasion five in a day.

Four Sabres sat permanently at readiness on the runway, the Alert Patrol, in case of some sudden report of an enemy takeoff by the radar controllers. The pilots recognized the key role of the controllers in making their scores possible—Low took them a few cases of beer whenever he made a kill. Each flier had pet preferences about his aircraft and his weapons. Some loaded extra tracer in the guns. Many carried solid tracer at the end of their belts to give warning that their 300 rounds were close to exhaustion. Most pilots wore silk scarves, and many affected the old soft leather World War II helmets until they were ordered to change to modern molded designs.

The enthusiasm of the enemy varied greatly from month to month. Sometimes weeks would go by without a UN squadron seeing combat. Then, without warning, the MIGs would embark on a flurry of activity. In a characteristic month—December 1952— the statistics tell the story: 3,997 MIGs were reported seen in the air by UN pilots; attempts were made to engage 1,849; twenty-seven were confirmed destroyed. Enormous effort was expended to achieve modest results in direct damage to the enemy. But much more important, air supremacy over Korea was constantly maintained. Men like Jim Low, with his flamboyant taste for enormous Havana cigars, his growing reputation as a "honcho"—a top pilot—revelled in the struggle. "I enjoyed all of it," he said later, "the flying, shooting down aircraft. I was too young to think about the politics. It was just a job we were over there to do."[9] Each pilot flew around 100 missions, perhaps six months' combat duty, before being rotated back to the United States. There was, perhaps, less tension among the squadrons in Korea than in World War II because the dominance of the American pilots was so great, their casualties less alarming. Some celebrated pilots were lost: Bud Mahurin, a World War II group commander, was shot down by ground fire; George Davis, one of the most celebrated aces, was brought down by a MIG when his score stood at fourteen victories. But the odds on survival were good. Even those who were lost were scarcely missed when men were coming and going constantly on routine rotations. And as Flight Lieutenant John Nicholls of the RAF, who flew the Sabre with the Americans, put it, "In England after a flying accident, there was a funeral. But in Korea, somebody just wasn't there anymore." Jim Low went home after ninety-five missions with five

MIGs to his credit, and not a scratch on him. He went on to fly fighters over Vietnam and survive five years in a Communist prison camp. The Sabre remained unchallenged as the outstanding aircraft of the Korean War: of 900 enemy aircraft claimed destroyed during the war by U.S.A.F. pilots, 792 were MIG-15s destroyed by Sabres, for the loss of just seventy-eight of their own aircraft. It was, inevitably, a Sabre pilot who became the war's top-scoring ace, Captain Joseph McConnell, with sixteen confirmed "victories."

If at least a proportion of fighter pilots found their occupation glamorous, it is unlikely that any of the heavy bomber crews would have said the same about theirs, flying a dreary daily shuttle to industrial and military targets in North Korea. Joe Hilliard was a twenty-seven-year-old Texas farmboy who just missed World War II and spent his first flying years as a navigator in what was then the U.S.A.F.'s only designated nuclear bomber group. He was newly returned from a tour of duty in England when Korea came, and he was rushed to Okinawa with the 307th Bomb Wing. They met none of the traditional comforts of combat aircrew: the only permanent accommodation on the base was occupied by another wing. They found themselves living in tents, which were razed to the ground at regular intervals by hurricanes. Their B-50 aircraft were taken from them and they were given instead old B-29s, just out of mothballs, which posed chronic problems with mechanical defects: "We were really mad about that. We got the feeling that the U.S.A.F. just didn't want to waste its first-line equipment on Korea."[10] To their disgust, they found that even the flight rations with which they were provided were of World War II manufacture.

Almost every morning the wing—part of the five B-29 groups operating over Korea—dispatched a formation of nine aircraft on a daylight bombing mission, in accordance with orders from Fifth Air Force headquarters in Tokyo. Then, with the coming of darkness, a succession of single aircraft was sent off, at intervals of ninety minutes. They flew and bombed under ground control. The next day it was the turn of another squadron to provide the force, and so on in rotation. It was a round-the-clock war. The lights burned in the operations room twenty-four hours a day, seven days a week.

Yet it was also war reduced to a cold-blooded, mechanical discipline. Daily orders laid down the grid coordinates of the target, the altitude—perhaps 28,000 feet—the bombload—probably 144 hundred-pound bombs, or 40 five-hundred-pounders—and the fuse settings, usually variable delays up to seventy-two hours. An average mission lasted around eight hours, from takeoff to touchdown, which hardly seemed a serious business to men who had been training under LeMay to fly seventeen- or eighteen-hour missions to Russia. They flew the first 500 miles, from Okinawa to the southern tip of Korea, at 4,000 feet, then began climbing to reach designated altitude around the 38th Parallel, flying at around 240 knots. The navigator and bombardier clambered down the fuselage to the bomb bay to remove the cotter pins from the nose and tail fins of the load, their flying suits wringing wet from the exertion. In winter they found flying very cold. In summer it was intolerably hot: "For most men, it was boring going up, boring coming down," said Hilliard. "One night our wireless operator slept all through the flight, after a heavy drunk."

In daylight they flew in a formation of three loose vics, which tightened only as they approached the target. They attacked on the orders of a "lead crew." For a big operation, a "Maximum Effort," there might be as many as seventy-two aircraft in the stream. The flak seldom troubled them. Most days they saw no sign of enemy fighters. But one morning, suddenly, they might reach "MIG Alley," twenty minutes short of the target, and hear their own radar controllers report urgently, "Twelve trains leaving the station." Then they knew that within a few minutes, the Communist fighters would be swinging in to intercept. If the enemy was in a determined mood, the Sabre top cover was seldom completely successful in keeping him away. The eternal controversy about the most effective means of giving fighter protection to bombers continued vigorously in Korea. The bomber men wanted escorts close in where they could see them. The fighter men insisted that they could do much more for the bombers by ranging wide and aggressively in their own manner than they could achieve—with fuel for only twenty-five minutes "loiter" over MIG Alley—hanging on to the edges of the bomber wings. Both methods were tried, and neither prevented some MIGs from breaking through. When they did so, for all the B-29's formidable weight of defensive armament, the gunners placed little faith in their ability to do more than throw off the aim of the MIG pilots. In the autumn of 1951 the bombers found themselves under growing pressure from MIGs, until in October casualties began to mount alarmingly. Five B-29s were lost in the month to MIG attack. The figure was a fraction of relative World War II bomber losses, but the aircraft were vastly more expensive and the commitment less absolute. Daylight operations were canceled abruptly. Thereafter the big bombers attacked by night.

The crews' enthusiasm was not increased by the living conditions on the base: rats in the tents, cold showers, naked light bulbs. One night when a typhoon blew, all the crews had to man their aircraft and sit in them through the night, engines turning into the wind for fifteen hours. Off base, there were a few whores and a few restaurants, and the chance of an occasional trip to Japan. Many men had wives at home in the United States who were less than enthusiastic about their husbands' role in Korea. Hilliard's was sharing a house in New Mexico with his flight engineer's wife. In World War II there had been a sense of hardships shared among fighting men, in whichever theater they were. Every man fighting in Korea was conscious that most of his fellow soldiers and aviators around the world were living lives of infinitely greater comfort.

A man flew thirty-five missions to complete a bomber tour—ten more than the European wartime standard, a recognition of the better prospects of survival. There were few of the problems of stress that afflicted World War II bomber squadrons. One officer in Joe Hilliard's squadron suddenly declined to fly any further missions and was simply given a ground job. But in Hilliard's view, "morale wasn't good. We didn't think we had enough support.

"When Vandenburg came down to inspect us, we really let him have it about that. A lot of us thought that if we were taking this thing seriously, we should have been able to bomb across the Yalu. We felt we should have had some better targets, or else some people felt that we shouldn't have been there at all. It was very discouraging when we found that they were repairing so many of the targets that we were hitting. There was a lot of criticism of Truman. Later, one looked back and felt that the whole thing had been a rehearsal for Vietnam—we just weren't getting the support from our government. Maybe if we had really hit North Korea with everything we had, it would have saved lives—there wouldn't have been any Vietnam."[11]

It was a source of constant irritation to the aircrew that they could approach targets close to the Chinese border only on an east-west course to avoid the risk of infringing Chinese airspace. Again and again they were compelled to watch the enemy's fighters scrambling from the invulnerable sanctuary of their base at Antung. The American fliers' great fear was of capture, not death. Joe Hilliard was haunted by a vision of years of confinement on a diet of cold, soggy rice: "I resolved I would starve rather than eat it." The experience of some Americans who were indeed taken prisoner suggests that Hilliard's fears reflected the reality. The bomber crews received lectures on escape and evasion from comrades who had bailed out and survived. Most of those who had not suffered such a trauma found it chilling to think too much about the prospect. It was easier to get through a tour if you treated it as a job, a routine, and brooded as little as possible about the brutality of the enemy beneath. Yet it was the strange irony of the bomber men's business that, in six months of raining death and destruction upon the Communist enemy in Korea, they never, even once, set eyes on the face of a Korean.

Throughout the Korean conflict one of the most important assets of the UN Command was its ability to deploy aircraft carriers relatively close inshore, almost parallel to the front lines, wherever these might be. The Americans and British— the dominant naval forces, with some support from the Canadians and Australians—divided their areas of responsibility from the beginning of the war. The British Far East Fleet operated west of Korea, in the Yellow Sea, and normally deployed two aircraft carriers and their escorts on a rotating basis. The American Seventh Fleet cruised on station in the Sea of Japan, east of Korea, with up to three carriers at any one time providing strike aircraft. From the outset the U.S. Navy vigorously defended the claims of its carrier-based aircraft to operate independently of the land-based air forces. "Command and control became a major problem in Korea," as a senior air force officer wrote.[12] Only relatively late in the war did the Navy concede the logic of joint target planning with Far East Air Force. The case for the independence of seaborne air operations normally rests upon the independence of the naval operations which the aircraft are supporting. Yet in Korea the allied fleets were merely providing mobile platforms for aerial sorties in support of the ground war. Without absolute command of the sea, the UN campaign could scarcely have been fought, since almost every soldier who fought, and every ton of supplies he consumed, was brought into Korea by ship. But since the Communists never significantly challenged the UN's naval forces, their principal role became that of providing floating air bases.

For most of the ships' crews it was a curiously unreal war. While the smaller vessels, destroyers and minesweepers, often worked close inshore and sometimes found themselves under fire from enemy shore batteries, the big bombarding cruisers and carriers steamed their racetrack courses, round and round a few square miles of sea, living out a daily routine that involved much hard work, much boredom, and only the smallest risk of enemy action. Yet aboard each of the carriers lived a few score men who were seeing the war at the closest and harshest proximity. The men of the air groups flew each day to the battle, then returned to the strange, cozy cocoon of their parent ship, where 2,000 men labored, most of whom never heard a shot fired in anger. As a British Fleet Air Arm pilot put it, "You could fly four sorties in a day, then come below, change into mess undress, and sit down for an evening of sherry, bridge, and brandy." The American Navy and Marine pilots, of course, on their "dry" ships, were denied the Royal Navy's alcoholic refinements. But the seesaw contrast in their lives between days of war and nights of naval comfort imposed almost a greater strain than the monotone discomfort of life on the line.

The vast majority of the 1,040,708 aerial sorties flown by UN aircraft in the course of the Korean War were close support, or fighter cover. Their importance was undisputed. But America's leading airmen persistently urged a more ambitious role for their forces in Korea and chafed at the frustrations of ground support. General Jacob Smart, Far East Air Force's Deputy Chief of Staff (Operations) for most of 1952, complained bitterly about "the opinion so often expressed or implied, that the Eighth Army is responsible for winning the Korean War, and that the role of the other services is to support it in its effort."[13] Here, yet again, was the airmen's search for a decisive independent role. Yet between June 1951 and the summer of 1952, the U.S. Air Force attempted overwhelmingly its most ambitious independent contribution to the struggle, and suffered the most galling failure.

"Operation Strangle" was a systematic attempt to cut off the Communist ground forces in the front line from their supplies by the sustained exercise of air power. It began with a campaign of bombing the road network in North Korea, and in August 1951 was extended to the railways. Three quarters of all land-based bomber effort and the entire carrier capability were dedicated to this task. Day after day and night after night, the enemy's communications were pounded from the air. In a fashion disturbingly reminiscent of World War II, and prescient of Vietnam, air force intelligence officers produced extraordinary graphs and statistics to demonstrate the crushing impact of the campaign on Communist movement. Yet, by the summer of 1952, none of this could mask the reality on the ground: the enemy's supplies were still getting through—between 1,000 and 2,000 tons a day continued to cross the Yalu at the height of "Strangle," it was later discovered. Prodigious feats of repair by civilian labor gangs working around the clock kept just enough of the road and rail network open to move food and ammunition. Constantly improving Communist antiaircraft defenses emphasized the eternal conundrum: to bomb low meant accepting unacceptable casualties; to bomb high meant a fatal loss of accuracy. "Strangle" cost the UN air forces 343 aircraft destroyed and 290 damaged, mostly fighter-bombers. It proved to objective observers such as Ridgway that there was "simply no such thing as choking off supply lines in a country as wild as North Korea."[14] In World War II, Allied intelligence estimates of German transport requirements proved to have been hopelessly distorted because a German division required only a quarter of the daily supply of its Allied counterpart. In Korea the ratio was even more dramatic: a Chinese division operated with a mere 50 tons of supply a day, against 610 for its American counterpart. The only means by which "Strangle" might have been made effective was to match the bombing of supply routes with intense pressure on the ground to force up Communist consumption of supplies. The will for this— or, rather, the will to accept the UN casualties involved—never existed.

"Strangle" was finally abandoned in the summer of 1952 in the face of severe aircraft losses for dubious strategic return. The airmen claimed that the campaign had at least prevented the Communists from building up supplies to mount a major offensive, but most thoughtful observers doubted that this had been the enemy's intention. The air forces turned instead to a succession of selective attacks upon power plants and dams in North Korea, about whose destruction the Communists were expected to be especially sensitive. Operation "Pressure Pump" was designed to impress upon the Communist delegation at Panmunjom the urgency of signing an armistice. Bomber attack, wrote Bradley as Chief of the JCS in November 1952, "constitutes the most potent means at present available to UNC, of maintaining the degree of military pressure which might impel the Communists to agree, finally, to acceptable armistice terms."[15] Yet American attacks upon the huge Suiho hydroelectric plant on the Yalu in June 1952 aroused intense controversy around the world, and especially in Britain, where strategic bombing in Korea was a sensitive issue. Installations in Pyongyang were hit again by massed bomber raids in July and August, along with key mineral workings. By the end of 1952 every worthwhile industrial target in the North seemed to the planners in Tokyo, poring over their photo mosaics, to have been battered into ruin. Pyongyang and other major cities had been flattened, hundreds of thousands of North Korean civilians killed. Yet there remained no evidence of the predicted collapse in the Communist will to win. In the summer of 1953 the airmen claimed that the Communist signature on the armistice document represented a last victory for air power, following a new campaign of attacks on dams critical for the irrigation of North Korea. There remains no decisive evidence to support or deny their claims. It is probably fair to assume that once the Communists had reached a political decision to accept the armistice, the prospect of further serious damage to North Korea's national infrastructure can scarcely have encouraged them to delay.

The lessons of the Korean War for air power seemed self-evident to the ground force commanders, and to those politicians who took the trouble to inform themselves about such things. The experience of World War II showed that intensive strategic bombing could kill large numbers of civilians without decisive impact upon the battlefield, or even upon the war-making capacity of an industrial power. Bombing could inflict a catastrophe upon a society without defeating it. North Korea was a relatively primitive society that contained only a fraction of the identifiable worthwhile targets of Germany or Japan. Nor could the airmen claim that this problem had never been foreseen. Alexander de Seversky was only one among many thoughtful students of air warfare. As early as 1942 he wrote, "Total war from the air against an undeveloped country or region is well nigh futile; it is one of the curious features of the most modern weapon that it is especially effective against the most modern types of civilization."[16] In Korea the U.S.A.F. belief in "victory through air power" was put to the test and found sorely wanting by many of those who were promised so much from it.

"The Eighth Army soldier [wrote an American officer in 1953] cannot but accept the destruction of that 'doctrine' [of air power] through demonstrations, costly to him, staged by his enemies the armies of Red North Korea and Communist China. For their troops and supplies moved, despite harassment from our air, consistently and in quantities sufficient to meet their needs. . . . Notwithstanding the all-out efforts of the air force in Korea, there was never a day when the trains did not run and the trucks did not roll behind the enemy lines in North Korea, from the forward enemy areas. . . . The air force in Korea did not fail to apply all the power of which it was capable. But it is plain that it could not, or at least did not, accomplish the mission Air Force theorists had repeatedly told the Army and the American people was sure to be accomplished, under conditions of such overwhelmingly one-sided aerial strength."[17]

*   *   *

No one could seriously dispute that to be bombed was a deeply distressing experience, and UN strategic bombing added greatly to the Communists' difficulties in sustaining the war. But of all the governments upon earth, those in Peking and Pyongyang were among the least likely to be deterred from continuing a commitment to the conflict merely because of the distress it caused to their peoples. Given time and labor to introduce countermeasures, above all putting key installations underground, the air-dropped conventional bomb proved as limited a weapon in the second half of the twentieth century as in the first. It is not surprising that the airmen's limitless faith in what they could achieve remained undiminished after Korea, as it had after World War II. If they admitted some of the bitter truths revealed by those wars, a critical part of the U.S.A.F. rationale for its own independent operations would cease to exist. But it remains astonishing that ten years later, in Vietnam, they were allowed to mount a campaign under almost identical circumstances to those of Korea, with identical promises of potential and delusions of achievement, and with exactly repeated lack of success.

15

THE WAR ON THE HILLS

Through the last two years of the war, for all the periodic surges of tactical activity, the ferocious struggles that cost thousands of men on both sides their lives in pursuit of hill numbers or map references, the strategic situation in Korea remained unchanged. From time to time the planners in Washington and Tokyo conceived grand initiatives for airborne drops or amphibious landings behind the enemy flank, designed dramatically to concentrate Peking's minds upon the negotiating table. Among many parallels between Korea and the later experience of Vietnam, as Dr. Rosemary Foot has written, was "the maintenance of the assumption expressed in the 1950s that using increased force can generate concessions at the negotiating table." The confidence of many American commanders in their ability to smash the Chinese line and reach the Yalu once more, if the leashes were slipped and the UN armies plunged all out for victory, remained a source of deep frustration. But the political realities ensured that their hopes were stillborn. The American public was weary of Korea. It was narrowly possible to sustain America's national will for the defense of a line across the peninsula until a compromise was reached, for avoiding the concession of defeat to the Communists. But the political consequences of any action involving many thousands of casualties—as an all-out offensive must—were intolerable. There was no possibility that America's allies would countenance any dramatic expedient. It was proving difficult enough, diplomatically, to sustain the United Nations' support for a tough stance at Panmunjom. The possibility of a decisive outcome had vanished in the spring of 1951 when the recall of MacArthur plainly demonstrated Washington's rejection of all-out war with China as the price of victory in Korea. The Western Powers were unhappily reconciled to the concept of Korea as a limited war, in which their highest aspiration was to demonstrate that their own will to defend the *status quo ante* would remain unbroken.

For many Americans at home, coming to terms with the limits of their own nation's power was a bitter process. Yet it was much more so for hundreds of thousands of men in the bunkers and foxholes from sea to sea across the Korean peninsula. Each day they faced the prospect of death or disablement without the prospect of compensating glory or even respect at home. A British officer spoke of the unhappiness among some of his subordinates in 29 Brigade when they received letters from their wives at home describing the public indifference and ignorance about Korea. In the Second World War men were sustained by the knowledge that their entire nation, on the home front, was committed to the struggle and understood what those on the battlefield were seeking to do. The wives of men in Korea found, instead, that some neighbors inquired clumsily where their husbands were and showed surprise to be reminded that a war was still being waged in Asia. For the professionals, of course, this was less disturbing. If a British Regular soldier was not in Korea, he would be in Malaya, or on the Rhine, or in the deserts of the Middle East. A Frenchman might be in central Africa or Indochina. An American might merely be stagnating at Fort Bragg. Korea offered career soldiers opportunities for combat experience and for distinction. But for those who were conscripted, the equation was different. British National Servicemen in Korea were irked by the meager pay they received, alongside that of Regulars sharing the same risks. Death along the 38th Parallel signified the termination of an adult life before it had usefully begun. The Western nations in Korea had borrowed the lives of some thousands of their young men in a cause few of them appreciated. Yet for more than a few, the loan was transformed into permanent confiscation.

In many ways it was remarkable that the morale of the UN forces held up as well as it did, until the summer of 1953. Private James Stuhler of the U.S. 3rd Division, who later served in Vietnam, remarked that his generation of soldiers had been brought up in the "Yours Not to Reason Why" tradition: "The army in Korea was much less well-informed than the army in Vietnam. In Korea, guys on line read comic books. In Vietnam, you'd see men reading *The Wall Street Journal*. That later generation was better educated, much more questioning. We just got on and did it without thinking much about why we were being asked to do it."[1] Some officer veterans of both wars suggested another important contrast with Vietnam: "In Korea, there was nothing to do but fight."

For some miles behind the front a zone had been systematically cleared of all civilians, so that the defenders could be certain that any unidentified figure was hostile. With dogged cunning, a few prostitutes periodically defied the expulsion orders to ply their trade in primitive "rabbit hutches" a few hundred yards behind the line. A sprinkling of refugees and infiltrators continued to test the vigilance of the outposts, despite the brutal risk that if they fell into South Korean hands and their *bona fides* was suspect, they would be shot out of hand. But for the most part, the forward area remained resolutely military territory under military discipline. There were no officers' clubs or bars, no drugs or movies or diversions. There were only the mountain ridges, surmounted by the defenses which both sides now dug with extraordinary care and caution.

Along most of the line, the United Nations and the Chinese faced each other a mile or so apart, from foxholes and observation posts sited on the forward slopes. But these were no longer the casual scrapes of troops in constant motion across a battlefield: they were fortresses, honeycombs of bunkers and tunnels bored into earth and rock by engineers with bulldozers and pneumatic drills, roofed with steel supports and timber, surmounted by many feet of earth or sandbags. They resembled the diggings of an army of monstrous moles, the setts of a great legion of badgers. Some were surmounted by carefully emplaced tanks, providing not only direct fire support but night illumination from big searchlights mounted upon their hulls. By day the only sign of human occupation of the ridgeline was an occasional fluttering national flag, or a defiant gesture by a man recklessly exposing himself on the skyline. Most men were asleep below ground on bunks woven from planks and telephone wire, or standing watch at a BC scope whose lenses filled the narrow firing slit in front of a bunker. "You could always tell how dangerous a position was by the size of its front apertures," said Sergeant Tom Pentony of the 5th Marines. "A big aperture meant no one was doing much shooting. A small aperture meant you were in trouble."[2] When the World War I veteran Field Marshal Lord Alexander visited Korea, he observed at once that the manner of warfare reminded him of Flanders.

It was only at night that intense, muffled activity began, with men shuffling forward in the darkness to work on improving defenses or leading patrols through the wire into no-man's-land. Down the slope from the bunkers, a host of ingenious and intricate devices had been created and deployed to break the momentum of an assault: wire, minefields, trip flares, booby traps, and a few uniquely Korean innovations, such as barrels of napalm or white phosphorus that could be unleashed and ignited by a wire pulled from a foxhole. The slightest movement observed or imagined in no-man's-land attracted the sudden pop and dazzling light of a flare. For no apparent reason, a sector of the front would suddenly erupt into an artillery duel that might last for weeks, with men lying in their bunkers while shells pounded overhead for four, five, six hours a day. Even the knowledge that the positions could withstand bombardment on this scale was scant comfort for the nerves of those within, or for the patience of the unit signalers, who knew that they must emerge, when it was all over, to replace every telephone wire in the area for the hundredth time of their tour.

On the reverse slopes behind the position more open movement was usually possible. Here, company headquarters were sited, with telephone wires running back to battalion, perhaps a ridgeline farther to the rear. By day files of men seemed to be toiling up and down incessantly in the Sisyphean labor of moving food, water, and ammunition from the nearest point in the valley below that a truck could reach. American or Commonwealth fatigue parties were assisted by hundreds of the inevitable "chiggies," the Korean porters with their A-frames on their backs, whose dogged support even under fire became one of the most vivid of all foreign veterans' memories of Korea. Most units spent between two and three months at a time "on line" before being withdrawn into reserve or to a rest camp. Even when there was little fighting it was extraordinary how great remained the strain and exhaustion of maintaining positions, standing watch, mounting patrols. There were aircraft recognition panels to be set out each day in different patterns, laundry to be gathered for the Korean "dhobie-wallahs," physical-training sessions in most British units, and always digging, digging, and more digging. It was a modified animal existence. When there were scant facilities for washing, many men did not trouble to shave, and almost relished their shagginess. Ignoring personal risk, some of the British heated their bunkers and cooked on tins of petrol. For the men of all the UN formations in winter, life centered upon the precious space heaters that were among the vital weapons of survival. They carried a spoon on a D ring on their belts as a universal eating tool, occasionally supplemented with a bayonet. They wrote interminable letters home, detailing the tedium of their existences and the weary speculation about the end of the war. After a time they scarcely noticed the tinny bellow of the propaganda loudspeakers from the Chinese lines: "Come over, British soldier [or American, or Australian, or Turk, or whoever they might be], you are on the wrong side!" Radio operators sometimes found a Chinese voice coming up on their frequencies: "Hello, Tommy. You must be very cold. Missing your wife?" It was all very odd. But the young Private Alan Maybury was frightened on his first day in the line when he heard the Communist loudspeaker proclaim: "Welcome, 1st Battalion Durham Light Infantry!"[3] The enemy did his best to create a propaganda impression of omniscience.

Amid it all there remained the ceaseless danger of a sudden Chinese attack, a night when, without warning, a wave of screaming, bugle-blowing Communist infantry would hurl themselves upon the wire, seeking to rush a position before its inhabitants could call down their devastating artillery fire support. Each platoon on each hill lived a self-contained existence, very conscious of its isolation. Few men took off their boots at night, and many slept on top of their sleeping bags rather than inside them, for fear of being surprised. The Commonwealth Division circulated repeated warnings to units about the need never to relax vigilance: ". . . Constant occupation of the same defensive positions tends to make infantry overconfident of their defensive works. Few positions will stand up to concentrated shelling, and many fire bays, weapons, and stocks of ammunition are bound to be buried during the softening-up stages of an enemy attack." ". . . counterattack troops must be moved into assembly positions immediately there is the slightest real suspicion of an enemy attack, and must be launched BEFORE or AS the enemy penetrates the position. False alarms will be many, but this must be accepted."[4]

Major John Sloane of the Argylls had formed his knowledge of Chinese soldiers in Burma, "where they were always half an hour late for the attack." But those men had been Kuomintang. Their successors of the PLA "Volunteers" in Korea were different. Western respect for the enemy had increased immeasurably: "The Chinese infantryman is well-trained, well-equipped and efficient," declared a Commonwealth Division report. "He is an excellent night fighter, very brave, with good morale and good at finding his way in the confusion of battle. His limitations are due to lack of equipment and communications. The Chinese are prepared to take casualties and can therefore patrol in strength. There is little doubt that the war in Korea has been fought to suit the Chinese. His limitations in communications, his lack of air support and absence of heavy equipment and vehicles would make him a very vulnerable opponent in a war of movement."[5]

On the night of Sunday, November 4, 1951, the Commonwealth Division suffered a characteristic surprise Chinese attack. The 1st King's Own Scottish Borderers were manning their positions on Hill 355, seized from the Chinese during Van Fleet's October limited offensive. For three hours an intense bombardment rained down upon their bunkers. Then, with the usual horn and bugle accompaniment, the Chinese infantrymen stormed through what remained of their protective barbed wire. The KOSB's mortars ran red-hot as they fired their counterbombardment, until the mortar platoon commander felt compelled to order his men to pour their precious beer ration down the tubes to cool them. Two platoons of B Company were driven from their positions. In the early hours of the morning, the company runner, a vast, slow Cheshireman named Bill Speakman, with a fearsome record of disciplinary offenses, clambered to his feet in company headquarters, stuffed his pouches, shirt, and pockets with grenades, and strode purposefully out into the darkness. "And where the hell do you think you're going?" demanded the company sergeant major. "Going to shift some of them bloody chinks," replied Speakman. He charged alone onto the ridge, grenading as he went, then returned for more ammunition. This time, others went with him. After repeated counterattacks through the night, at first light the KOSB's positions were once more in British hands, at a cost of seven killed, 87 wounded, 44 missing. Four DSOs were awarded for the night's work. Private Speakman, twice wounded, received the Victoria Cross. The story of his lonely action—and the legend of the alcoholic stimulus that played some part in it—passed into the history of the British Army. The battle? The battle was nothing, in the context of Korea—the kind of local action that units up and down the front found themselves compelled to fight at regular intervals through two years of positional war. If they won, they could pride themselves on a job well done. If they lost, the Communists had gained another hill and some other hapless unit would sooner or later have to pay the price for displacing them from it.

The UN troops were impressed by the dedication with which many Chinese soldiers would fight, and the lengths to which they would go to avoid being taken prisoner. Wounded Communists sometimes struggled to resist the attentions of British or American medical orderlies. Nor did this always appear to be the product of mindless fanaticism but of skilled indoctrination: "On the average," concluded a British intelligence report on deserters, "the Chinese Communist soldier disposes of more information regarding commanders' plans and intentions than would normally be available to similar ranking soldiers in non-Communist armies. Once again this is believed to be the result of the frequent political meetings, when all ranks are encouraged to discuss future operations, even to the extent of criticising commanders' plans."[6]

The familiar military routine of briefing took on a new meaning in Chinese hands. It was an article of faith among the leaders of the PLA's "volunteers" in Korea that hours each week were devoted to before- and after-action discussions on tactics and political education. Such familiar slogans as "Aid Korea to Fight America and Defend Our Motherland," "Love the Korean People, Love Everything in Korea" provided texts for regular harangues in a fashion not so very different from that in which verses from the Bible armed Christian padres for their sermons. It remains a measure of the success of political indoctrination that it proved so difficult for the UN forces to take prisoners, and that defectors remained few in number, despite the torrent of propaganda leaflets promising good treatment with which the UN deluged the Chinese lines.

For the Communists, life on the line was troglodyte in an even more absolute fashion than for the UN. The UN's command of the air made it possible for its soldiers to move with relative freedom during daylight, as long as they were out of direct sight of the enemy. The Chinese had no artillery ammunition to waste upon random barrages. For Peng's men, however, every inch of territory in the forward areas was under constant threat from the air. Camouflage became an obsession, for they knew that if the Americans observed even a single moving figure in the open, a devastating barrage of bombs or artillery would follow. The Chinese lived, until darkness fell and often beyond, in the incredible honeycomb of tunnels that they created along their front, exceeding all that mechanical ingenuity achieved on the UN side. "The tunnel became a great Chinese institution," Hu Seng, one of Marshal Peng's staff, said wryly. Within its confines, the men of the "Volunteers" passed their day in a mirror image of life on the UN side: listening to Peking radio, reading, playing poker, singing and dancing to music made on Chinese violins and instruments fashioned out of shell cases. Many men who went to Korea as illiterates used the opportunity lent to them by boredom to learn to read and write in the flickering candlelight beneath the mountains. Disease, in those dripping caverns, was a chronic problem. Fever thrived in summer, and men welcomed the healthier chill of winter. If they were ill, or wounded, they depended almost entirely upon traditional Chinese herbal remedies for a cure. Modern drugs were almost nonexistent. Many men, much of the time, went hungry.

The Chinese suffered almost as acutely from the sense of distance from home as the men of the UN. "Because we were fighting abroad, it was more difficult to sustain morale than during the Liberation War," said Li Ben Wen, a regimental propaganda officer.[7] Few men even possessed a photograph of their families, for cameras were a rare luxury. Once every two weeks or so they might receive mail from home—letters written, for the most part, by their village's professional letter writer. Leave was almost unknown. Rarely, a man might be allowed to visit his village for compassionate reasons, if a close family member died. Wang Zhu Guang, a staff officer at 23rd Army Group, spent six years in Korea and went home only twice. His wife, a factory worker, sent him such occasional remittances as she should spare from the upkeep of herself and their small daughter. Wang, like the rest of the "Volunteers," received no pay—only cigarettes.

In assault, the Chinese specialized in infiltration and envelopment, at least one attacking group making immediately for the defender's line of reinforcement. Thus, all-round defense was essential. As the war progressed, organization and training improved markedly, with rehearsals for attacks being carried out behind the lines. Messages were passed in plain language over such radios as they possessed, or more often by telephone. "Encirclement and deep penetration are standard," in the words of a British assessment of Chinese tactics.

The Chinese claimed to find *mei juin*—the Americans—less formidable foes than the Japanese: "They lacked the fighting will of the Japanese," according to Li Hebei of the 587th Regiment. The Communists developed night fighting to a fine art, because only in darkness could they overcome the overwhelming problem of UN air superiority. As the war progressed, their antiaircraft capability increased dramatically: 35-mm, 37-mm, 100-mm guns provided by the Soviets. "We also became more and more experienced in dealing with 'choke points,' " said Wang Zhu Guang. "We became accustomed to the way the Americans would bomb in fixed places at fixed times, and more skilled in moving trucks in the intervals." Asked what shortages the Chinese felt most acutely, he replied unhesitatingly,

"Aircraft." The size of China's forces in Korea was restricted by the number of men for whom supplies could be moved south across the Yalu. Manpower as such was never a problem—thus, the vast, ruthless sacrifice of lives in attack. "We suffered very heavy casualties," conceded Wang Zhu Guang, "but it was worth it. We won the battle."[8] More objective observers might reject his assessment. Even many Chinese officers today appear to look back on the tactics of the Korean period with some embarrassment.

On the UN side of the line, opinion varied from unit to unit about the scale of risk that was acceptable in pursuit of the domination of no-man's-land by night. Among the Americans, Southerners often seemed the most enthusiastic soldiers. There was a West Virginian in Private First Class Mario Scarselleta's platoon of the 35th Infantry who was constantly volunteering for patrols: "He'd say, 'Oh Lord, please send over fifty gooks!' He loved it. I wish we'd had 50,000 like him, so the rest of us could have gone home." Many men felt infinitely less inclined to take risks after the armistice negotiations began. "It made it awfully hard to get people to do things, to go out on patrol," said Corporal Bill Patterson of the 27th Infantry. "A man would just say, 'Aw, I'm on short time.' "[9]

Yet because it was plainly indefensible to expend men's lives except in pursuit of worthwhile objectives—whatever these might be—senior commanders in Korea also faced serious difficulty in checking the ambitions of professional soldiers who came to the country bent upon achieving a battlefield reputation. There were not a few American major generals who arrived to take over divisions for a tour in the line and had to be decisively checked in their determination to mount an attack in order to further their own reputations. An officer with an outstanding reputation for courage earned as a battalion commander in World War II came to take over a brigade of the Commonwealth Division: "Brave as a lion," as one of his colleagues said of him. Yet as a brigadier in Korea, his offensive instincts, his determination to carry the war to the enemy, appalled his subordinates. When he organized an attack on the Chinese positions which they believed would decimate their units, his battalion commanders protested strongly to the divisional commander. The brigadier was quietly relieved of his post. By the standards of conventional war, his enthusiasm was admirable. By those of Korea, it was merely foolish. Lieutenant Paul Sheehy of the U.S. 7th Division reflected the feelings of many UN soldiers about overzealous officers when he wrote to his parents in Maine in June 1952:

We have a new battalion commander who is a "son of a gun." He came over to Korea in Sept 1950 when the division landed at Inchon, and he refuses to go home. He came over as a master sgt and is now a major. He is crazy for power and loves war. I believe he is actually crazy and should be sent home to a hospital. He talks with a gleam in his eyes about the killing of Chinks in the coming operation. He hasn't any heart, and sent a brand-new 2nd lt., fresh from the States, out on a patrol the night he came to the battalion. And this crazy man is in charge. The high brass think he is No. 1 soldier. Boy will I be glad to get out of this outfit, I've sure had enough of Korea,

God bless you both, your loving son, Paul[10]

The British Commander in Chief in the Far East, General Sir Charles Keightley, visited Korea in April 1952 and reported to the War Office that "the views of commanders there from top to bottom are really all in line: that the Chinese Communist policy is directed from Moscow, and a forecast as to what will happen is as unpredictable as the rest of their actions throughout the world. The majority guess that it will be a stalemate. This sort of war, where the enemy is prepared to launch attacks apparently quite regardless of whether the losses are worth the objective, is a new one to us, and produces some quite new lines of thought. I was much impressed by the fact that the Chinese was showing himself a very skilful as well as tough fighter."[11] Keightley described the main tactical problem as enemy infiltration at night, which was being met by "wiring on the 1914–18 standards, thickened up with mines." He was impressed with the men's morale, but dismayed by the extent of the chronic problem of venereal disease throughout the American and Commonwealth contingents. Keightley suggested making the cure more unpleasant, "reintroducing some of the pre-war methods instead of penicillin." The UN Command was constantly preoccupied with the problem of staleness among the men on the line: "Ridgway says that if he had his way, he would change every man, divisional commanders included, every 90 days!" Senior officers were exasperated by the number of gunshot accidents; a senior army doctor visiting a hospital found fifty-nine cases resulting from enemy action and twenty-four accidental gunshot wounds, "the great majority of which were self-inflicted."[12] It was so in every war of this kind, that for every man who died facing the enemy, another was killed in some wretched truck accident, bar brawl behind the lines, mishap with munitions, or a fatal step into an unmarked minefield.

Many of the British of the World War II generation, serving as infinitely junior partners to the Americans in Korea, found the experience of decline too recent not to gaze somewhat sidelong at the new dominant force on the globe and cherish unworthy thoughts about how much better the old team had done it. An American unit in the Commonwealth Division area posted a sign over its camp entrance proclaiming itself "SECOND TO NONE." The Australian radio relay station a few hundred yards farther down posted a sign proclaiming itself "NONE."

If there's any two things that I can't stand

ran a characteristic little ditty in the Commonwealth Division newssheet, *Crown News,*

it's a North Korean and a Chinaman.
We're moving on, we're moving on.

See the chinks coming up 355,
the yanks pulling out in overdrive,
they're moving on, they're moving on.

The last verse, of course, referred to a hill crest the Americans had allegedly abandoned without reasonable cause. From General Cassels downward, the Commonwealth Division argued that it was more economical to hold a position under attack than to adopt the American tactic of maintaining only a light screen in forward positions, which gave ground under pressure and left it to a set-piece counterattack in strength to regain. A British company commander who found himself posted alongside the Turkish Brigade was exasperated to receive constant phone calls from its liaison officer, accustomed to take a skeptical view of American tactics, demanding, "You still there, Tommy? You still there?" The Englishman assented crossly, adding, "And let us be clear that we have not the slightest intention of going." Colonel William Pike, Cassels's CRA, said, "It is a paradox that the British like Americans very much, but do not have great respect for them as soldiers."[13] Pike and many of his British colleagues, with their reluctance to accept casualties in pursuit of objectives which seemed to lack any wider strategic value, much disliked the local attacks they were periodically called upon to mount: "If one had wanted to finish that campaign, it would have been perfectly possible to concentrate a corps and drive through. Instead, we would be asked merely to capture some hill. The Chinese would allow us to get on top, then retire into their bunkers while they called down mortar and artillery fire. These small attacks seemed to us singularly expensive. It would have been far more logical militarily to mount one good, big set-piece attack which could have taken us to the Yalu."[14] But by 1952 the war in Korea was not an exercise of military logic but of national will.

The static campaign in Korea was justly described as a platoon commander's war because so much of the fighting followed small-unit encounters in no-man's-land. Some units awarded seven days' leave to any man who could bring in a prisoner, and patrols went to extraordinary lengths to achieve this ambition, cutting Chinese telephone wires and then laying ambushes for the wiring parties that came to repair them, spending night after night with blackjacks clutched in their hands, awaiting an opportunity.

Spring came with dramatic suddenness to Korea. The thaw followed by the monsoon rains played havoc with the fabric of laboriously dug positions. Yet this was the most welcome, indeed perhaps the only really enjoyable, season in Korea. The hillsides burst forth in a riot of colors. Men were astonished by the speed with which vegetation grew, and the variety and profusion of wildflowers. Then, with the coming of summer, the heat became crippling. Western soldiers toiling up the mountainsides under loads envied the infinitely greater endurance and carrying power of the little Korean porters. Infection and disease prospered in the damp warmth of the bunkers. The insects proved marginally more endurable than the stink of the repellent issued to suppress them, which was principally employed to soak rifle patches and make night-lights. Rats scurried among the garbage behind the positions, and often in the tunnels beneath them. Some fortunate units possessed streams near enough to hand, and sufficiently screened from hostile observation, to wash. Those who did not were periodically ferried to the rear for showers. But most men were coated in sweat-soaked dirt most of their time on line. NCOs checked feet and socks to guard against chronic foot infections. Dust coated weapons, vehicles, food, clothing. Men in the forward positions counted off the days until they were rotated into reserve. But when their turn came, and they found themselves facing the same discomforts a few miles to the rear, constantly employed on fatigue parties, yet earning only half as many points toward their release date, they began to feel that it was better to be on line. Even the hardiest Chinese soldiers in the opposing positions declared that the Korean summer was unbearable.

Until winter came, that is. Then, as men plodded between positions with the studied clumsiness of spacemen, movements muffled by innumerable layers of clothing, they gazed in awed disbelief as the thermometers plunged to new depths. Starting a vehicle engine became a major undertaking. Laying or clearing mines was a nightmare in the frozen earth. The British cursed their ridiculous 1939 vintage "Finnish pattern" snowboots, their inadequate camouflaged windproofs. The gunners found that the range of their weapons could vary by as much as 2,000 yards, according to the air temperature. An hour of carelessness in exposing a corner of flesh to the naked air was punished by frostbite. They experimented with hand warmers, foot warmers, belts stuffed with body warmers. They relieved the monotony of the rations by shooting the quail, pheasants, and ducks that populated the countryside in such profusion. They devised crude practical jokes to make each other laugh—putting an electrical charge through a latrine seat by attaching it to a communication wire, lighting the ends of a screwed-up newspaper between a sleeping man's toes. But there were pitifully few trees to chop for firewood, pathetically few diversions beyond lying on one's back in a bunker listening to Hank Snow singing "Moving On," Patti Page or Teresa Brewer, Connie Stevens or Eddie Fisher heart-throbbing across the airwaves from a real world a planet away. All the UN forces observed a "one winter" rule in Korea. No man, it was decreed, should be asked to endure more than one season of that terrible cold in the forward areas.

Every few months most men were granted a week's "R & R"—rest and recuperation—which almost all of them spent in Japan. The memory of Japan in the early 1950s is the most lyrical that most veterans brought back from Korea. "At that time," said Colonel William Pike, "it really did still have something of the romance of the Orient." Men who sought a civilized release from the animality of the line found it in Japan, together with a real friendliness and kindness from the Japanese. For the British, it was a little painful to see recent enemies already in possession of consumer goods that were unobtainable in their own country, food beyond the dreams of rationed families in London or Glasgow.

But most men went to Japan seeking, above all, a woman and a drink. Many retained memories of the bar girls they met there until the end of their lives. A man stepped off the transport from Seoul, took the truck into town, and made a bargain with a girl for the three, four, five days he was at liberty: "It was the land of the big PX," said Private Warren Avery of the 29th Infantry. "You drove to the Hotel Sun, got a girl, a room, and all the beer you could drink for five days for sixty dollars. I fell in love with Japan."[15] So did hundreds of thousands of UN servicemen who fought in Korea. And for Japan itself, the war provided a staggering economic opportunity. The first, critical phase in the creation of Japan, Inc. was made possible by the wealth the Korean War poured into the country when it served as aircraft carrier, repair base, store depot, commissariat, hospital, headquarters, and recreation center for the United Nations forces in the Far East.

In February 1953, Van Fleet handed over command of the Eighth Army in Korea to the veteran paratrooper Maxwell Taylor. The outgoing general disappeared into retirement with bitter complaints that he had been prevented from launching an all-out offensive to drive the Chinese out of Korea once and for all. His frustration was widely shared by other senior officers. It seemed profoundly un-soldierlike to that generation, which had come to maturity in World War II, in which defeat and victory were absolutes, to allow an army to stagnate upon the mountains of Korea, restricted to patrolling. Van Fleet was probably correct in believing that, with the vast firepower at his disposal, the Chinese line could have been breached and eventually rolled up. But such a campaign would have cost many thousands of UN casualties. There was never the remotest possibility that Washington or the allied capitals would entertain the plan. Yet the last months of the war saw some of the fiercest fighting since the 1951 spring offensive. The Chinese made a series of determined attempts to test the UN's will on the battlefield as negotiations at Panmunjom reached a critical stage. On each occasion they were thrown back— but only after bitter struggles.

"Old Baldy," a hilltop in the midst of the peninsula that possessed no unique strategic significance, nonetheless became the focus of intense Chinese offensive effort in the summer and autumn of 1952. In March 1953 they at last gained possession of it after the collapse of a Colombian regiment rashly entrusted with its defense. Taylor was reluctant to lavish lives upon its recapture. But the Communists quickly made it clear that they proposed to make use of the advantage that they had gained to advance another bound: Old Baldy overlooked a feature named "Pork Chop Hill," garrisoned by two understrength platoons of the 31st Infantry of 7th Division. Soon after 10 P.M. on the night of April 16, 1953, an American patrol moving into the valley between Pork Chop and the enemy positions opposite encountered two companies of Chinese sweeping forward to assault the hill. Within minutes the ninety-six Americans on Pork Chop found themselves isolated under furious attack. The lieutenant in command lost radio and telephone contact with the rear, but summoned emergency artillery cover by flare. But when the barrage at last lifted, the Chinese stormed forward again. By 2 A.M. they held most of the hill. Two hours later an American counterattack managed to link with the surviving defenders on the high ground, but was not strong enough to recapture the lost positions.

All through the next day some fifty-five Americans clung to their precarious foothold on Pork Chop, pinned down by the Chinese. At Eighth Army, the decision was made that at all costs, American dominance of the position must be reestablished. It was essential that the Communist delegation at Panmunjom should be denied the opportunity to claim a victory on the battlefield. At 9:30 P.M. on the night of April 17 two companies of the 17th Infantry struck the western end of the feature from both sides. The battle continued all through the following day, with a stream of reinforcements being thrown in by both sides. By the night of April 18 the Chinese had conceded tactical defeat. They withdrew their surviving elements from Pork Chop while the Americans began an intensive struggle to rebuild the defenses before the next assault came.

The battle for Pork Chop continued at bitter intensity deep into the summer of 1953. The U.S. garrison of its blasted slopes grew to five battalions, under incessant Communist mortar and artillery fire. On July 10, a fortnight before the armistice was signed, Taylor and his commanders concluded that the cost of maintaining it, still under constant surveillance from Old Baldy, outweighed even the moral benefits. It was evacuated. The struggle for Pork Chop became part of the legend of the U.S. Army in Korea, reflecting the courage of the defenders and the tactical futility of so many small-unit actions of the kind that dominated the last two years of the war. It was said that there were eleven stars' worth of American generals at the regimental headquarters behind Pork Chop at the height of the battle. The divisional commander, Arthur Trudeau, won a Silver Star for personally leading a counterattack battalion reconnaissance party onto Pork Chop under fire, after switching helmets with his driver. Some of the allies were deeply skeptical about the price the Americans paid to regain the position. General Mike West, who succeeded Cassels in command of the Commonwealth Division, was asked what he would have done to recapture it and answered, "Nothing. It was only an outpost.'' But this view reflected, yet again, the interminable conflict between military reason and political interest.

A succession of almost equally bitter battles was conducted for possession of a ridge within a few miles of the western coast of Korea named "the Hook.'' On the night of October 26,1952, the U.S. 7th Marines fought a successful defensive action under the most unfavorable conditions. Thereafter, the Hook passed into the hands of the Commonwealth Division. The British lost more casualties on its steep flanks than on any other single battlefield in Korea.

In the last months of the war the names of the hills Carson, Vegas, and Reno became forever identified with the U.S. Marine Corps, who fought so hard to retain them. Sergeant Tom Pentony was an artillery forward observer with the 5th Marines. He had found boot camp untroublesome after the rigors of a Catholic upbringing in New Jersey, "where the nuns taught you that you would die as a martyr if you went fighting communism.'' On March 26, 1953, Pentony was with the 3/5th behind Vegas when the Chinese overran the American "Combat Outposts'' and the Marines went in to retake the position. Pentony watched, appalled, as the Americans fought their way up the hill under punishing Chinese fire: "I used to think officers were smart. Now I felt, 'This is stupid. Do they have any plan?' They just seemed to think, 'The Marines will take that hill, frontal assault, that's it.' ''[16] On the afternoon of March 27, Pentony's senior gunnery officer, a major, was so appalled by the spectacle of infantry still struggling forward, having lost all their own officers, that he received special permission to go forward and lead them himself. His radio operator returned two days later with his pistol and watch. The March battles for Carson, Reno, and Vegas cost the Marine Corps 116 men killed out of a total of over a thousand casualties, and inspired some of the most remarkable feats of American courage to come out of the Korean War.

Pentony found that his own mood, his attitude to the war, vacillated greatly from day to day: "It was like indigestion: some days you felt very brave, nothing bothered you, sounds at night didn't worry you. Then on other days, for no special reason you were scary, jumpy—the smallest thing bothered you.'' The atmosphere on the Marine positions was consciously "macho'' by comparison with that in the army lines. When the Chinese propaganda loudspeakers began to blare forth their raucous messages with their customary exhortation—"American soldiers and officers!''—the Marines at once interrupted to shout back, "We're not soldiers! We're marines!'' Many men were reluctant to be switched out of the line into reserve, not only because they were earning less points toward their day of release, but because reserve units were nagged by training and inspections and were still liable to be called forward to fill sandbags and dig trenches, often more dangerously exposing them than the men on line.

The American points system was regarded as one of the most pernicious innovations of the campaign: a man needed thirty-six to go home; on line, he earned four a month; in the combat zone, three; in country but beyond reach of enemy action, two. Thus most men serving with an American combat formation might expect to go home after about a year in Korea, while support personnel served eighteen months. It was a discipline which earned intense dislike among professional soldiers and commanders because it caused men to become increasingly cautious and reluctant to accept risk as they grew "short" and approached release date. It mitigated strongly against the unit cohesion the British achieved, by shipping men in and out of Korea by battalions, because each soldier focused upon the schedule of his own tour in the country. Yet the system persisted in Vietnam throughout the 1960s, with equally negative effects upon the U.S. Army there.

Private James Stuhler was a New York high school dropout who had run away to join the Marines at sixteen, been sent home again, and finally went to Korea for the last few months of the war with the 3rd Division in the Kunwa Valley. An initial irony struck him on his way to the front when the truck in which he and his draft of replacements were being carried forward was stopped and booked by the military police for speeding. Even at this late stage of the war, the routines and strains of life and death on the line were undiminished. They spent their first days in new positions digging incessantly, for the only contribution the unit they relieved had made to its own defense was to hang out a Chinese skull on a long pole. A squad leader in his platoon, obsessed with fear of being killed, deliberately shot himself in the hand, maiming himself for life. To pass the time, they fitted a telescopic sight on a .50-caliber machine gun, stabilized its tripod with sandbags, and sought to snipe at Chinese forward observers.

Then their company commander, an eager young first lieutenant, planned a raid to relieve the monotony. It went disastrously wrong. During their advance through the darkness, they walked into the American covering bombardment. Dankowski, their platoon leader, was killed almost immediately. "O.B., what the f**k are we going to do?" Stuhler cried desperately to O'Brien, their radio operator. The Chinese were now firing into them, hitting their squad leader as he ran along a ridgeline. Stuhler's machine gun jammed. He pulled out a .45 pistol and fired in sheer fear and frustration. To his horror, he found that he had narrowly missed shooting an American lying in front of him. Then a rock splinter struck him on the finger, numbing his entire arm. A grenade exploded, horribly wounding his fellow machine gunner in the face. Stuhler looked in horror at the man's eye, hanging loose from its socket. "Pull back! Pull back!" shouted O'Brien among the chaos of explosion and pyrotechnics now breaking up the night sky. Discipline collapsed as they stumbled away into the valley toward their own lines. Stuhler hastily wrapped a field dressing on his companion's ragged face and told the man to hold his collar while he guided him out. His helmet had fallen off, and a moment later he was stunned by a flying rock hitting him on the head. The New Yorker never knew how he got back. He and his companion waded chest-high through a creek, and were told later that they had walked through a minefield. Toward dawn a sudden burst of machine-gun fire ripped over the exhausted men's heads. They threw themselves flat, the wounded man groaning, "We're gonna get killed! We're gonna get killed!" Stuhler yelled to the Americans in front of him to hold their fire. They dragged the casualty in. "Oh for chrissake, will you look at this guy?" said the shocked medical orderly who examined his face. The victim was still conscious, and Stuhler said furiously, "You're not supposed to say things like that." Around half the platoon that had set out were dead or wounded. Stuhler received a Bronze Star for bringing back his buddy. To their fury, the company commander, who had never left the lines, was awarded a Silver Star. The battalion area was named Camp Dankowski in memory of their squandered platoon commander. This pathetic little drama unfolded barely a month before the armistice was signed. Of such stuff was the Army's weary disillusion with the Korean War made, by the summer of 1953.

16

THE PRISONERS

One day in the summer of 1951 a British lieutenant named Brian Hawkins found a tin can in no-man's-land, containing a message from the Chinese. "Officers and men of the 1st Division of the United Kingdom," it proclaimed,

> in the April battle 701 officers and men of the British 29th Brigade were captured by one of our units. We had sent them to the safe rear for learning. They received the best treatment from us. They play ball and amuse themselves after studying every day. So, don't worry about them please. We write the name of the officers here, expecting you to tell their parents and wives that they are safe and will go home in the future. Life is invaluable. You should keep your safety for a good turn. You may hide yourselves while you are ordered to fight. When you see China volunteers or Korean People's Army men, lay down your weapons and come over to us. We absolutely guarantee no harm, no abuse, and plenty of food for you. Otherwise, "Death" is the only way before you
>
> The Chinese People's Volunteer Forces[1]

In a curious sense, the Chinese in the forward areas of Korea were sincere in the pursuit of their "lenient policy" toward prisoners. There were repeated examples, throughout the war, of Chinese—though never North Koreans—not killing UN soldiers when they had the opportunity to do so, even releasing them and sending them back to the UN lines for propaganda purposes. Yet the clumsy efforts to display humanity that sometimes took place at the front masked a terrible reality in the rear. "We do not know about Geneva Convention," a contemptuous Communist officer told Padre Sam Davies when he was captured on the Imjin, and then pointed to his interrogator: "You must obey his orders."[2] No aspect of the Korean conflict caused greater bitterness—bordering upon hysteria in the United States—than the postwar revelation of the treatment of United Nations prisoners by their Communist captors. The bald figures speak more eloquently than any narrative. Of 7,140 American prisoners to fall into enemy hands, 2,701 died in captivity. Some fifty of the 1,188 Commonwealth officers and other ranks posted as missing or prisoners died in enemy hands. The West was appalled to hear of the discovery in a railway tunnel, during the 1950 advance into North Korea, of the bodies of a hundred American prisoners massacred by the retreating Communists. From the outbreak of war, Kim Il Sung's army made it plain that it killed American prisoners whenever it suited its convenience to do so.

The North Koreans were a law unto themselves. The only mitigating factor in judging their behavior toward their prisoners is the parallel attitude of many UN soldiers toward Communist captives. Many American officers and men interviewed for this book admitted knowledge of, or participation in, the shooting of Communist prisoners when it was inconvenient to keep them alive. It is fair to suggest that many UN soldiers did not regard North Korean soldiers as fellow combatants, entitled to humane treatment, but as near-animals, to be treated as such. As usual in most wars, when the atmosphere at the front was relaxed, Communist prisoners were perfectly properly used and sent to the camps in the rear. But at periods of special stress or fear, especially in the first six months of the war, many UN soldiers shot down enemy prisoners—or even Korean civilians—with barely a moment's scruple. "I couldn't get over how cruel we were to the prisoners we captured," said Private Mario Scarselleta of the 35th Infantry. "We'd strip them and tie them on the hood of a jeep and drive them around. A group would be taken back for interrogation and shot. My outfit didn't take too many prisoners."[3] Scarselleta's outfit was not atypical. Private Warren Avery of the 29th Infantry said flatly, "We took no prisoners. Our interpreter, Lieutenant Moon, was always asking for a prisoner, but we never gave him one. Geneva Convention, my ass. I shot an old woman carrying an A-frame. We killed an awful lot of civilians over there. You just couldn't trust them. After you'd seen them kill a tank crew, you didn't take chances again. Anybody you saw wearing mustard-colored sneakers, you shot."[4] It remains important and valid to make some distinction between the random acts of individual UN troops and the systematic brutality of the North Koreans. But in Korea, as later in Vietnam, it seems essential, more than thirty years later, to set the behavior of the West's forces in context when judging that of the Communists.

Beyond anything that took place on the battlefield, Korea became notorious as the first major modern conflict in which a combatant made a systematic attempt to convert prisoners to his own ideology. The Chinese success in this may be partly measured by the statistics: twenty-one Americans and one Briton refused repatriation at the end of hostilities. By 1959 the Americans claimed to have identified seventy-five former prisoners in Korea as Communist agents. The most serious case was that of George Blake, former British vice-consul in Seoul, who was seized and interned in June 1950, and remained in Communist hands until 1953. A decade later Blake was unmasked as a key Soviet agent inside the British Foreign Office. The deep fear that similar traitors still lurked undiscovered within the bureaucracies and bodies politic of the West persisted for a generation and spawned such books and films as *Time Limit, The Rack,* and *The Manchurian Candidate.* As the experiences of UN prisoners were revealed after the Panmunjom armistice, Americans were even more dismayed by the number of their own men who were found to have collaborated with the enemy, in greater or lesser measure, while behind the wire. Had the Communists indeed, by their "brainwashing" techniques in the cluster of camps along the Yalu, discovered a psychological formula for changing the loyalties of soldiers fighting for freedom? If this was indeed so, the implications for the future struggle against communism were disturbing indeed.

When Marine Andrew Condron was captured in Hellfire Valley on November 30, 1950, along with some fifty Americans, during the Chosin Reservoir campaign, a Chinese officer harangued the group in English, considerably to their bewilderment, about their bond with their captors, as fellow members of the proletariat. "Proletarians like us?" demanded a bewildered GI. "I thought they were f***ing Communists." The Chinese shook hands with them all, and handed over some captured cigarettes and canned food before shutting them up in a nearby hut. Their first conflict with their captors came, wholly unexpectedly, when a guard brought in a steaming gourd of hot water. Somebody had some soap. To the delight of the prisoners, they were able to wash off the filth of days. Then the guard returned and gazed on the scene with sheer horror. He fixed his bayonet, and for a tense moment the prisoners were convinced that he intended to use it. They were herded against the wall while the guard screamed and shouted at them. Then he vanished.

When his officer returned they were rebuked in English. The guard had taken the risk and trouble of lighting a fire to heat water for them. By using it to wash in, rather than to drink, the prisoners had insulted him. "It really was East meets West," said Condron. "We simply didn't know."[5] Belatedly, they were searched. Knives, watches, lighters were taken away. So, too, were the wounded. To the best of Condron's knowledge, none survived. In justice to the Chinese, with their primitive medical facilities, few of their own casualties were likely to fare better. One night all the unwounded prisoners were ordered to start marching. They continued to do so for almost a month.

Hundreds of men, above all the wounded, died on these marches from the battlefield before they ever reached a camp. "The signal for death was the oxcart following the column," said James Majury, Captain of Ulster Riflemen. "If you had to be placed upon that, you would freeze to death." Pneumonia and dysentery took an early toll. Throughout the march toward the camps, every prisoner retained a keen sense of imminent death. One morning when a call came—"All British outside! All British outside!"—the two dozen or so Royal Marines in Andrew Condron's party were convinced that they were about to be executed. The Chinese looked excited and nervous. For two hours a Chinese officer delivered a political harangue. He seemed convinced there was an officer among their group, which there was not: "I no believe you! Which one is officer?" In a long single rank, the British prisoners were marched along a railway line. Condron became maudlin as he thought of breakfast at home in West Lothian—black pudding, sausage and eggs. Why had he not joined the Air Force, like most of his friends? His sense of self-pity was deepened by the sight of a cluster of Korean children laughing and giggling at them from a ridge above. Around a corner, they reached a huge hole, a bomb crater. Condron was convinced it was to be their grave. Then the guards motioned them onward, into a house. They sagged with compulsive relief. Another Marine, Dick Richards, muttered to Condron, "Red, were you thinking what I was thinking?" After that moment they began to feel a flicker of confidence that they might live.

In the three or four months that followed, they had no chance to wash or take off their clothes—they could only rub their hands with snow. Yet the Scottish Socialist in Condron was impressed that on the march their captors never asked them to carry their heavy equipment, and that as a matter of course the guards and their officers joined the daily queue for sorghum along with the prisoners. Condron admitted that it was only later that he understood the conscious political purpose behind this.

Among their party were two U.S. Marines who had been prisoners of the Japanese and could communicate with the Chinese. The Marines seemed to respond to the situation with less difficulty than the U.S. Army prisoners. "The American soldiers seemed to see the way out of the experience as individuals," said Condron. "If one stole a bit of food, he would scuffle into a corner and eat it alone. The British and American Marines took it in groups. We stuck together. When the marching was looking rough, we'd say to each other, 'Come off it—the f***ing commando school was tougher than this.' "

Their group's morale soared when they heard, through their American Japanese-speakers, that "all prisoners go home." To their utter astonishment, they were suddenly marched to a train. It began to head south. For four or five nights they traveled, halting throughout the daylight hours in tunnels. Near Pyongyang they were shuttled into marshaling yards, where they remained for a week. Then a handful of men were picked out, for no evident logical reason, and taken away. These men were indeed returned to the UN lines, apparently as a propaganda move to convince the West that rumors that all prisoners were being shot were unfounded. The remainder began to receive more food—a little rice, chicken, soup. Some of the Americans were now euphoric, composing cables and letters to their families, ready for dispatch at the moment of their release. Some men spent hours discussing the menu for their first meal on their release. The British imposed a self-denying ordinance on themselves not to discuss food. Suddenly the Chinese brought news: "You go north—prisoner-of-war camp." The shock to those who had convinced themselves that they were going home was appalling. A few weeks later Condron helped to bury one American, whom he had watched on the train working out the hour-by-hour program for his first week of freedom.

Now, for the first time, they were interrogated. They were apprehensive at the prospect, and bewildered by the reality. They had spent some time discussing with an American captain how they should respond to military questions. Yet there were none. Instead, an amiable Chinese officer sat on the floor, offered each man a glass of hot water, and asked, "What sort of work does your father do?"

"What sort of work does your mother do?"

"My mother does not work," answered Andrew Condron.

"Why your mother no work?"

"She is a housewife."

"What is housewife?"

"She just stays home."

"How much land your family own?"

"There's the back garden."

"What you grow?"

"Potatoes, rhubarb."

"How many cows have your family got?"

"We get milk from the dairy."

"What is dairy? How many pigs you have? How many cows?"

At last, with a self-satisfied grin, the Chinese concluded, "Ah, your family very small land. You are poor peasant." The British laughed for weeks about the Cockney Marine who was asked about his family's land and vividly described his window box.

Yet if it is easy to find comedy in the naiveté of all this, among the prisoners a powerful undercurrent of fear was never far distant. Condron's group were relatively well treated by their Chinese guardians. Many men who fell into the hands of the North Koreans suffered dreadfully. Aircrew and those with special technical knowledge were singled out for far more sophisticated and brutal questioning. In the first months of captivity many officers were treated with savage cruelty and subjected to months of solitary confinement. The worst brutalities were suffered by those confined in the hands of the North Koreans in the transit or penal compounds around Pyongyang—"Pak's Palace," "The Caves," Camp 9 at Kangdong.

Jerry Morgan was a twenty-five-year-old technical sergeant in the 24th Infantry, a black regiment, when his company heard the cry "Every man for himself!" on the night of November 27, 1950. Most of them were rapidly rounded up by the Chinese and marched north. They spent a month in the houses of a village at a place they called "Death Valley," for many Americans died there. Then they were moved some twenty miles to their permanent home on the Yalu: Camp 5, "Pyongdong University." Here, in the hands of the North Koreans, they suffered through the rest of that first, terrible winter.

When Andrew Condron and his group were taken north again in March 1951 to Camp 5, they were appalled by what they found. They joined some 700 men at the limits of misery and hunger, among whom prisoners were dying every day. The camp was sited in a valley, on a peninsula overlooked by two hills. It was a place of great natural beauty, had the circumstances been such as to make them appreciate it. Here, confined chiefly by the geography and certainty of the impossibility of escape, with a single strand of wire marking the permissible limits of movement, many men stayed for up to three years. Only when the Chinese assumed control of Camp 5 in the spring of 1951 did conditions improve marginally, and the worst excesses perpetrated by the North Koreans cease.

The more thoughtful prisoners perceived from the outset that their wounded died for lack of medical attention and not, on the whole, as a matter of enemy policy. The Communists themselves were entirely bereft of drugs and equipment, even for their own men. But it was also evident that in the first winter of 1950–51, the North Koreans were indifferent as to whether their captives lived or died of starvation. Men who had been receiving a U.S. Army daily combat ration of 3,500 calories now found themselves provided with only 1,200 calories of corn and millet. It was a diet devoid of vegetables, almost barren of proteins, minerals, or vitamins. Leadership among the prisoners collapsed. A dreadful struggle for survival took over, the strongest ruthlessly stripping the weak of food. Up to thirty men a day were dying.

By far the most deadly killer, above all in those first months of 1951, was the dreaded "give-upitis," which afflicted thousands of prisoners. In an extraordinary fashion, they lost the will to live, above all the will to eat. Many Americans simply declined to eat the mess of sorghum and rice with which they were provided. They chose instead to starve. The British would say laconically, "If you don't eat, you don't shit. If you don't shit, you die." Some men were fortunate enough to have friends and comrades who cosseted and cajoled them into eating. Private First Class Graham Cockfield of the 34th Infantry noticed that it was the younger prisoners who seemed most vulnerable: "You'd hear them sitting all day, planning the meal they were going to have when they got out. Then somebody came around with the millet, and they wouldn't touch it. We simply did our best to force food down any individual we knew wasn't eating. Natural physique had nothing to do with who survived and who didn't. It was all in the mind."[6] Private Henry O'Kane of the Royal Ulster Rifles was near the margin of survival when he reached Camp 1: his mouth was sore from lack of vitamins; like every other man, he was suffering from dysentery and beriberi. All around him lay cases of malaria, jaundice, bone fever. O'Kane was placed in a hut with some forty Filipinos and Puerto Ricans: "They saved my life. They were peasant characters, rice eaters, who simply understood that kind of life, could make medicine from herbs to keep themselves alive. That is what they did for me."

But other prisoners refused help, resisted every blandishment. The "no hopers" merely lay down, staring emptily into space, until one morning they were dead. "It was easier to die than it was to live," in the words of Lieutenant Walt Mayo of the 8th Cavalry. "We tried to do as much amateur psychology as we could, but the problem was sheer despair."[7] It was an extraordinary phenomenon. A few men in the Communist camps in Korea died as a result of deliberate brutality. Many suffered terrible beatings, punishments involving exposure to cold or heat that amounted to torture. Almost all were terribly weakened by hunger and disease. Yet there was never any equivalent of the systematic, wholesale brutality that the Japanese practiced upon their prisoners in World War II.

The atmosphere in the camps, above all in the first months of most bitter starvation, was savage. As men's boots wore out, they saved the taps from the soles and sharpened them into shivs, as tools for self-defense. There were endless petty power struggles, most about food. Terrible acts were perpetrated by prisoners upon each other. In one of the most notorious cases, U.S. Army Sergeant James Gallagher was later convicted by court-martial of killing two seriously ill prisoners by throwing them out into the snow. "I learned more about the way society operates in that camp than I could have learned in any university," said Andrew Condron. With a kind of insanity, some prisoners sold scraps of food to others for money or scrip that was utterly worthless to them. In those first months of 1951 every man was entirely preoccupied with the struggle for survival. Racked with dysentery, a man's intestine would hang down inches below his anus, to be stuffed back with a surge of agony when the next call to defecate came. It was not uncommon to stagger thirty, forty times a day to the latrine, men finding themselves unable even to cross the compound without dropping their trousers. Prisoners drowned by falling in the latrine pits. Lice and bedbugs thrived. They held competitions to kill them—123, 124, 125: their thumbs became black with ingrained blood. Condron became obsessed with this. "If I live," he thought, "I shall never get rid of that blood." They itched ceaselessly as they sat and talked;

exchanged the plots of old films; signaled extracts from old newspapers to each other in Morse or semaphore—anything to pass the dreadful, savagely cold days, until the time came to huddle desperately together for warmth through the icier nights.

For the weakened men, the greatest hardship was the regular wood detail. Their lives depended upon collecting sufficient fuel to keep their fires and cookers alive. Yet with each trip they were compelled to forage farther and farther afield into the mountains. The supply began to falter. Crossly, the Chinese summoned a meeting and harangued the prisoners upon their negative attitude to labor, pointing out that it was not for the captors' benefit, but that of the captives. Then, as spring came, there was a surge of volunteers for the wood detail. The Chinese were delighted to discover that "your attitude toward labor has improved." Yet it was not wood that called the men, but the discovery of marijuana. First identified by some of the Mexican prisoners, it grew wild on the hills. Through the next two years it became, for some men, the only means of making captivity endurable. It caused some excesses that puzzled the Chinese—sudden exuberant singsongs from groups of black prisoners, one morning a helplessly stoned figure racing around the compound screaming, "The Indians are coming! The Indians are coming!" But the Chinese were told that he was shell-shocked. Curiously enough, in two years they never appeared to grasp the truth.

In the spring of 1951 officers and men were held in the same camp areas. Each morning they were herded together in the hundreds for political lectures, huddled shivering together for four hours at a stretch—two hours in Chinese, two hours of translation—and any man found sitting back on his hands received a kick. "Study hard, Comrades, with open minds, and you will get home soon," the Chinese commandant told them. "But if you don't, we'll dig a ditch for you so deep that even your bourgeois bodies won't stink."

In the summer of 1951 there was a dramatic change in Chinese policy toward the prisoners of war. It was determined that if possible, they should be permitted to live. Conditions in all the camps improved markedly. Thereafter, the number of deaths among prisoners declined to a trickle: 99 percent of all American prisoner deaths took place in the first year of the war. As Captain James Majury of the Ulsters put it laconically, "The Chinese realized that they needed some survivors if their propaganda about 'the lenient treatment' was to have any meaning." At last they were given the means to delouse themselves—and lice had been one of the most corrosive destructors of morale. By the winter of 1951, to their astonishment, the prisoners found themselves receiving sufficient food to sustain life. The Chinese killed an occasional pig, and its fat was distributed among the prisoners by self-administered roster. They began to receive a rice ration instead of millet. In August, Captain Majury was at last able to dispatch a letter from the officers' camp which reached home and received his first from his family in October.

Then, as the Chinese arrangements became more organized, the prisoners were broken down into "companies" for daily political study sessions, at which they were required to write long, allegedly self-analytical political tracts. As part of the deliberate Communist policy of destroying their existing leadership, in October the British and American officers were gathered together and marched some hundred miles into the mountains to the new Camp 2, which remained the officers' camp for the remainder of the war. Their uniforms were replaced by Chinese quilted suits and caps, a further blow to their identity as soldiers. The Chinese appointed company and platoon leaders from among the prisoners.

From beginning to end, the Chinese purpose was to reindoctrinate their prisoners politically, to convert them from their traditional political values to those of communism. Beyond obvious political instruction, the Communists sought to destroy all existing structures of rank and command. No officer's rank was recognized. Any internal attempt by the prisoners to organize their own leadership without approval from the Chinese was interpreted as a "hostile attitude." When Sergeant Jim Taylor of the 8th Hussars, the senior British ranker in Camp 5, refused to salute a Chinese one morning, he was sent to "the hole" for three days, literally to roast in the summer heat in a hole covered with a sheet of corrugated iron. Some men were kept in it for weeks at a time.

The problem of "hostile attitudes" occurred most often among the officers in Camp 2, and resulted in the frequent removal of officers to "the cages," where they were held in solitary confinement, sometimes for months. Major Denis Harding, a Gloucesters company commander, was held in solitary confinement, mostly in a hillside cowshed, from January 1952 until his release in the summer of 1953. Major Guy Ward, R.A., had already endured four years of captivity in World War II. Throughout that experience he was sustained by a feeling "that we were all together, like a family, that in the end things would be all right. In Korea, we asked ourselves, 'How many years might this go on? Will it ever end?' " That first winter in the officers' camp, Ward, like his fellow prisoners, would find himself suddenly hauled from his bed at 3 A.M., when human resistance was lowest, and taken to an underground bunker for interrogation. Once again, this was overwhelmingly social and wearily repetitive:

"What car does your father have?"

"Are you a large family?"

"How much capital have you?"

Ward said later, "The only Chinese who understood us were the younger ones who had been educated in the United States. We were conscious that the way they treated us was the way they treated their own people. You might see fifteen or twenty Chinese by the roadside being kicked about in just the same way that they kicked us."

The sheer dreary monotony of the political lectures aroused their contempt: "The Democratic Reformation and Democratic Structure in North Korea and the Peaceful Unification Policy of the North Korean Government"; "The Chinese People's Right to Formosa"; "Corruption of the UN by the American war-mongers." They were permitted only Communist newspapers—the *Daily Worker* and *Chinese Pictorial*. The loudspeakers blared forth each day with news that announced fresh American defeats, never conceded a glimmer of United Nations success. Yet often they would glimpse the white contrails of high-flying aircraft, and occasionally they would see a dogfight, even see a Communist MIG brought down. Thus they were reminded that the war was not yet over, that the Communist armies had not yet triumphed.

There were a few tattered, dog-eared books which passed from hand to hand. Andrew Condron read Daphne Du Maurier's *Rebecca,* and was driven mad by the absence of the very last page, torn out by his captors. Years later Condron discovered that it contained a casually hostile reference to Communists. Generally, they were allowed to keep books the Chinese considered ideologically sound: *Uncle Tom's Cabin, War and Peace,* Lenin's *One Step Forward, Two Steps Back,* some Steinbecks, those works of Dickens which were thought to present a sufficiently bleak portrait of the plight of the proletariat.

Men's reaction to imprisonment varied enormously. It was difficult to generalize about the kind of man who held together best. A U.S. Marine pilot, who was little regarded at first by his fellow prisoners because of his taciturn manner, his apparent inability ever to say more than "Uh-huh?" or "Shit," proved one of the most rugged and respected "reactionaries" in the officers' camp. A British officer who had been a prisoner of the Germans in World War II was one of the most visible resisters for months. Then, imperceptibly, he began to deteriorate. Like so many others, his will was weakened by illness and hunger. By the end he seemed one of the most broken-spirited. To many British prisoners it seemed a criminal blunder by the War Office to have recalled for service in Korea so many ex-World War II POWs. It was an unspeakable experience for men who had already endured two, three, four years of their youth in captivity now to be exposed to the same misery once more. It was worst of all for those who had been held by the Japanese. They, from the outset, remembered the Korean guards as their most atrocious and brutal tormentors. Colonel Fred Carne of the Gloucesters seemed, to most of his companions, astoundingly untroubled by captivity. The Chinese singled out Carne for special treatment, as their highest-ranking British captive. He spent much of his time in their hands in solitary confinement. Yet Carne behaved throughout with his customary taciturn serenity. His example impressed his fellow prisoners for the rest of their lives. Major Denis Harding's weight fell from 154 pounds to 98 pounds during his time in captivity.

By common consent, most of the doctors and chaplains—those with a very obvious and visible role to play in the camps—behaved well, some outstandingly so. Despite the pitiful absence of drugs and equipment, the doctors spent hours attempting to persuade men stricken with "give-upitis" to eat. Among the padres, Sam Davies of the Gloucesters was remembered by his fellow prisoners with immense affection and respect. But perhaps the most beloved of all was Father Emil Kapaun, Catholic chaplain of the U.S. 1st Cavalry. Kapaun's cheerful selflessness, his genius for scrounging and devotion to the suffering, his nightly sick rounds, became a legend. He died in Camp 5 in May 1951, worn out by dysentery and a blood clot in his leg. In Camp 2 the prisoners hoarded rice paper on which to compile a copy of the Book of Common Prayer. When Padre Davies was dispatched to solitary confinement, James Majury took over the conduct of his services. Davies secretly baptized six Americans and prepared nineteen British and American officers for confirmation in the camp. He was bitterly chagrined that, because of his officer status, the Chinese would never allow him to go among the other ranks.

Lieutenant Bill Cooper of the Northumberland Fusiliers found it helpful to demand of himself at the beginning of each day, "What worthwhile thing are you going to do today?" He would often accept the job of washing the ghastly rags of men crippled by dysentery: "It was horrible, but you felt that it was a job worth doing."[8] For most men, the nights were the worst. It was then that they lay silent but awake, brooding in the loneliness about their families and their societies, going indifferently about their business so many thousands of miles away. Desperately as they hungered for letters, life became almost more intolerable on the rare occasions when these came. In two years Bill Cooper received three letters from home, and five of those he wrote reached his family. Jerry Morgan received his first letter from home in April 1952, enclosing a photograph of the son born in the United States whom he had never seen. Many men did not even achieve this level of contact. There was so much a man yearned to know that was not in the simple scraps of paper they received.

"Dear Robert," Lance Corporal Bob Erricker's father wrote from his little house in Surrey to his son in Camp 5 on the Yalu, "I have just received the news via the War Office that you are a Prisoner of War in North Korea, it's wonderful and we are so thankful to know you are safe and well, shall be watching every day for the post. . . . Look after No. 1. I had a nice letter from Lt. Alexander's father. His death was in *The Times*. P. C. O'Halloran has been made Sergeant and is going to live at Milford. Daisy has got another Girl two month old. Mrs. Terry has left Alford and Eileen Brunet is living in their bungalow. We celebrated the good news of your safety by going to the Daily Mail Ideal Home Exhibition at Olympia. Mum was 'Frisking about' like a 2-year-old, bought a Hoover Washing Machine for £31, and she aint got 4d."

It was a kind of agony to hear this simple domestic small change amid the sorghum and dysentery of a hut on the Yalu. Camp 5 was for "progressives," the men whom the Chinese considered to be adopting the most positive attitude to their own political education. If its inmates were marginally better treated than those in "reactionary" camps, there is little evidence that most of them treated the Chinese any more seriously. Many British and American rankers simply decided that there was no harm in playing the Chinese game if by doing so they could gain better food and marginally improve their own chances of survival. Even when attendance at political lectures was made voluntary, in the later stages of imprisonment, some men continued to attend merely to pass the day.[9]

The first serious shock to Western consciousness about the POWs in Korea was the transmission by Radio Peking of broadcasts by American and British captives. Some made recordings at the behest of the Chinese because they could sincerely see no harm in them. Some represented Communist successes in political indoctrination. Some were merely willing to pay any moral price for a greater prospect of survival. But the revelation in the West that some captives were cooperating, if not collaborating, with the Communists was a profound shock. What was happening to men in the hands of the enemy that they could be persuaded to speak to their own people across the airwaves in such terms?

"Hello. This is Marine Andrew Condron speaking. Hello, Mum, Dad, and all at home. By courtesy of the Chinese People's 'Volunteers,' I am broadcasting to you now to tell you how we are getting on here, and about our preparations for Christmas. . . ."

A further confusing element in the lives and loyalties of the prisoners were the visits of Western Communists to the camps. In World War II the handful of British renegades who chose to put themselves at the disposal of the Germans were unhesitatingly branded as traitors, and several—including the son of a British Cabinet minister—were hanged in 1945. Yet during the Korean War, as during Vietnam, the Communists extracted a major propaganda advantage from invitations to Western left-wingers to visit their martyred country. It is difficult to regard the behavior of the visitors to a nation with which their country was at war with much enthusiasm. It contributed something, at least, to the Communist purpose of confusing the minds of the UN prisoners, as well as the world, about the unity of national purpose behind the UN war effort in Korea.

So much of the prisoners' experience teetered uneasily between tragedy and farce. "You see that now?" said Comrade Lim to a Camp 5 group one morning, stabbing his blackboard as he denoted some refinement of proletarian organization. A bee on the blackboard stung him, to the delight of his audience. "You see that now?" demanded Lim furiously. "That is a capitalist bee." Chinese prurience was persistently affronted by the prisoners' language: "Why all the time you effing, effing, effing?'' The Chinese regarded the constant obscenities as a deliberate insult to themselves. The prisoners, in their turn, laughed at the Chinese habit of walking into the compound holding hands with each other: ''We thought they were a load of blooming fairies,'' said Bob Erricker. The Chinese discovery of this belief led to yet another lecture, to ''correct their attitude.''

A fanatical young Marxist named Comrade Sun was Chief Political Commissar at Camp 2. His classes were conducted with weary, unrelenting zeal. The more senior an officer, the more likely to be singled out for correction:

'' 'Davies, stand up,' he commanded the Gloucesters' padre one morning. I rose.

'What is your opinion of the chapter we have just read?' [It was from William Z. Foster's *Outline History of the Americas.*]

Long pause, then:

'I'm afraid I was not listening.'

'Why not?'

'Well, I'm a British POW and I have other interests than American history.' Silence.

'You will pay attention. You must correct your attitude.'

Ponderously:

'I confess my crime.'

'Sit down.' ''[10]

The Chinese made determined efforts to destroy prisoners' faith in religion. ''If you believe in God, why doesn't he help you now?'' the commandant taunted NCO prisoners in Camp 4. Lieutenant John Thornton, U.S. Navy, noticed that the black prisoners—whom the Chinese worked steadily to distance from their white compatriots—held on to their religious faith better than many whites. One of the best-loved prisoners was Captain John Stanley, who delighted his comrades with his guitar playing and exasperated the Chinese by his dogged insistence: ''I am an American, not a Negro.''

Men became intensely moody, their spirits vacillating dramatically from one day to the next. Personal relations could become obsessive. Close friendships would form and persist for weeks, until broken by some fit of temper. But there was virtually no homosexuality. Most men found, very early in their imprisonment, that they lost all interest in sex. It was only in the last weeks before their release, when the end was obviously near, that prisoners allowed themselves to think again about women. Most men believed that they learned from their time in captivity to count the blessings of daily life in freedom. Padre Sam Davies used to say, ''When I get out of here, I shall never again moan about waiting for a bus in the rain.''[11]

The attitudes of the ''reactionaries''—those who continued openly to defy the

Chinese throughout their captivity—varied greatly. The most systematic defiance, not surprisingly, came from inhabitants of the officers' camp. Some British and American officers, for instance, refused to speak to a Chinese at all, if this could be avoided. Others, like Captain Anthony Farrar-Hockley, talked and argued with them at every opportunity. It was a matter of personal inclination. The behavior of all prisoners tends inevitably toward the juvenile because they are unwillingly placed in the position of captive children, unable to make their own decisions. Thus, too, some of their acts of defiance were childish. One morning a dozen men would work furiously for hours, digging in a deep hole in the midst of the compound. Then, with great ceremony, they would place a piece of paper in it and fill it in again. Inevitably, the curious Chinese would excavate it, to discover the simple message "Mind Your Own Business." Some days prisoners would reduce "loll call" to chaos, only to parade with perfect discipline the next time. One morning a group of men would run out into the compound and spend an hour "flying" around, pretending to be helicopters, amid the bewildered gaze of their guards. Another day a crowd of spectators might stand watching two prisoners play Ping-Pong, their heads moving to and fro with the ball—except that there was no ball, no bats, no table—merely a mime show to needle the Chinese. Taking invisible dogs for a walk was always popular. One morning at Camp 3 "all of us decided to go crazy," according to Private David Fortune. "We rode round on invisible motorbikes, sat playing invisible cards. Some men really were that crazy. . . ."[12]

Perhaps the most imaginative pinprick "tease" of their captors was perpetrated from the officers' camp at the height of the Chinese propaganda campaign alleging that the Americans were employing bacteriological warfare in Korea. Some prisoners attached a dead mouse to a small parachute, and one morning when unobserved they hurled it some yards beyond the wire of the compound. They were rewarded by the spectacle of an earnest cluster of Chinese surrounding a doctor in a face mask who arrived to examine and at last, with infinite caution and ceremony, remove the specimen. It was another contribution to the prisoners' tiny, sometimes pathetic efforts to demonstrate to themselves, as well as to their captors, that they had not yet surrendered all control of their own affairs.

Although there were many friendships among prisoners that transcended nationality, in general each group hung closely together. The Turks were greatly admired for their indomitable toughness and resistance to the Chinese. Their only collaborator was quietly killed by his compatriots. When one of their men was sick, two of his comrades undertook responsibility for his survival. The British seemed to suffer fewer difficulties than the Americans with "give-upitis." Resignation and adjustment to the inevitable is a British national characteristic. Most British prisoners took it for granted that it was preferable to eat the unspeakable food they were offered rather than to die. There were subdivisions within the national groups: the American aircrew, for instance, tended to distance themselves from their army counterparts. Each nationality tended to keep its own secrets, above all in Camp 2, the officers' camp. There was deep suspicion of a handful of American officers, one senior, who were believed to be collaborating with the Chinese, even to the extent of betraying escape plans.

The nationalities often argued about what approach to adopt to specific Chinese demands. In the officers' camp there was a protracted debate when the Chinese demanded that prisoners' group commanders should assemble and count them each morning. The Americans were uncertain whether or not this was a reasonable demand. The British flatly refused. They said, "If the Chinese want to count us, okay. But we will not do it for them." Two British officers were dispatched to solitary confinement in the course of that dispute. It would be foolish to deny that there were considerable tensions between the British and American officers in Camp 2. While the British greatly admired individuals, such as Marine Major John McLoughlin and Tom Harrison of the U.S.A.F., limping on his wooden leg, there was considerable mistrust at group level. The Americans considered some British behavior and acts of passive resistance absurd and counterproductive. The British simply did not confide in some Americans about their plans or intentions because they did not trust them. The British, historically conditioned to despise the open display of emotion, were bemused by the American readiness to weep. Lieutenant Bill Cooper was bewildered to see a U.S. Army Captain cry one afternoon when one of his team dropped a catch during a softball game. Another officer burst into tears when he found his bedding had been switched when he wanted to sleep next door to a friend. It was a difference of cultures. Lieutenant John Thornton, an American helicopter pilot universally known as "Rotorhead," who behaved with great courage throughout his captivity, said afterward, "We were very poor POWs—we envied the British regimental tradition. The attitude among most of our men was 'Hooray for me. Screw you.' The Communists were largely successful in isolating us from each other."[13] Private Dave Fortune said, "Among many Americans, one saw every principle of the code of conduct for POWs break down. The whole idea of having faith in one's fellow man collapsed."

In the course of the entire war there was not a single successful escape back to the UN lines by a prisoner in the Yalu camps. But there were many attempts. Some prisoners such as Captain Farrar-Hockley tried again and again, and remained at liberty for some days. Private David Fortune, a 35th Infantryman captured on January 2, 1951, got out of Camp 3 with a comrade and remained at liberty for three days and nights in the winter of 1952. On the third night the two men were peering curiously at a Chinese antiaircraft battery when they were spotted and seized by North Korean militiamen. The Koreans behaved with predictable savagery. The Americans were stripped naked, paraded through the nearby village, and beaten up. Then they were tied up, to be mocked and spat upon by the local children for a few hours before being returned to the Chinese. Back at the camp, they were rewarded with two weeks' solitary confinement. The Chinese liked to say to the prisoners, "The guards are not here to keep you in, but to save you from the Korean people." There was a disagreeable strand of truth in this.

One of the most notable Chinese failures was the establishment, in August 1952, of a "penal camp" for "reactionary" noncommissioned prisoners. This was a fenced compound where men were compelled to do hard labor, often as meaningless as digging holes and filling them in again. Yet the very qualities in a prisoner that qualified him for the penal camp were those that bound him to his fellow "reactionaries" with a coherence that was achieved in no other compound. "Everybody in that camp was a good man," said Dave Fortune. "Morale was much higher." There were no informers, no collaborators, no burden of mutual mistrust. After a few months the Chinese realized their mistake and redistributed the 130-odd inmates among the other camps once more.

The notion that the Chinese "brainwashed" the bulk of their prisoners in Korea is simply unfounded. They appear to have employed the sophisticated techniques generally associated with this term only in one case—that of the American aircrew from whom they extracted confessions of participation in bacteriological warfare, their most notable propaganda achievement. In the Korean prison camps the Chinese attempted large-scale thought reform, with a very modest degree of success. What was astonishing about their attempts to convert their prisoners to the cause of communism was the crudity, the clumsiness, the stupidity with which they were conducted. There is no difficulty in understanding their approach—the "lenient treatment," the efforts to build a sense of community between captors and captives. It was precisely that by which the Communists achieved such success during their civil war with the kuomintang, by the end of which millions of Chiang Kai Shek's soldiers were successfully absorbed into the armies of Mao Tse Tung. It was founded upon the willingness of the defeated, throughout China's historical experience, to throw in their lot with the victors, to recognize a new leadership, a new source of power and patronage. Yet for the overwhelming bulk of the UN prisoners in Chinese hands, the notion that they had anything to learn from Mao Tse Tung's society was risible. Themselves the products of a highly technical, relatively educated society, they saw the absolute poverty, the pathetic ignorance of their guards and indoctrinators—and despised them. "One or two of the Chinese were laughably pleasant," said Major Guy Ward. "But not one of them showed the intelligence really to make us like and respect them."

"The Chinese were trying to persuade us, 'Our world is better than your world' [said Captain James Majury]. In my own mind, I would say, 'Okay, anything you've done with your own society has got to be better for you than Warlordism.' But there was no way that a Chinese could ever convince me that his world would be better for *me*. Very few people were truly brainwashed. I said to the Chinese toward the end, 'Surely you must realize that you will never change us?' And yes, I think they had given up. If they had really been smart, if they had really wanted to make an impact, they would have pampered us from the beginning.''[14]

Yet two years of grinding repetition of political dogma, two years of isolation from their own society, two years of Chinese scorn—''You know that your country is not interested in you''—made a decisive impact upon some men. ''Do not think that, because you get home, we cannot reach you—we can always get you if we want you,'' they were told. In their impotence, some prisoners found this perfectly believable. The most effective means of breaking a man's will was the appeal to his physical weakness—offering secret access to the commodity whose absence dominated their lives: food. A prisoner who accepted an egg, a fistful of tobacco from a Chinese in return for some tiny act of betrayal was half doomed already. His own self-respect was cracked. It remained only for his captors to make the treason absolute, to extract some hint about an escape plan, secret religious services, ''hostile attitudes.''

Why did such a man as Andrew Condron, the twenty-three-year-old barrack-room Socialist from West Lothian, become, in the eyes of his countrymen, a traitor by refusing repatriation at the end of the war, along with twenty-one Americans? The simple answer, perhaps, is that he was ripe for it. Condron always refused to see himself as a traitor. He declared his lifelong pride in his country, in his service in the Royal Marines. But he had always been a member of ''the awkward squad''—''Red'' Condron, the man forever asking questions, who instinctively resisted authority in any form. In Camp 5 he became fascinated by Marxism:

''I had seen the suffering and hardship among people in the Mediterranean, and I related to it. Why were there the very rich and very poor? Surely life could be better organized than that. There was a large element of romanticism about China, a sense of adventure. At that time, I thought I'd go to China for a year or so, then come home. Had things not turned out the way they did, I might have become a missionary. I wanted to go and live in Russia afterwards. What I wanted to know was—Did it work? I wasn't a convinced Communist, but a convinced Marxist. I have remained one all my life. I had lost my Catholic faith even before I went in the Army. Perhaps I needed something to latch onto.''[15]

Thirty-five years later it seems much easier to accept the naive simplicity of Condron's reasoning than it was for his contemporaries. They perceived an enormity about his act, a sense of national disgrace which was shared by

Americans toward their own prisoners who chose to remain in China. Condron "the Bolshie," the instinctively bloody-minded, made a gesture which seems, with hindsight, to owe far less to the wiles of his Communist captors than to his own willfulness. It is striking that most of his British fellow prisoners, even "the reactionaries" who fiercely declined to cooperate with their captors, bear Condron little or no resentment today. At no time during their imprisonment was he suspected of the acts of personal betrayal of his comrades of which many other prisoners were guilty, who returned to their countries free of the stain of treason. It was their crimes that their peers found impossible to forgive. And these owed nothing to ideology, but everything to a pathetic collapse of will and self-discipline in the face of suffering and privation.

Guy Ward was cynically amused, on the eve of his release, to discover that the Chinese provided the same sort of demonstration of their own honesty that he had received from the Germans in 1945. They scrupulously returned all the prisoners' possessions removed on their capture—lighters, pens, watches. Some of their captors sought to make amends for all that had happened in the previous two years: "We are sorry, very sorry this has happened. We are friends. It is the American imperialists." But even thirty-five years later Ward would think of the Chinese and say simply, "I loathe them."

What was remarkable was not how many men were scarred for life by the experience of Communist captivity, but how many shrugged it off with little long-term effect. General William Dean, the commander of the U.S. 24th Division captured at Taejon in July 1950, was held for three years in solitary confinement near Pyongyang, subjected to intense Marxist-Leninist indoctrination. Yet Dean, on his release, merely remarked lightly, "I'm an authority now on the history of the Communist Party and much of its doctrine."

"I took the simple professional soldier's view," said Captain James Majury. "I certainly came out saying, 'I shall never leave food on my plate again.' But I felt that if one had been stupid enough to be taken prisoner, one must accept the consequences. It was an experience that I would not want to repeat, but it probably did not do me much permanent harm." The most lasting mark of imprisonment upon Lieutenant Bill Cooper was the destruction of trust in his fellow men: "It made me look at people and say, 'You are guilty until I have found you innocent.' It also made me not care about things. If somebody said to me, 'You mustn't do that,' I would say, 'Why? I'll make my own decision.' " Private Bill Shirk of the 15th Field Artillery found the whole experience "a bad, bad, dream. All the time, I kept asking, 'Why don't they come and get us out?' We were fighting these primitive people, for chrissakes. I made up my mind: if I ever get out of this place, I won't ever put myself out for anybody. What the hell did we want with this country, anyway? I sure felt let down."

The exact number of British prisoners who died in captivity is uncertain, but it was probably around fifty, against a total of 1,036 who were repatriated by the Communists in 1953. Of the 7,190 American prisoners who fell into Communist hands, 2,730 did not return. At least some hundreds of these were murdered in cold blood by the North Koreans. Many more died on the terrible journey to the camps or in the first winter of the war. American history students judge the casualties to represent the highest prisoner death rate in any conflict in the nation's history, including the Revolutionary War. Yet why was it that none of the 229 Turkish prisoners died, and only 13 percent of U.S. Marines, against 38 percent of army prisoners? Part of the answer—a significant part—was that most of the non-American prisoners were captured after the winter of 1950, when the Communists had begun to make greater efforts to keep prisoners alive. But also, "the Army felt that its losses were due not so much to the Communists' disregard of the Geneva Convention—although this was unquestionably contributory," wrote an American writer who investigated the issue in detail,[16] "as to the breakdown of discipline among the prisoners themselves. Many men after capture appeared to have lost all sense of allegiance, not only to their country but to their fellow prisoners." One in seven of all U.S. prisoners was considered by subsequent army investigations to have been guilty of "serious collaboration." The U.S. Army's postwar reports upon the conduct of its own men in captivity inflicted a major trauma. It was felt necessary, in its aftermath, to draw up a Code of Conduct for U.S. servicemen, reminding them of their obligations to their comrades, and to their country, if they fell into the hands of the enemy. It must be a measure of the success achieved by training in prisoner behavior after Korea that U.S. prisoners in Hanoi conducted themselves, as a group, incomparably better than those in the camps along the Yalu.

The revelation of what the Communists had done to the UN prisoners in their hands had a profound influence upon the West's perception of the Korean War and of the Chinese. For much of the conflict, the men on the line felt little hatred for their Chinese opponents, although the North Koreans enjoyed an unchallenged reputation for barbarism. But the shock of discovery of the plight of the prisoners placed Chinese conduct in a new, infinitely more sinister light. Mao Tse Tung's China acquired a new, far more frightening and disturbing aspect. From this, arguably, its image in the West never recovered. Long after the Korean War receded into memory, the fear of "the Manchurian candidate" remained.

17

THE PURSUIT OF PEACE

Koje-do

No aspect of the Korean War was more grotesque than the manner in which the struggle was allowed to continue for a further sixteen months after the last substantial territorial obstacle to an armistice had been removed by negotiation in February 1952. From that date until the end in July 1953, on-the-line men endured the miseries of summer heat and winter cold, were maimed by mines and killed by napalm, small arms, and high explosives, while at Panmunjom the combatants wrangled around one bitterly contentious issue: the post-armistice exchange of prisoners.

Long after both sides had forsaken any hope of achieving decisive territorial gains on the battlefield, the impulse toward gaining a moral victory—or at least avoiding a moral defeat—persisted. In the matter of the prisoners, there were two vital objectives for the UN Command: first, to gain the return to freedom of every man of their own held by the Communists, and second, among Chinese and Korean prisoners held in the South, to ensure that only willing prisoners were returned to Communist hands. The memory of Yalta, of hundreds of thousands of doomed, desperate Russians being herded by the Western Allies back into the bloody maw of Stalin in 1945, hung heavy over the governments of the West.

The first list of prisoners in Communist hands handed over to the UN Command on December 18, 1951, contained just 11,559 names. Yet in March

1951, Peking and Pyongyang had claimed to be holding 65,000 captives. Even by Communist standards, this was a huge discrepancy. Apart from South Korean captives, it left more than 8,000 missing Americans unaccounted for. The Chinese claimed that thousands of ROK Army prisoners had been allowed to go home and that the unlisted foreigners had died, escaped, been killed in air raids or released at the front. But Peking can never have supposed that this explanation would be acceptable in South Korea or the United States.

Even more contentious and complex, however, was the fate of the Communist prisoners in UN hands. From the standpoint of Peking and Pyongyang, it was a matter of immense importance that all these should be seen to return to the bosom of the people's republics. The propaganda cost of many thousands being seen to "choose freedom," to decline repatriation, appeared intolerable. On April 2, 1952, the Communist delegation at Panmunjom demanded that the UN Command should prepare lists of prisoners willing to return north. To the astonishment of both delegations, only 70,000 of the total of 132,000 agreed to do so. There was no possibility that such a situation could be accepted by the Communist governments. A long, wretched struggle of wills began, in which the attention of the world became focused upon the vast UN prison compounds on the offshore islands of South Korea.

Until the war was well advanced, Koje-do remained one of the prettiest possessions of South Korea. A little fishing community a few miles across the sea from the port of Pusan, it had gone untroubled by most of the dramas and horrors that had befallen the mainland. Communist prisoners were shipped in batches to Pusan by truck or train. At a compound on the edge of the city, the bewildered and demoralized men spent an average of two days while joint American and South Korean CIC teams interrogated them. They were given old American-style fatigues to replace their tattered uniforms, segregated by rank and ethnic group, and housed in big tents from which they were brought forth, in their turn, to be questioned.

Millions of words have been written about the plight of UN prisoners in the hands of the Communists in Korea. Much less has been said about the treatment of Communist prisoners in the hands of the UN. Under the UN, nothing remotely resembling the indoctrination program carried out in the Yalu camps took place. It may justly be claimed that the North Korean and Chinese prisoners in the southern camps were confined, for the most part, in conditions little worse, and with more and better food, than many would have enjoyed at home. Yet amid the profound humanitarian concern for the British, Americans, Turks being maltreated in the North, little has been said about the casual brutality to which thousands of Communist prisoners were subjected. A host of UN veterans of Korea testify to the hostility and contempt in which most soldiers held "the gooks," whether North or South Korean.

Western treatment of the Koreans and the Chinese was dictated by a deeply rooted conviction that these were not people like themselves, but near-animals who could be held at bay only by the use of the kind of brutality they were wont to employ against each other. At the front prisoners became better treated, indeed greatly valued for intelligence purposes, from the spring of 1951 onward. But in the camps of South Korea, many suffered as severely as their counterparts on the Yalu. "The compounds at Pusan were run by military police who were very rough on the prisoners, often beat them up very badly," said Private Alan Maggio, who served among the POWs as a medical orderly for ten months from May 1951. "Those MPs were just waiting for trouble. They wanted something to happen. The enlisted men ran the system. There were no officers who bothered to walk round or check what was going on."[1]

From the Pusan compounds the prisoners were herded into landing craft at the dockside and ferried for three hours across the sea to Koje-do. Here, beneath the shadow of the high hills that dominated the island, thirty-seven vast, adjoining, wired compounds had been constructed. Within these were confined, early in 1952, some 70,000 Chinese and North Korean prisoners. They were held at a density four times greater than that tolerated in U.S. federal penitentiaries. A further 100,000, including 38,000 born in South Korea and conscripted into the North Korean Army during the Communist occupation, had already been screened and removed from the island.

They drifted upon an unbroken swell of boredom. There were a few daily fatigue parties—the details marching out of the compounds each morning carrying great drums of excrement slung between poles, the men working on the drainage ditches in endless, hopeless attempts to clear the mud which overlay the entire camp. But most prisoners sat in their tents all day playing a Korean version of mah-jongg, carving wooden figures, reading, playing cards, cooking over their little fires. Within each compound the Americans left the prisoners entirely to themselves. But their lot was not enviable. From one of the little dispensaries outside the compound gates, Private Maggio found ample opportunities for exercising his medical skills:

"Koje-do wasn't managed properly—there were far too many men in one enclosure. There was a lot of bronchitis, pneumonia, malaria, dysentery, pinkeye. TB was widespread. There were men with open wounds that were still draining. All of them had lice. The problem was washing their clothes—it should have been compulsory, but it wasn't. The prisoners hated the delousing powder. Then there were always problems with the rats, which wasn't helped by the way they all hid food under their mats. The Chinese prisoners had the cleanest compound and highest morale. They were by far the most disciplined group on that island."[2]

The UN Command could claim that despite all the medical problems, only a very small number of Communist prisoners died from disease on Koje-do, by comparison with the terrible toll on the Yalu. But the eyewitness evidence is also overwhelming that conditions among the prisoners would have been considered barbaric by, say, the inmates of a POW camp in Germany in 1943. Their captors had simply installed the Chinese and North Koreans in the circumstances they considered appropriate to Asian peasants.

More serious than this was the rabble of the American and Korean armies who were entrusted with their custody. Maggio and other eyewitnesses describe the ferocious racial tensions between American groups among the guards—notably the blacks and Chicanos against the whites. For them, duty on Koje-do was almost as intolerable as for the prisoners. No serious attempt was made by officers to impose leadership or discipline. Gambling and local whores were the only diversions. Knife fights and brawls were commonplace. ''The disciplinary situation was unbelievable,'' said Maggio. ''I found the whole place a living hell—I was in fear constantly. There were fights in the barracks, fights in the compounds. Anybody who couldn't make it on the line was sent down to do duty on Koje-do. We ended up with the scum of the Army—the drunks, the drug addicts, the nutters, the deadbeats.'' To his overwhelming relief, in February 1952 Maggio was able to gain a transfer to an ammunition trucking company.

Sergeant Robert Hoop was posted to the 595th Military Police Company on Koje-do in October 1951, after being wounded in combat for the second time, serving with the 15th Infantry. In five months on the island, he only once set foot inside the wire of a compound, escorting a medical orderly—''I was very scared every second I was in there. I just couldn't wait to get out.''[3] Hoop had constant disciplinary problems with his men—''getting mixed up with whores and getting drunk on duty.'' In his sector of the camp, there were just three MP companies, American and South Korean, to control and guard some 24,000 prisoners. By the spring of 1952 it was debatable whose predicament was more wretched—that of the prisoners within the wire or the guards outside it.

The root of the huge difficulties that burst upon the UN prison camps in 1952 was that, once the prisoners had been sent to the rear areas and interrogated, their custody and welfare became very low priorities for the UN Command. The officers and men who were entrusted with running the camps were, for the most part, among the least impressive manpower in the U.S. and Korean armies. Many of the guards treated the prisoners as animals. The chief objective of their officers was to distance themselves as far as possible from the prisoners and leave them in their compounds to administer their own affairs. Thus it was that when, in the spring of 1952, the Communists began infiltrating men who deliberately allowed themselves to be taken prisoner, with orders to seize internal control of the POW compounds, they were able to do so without the slightest difficulty. An extraordinary storm broke upon Koje-do Island, of a kind never witnessed before in any military prison camp in history.

The officers responsible for Koje-do had plenty of warning of the impending furor. In the first months of the year there was growing evidence of ideological and military activity inside the compounds. Prisoners manufactured dummy rifles, uniform caps headed with bottle-top badges bearing the red star, flags, banners. Openly, by squads and companies, they began to drill inside the wire. Their commissars harangued them. The first evidence of ruthless internal discipline appeared: prisoners were badly beaten up, even murdered within the wire. Yet in the face of all this, their custodians did nothing. The inmates were left undisturbed. The prisoner's leaders began to make increasingly strident demands for improved conditions: writing paper, better food, changed routines. They were probing, testing the will of the Americans. It was found wanting. One morning a crowd of prisoners began hurling cans of sardines and salmon back over the wire. The food was unsuitable, they proclaimed. They wanted fresh fish sent from Japan. The prisoners staged strikes in support of their demands. Their custodians, baffled, fearful of the wrath of this vast horde of apparent fanatics, desperate for tranquility at any price, sought earnestly to appease them. An extraordinary psychological situation developed, in which it was the prisoners behind the wire who held the initiative. Their captors danced impotently to their tune.

There were violent incidents as early as the summer of 1951. In June, after a prisoners' attack on a UN work detail, seven men were killed and four wounded by ROK fire. In August there were demonstrations which ended with nine dead and twenty-five wounded on Koje-do, eight killed and twenty-two wounded at Pusan. Struggles in September caused twenty more deaths. In a more sinister development, on December 23 UN medical staff were unable to save the lives of ten prisoners fatally beaten by their fellow inmates. No serious attempt was made to seek or punish the murderers. The same night, in a mass demonstration in another compound, fourteen prisoners were killed and twenty-four injured.

In the first months of 1952 the tempo of violence on Koje-do rose sharply. In February the UN began its first attempts to screen the prisoners one by one, to determine who wished to be repatriated to North Korea and China. To the astonishment of the guards, the Communist leaders of the first compound they entered launched a headlong assault with steel pickets, spiked clubs, barbed-wire flails, and blackjacks. One American was killed—and seventy-five prisoners. On April 10, when American medical orderlies entered Compound 95 on a routine visit to remove a wounded man, a wave of screaming prisoners charged them. Koje-do's commandant, Brigadier Francis T. Dodd, sent 100 unarmed ROKs into the compound to retrieve the prisoners. One ROK soldier simply disappeared in the ensuing struggle. He was never seen again. Eventually, the guards on the perimeter tried to give their men inside covering fire. An American officer and several ROKs were wounded. In another incident, prisoners staged a massed rush on a compound gate. An American officer and two men fought them off with a jeep-mounted .30-caliber machine gun. Three prisoners were killed and sixty wounded, along with four ROK guards.

Koje-do was becoming, as the Communists intended, a second front in the

Korean War. Their purpose was to achieve a major propaganda victory—to project the United Nations as the brutal persecutors and murderers of their prisoners. To this end, the fanatics within the compound were able to inspire or intimidate thousands of their wretched fellow prisoners to hurl themselves, often under suicidal circumstances, upon the guns of their captors. Those responsible for the camps now faced the worst of all possible worlds. In their fear they made absurd concessions to the prisoners and allowed their leaders ludicrous liberty to create an ideological hell within the perimeter fence. But Koje-do was also becoming the focus of growing world controversy, as reports grew of the casualty lists in the island disturbances.

On May 7, 1952, a far more serious, indeed grotesque, episode took place. In the midst of preparations for fresh political screening of the prisoners in Compound 76, which housed 6,400 of the most fanatical prisoners, the commandant, Brigadier Dodd, went in to reason with them. At 3:15 in the afternoon, as he prepared to leave, a whistle was blown. There was a rush of North Koreans around him. He was seized by the Communists and held hostage. A sign painted on ponchos, obviously preprepared, was hoisted: WE CAPTURE DODD AS LONG AS OUR DEMAND WILL BE SOLVED HIS SAFETY IS SECURED, IF THERE HAPPEN BRUTAL ACT SUCH AS SHOOTING, HIS LIFE IS IN DANGER. The following day, with the compound now under siege by tanks, guards, and offshore gunboats, and the island under the temporary command of Dodd's deputy, Colonel Craig, Dodd was allowed to communicate the POWs' near-farcical demands: to be permitted to form an association, to be provided with office supplies and a telephone. From Tokyo, Ridgway instructed Van Fleet to take whatever measures were necessary to regain control. On May 9, Van Fleet arrived personally to investigate the situation. There were now some 15,000 heavily armed UN troops on the island, facing the mass of unarmed Communists behind the wire. On the night of the tenth, after negotiations, Dodd was released unharmed. But to the profound embarrassment of the Americans, it was found that he had signed a document which appeared to acknowledge a measure of justice in the prisoners' case.

The Communists had scored a propaganda triumph, and focused the spotlight of foreign attention upon Koje-do. In the days that followed a procession of official and unofficial visitors descended upon the island, and without exception castigated the authorities for the collapse of control. The British Air Vice Marshal Bouchier reported on the lack of parades and roll calls, the open display of Communist flags and military drilling by prisoners: "In short, the Communist POWs in these compounds have held, and still hold, undisputed control within their own compounds."[4] Van Itterson, the Dutch representative to the UN Korean Commission, who was a former POW of the Japanese, declared, "The Americans have no idea how to treat Asiatic POWs. The fact that they still don't act strongly enough causes an ever-increasing audaciousness of behaviour by the prisoners. It is clear that only drastic measures can help."[5]

In the months that followed the Dodd seizure, far from improving, the situation appeared to deteriorate: 115 prisoners died in rioting between July 1951 and July 1952. American attempts to reassert authority generated only more unfavorable publicity. On June 9, 1952, *Pravda* reported gleefully that the Americans were employing gas chambers and torture, and forcibly preventing prisoners from expressing their wish to be repatriated. When General Mark Clark expressed his desire for token British and Canadian contingents to join the UN guard force on Koje-do, the British reluctantly complied, but the Canadian government agonized for days about whether it was willing to allow its troops to be associated with the unsavory situation on the island. Renewed Communist rioting was met with strong American repressive action, and scores more deaths. The Communist "journalist" Wilfred Burchett wrote in the *Daily Worker,* "Two hitherto unreported massacres of Korean and Chinese prisoners in the American compounds on Koje-do have now come to light. . . . The brutality used to make a prisoner agree not to return home is now clearly revealed." Strained relations between London and Washington were worsened by the difficulty of gaining accurate reports about what was going on at Koje-do. The Washington Embassy minuted the Foreign Office, "I think this is just one more instance of the difficulty of getting detailed information in Washington about operations in Korea."[6]

One of the most interesting outsider's views of the Koje-do drama was presented in a report by Major D. R. Bancroft, the British commander of a company of the King's Own Shropshire Light Infantry sent to the island on May 25, 1952. Within hours of their own arrival, the KSLI had "invaded" a compound and removed reserve food supplies, escape maps, and contraband which it was plain had been sold to the prisoners by ROK guards. An hour later two prisoners broke away from the compound and sought asylum with the British. They reported that the Communist commissars were furious at having lost face and had ordered that the prisoners must forcibly resist the next "invasion." Bancroft was appalled to discover that each compound possessed its own blacksmith's shop, in which prisoners could forge weapons, and that American supply vehicles were providing them with petrol with which to start their fires. Accidental discharges from the weapons of guards, causing death or serious injury, appeared commonplace. On June 10 some prisoners who sought refuge from the commissars were speared to death by the inmates under the eyes of the guards. American troops entered the compound to restore order, and a battle followed. The Americans' "bearing and control was of the highest order," reported Bancroft. "The fanaticism displayed by the prisoners was alarming. . . . Even when half the compound had been cleared and there were over 100 dead and wounded lying around, the commissars harangued the masses to greater endeavours.'' On June 11 fifteen prisoners in one compound were murdered overnight by the commissars.

The British attempted a new approach in the compound under their control to contest the commissars' supremacy. They ordered and supervised the election of prisoners' leaders by secret ballot. Thereafter, when the compound misbehaved, the prisoners' representatives were compelled to stand mute in the corner of the athletics field without food or water for up to twelve hours. The loss of face obviously caused them bitter pain. When the prisoners hoisted Communist flags in their compounds, the British tossed in tear-gas grenades until they were taken down. Matters began to improve generally on Koje-do with the appointment of a new commandant, General Boatner. It was considered a damning comment upon the situation that prevailed before his appointment that, within a few days of his arrival, every single member of the former commandant's staff had been sacked and replaced. Efforts began to remove the 8,000 prostitutes who had taken up residence close by the compounds, for whose services so many sentries had been accustomed to abandon their posts.

But the problem of the attitude of the guards to the prisoners persisted. *''All* U.S. troops,'' reported Major Bancroft, ''were apt to regard the PWs as cattle, and treated them as such. They were offensive in speech and manner towards the prisoners, and handled them, including cripples who had been badly wounded, extremely roughly. When witnessing this tendency, I asked both officers and men if they expected similar treatment to be meted out to their PWs in North Korea. Their reply was invariably, 'Well, these people are savages'; and on one occasion, 'Congress has never ratified the Geneva Convention anyway.'

''It was quite clear that the leaders [of the prisoners] could whip up mass hysteria among the PWs. It is therefore essential to segregate the ardent Communist leaders as soon as they begin to make trouble. Their cruelty is beyond belief. Normal torture was to hang offenders to the ridgepoles of tents by their testicles, place water hoses in offenders' mouths who were left to drown slowly, etc. As soon as it is known that atrocities are being committed, immediate action must be taken to release the victims. This was seldom done. The PWs organised the running of their camps extremely well. Morale was high under the most adverse conditions. Physical fitness through organised PT was compulsory. . . . I formed the opinion that the North Korean was more honest, more militant, cleaner and better-educated than the South Korean.''[7]

Major Bancroft's extremely disturbing report was forwarded to the Foreign Office in August 1952. An official attached a minute to the text: ''The report confirms other accounts we have had of the 'Hate Asia' attitude so freely displayed by Americans in the Far East. The harm which such behaviour does to our joint cause needs no emphasising. It seems to us that if the United States' Joint Chiefs of Staff were to take practical measures of indoctrination, a good deal might be done towards improving the behaviour of the U.S. Armed forces.''[8] If these remarks—intended only, of course, for internal Whitehall consumption—sound somewhat complacent and patronizing, the seriousness of the problem of U.S. attitudes to the prisoners on Koje-do is confirmed by American reports to Washington. A fatal combination of incompetence, lassitude, and casual brutality by their captors had enabled the Communists to gain a bloody triumph in their propaganda struggle.

From the summer of 1952 the Americans sought to regain control over their prisoners by dividing and relocating them among a number of offshore island camps. Yet the savage revolts continued. On December 14 some 3,600 of the 9,000 prisoners on Pongan-do fought a pitched battle with guards in which they advanced, arms locked together, hurling a barrage of rocks and missiles. Eighty-four prisoners died, and a further 120 were wounded before peace was restored. Public controversy persisted about the treatment of Communist POWs. "The United Nations refuse to return captives who would almost certainly be shot when they got home," commented the London *Daily Mail* on December 18. "But the effect of this humanitarian policy will be weakened by continual shooting of prisoners, even in self-defence." Yet how, in the face of the fanatical and murderous behavior of the commissars behind the wire, was control of the prisoners to be maintained? An International Red Cross delegate, Colonel Fred Bieri, reported from Koje-do:

"Many prisoners' spokesmen have informed the delegate of their grave concern on the question of repatriation. According to their statements, it appears that there are North and South Koreans (both POW and Civilian Internees) who wish to return to North Korea, and North and South Koreans who desire to remain in South Korea. Many Chinese POWs desire to be sent to Formosa. Many men at present living in close contact with those of opposite political ideology are scared to express their real opinions; others have been forced by their comrades to make statements which are contrary to their wishes. Our delegate states that the effects of political pressure (from both sides) as applied to POWs by POWs themselves can be clearly observed. Most of the incidents which have occurred so far were actuated by purely political motives."

Bieri and General Boatner discussed the seemingly intractable problem of Communist terrorization within the compounds: "The Commandant regretted these incidents, but explained how difficult it is to keep each tent under observation in complete darkness. These beatings, which, unfortunately, often cause deaths, happen quickly and are carried out by well-organized groups. Even should culprits be recognized by tent inmates, fear prevents eyewitnesses from giving evidence."[9]

In the last months of the war, control was tenuously maintained among the Communist prisoners of the UN. But the Western powers had been dealt another bitter reminder that the conflict in Korea was being fought by new rules, far outside the historic experience of the democracies.

"I Shall Go to Korea"

By the summer of 1952 the weariness of the United Nations, and above all the United States, with the war in Korea was becoming intolerable. So, too, was the embarrassment of defending the excesses of President Syngman Rhee. In Tokyo, General Mark Clark, veteran of the World War II Italian campaign, had replaced Ridgway when the paratrooper departed for Europe to succeed General Dwight Eisenhower in command of the NATO armies. As the corrupt farce of a South Korean election loomed, Clark discussed by cable with Van Fleet at Eighth Army the possible implications of Rhee's defeat, in the unlikely event that the people of South Korea were allowed to achieve such a verdict:

"In the remote possibility that President Rhee accepts defeat gracefully," said Clark sardonically, "it is recommended that he should be urged to serve his country by making a worldwide lecture tour at UN expense to explain his country's problems and needs."

But if Rhee forcibly resisted ejection, the UN would face serious problems: "We do not have the troops to withstand a major Communist offensive, to retain uncontested control of the prisoners of war on Koje-do, and to handle major civil disturbances in our rear areas at the same time. Therefore, we must swallow our pride to a certain extent until Rhee, through his illegal and diabolical action, has catapulted us into a situation where positive action must be taken."

In other words, the U.S. and UN must bitterly stomach almost any political excesses in Seoul. The military situation was causing equal dismay. "It appears that, within current capabilities (in the true sense) and existing policies, there are no military courses of action that will ensure a satisfactory conclusion to the Korean struggle," the Assistant Chief of Staff (Plans) minuted on September 15, 1952. "The problem of Korea is essentially part of a larger problem in Asia having its genesis in the aggressive posture and actions of Communist China. The JCS recorded that the United States' objectives, policies, and courses of action in Asia should be reviewed, in order to determine the extent to which the United States military resources should be committed to deter or repel Chinese Communist aggression." [10]

Here was a heart cry from the Pentagon to the Administration: What are we doing in Korea? How quickly can we get out? This private debate in the offices and corridors of Washington matched the great public one, fought out all that year, on the election platforms of the country.

In the early months of 1952 there was intense public debate on President Truman's prospects of gaining a third term. Toward the end of 1950 his "favorable" ratings in the Gallup poll were running at 46 percent, the highest he ever achieved. For the remainder of his term electoral approval of his performance never rose above 32 percent, and sometimes fell as low as 23 percent. On March

29, 1952, Truman chose the annual Jefferson-Jackson Day dinner at Washington National Guard Armory to announce that he would not run for reelection. He always claimed thereafter that he made his decision because he believed two terms enough for any President and that he could have retained the White House had he chosen to fight. This was unlikely, above all when it became apparent that his Republican opponent would be America's most celebrated living soldier, Dwight D. Eisenhower. Early in April, Eisenhower asked to be relieved of his military duties as NATO's first commander because of his "surprising development as a political figure." For most of that year Eisenhower sought to create the impression that he had somehow been drafted by popular acclaim rather than made a conscious and ambitious decision to run. Likewise, he did his utmost to avoid explicit statements of political policy or intention. He was just Ike, and he believed that he could be elected for what he was, not for what he promised. He was almost right. Adlai Stevenson, the Illinois governor whom Truman had selected to succeed him, could not unite even his own Democratic Party behind him, far less the nation. Eisenhower, with his great grin and good-natured professions of pious intention, his prudent equivocation about McCarthyism, and his invulnerable status as a national hero, was unstoppable. Pathetically, Douglas MacArthur still cherished hopes of the GOP nomination. At the convention he received just 10 votes. Ike won on the first ballot, by 595 votes to Taft's 500.

It would be wrong to suggest that the pursuit of an escape route from the war dominated the 1952 U.S. Presidential election campaign. Indeed, by that year one of the foremost grievances of the men freezing or sweltering on the line was that so many of their own countrymen appeared to have forgotten that they were there. But weariness with Korea played its part, not only in the political decline of Harry Truman, but in the election of Dwight Eisenhower. Korea was one of the "four Cs," alongside Corruption, Crime, and Communism. The last glories of the New Deal had vanished in a welter of seedy Administration corruption scandals. Few Americans, few Westerners, any longer drew sustenance from a sense of high purpose in Korea. The cause was now tarnished by so many of the stains and blemishes that would assert themselves again in Indochina a generation later: the inglorious nature of a struggle that denied the promise of military success; the embarrassment of fighting for a regime whose corruption and incompetence were bywords; the difficulty of welding the South Korean Army into a fighting force capable of meeting the Chinese on anything like equal terms; the reluctance of America's allies to shoulder anything resembling a just share of the burden. Before Vietnam was ever heard of, Americans discovered in Korea an unprecedented frustration of national will.

Despite the honorable character of both candidates, America's 1952 presidential campaign was one of the most distasteful of modern times, dominated by the shadow of McCarthyism and the anti-Communist crusade. MacArthur's objections to Eisenhower were partly founded upon the belief that Ike was insufficiently zealous in his hostility to communism, at home and abroad. Yet, paradoxically, few American conservatives cried out for a more vigorous military policy in Korea, the one battlefield on which communism was being confronted at gunpoint. McCarthy and his acolytes declared that American blood was being wasted in a struggle that the Administration was conducting without conviction. Their isolationism mitigated against any display of enthusiasm for an increased American commitment to a campaign in Asia. Like most of their fellow countrymen, they wanted to see America out of Korea. They sought only an escape without intolerable loss of face.

John Foster Dulles, the architect of Eisenhower's foreign policy for much of his election campaign and presidency, believed that Truman's decision to intervene in Korea had been ''courageous, righteous, and in the national interest.'' But Dulles also considered that the broader Truman-Acheson strategy of contain-ment of the Soviet Union by limited action and reaction had enabled the Russians to choose where, when, and how to confront the United States. Dulles wished to see America's military and foreign policy organized in a fashion that would enable the country to deploy its full might. He was the creator of the concept of ''massive retaliation,'' which somewhat troubled Eisenhower. Dulles proposed to keep the Soviet Union in a condition of permanent uncertainty and apprehension about where and when the United States would meet Communist aggression with unbridled atomic retaliation. As a corollary of this policy, it was no longer in America's interest to become bogged down in limited local wars on distant battlefields against Soviet surrogates. Dulles favored disengagement from Korea.

Eisenhower's early campaign statements on Korea were marked not merely by vagueness but foolishness. In one speech in August he claimed that the Administration had committed itself to the serious error of withdrawing U.S. troops from Korea in 1949 ''despite menacing signs from the North.''[11] In reality, of course, Eisenhower himself had been a member of the Joint Chiefs of Staff who advised the Administration in September 1947 that the United States had ''little strategic interest'' in maintaining a military presence in Korea. Truman was disgusted by Eisenhower's posture. He and the Democrats continued to demand insistently that Eisenhower should declare precisely what, if elected, he proposed to do about the war.

Truman's question was answered by Emmet John Hughes, a *Life* magazine editor who had become a speechwriter for Eisenhower, and Herbert Brownell, his campaign manager. In a long discussion over dinner in Brownell's New York apartment, the two men groped for a decisive declaration that their candidate could make, that would yet commit him to nothing. It was Hughes who seized upon the idea that Eisenhower should promise to go to Korea and make a personal assessment of the war. He and Brownell then distilled a single, simple, short phrase for Ike: "I shall go to Korea." The candidate himself proved uneasy about the idea, and the speech that was built for him around it. But on October 24 in Detroit, despite the doubts of some of his advisers, he took the plunge. In a speech at the Masonic Temple that was broadcast on nationwide television, he concluded with the declaration that his first priority upon taking office as President would be to bring an end to the war in Korea: "That job requires a personal trip to Korea. I shall make that trip. Only in that way could I learn best how to serve the American people in the cause of peace. I shall go to Korea."

The phrase passed into the textbooks of American politics, for it set the seal upon Eisenhower's victorious campaign. Two weeks later he was elected President of the United States by 33,936,234 votes to 27,314,992. On November 29, 1952, he fulfilled his pledge. Under conditions of deep secrecy, his absence from New York concealed by an elaborate cover plan involving a procession of distinguished visitors to his empty apartment, Eisenhower flew to Korea.

The President-elect spent three days in the country. He visited a Mobile Army Surgical Hospital and talked to wounded men. He traveled to within earshot of artillery fire in the forward area and inspected some troops. He passed an hour with a bitter and suspicious Syngman Rhee. He spent most of his time in the country with General Mark Clark. He saw General James Van Fleet, commanding the Eighth Army. He gave a press conference at which he conceded the unlikelihood of achieving "a positive and definite victory without possibly running the grave risk of enlarging the war." But he declared that America "will see it through." Then he flew home to New York.

The gesture had been made. That it was no more than a gesture was made evident by the subsequent testimony of Clark and Van Fleet, who had expected to take part in protracted debate about military options, only to discover that Eisenhower's mind was fixed upon the best means of achieving a truce. The exalted visitor had flown from Seoul to Wake Island, where he joined John Foster Dulles and other prominent advisers for a three-day cruise to Hawaii on the cruiser *Helena*. The world believed that the voyage was spent in intensive debate about Korea. In reality, however, it seems that little of substance was discussed. The new Administration's objective for Korea was already set: cease-fire. All that remained to be decided was how the Communists could be persuaded to accede.

MacArthur was among the foremost to propose a solution. While Eisenhower was still at sea, he announced publicly that he had his own plan for ending the war when the new President was willing to hear it. On December 17 the two generals met at Dulles's home. MacArthur presented Eisenhower with a lengthy memorandum. He argued that the United States should demand from the Soviet Union the unification of Korea—and Germany. Their neutrality would be guaranteed by the two superpowers. Failing Moscow's agreement, "it would be our intention to clear North Korea of enemy forces. This could be accomplished through the atomic bombing of enemy military concentrations and installations in North Korea and the sowing of fields of suitable radioactive materials, the by-product of atomic manufacture, to close major lines of enemy supply and communications leading south from the Yalu, with simultaneous landings on both coasts of Korea.''

It was a sad postscript to a great military career, this spectacle of an aged warrior casting his Jovian thunderbolts into oblivion. ''General,'' said Eisenhower carefully, ''this is something of a new thing. I'll have to look at the understanding between ourselves and our allies, on the prosecution of this war, because if we're going to bomb bases on the other side of the Yalu, if we're going to extend the war we have to make sure we're not offending the whole . . . free world or breaking faith.'' MacArthur went away home empty-handed. Two weeks later Truman departed from office filled with distaste for both generals, Eisenhower perhaps most of all. Ike, Truman considered, knew better. Ike, who had sought to pretend that an inconclusive settlement in Korea could be avoided, was in reality entirely committed to bringing this about.

The first plank of the new Administration's Korean policy was a dramatic expansion of the ROK Army to a strength of some 655,000 men, at an estimated cost of $1 billion a year. Thus, it was hoped, the principal military burden of the war could be transferred from the United States to the Korean people. ''Korean-ization'' possessed precisely the same shortcomings as ''Vietnamization'' twenty years later. While the ROK Army was a greatly improved fighting force since its lowest ebb in 1950–51, all the evidence on the battlefield continued to suggest that Korean formations were incapable of meeting their Chinese opponents on equal terms. But, unlike Vietnamization, Koreanization would not be put to a decisive military test. The expansion program began in the spring of 1953.

A development of much more direct impact upon the Korean peace negotiations was America's test detonation, in January, of the first nuclear device of a size capable of adaptation for artillery—a tactical atomic weapon. The Joint Chiefs of Staff recognized its relevance to the Korean stalemate in a study issued on March 27:

''The efficacy of atomic weapons in achieving greater results at less cost of effort in furtherance of U.S. objectives in connection with Korea point to the desirability of reevaluating the policy which now restricts the use of atomic weapons in the Far East. . . .

''In view of the extensive implications of developing an effective conven-tional capability in the Far East, the timely use of atomic weapons should be considered against military targets affecting operations in Korea, and operationally planned as an adjunct to any possible military course of action involving direct action against Communist China and Manchuria.''

On May 19, the Joint Chiefs recommended direct air and naval operations against China and Manchuria, including the use of nuclear weapons. There should be no gradual escalation of force, they argued, but a dramatic surprise attack. The next day the National Security Council endorsed the JCS recommendation.

Dulles, the Secretary of State, was visiting India. He told her Prime Minister, Nehru, that a warning should be conveyed to Chou En Lai: if peace was not speedily attained at Panmunjom, the United States would begin to bomb north of the Yalu. The Pentagon had recently carried out successful tests of atomic artillery shells. The implication was plain. So, too, was the significance of Eisenhower's public announcement that the Seventh Fleet would no longer be committed to preventing military operations between Formosa and the mainland of China. Nationalist guerrillas, armed and trained by the CIA, embarked upon an intensified program of raids against the mainland, more than 200 in the first five months of 1953, according to Peking.

It will never be certain how close the United States came to employing nuclear weapons against China in the spring and summer of 1953, or how far the JCS study and the Dulles warning were intended as bluffs. If such they were, there is no doubt of their success. Through its agents in the United States and Europe, Moscow was undoubtedly informed of American progress on tactical nuclear weapons and Washington's change of policy toward active consideration of their use. The Russians feared Dulles and were disposed to believe that he meant business. There was a new confidence about American policy. In 1950 the uncertainty within the Administration was profoundly influenced by its perception of its own military vulnerability. By 1953 the rearmament program was well advanced; aircraft production was at a postwar high; the United States felt less afraid of the Russians, more assured of its own ability to confront them. Eisenhower said after his return from Korea, "We face an enemy whom we cannot hope to impress by words, however eloquent, but only by deeds—executed under circumstances of our own choosing."[12] At a National Security Council meeting early in February, Dulles spoke of the need to make the idea of nuclear weapons more acceptable. He "discussed the moral problem, and the inhibition on the use of the atomic bomb, and Soviet success to date in setting atomic weapons apart from all other weapons as being in a special category. It was his opinion that we should try to break down this distinction." At the same meeting Eisenhower suggested the Kaesong area of North Korea as an appropriate demonstration ground for a tactical nuclear bomb—it "provided a good target for this type of weapon."[13] By March, Eisenhower and Dulles were "in complete agreement that somehow or other the tabu which surrounds the use of atomic weapons would have to be destroyed."[14] At a special NSC meeting in March, Eisenhower said that although "there were not many good tactical targets . . . he felt it would be worth the cost" if a major victory could be gained in Korea.[15]

Here then is clear evidence that Eisenhower and his senior advisers talked with considerable open-mindedness about the possible use of nuclear weapons in

Korea. Yet today it remains difficult to believe that, had the military situation in Korea remained unchanged, Eisenhower would have authorized their employment. It is entirely probable that he would have done so had the Chinese offered some new and dangerous military provocation. But if America had detonated a nuclear weapon in cold blood, at a time of military stalemate on the battlefield, Eisenhower would have faced the certain, bitter, lasting anger and hostility of America's allies around the world. He was a cautious, humane man. It seems unlikely that he would have taken so drastic a step.

But in the spring of 1953 the Russians and Chinese almost certainly allowed themselves to be persuaded that the new Administration was willing to use nuclear weapons if the United States was denied an honorable escape from Korea. After so many months of deadlock, the talks at Panmunjom suddenly began to move with remarkable speed.

The Last Act

For almost two years it had been apparent that the Korean War could not be settled on any terms that provided for the reunification of the country, nor which dispossessed either client regime in north or south. In the interminable struggle in which each side labored for face, the fate of the prisoners held at the two extremities of the Korean peninsula remained the dominant issue. The prisoners. It always came back to the prisoners. They were no longer even prisoners of war, in any historic sense. Each side's captives had become hostages whose treatment and disposal became the focal point of ruthless bargaining in those last, sterile months of the Korean War.

In December 1952, when the Red Cross in Geneva urged the exchange of sick and wounded prisoners in Korea as a "gesture for peace," Mark Clark warmly welcomed the proposal, but the Soviets and Chinese firmly rejected it. But on March 28, without warning, Kim Il Sung and Marshal Peng not only announced their acceptance of the swap but also declared that this should pave the way to a settlement of the future of all POWs and a cease-fire "for which people throughout are longing." Chou En Lai endorsed this commitment in a Peking radio broadcast on March 30. Though he restated Chinese rejection of any exchange which left any Chinese or North Korean prisoner in UN hands, he now proposed that any prisoner whose will was in doubt should be placed in the hands of a neutral state for further investigation. For the Soviets, on April 1, Foreign Minister Molotov endorsed Chou's proposal and offered Moscow's support in seeing it carried out.

Washington at first regarded the Chinese declaration with deep suspicion. Again and again over the past two years an apparently straightforward proposal from Peking had proved, on closer inspection, to be capable of such different interpretation as to be worthless. Yet on April 11, at Panmunjom, the liaison officers at the conference table were astonished to reach rapid agreement with the Communists for "Operation Little Switch": 700 Chinese and 5,100 Koreans were to be sent north; 450 Korean and 150 non-Korean soldiers were to come south. Between April 20 and May 3, the exchange was completed at Panmunjom.

A new wave of revulsion for the Communist conduct of war swept the West when the world beheld the condition of the UN prisoners who were released. In addition to wounds and disabilities that had effectively gone untreated for months, even years, many men were corroded by prolonged starvation or psychologically crippled. Yet negotiations for the next exchange began at once, and the full UN and Communist delegations met at Panmunjom on April 26 for the first time in six months. The main point at issue was the selection of a neutral "quarantine nation" where prisoners refusing repatriation should be held. The UN opened by proposing Switzerland, with no man to be held in quarantine for more than two months. The Chinese rejected Switzerland and demanded six months. Pressed for an alternative neutral site, they named Pakistan. Then the Communist delegates appeared to undergo a sudden change of heart. They no longer insisted that the prisoners' political screening process should take place outside Korea, cut the proposed period from six months to four, and demanded the creation of a Neutral Nations Repatriation Commission made up of Poland, Switzerland, Czechoslovakia, Sweden, and India.

The Americans were at last convinced that the Communists genuinely sought peace. Stalin was dead, and in the dark shadows of the Kremlin new forces, albeit no less hostile to the West, were setting policy. Perversely, at this moment Dulles experienced a twinge of doubt about the wisdom of making a Korean peace based upon the status quo on the battlefield. Korea was the only shooting war that the United States was conducting with the Communists anywhere in the world. Was she now sacrificing a unique opportunity militarily to humble the enemy before the world? "I don't think we can get much out of a Korean settlement until we have shown—before all Asia—our clear superiority by giving the Chinese one hell of a licking," the Secretary of State told Emmet Hughes. But Eisenhower was by now wholly committed to a Korean settlement. Dulles buried his misgivings.

At last the Americans perceived that they possessed the balance of advantage at the negotiating table. It seemed that time was pressing the Communists even more urgently than the UN. Mark Clark requested, and received from Washington, permission to drive home the advantage. The bombing campaign of Far East Air Force was intensified, with attacks on dams in North Korea deliberately intended to destroy crops and food supplies. The UN delegation at Panmunjom tabled a new, and declaredly final, proposal: a single neutral power would screen all reluctant POW repatriates within ninety days, inside Korea. If this proposal was rejected, all unwilling North Korean repatriates would be unilaterally freed inside Korea within a month. The UN air attack on the North would also be intensified.

Yet even as the Western world waited impatiently and expectantly for decisive news from Panmunjom, for an end to the long stalemate of which the Allies had grown so weary, inside South Korea entirely different emotions reached the boiling point. For President Syngman Rhee and his followers, the prospective settlement that offered peace to Seoul's foreign allies signaled the collapse of all their hopes. Always an obsessively stubborn man, Rhee was now also a bitter one. He saw plainly that Eisenhower proposed to accept a cease-fire based on the permanent division of Korea and a continuance of a permanent Communist threat to the Seoul government. He declared again and again that he would never countenance a settlement that did not remove the Chinese from North Korea and effectively demilitarize the North. His persistent warnings of imminent American betrayal made a profound impact even on those of his countrymen who detested him. If the anti-American rallies in major cities were inspired by Rhee's agents, they were attended by many Koreans full of genuine fears for their society's future if the Americans withdrew, leaving South Korea at the mercy of the Communists beyond the cease-fire line. Even opposition politicians in the National Assembly joined the desperate clamor. Rhee now directly threatened Eisenhower: if a deal was made at Panmunjom which permitted the Chinese to remain in North Korea, the ROK Army would continue the fight unaided, if need be, until the Communists 'were pushed north of the Yalu. However vain this threat in pure military terms, it caused the utmost alarm in diplomatic and political ones. Rhee's behavior, it seemed, might now shatter the entire delicate fabric of the peace talks.

Mark Clark did his utmost to assuage the Korean President's fears. The expansion of the ROK Army would proceed whatever the outcome at Panmunjom, the American assured him. He believed that he had been successful in persuading Rhee of the futility of seeking to sabotage the peace negotiations. Clark cabled the JCS, "He is bargaining now to get a security pact, to obtain more economic aid, and to make his people feel he is having a voice in the armistice negotiations." The infinitely obstinate Korean was not finished yet.

Nor were the Chinese. On April 26 their delegation at the peace talks entered a new proposal about the prisoners: three months after a cease-fire those who refused repatriation should be moved for another six months to a neutral state, where representatives of their own government would have access to them. Those who still refused repatriation at the end of this process would remain in confinement while further negotiations were held to decide their fate. American counterproposals were rejected. For four days the Communists harangued the UN delegation across the conference table, in a return to the exchanges of stultifying rhetoric that characterized the earlier stages of the talks. Finally, the talks were adjourned. Clark consulted with Washington.

To the American's acute embarrassment, his government now determined to make the very concession that it had refused for so long, that was certain to provoke a new upheaval in relations with President Rhee: the UN delegation was to agree that Koreans, as well as Chinese, who refused repatriation should be handed over to the Indian neutral supervisory commission. Rhee's rage, when this news was broken to him, brought relations between Washington and Seoul to their lowest ebb since the war began. The Korean threatened to withdraw his army from the UN Command. The Americans, in their turn, undertook hasty secret preparations to implement Plan Ever-ready, a politico-military operation to seize control of South Korea from Rhee's regime. If it proved necessary to launch Ever-ready, the Korean President "would be held in protective custody, incommunicado" unless he agreed to accept the terms reached at Panmunjom. Either his Prime Minister, Chang Taek Sang, would be installed as head of government or, failing his consent, a military regime would be established. On May 29, Dulles and Wilson—the Defense Secretary—gave Clark authority to take whatever steps he considered necessary in Korea in the event of a "grave emergency." They did not explicitly approve the proposal for Rhee's detention. But they gave their commander in chief almost unlimited discretion to act as he saw fit in an internal crisis in Korea.

By May 25 it was apparent that the Communists were ready to accept the modified American proposals for the exchange of prisoners. Mark Clark drove to Rhee's home to present the bitterly unwelcome news. Rhee received him alone, forcefully denounced the armistice proposals and the United States' foolish course of appeasement of the Communists. Clark departed, still uncertain what the Korean intended to do. The negotiations at Panmunjom continued. On June 8 agreement was at last reached on the terms for repatriation of prisoners. Those who wished to go home could be exchanged immediately. Those who did not would be left in the hands of the Repatriation Commission for ninety days, during which their governments would have free access to them. Their future would then be discussed for a further thirty days by a "political conference." After that period those who remained would be considered civilians.

The details of this arrangement were still being concluded on the night of June 18, 1953 when, to the astonishment and bewilderment of the handful of Americans at the huge Pusan POW compound, they saw that the main gates were open and a vast herd of North Koreans were streaming out into the countryside, watched with supine indifference by their South Korean guards. The same process was taking place at three other compounds around the country. Some 25,000 North Koreans who had expressed unwillingness to return to their homeland after the armistice disappeared into the darkness. President Rhee had acted. Seoul radio warned escapees to beware of American soldiers seeking to apprehend them. Seoul's soldiers and police gave the men clothing and directed them toward shelter. Even as U.S. troops were rushed to the compounds to take over guard duties, liberation operations continued. By June 22 only 9,000 North Koreans remained in captivity, out of a total of 35,400. Only 1,000 of those who had gone were rounded up. The mass liberation had been one of the most efficiently organized exercises in the history of the ramshackle Seoul regime.

In Washington it caused genuine consternation. What now, if the Communists regarded Rhee's action as sufficient cause to break off the negotiations? The Administration hastened publicly to deplore the Korean's action and dissociate the United States from it. For days Washington waited anxiously for a sign from Peking. When at last it came, deep sighs of relief were audible at the State Department. Broadcasts from the New China News Agency deplored the episode but displayed a willingness to listen to American explanations. The delegation at Panmunjom provided them. They were accepted. The peace talks entered their final phase.

Yet now the critical conversations were taking place not at Panmunjom but in Syngman Rhee's office. It was a matter of paramount importance to secure the Korean President's public consent. To achieve this, the Americans were prepared to threaten to abandon absolutely the Seoul regime if it was not forthcoming. Yet it was essential that no word of the strength of American determination should leak out to the Communists, for it would immeasurably strengthen their hand . . . and their determination. Through the last days of June and the early days of July, Rhee spent hours closeted in private talks with Mark Clark and President Eisenhower's special envoy, Walter Robertson. Into Robertson's ear Rhee poured his interminable grievances against the United States. At each session the elderly President appeared to change the grounds of his demands.

Rhee's obduracy now remained the sole obstacle to the signing of an armistice. Even as he and his American guests talked in Seoul, on the battlefield United Nations troops were repelling the heaviest Chinese offensive for two years. After a long period of stagnation at the front, the Communists plainly had determined to drive home to the South Koreans their military vulnerability. Some 100,000 Communist troops struck across the front of five ROK divisions. The South Koreans were thrown back in disarray up to five miles before a vast UN artillery concentration was laid in the path of the enemy offensive. In June 2.7 million rounds were fired on the UN front, a million more than in any month of the war thus far. While the Communists sought to demonstrate their will to prevail on the battlefield if they were denied an acceptable peace at the conference table, the UN proved its ability to deploy massed firepower to thwart them. Heavy fighting continued into July. The UN suffered 17,000 casualties, including 3,333 killed, in the twenty days between agreement in principle being reached between the delegations at Panmunjom and Syngman Rhee acknowledging his readiness to accept it.

For accept Rhee finally did, on July 9. He would not sign the armistice, he declared. But he would no longer obstruct it. On July 12 the United States and the

Republic of Korea announced their agreement on truce terms. Privately, the UN Command allowed the Communists to know that they would give no support to independent offensive action by the ROK Army.

Glimpses of sun broke through the heavy clouds overhanging Panmunjom on the early morning of July 27. During the night carpenters had worked in the rain to complete the building where the armistice was to be signed. Before the ceremony could take place, however, Mark Clark insisted upon the removal of two Communist "peace dove" propaganda symbols from the pagoda and the creation of a new entrance to avoid the necessity for his delegation to pass through the enemy area of the building. If such details seemed petty, their importance in negotiation with the Communists had been grasped over two painful years of experience. A guard of honor, composed of representatives of each army that had fought for the UN cause, flanked the southern approach. Only the South Koreans were missing. Rhee would allow his soldiers no part in a process he detested.

At 10 A.M. precisely the two delegations entered the building from opposite sides. It was two years and seventeen days since talks began. Some pedant or public relations man calculated that 18,000,000 words had been exchanged at 575 separate meetings. Now Lieutenant General William K. Harrison led in the UN contingent with studied casualness. His party strolled forward, then sat back easily in their chairs, while the Communists, wooden-faced, took their places with an air of rigid formality. Harrison sat down at a table marked by a small UN flag and began to sign the first of the nine blue-backed copies of the armistice agreement. General Nam Il sat at the North Korean-flagged table. Without a word or a sign, the two men went through the formalities, while in the distance the crump of the guns went on. By 10:12 A.M. it was all over. Still without a word, the two men got up and departed through their allotted exits. It was done.

A few hours later Mark Clark signed the documents at UN Advanced Headquarters at Mansan-ni. The former wartime commander of the Fifth Army found the experience repugnant. "I cannot find it in me to exult in this hour," he said in a short radio broadcast afterward. "Rather it is a time for prayer, that we may succeed in our difficult endeavor to turn this armistice to the advantage of mankind." Later, in his memoirs, he declared that the moment "capped my career, but it was a cap without a feather." He bitterly regretted becoming "the first U.S. Army commander in history to sign an armistice without victory." Clark was among those who had always believed that the UN should have bombed beyond the Yalu, who shared many of Joseph McCarthy's fears of secret enemies at the heart of America's government. To the lanky, single-minded general, this inconclusive conclusion of the long and bloody experience of Korea was infinitely distasteful. To the end of their days he and other senior American military men would continue to cherish the conviction that there was another, a better way to peace—through military victory. At the Korean Embassy in Washington, Han Pyo

Wook sat in the office he had occupied through three years of war and in which he had witnessed the first diplomatic acts of the drama: "There was no celebration," he said, "only bleak looks. We had fought the armistice to the end. How could we survive, with a million Chinese in North Korea? There was a very great sense of disappointment."[16] But many others, the men on the mountains from coast to coast of Korea, were merely content that there was peace.

In the last few hours before the cease-fire came into effect at 10 P.M., on some sectors of the front the artillery of both sides fired with redoubled, passionate futility. "It was like the Fourth of July and New Year's Eve rolled into one," said Lieutenant Bill Livsey of the 7th Infantry. He and many of the men around him could not believe that this vast, insensate din could be hushed according to a schedule. They were astonished, almost awed, to discover that at 10 P.M., 2200 hours, a sudden deafening silence fell upon the line. "There was no elation. We were just so damn happy that it was over," said Livsey.[17] In the Duke of Wellington's Regiment sector, word came over the radio from battalion headquarters that other ranks might venture into no-man's-land, but no officers were to do so. Within a few hours little clusters of Chinese appeared in front of the wire, bearing bottles of rice spirit and little glass rings inscribed with the word "peace."

At dawn on July 28, Lieutenant Chris Snider of the Canadian Brigade watched, fascinated, with his men as the bare hillside opposite suddenly grew a forest of Chinese figures: "They all came out. My God, there were thousands of them, more than I ever thought possible, on every hill, standing gazing at us. Some of our people thought they must have been brought forward specially, to impress us."[18]

On the U.S. 7th Division's sector of the front, the commanding general, Arthur Trudeau, ritually pulled the lanyard to fire his formation's last round of the war, picked up the shell case as a souvenir, and drove back to his command post for a few celebratory drinks with his staff, to musical accompaniment from the CP band, in which he played the banjo. "I was happy it was over," he said. "It was apparent that all we were going to do was sit there and hold positions. There wasn't going to be any victory. All we could do was go on losing more lives. In those last few months, I lost men faster than Westmoreland at any stage of the Vietnam War except Tet."[19] Private Alan Maybury of the Durham Light Infantry said, "We didn't celebrate victory. We celebrated being able to go home."[20]

Lieutenant Clyde Fore of the 27th Infantry was on his way home to America aboard a hospital ship when the truce was signed. "There was no rejoicing—we were just sad and quiet. This was the first time Americans had ever accepted a no-win war. Everybody else was acclimatized to no-win wars, but we were not. To me, Korea had been an abomination. So many people had died, for what?"[21]

Many of the same mixed feelings pervaded the ranks of the opposing army.

Were the men of the Chinese 23rd Army Group disappointed to go home without victory? Wang Zhu Guang, one of its staff officers, lingers before answering, "We did our best. We felt that it was difficult to continue the war, to conquer the whole of Korea. We did our best. I was happy it was over. We talked to the men in the most down-to-earth manner, explained the situation. They were happy. We never expected to get the whole of Korea. We were told that we were going to support the Korean people in getting the Americans out of Korea, stopping the American invasion. But exactly how far—that was not made clear."[22]

When dawn came men on the UN line peered out across the silent valleys between themselves and the Chinese. In many places little clusters of bold spirits slipped forward through the wire and the minefields, searching with intense curiosity for their former enemies. What did they look like, these strange creatures who had been glimpsed only momentarily through binoculars or as screaming shadows in the darkness of an attack? The same curiosity possessed their enemies. On the low ground between positions, there were stilted little encounters. The Chinese passed over beer and bottles of rice wine. UN troops offered chocolate and cigarettes. Some Chinese made it apparent that they were as delighted that the war was ended as the Westerners. But these meetings could scarcely be called fraternization. They were impelled not by fellow feeling for the enemy, but by the same impulses that would provoke any earthman to inspect visiting aliens.

Inevitably, the most intense emotional drama of the days after the armistice surrounded the release of the prisoners. The Communists, truckload after truckload of them being driven north to the release point at Panmunjom, were in haste to dispel any suggestion that they had been well treated in the South. Some gashed their new fatigues into ribbons to make clear that they had been clad in rags. Others cast out of the trucks the cigarettes, toothpaste, chocolate with which they had been provided. The most dramatic gestures of all were made in the last miles before the convoy reached the exchange point. Thousands of North Korean and Chinese prisoners stripped off their clothes and boots and hurled them away onto the road. They chose to return naked to their own people, uncontaminated by the contemptible handouts of capitalism. When the convoys had passed, one of the most unforgettable images of the post-armistice exchange was that of the empty road, strewn for miles with discarded fatigues and footwear.

Yet the other, still more memorable moment was that of the return of the United Nations prisoners from the North: some gaunt men, some broken men, some clutching the bitter shame and memory of collaboration, others physically devastated by paying the price of resistance. Some came weeping into "Freedom Village," the encampment south of the exchange line, where beneath the "Welcome Home" arch a small army of interrogators, doctors, and psychiatrists waited to receive them. Some strode boldly in, others shambled uncertainly into a life whose reality they had almost been taught to deny. "Ninety percent of us would have much preferred to be liberated by our own forces than released by the Chinese," said Private First Class David Fortune. "The shame, if it was shame, lay in being let go."[23] But it was enough to be free. They gorged themselves on bowl after bowl of ice cream while the psychiatrists talked to them. Each man was processed and examined to check whether he was fit for press interviews or immediate repatriation. The first bitter denunciations of collaboration spilled forth, from prisoners who had been containing their hatred and disgust for years, in anticipation of this moment. Others—those who nursed private guilts—began to mumble the excuses and explanations that would haunt the balance of their lives. "The average POW was not really a human being when he was released," said Private Fortune. "He was a wild animal." Fortune, like many others, continued to lose weight for weeks after his release, and worked his way through many women and many bottles of whiskey before he felt sufficiently sated to come to terms with life at a normal tenor.

Within a month of the commencement of "Operation Big Switch" on August 5, 75,823 Communist prisoners had been sent north, 5,640 of these Chinese. The Communists, in their turn, handed over 12,773 men, 3,597 of them American, 7,862 South Korean. The Neutral Nations Repatriation Commission in the Demilitarized Zone took over 22,604 prisoners from the United Nations. Of these, 137 eventually agreed to repatriation. The remainder elected for resettlement in South Korea or Formosa. Of the prisoners in Communist hands, 359 initially declined to go home. Ten of these—two American and eight Korean—changed their minds while in the custody of the Repatriation Commission. But for the remainder—325 Koreans, 21 Americans, and one Briton (Andrew Condron)—there was no emotional arrival at Freedom Village. To the astonishment and profound dismay of their fellow countrymen, they chose to join the society of their former captors.

In the compound in the Demilitarized Zone where the British Marine Andrew Condron and the Americans refusing repatriation were held in Indian custody, the renegades appeared before a press conference to explain their conversion to the Communist cause. Their decision sent shock waves through their own societies. What diabolical techniques could the Communists have employed upon them to cause men to choose a life of rice and cotton suits in preference to a return to Glasgow or Jersey City? What sort of reflection was it upon American political motivation and military training that while twenty-one Americans had been successfully Communist indoctrinated, not a single Turkish prisoner had succumbed? At a moment when American political self-confidence was under great strain from McCarthyism, the growing alarm about "enemies within" their own society, here was hard evidence of the Communist capability to make conversions even amid the brutality of a prison-camp regime. Seeds of fear and doubt were sown in America which took years to root out.

The British were disposed to take a less alarmist view of the impact of Communist captivity upon their own men, proportionately fewer of whom proved to have been successfully indoctrinated than among the Americans. Yet, a decade later, British complacency would be sorely shaken by the revelation that the diplomat George Blake, captured in June 1950 when he was serving as vice-consul in Seoul, had been successfully "turned" during the three years that followed. He operated undetected for years as an important Soviet agent.

The Chinese, oddly enough, seemed profoundly embarrassed by their twenty-two foreign converts. They issued them with Western-style suits and fedoras and shipped them by train to Tsinan. From there they were dispersed around China to spend as many years as they could endure studying or translating or working at such jobs as the Chinese could find them. They were actively discouraged from learning Chinese. Contact with civilians, above all women civilians, remained very difficult. Over the years that followed, most quietly trickled back to the United States as their patience with Chinese life—and Chinese patience with their Western habits—expired.

General S. L. A. Marshall, perhaps America's finest combat historian of the twentieth century, described Korea as "the century's nastiest little war." In those days, before Vietnam, its claim to that title seemed unlikely to be eclipsed: 1,319,000 Americans had served in the Korean theater and 33,629 did not return. A further 105,785 were wounded. Forty-five percent of all U.S. casualties were incurred after the first armistice negotiations with the Communists took place. The South Korean Army lost 415,000 killed and 429,000 wounded. The Common-wealth—Britain, Canada, Australia, and New Zealand—lost 1,263 killed and 4,817 wounded. Belgium, Colombia, Ethiopia, France, Greece, Holland, the Philippines, Thailand, and Turkey among them lost 1,800 killed and 7,000 wounded, of whom almost half were Turks. The Americans estimated that more than 1.5 million Chinese and North Koreans had died. If this estimate is exaggerated, it seems reasonable to assume that China cannot have lost less than half a million men, given the manner in which she fought her war. Few people of any nationality, four years earlier, would have supposed that barren peninsula would ever be worth any fraction of those lives.

18

HINDSIGHT

Many United Nations veterans came home from Korea to discover that their experience was of no interest whatsoever to their fellow countrymen. The war seemed an unsatisfactory, inglorious, and thus unwelcome memory. It had begun as a crusade to save South Korea from communism, and enjoyed a brief public popularity in Europe as well as the United States. This died in the mud and blood of retreat in the winter of 1950. Thereafter, Korea was perceived only as a running sore, belatedly cauterized in July 1953. A woman saw Private Warren Avery in the street of his hometown in Connecticut when he was discharged from the service and remarked severely, "So you finally got out of jail?"[1] John "Rotorhead" Thornton of the U.S. Navy returned from captivity to hear his wife declare that he had been wasting his life. Once too often friends had asked her, "Gee, I haven't seen John for a while. Where is he?" The first night after his return, they argued into the night. Thornton said, "I guess I just couldn't accept the fact that we hadn't won, that we couldn't beat the Communists. The only people who welcomed me back were my neighbors in Philadelphia, who gave me a block party." His Navy Cross had been posted to his home through the mail. "I thought I would go round telling people what communism is—hanging Major Hume up by his thumbs until he froze, for instance. I ended up feeling like most returning POWs I know—that I was shoveling shit against the tide. You talk about Mao and the millions he killed, and they just say you're a McCarthyite." Many POWs came home to

330

discover that their wives had "made other arrangements." Most felt themselves returning to a new, unfamiliar world that cared little for their experience. "We went away to Glenn Miller. We came back to Elvis Presley," said Thornton without enthusiasm.

In the Southern states, perhaps, traditional patriotism was a more active force than in the East. Private First Class David Fortune was embarrassed by the display that greeted him in his home town of Pickens, South Carolina, after more than two years on the Yalu. They gave him a brand-new 1953 Ford Fairlane and treated him as a hero: "In my part of the country, I don't know anybody who opposed the war." He spent three years' pay in three months and declared proudly that at the end of it, he had nothing to show.

It is a source of widespread bitterness among Korean veterans in the United States that their memories and sacrifices seem so much less worthy of attention than those of Vietnam veterans. It was their misfortune to endure a war that aroused less public emotion, because in those early days of television it was infinitely less vividly projected, less impressed upon the consciousness of Americans. Even at the height of the Korean War, that Asian peninsula seemed an infinitely remote place, far less real than Vietnam became, beamed nightly for years into the nation's living rooms. Rather than acknowledging that too little attention has been lavished upon the victims of Korea, it may be more just to suggest that too much has been heaped upon the veterans of Vietnam. It is an absurd conceit to suppose that, in Indochina, combatants suffered in a fashion unknown to others in other conflicts. Almost all men are marked in some way by the experience of taking part in any war. Those who fought in Korea are no more and no less deserving of respect—and of a memorial—than those who fought in Vietnam, World War II, World War I. Subsequent historical debate about the political merits of a national cause should never be allowed to detract from the honor of those who risked their lives for it on the battlefield.

In the years that followed the Korean War, as the immediate sense of frustration and stagnation that attended the armistice faded, soldiers and politicians became more disposed to think favorably of its value as a demonstration of the West's commitment to the arrest of communism. If the United Nations had failed to achieve the reunification of Korea, they had prevented the North from imposing its will by force upon the South.

Yet it was also self-evident that for the United Nations, the Korean commitment was an experience that would never be repeated. UN forces might be granted an international mandate to carry out policing and peacekeeping tasks around the world. But never again was it conceivable that such a mandate would be granted for a military commitment in pursuit of ideological and political objectives. Even in the summer of 1950 it was only the accident of the Soviet boycott that made the UN vote possible, sending troops into Korea. The relatively small number of countries which then possessed UN membership, most of them sympathetic toward the United States, accepted American leadership in going to war for Korea. But only sixteen members provided any measure of military support, none of which could properly be called nonaligned. The Korean War was fought by the United States, with token support from her allies in the capitalist world. Within months of the outbreak these allies were displaying their dismay at the economic and military cost, and uncertainty about the merits of the regime they were committed to defend. The allied contingents in Korea, the Commonwealth Division most notable among them, were maintained in the field by their respective governments until 1953 only because their withdrawal would plainly inflict deep damage upon Allied solidarity in confronting communism. It is a measure of the desperate economic plight of Britain, in contrast to booming post-World War II America, that the Korean War and the rearmament program that it provoked drove the country to the brink of financial crisis.

Once the Korean War was ended, the old powers, preoccupied with the abandonment of their overseas empires, showed no stomach for fighting abroad alongside the Americans against communism. More than a decade after Korea, when President Johnson pleaded with British Prime Minister Harold Wilson for even a token British contingent in Vietnam, he received no comfort whatever. The United States was compelled to look to its Pacific and Asian allies for such military support as it could muster. As for the United Nations, it was now a larger body than the nucleus of nations which made up its membership in 1950. Many newly created nation members were chronically skeptical of American foreign policy.

Yet it remains a tribute to the respect the United States could call upon in 1950 that an international force was committed at all. For a brief historical moment the combination of foreign gratitude for America's military role in World War II and economic assistance in its aftermath, together with real fear of imminent conflict with the Soviet Union, enabled Washington to mobilize allied troops for an Asian war few Europeans believed in, once the first shock and alarm of June 1950 had ebbed away.

Only America's absolute dominance of the Korean campaign enabled it to be fought to a tolerable conclusion. Yet this very dominance also contributed greatly to Allied unhappiness about the course of the war. Beneath a thin veneer of respect for the authority of the United Nations, Americans conducted the war as they saw fit. Many American soldiers and politicians were exasperated by the prevarication and scruples of allies who were making so small a material contribution to the conflict. "It was a legacy of World War II that the United States was expected to accept the brunt of commitment and sacrifice," acknowledged the British diplomat Roger Makins. Yet this created the conundrum of alliance, that the manner in which the war was commanded and conducted by one dominant nation made the presence of the United Nations flag seem to many foreigners a charade. "Though we called ourselves the UN, there were so few of us," said the British Group Captain "Johnnie" Johnson, "I felt very much an observer of an American show." The British, not excluding their Prime Minister, deluded themselves in supposing in 1950–53 that they could exert a decisive influence even upon American nuclear policy. Other nations were even less likely to rally to the UN banner ever again because of the widespread perception that it was employed in Korea in the foreign policy interest of the United States, whether or not this was also the cause of natural justice.

Much academic research has been devoted to exploring the shifting currents within the U.S. military establishment, both in attitudes to embarking upon the Korean War and professional debate about its conduct. "Much of the analysis of military opinion," wrote Dr. Rosemary Foot, one of the most recent students of the period, "has confirmed the conclusion of other students of American foreign policy, that once a decision is made to use force, the generals want to use it more quickly and decisively than do their civilian counterparts . . . the navy and air force are likely to advocate more hawkish courses than the army."[2] Field commanders in Korea, as later in Vietnam, were consistently more bellicose in the strategies they advocated than the politicians—or even the Joint Chiefs of Staff—in Washington. The doctrine of Limited War will always find more favor among those responsible for national policy than with those charged with implementing it upon the battlefield.

As to the military conduct of the war, a senior American veteran of both Korea and Vietnam remarked, "We went into Korea with a very poor army, and came out with a pretty good one. We went into Vietnam with a pretty good army, and came out with a terrible one." The performance of most elements of the U.S. Army in the first year of fighting in Korea ranged between moderate and deplorable. Five years of fatal neglect between 1945 and 1950 had produced a rundown of men, training, leadership, and equipment that almost, but not quite, enabled the Chinese to inflict a wholesale disaster upon American arms in the winter campaign. But, having saved themselves narrowly from disaster, in the two years that followed the Americans in Korea made themselves a far more effective, and above all self-confident, fighting force. Ridgway deserves a great measure of credit for turning around a beaten army and directing it in such a fashion that it inflicted a series of shattering defeats upon the Communist invaders.

There are many important senses in which Korea was a rehearsal for Vietnam a generation later. It may be argued that the United States learned many of the wrong lessons from the experience of Korea, where a huge commitment of resources enabled her army to halt the Communists at tolerable cost in casualties. The fact that Syngman Rhee was the unpopular leader of a thoroughly corrupt

regime, whose army was incapable of effective self-defense on the battlefield, did
not prove a fatal disadvantage to sustaining the South Korean cause. Nor was it
only Americans who allowed themselves to be little concerned about the nature of
the regime the UN presence was supposedly supporting. "Of course we knew that
Syngman Rhee was a pretty monstrous figure," said Colonel William Pike of the
Commonwealth Division. "But weren't they all out there?" Many Americans,
inside and outside the Defense Department, concluded that with sufficient military
and economic support, almost any anti-Communist regime abroad could be kept
afloat, regardless of its intrinsic viability. The regime of President Thieu of
Vietnam was certainly no worse, indeed almost certainly less oppressive, than that
of President Rhee. But more sophisticated Communist techniques of subversion
and infinitely more skeptical world media attention undermined it. Thieu's regime
was finally exposed to a military test which that of Rhee escaped. Had the ROK
Army ever been left alone to combat a full-scale Communist offensive, its fate
would almost certainly have resembled that of the ARVN more than twenty years
later.

The American Army emerged from Korea convinced that its vastly superior
firepower and equipment could always defeat a poorly equipped Asian army if it
was provided with the opportunity to deploy them. Shrewd commanders were well
aware of historic weaknesses in American infantry, dating back to World War II
and before, in small-unit leadership and tactics, fieldcraft and battle discipline. But
most senior officers continued to believe that the historic American military
virtues, centering upon the massive concentration of scientific and technical
expertise, could more than compensate for these. They might have reflected, had
they chosen, upon the unusual convenience of the Korean battlefield, where the
mountains restricted movement on either side, and the narrow peninsula made it
possible to fortify and defend a relatively short front. In Vietnam there could be
no such fixed line. The very tactics of lightly armed hit-and-run, in which the
Communists proved so formidable in the mobile winter campaign of 1950, could
be employed daily in Indochina for years on end. "It was amazing that so many
of the mistakes we made in Korea, we repeated in Vietnam," said Colonel Al
Bowser of the U.S. Marines. "Why? I wish I could answer that. Something
seemed to come over people who went over there. During Vietnam, I used to say
to a colleague of mine, Lew Walt, 'Lew, what in the name of God are you doing
with all those tanks in a rice paddy?' I never got a good answer." Colonel John
Michaelis of the 27th Infantry argued that the U.S. Army failed to learn the lessons
of Korea because it became an unpopular war, and those who returned preferred
to forget it, inside as well as outside the service: "I don't think that, as an army
or a nation, we ever learn from our mistakes, from history. We didn't learn from
the Civil War, we didn't learn from World War I. The U.S. Army has still not
accepted the simple fact that its performance in Korea was lousy."

It may be argued that the Communists profited more than the United Nations from the painful military lessons they learned in Korea. Mao Tse Tung's conviction that any conflict could be conducted upon the principles, and with the organization, of guerrilla war was proved fallacious. Large-scale guerrilla tactics proved very effective in the first winter campaign of 1950, where rapid cross-country movement and surprise broke open MacArthur's army. But thereafter even the infinite willingness of the Communists to accept casualties went for naught when confronted with the air power and firepower of a Western army in prepared positions. To the end of the conflict, Mao Tse Tung retained a strong personal commitment to the massed "human wave" assaults characteristic of his army since its inception. His generals had discovered their limitations by painful experience in Korea. In the positional war the Chinese displayed remarkable skill and professionalism with their scanty resources. But they were quite unable to achieve a breakthrough and paid a vast price for their attempts.

"The survivors," General Sir Anthony Farrar-Hockley has written, "no longer believed that, armed with the philosophy of the Party, they could beat anybody however superior their technology. They knew it was not true. So, too, did their senior commanders. Peng Te' Huai eventually succeeded in convincing his Central Committee comrades that they must upgrade the basis of the army from that of a body armed with what it could capture to one enjoying standard equipment tables, not least a comprehensive communications system. For a time, he persuaded enough of his colleagues that they must initiate a rational system of recruitment based on conscription, and that a properly selected and trained professional officer corps was essential to the future of the armed forces."[3]

Yet Mao alone remained unconvinced of these lessons, and above all disputed Peng's downgrading of the importance of political officers, who in early stages of the Korean War constituted 10 percent of every formation's leadership down to sub-unit level. If the PLA was to be armed and organized like any other army, then it must depend upon Soviet weapons and equipment to an extent Mao found intolerable. When he purged Peng Te' Huai and other senior PLA officers, he reversed their policies and preserved the PLA in much the mold in which it was forged in the civil war. Yet in the words of Farrar-Hockley, the Korean War had "raised doubts in the PLA concerning the wisdom and competence of the Party leadership"[4] which would not go away.

Senior Chinese soldiers—if not their leader—emerged from Korea having absorbed the central, critical lesson for future Asian conflicts: that they must never face a Western army on its own terms. They must seek to fight when Western resources and technology count for least. They could exploit the West's greatest single weakness: the impatience of democracies. It had proved difficult for the United States and her allies to maintain public tolerance and support for the

Korean War for three years. Apathy and exasperation with a national effort which was yielding no evident result became apparent in the American electorate long before the armistice. The decisive reason that it was possible for Western statesmen to sustain their people's tolerance of the war was the memory of that devastating, indisputable act of Communist aggression which began it all in June 1950. Even the least sophisticated, most xenophobic Iowa farmer or Bradford bank clerk could comprehend the nature of the North Korean invasion. Without that simple *casus belli,* it seems highly doubtful that the Korean War could have been fought to an acceptable finish. This message the Communists surely absorbed: never again should they provide the West with so unclouded and comprehensible a reason to resist, and time must always be against the democracies in arms.

Thirty years later Oliver Franks, the former British Ambassador in Washington, had no doubts about the merit of Truman's Korean commitment: "The United States administration acted in Korea—the United Nations involvement was merely a fig leaf for executive action. It was a *bellum justum*—the use of force to put down a wrongful action, not a case of counteraggression."

"Worthwhile? It was more worthwhile than Vietnam," said Major Ed Simmonds of the U.S. Marine Corps. "In 1950 the individual GI couldn't see much to admire in the average Korean. But looking back on it, the war revitalized NATO. It caused us to drop the tradition of demobilizing at the end of a war. It hastened the schism between China and the Soviets. It saved Formosa. It contributed greatly to Japanese recovery: they got rich out of Korea, and fabulously rich out of Vietnam. It probably saved the Philippines for a time. Yes, it was worthwhile."

A less grammatical but almost more eloquently confused view, probably shared by thousands of American rankers who fought in Korea, came from Ecton Plaisance, a Louisianian whom 1950 found as a private soldier in 7th Cavalry: "A lot of us feels that Truman made a big mistake by not leting McArthur bomb the bridges on the Yalu river, allso not letting him bomb the Chinese that were mass in China. Another big mistake was in 1951, the Chinese made there last big offensive against us and we stop them cold, right after that we could have went north and set up a good line 20 miles north of Pyongyang. . . . My family did not understand the war, except that they knew that the communists wanted South Korea. They support our government in the war. The war set the Chinese back 10 to 20 years where in the United States the big companys get richer. Don't get me wrong I am not sorry I went and fought it was an honor to fight the communists because it had to be done, however I would not do it again for a million dollars."

Private First Class Bill Shirk, an Ohioan who spent more than two years in captivity, "thought of the war as a hell of a waste. I saw no reason for it when I went over, less when I went back. When Vietnam started, I just thought, 'Here we go again, the same damn nonsense. Who gives a shit if they're North Korean or South Korean? You can't take a person living like an animal and expect them to act like a human being. They don't place the value on human life that we do. Lots of men felt the same as I did.''

Many American career officers were deeply dismayed by the precedent Korea established: the United States had failed to fight a war to a victorious conclusion. Lieutenant General Arthur Trudeau, commanding the U.S. 7th Division, spoke of "that odious armistice . . . when we let the Russians and the Chinese off the hook in Korea, we opened the door for their victory over the French in Vietnam. We should have let MacArthur go to the Yalu and bomb the piss out of them on the other side." "I still feel very badly about Korea," said Colonel Paul Freeman. "I thought there had been a lot of unnecessary bloodletting for a stalemate. To have had this thing drag on and on, fighting for every bloody little hill over there, was all wrong. We should have knocked the Chinese out of there, whatever it took. But some of the European nations were scared that we were going to start something . . . the absurdity of trying to destroy those Yalu bridges without bombing the other side, that isn't the way to fight a war."

Freeman's, of course, is the voice of a generation of post-World War II American professional soldiers, infinitely frustrated by the inability of their nation effectively to deploy its vast military power in limited conflict. MacArthur was the foremost protagonist of their argument. For a brief window of time in the early 1950s, the United States possessed the unmatched atomic capability to take on and defeat the Communist powers. Sooner or later, they believed, it was the destiny of the United States, as the greatest capitalist power on earth, to fight the Communists. Better now, surely, when the nation possessed the means to achieve victory at minimal risk to the American continent, than a generation hence, at a time and place of the Communists' choosing.

Much that has taken place in the world since 1950 reinforces the conviction of supporters of the MacArthur doctrine. Soviet nuclear power is now such that the United States could never hope to fight the Russians without suffering intolerable casualties. Asian communism has inflicted a crippling humiliation upon the United States in Vietnam, achieving victory in a war that was fought on Communist terms. The political limitations imposed upon the deployment of American force in Korea were matched by the restrictions in Indochina that caused the United States to fight "with a hand tied behind its back," as so many Americans saw it.

Yet few uncommitted observers, looking back thirty-five years to Truman's dismissal of MacArthur, can doubt that the President was perfectly justified. If the old general's faculties remained undiminished, there is little question that his judgment had become fatally unstable. The shock of initial defeat in Korea, followed by the almost mystical triumph of Inchon against all odds, followed in turn by new humiliation at the hands of the Chinese, might have distorted the thinking of a much younger, more conventional mind than that of MacArthur. The general believed that he was facing the great historic issue of his time, from which Washington flinched. Yet his own preoccupation with the balance of world power, and the military means of changing this, blinded him to the huge, critical moral issue surrounding the use of nuclear weapons. Most of our post-Hiroshima generation are convinced that it is not acceptable to regard nuclear weapons, as did MacArthur and some of his contemporaries, as merely quantitative increments to the arsenal of war. A real political, military, and moral chasm exists, most of us believe, between the employment of conventional and nuclear weapons. What would have been the moral standing of the United States in the world today had she employed nuclear weapons in Asia in 1950–51, not even in self-defense, but in pursuit of foreign policy objectives related to the defeat of communism? In the answer each of us makes to that question must lie our own attitude to MacArthur and the controversy surrounding his dismissal by Truman.

The Korean War occupies a unique place in history, as the first superpower essay of the nuclear age in the employment of limited force to achieve limited objectives. The United States might have come away from Panmunjom in a more satisfied frame of mind had this perspective been clearly discernible at the time. Instead, however, many Americans were merely frustrated by discovering the post-World War II political limits of military power. A generation later, had America been able to do for South Vietnam what she had done for South Korea, the achievement would have been a cause for national self-congratulation.

Korea was a landmark in the post-1945 foreign policy of the United States. Before the North Korean invasion, though America mourned the ''loss'' of China, she did not regard Asia as the principal battlefront against communism. This lay in Europe. But events in Korea focused the attention of Americans upon the Far East. As the political frontiers in Europe stabilized, and the prospects of further Communist takeovers there by political or diplomatic means receded, Americans became increasingly preoccupied with Asia. They had always enjoyed a romantic fascination with the continent. Now they saw within it a host of precariously governed small nations, highly vulnerable to Communist intervention. The military and foreign policy energies of the United States became more and more dedicated to frustrating this turn of events.

Yet if this objective was not ignoble, it was founded upon one profound misjudgment: it greatly underestimated the influence of nationalist, as distinct from ideological, forces among the nations it sought to protect. Among all the thousands of reports and assessments of Korea in the archives of the United States and her allies, depressingly few pay even lip service to the needs or interests of the Korean people. Korea merely chanced to be the battlefield upon which the struggle against the international Communist conspiracy was being waged. In Korea, Americans revealed all the arrogance, the paternalism, the insensitivity in handling of local people—and the local army—which later revealed themselves in Vietnam. South Korea did not gain the immense self-respect she possesses today from her part in the war. Indeed, most South Koreans emerged from the war conditioned either to an absolutely cynical pursuit of personal survival or burdened by self-disgust. South Korea gained her self-respect from what she achieved by her own astonishing industrial efforts in the generation that followed the war. If the UN Army had abandoned the South Koreans before an armistice was signed, and left Rhee's regime to fend for itself, it would have collapsed as ignominiously as that of Saigon twenty years later, with or without Chinese military support for Pyongyang. South Korea escaped the fate of South Vietnam chiefly because the accident of geography made it infinitely easier to defend, and because the West, in 1950–53, still possessed a sufficient reservoir of crusading zeal to sustain an overseas campaign against communism. This reservoir was all but drained by the 1970s.

In determining the justice of what was done in Korea in the name of the United Nations, it is necessary to pull away a great tangle of subsidiary issues that confused contemporary observers as much as they have complicated the judgments of history. American occupation policy in South Korea from 1945 to 1949 was clumsy and insensitive. A political structure was created whose chief merit was that it professed hostility to communism. Yet it is too easy for historians to argue that Americans misread the signals from North Korea, that the Soviets had no initial intention of creating a satellite state in the Korean peninsula. If American reaction to Soviet behavior was at times alarmist, nothing alters the fundamental truth that in Eastern Europe, from 1945 to 1950, the Russians were engaged upon the ruthless construction of an empire. They were determined to build a military buffer zone around their own frontiers, without the slightest regard for the liberty or interests of millions of people whose misfortune it was to live within it. Given the scanty intelligence available from North Korea, it was asking a great deal of the Washington Administration to divine and acknowledge the Soviets' nonimperialistic intentions in Korea—if such indeed they were. If the Americans behaved clumsily in South Korea, their conduct was understandable in the worldwide context of the period. It remains debatable whether, even if a leader-based government had been created in South Korea, this would have been immune from North Korean aggression.

By 1950, if the regime of Syngman Rhee in the South was dictatorial, it was no more oppressive than that of Kim Il Sung. And the Southerners had been deliberately denied by the Americans the means, even if they possessed the will, to carry out aggressive acts beyond their own frontier. By any reasonable measure, Kim Il Sung's invasion of June 1950 was an unprovoked act of raw aggression, which the South lacked the means to resist. If the Soviets did not directly encourage the invasion, it could not have been carried out without their consent. From Moscow's perspective, the invasion of South Korea can be regarded—as it was interpreted in Washington at the time—as an experiment. If the Americans merely abandoned their puppets, so much the better. Even if they did not, it is unlikely that the Russians anticipated an American reaction on the scale that in reality took place. The Soviet view was characteristically cynical, and there is no reason to doubt the sincerity of Russian expressions of alarm in the weeks that followed, as it became apparent that the United States was determined to repel the North Koreans with whatever resources were required.

The Soviets seemed persistently unhappy about the war thereafter. They supplied the North Koreans and Chinese, and provided the pilots of an air corps. But if the Chinese had not chosen to intervene in the winter of 1950, it seems doubtful whether the Russians would have done so, even with Americans camped on the Yalu. Moscow had miscalculated the strength of American reaction at the outset. In the winter of 1950, fear of provoking American nuclear retaliation would almost certainly have dissuaded Stalin from going to war with the United States on the borders of Korea. The strongest evidence of Moscow's lack of enthusiasm for the Korean War lies in the sluggishness with which Stalin supplied materiel to Mao. Only in the autumn of 1951 did Soviet military supplies begin to move in quantity to China. And, to the bitter resentment of the Chinese, every ton had to be paid for. Korea precipitated the deep mutual mistrust between Soviet and Chinese Communists, which has been evident ever since.

Yet the Chinese, who were the most passive partners in the original North Korean invasion of the South, could argue a legitimate determination not to tolerate an American presence on the Yalu. It was MacArthur's commitment to sweep north from the 38th Parallel that introduced a new strand of confusion into the debate about the merits of the United Nations' operation in Korea. Until that moment few detached observers around the world could deny that the UN flag was flying in an honorable cause, the restitution of the status quo in Korea. But from the moment UN forces crossed the 38th Parallel, the highest ideals of the United Nations became submerged beneath the foreign policy purposes of the United States. Yet MacArthur must not bear sole responsibility for the decision to drive north. Not only in Washington, but in London and other Western capitals, in the flush of victory at Inchon it seemed possible to achieve a cheap, absolute success over the Communists. If some statesmen and diplomats possessed reservations, they did not express them very strongly. Their silence, or at least muted expressions of concern, could reasonably be interpreted as consent in Washington and at the Dai Ichi.

MacArthur's denunciation of the Chinese intervention as a treacherous act will not do. Peking gave repeated warnings of the limits of its patience. It could plead the interests of self-defense in crossing the Yalu with at least as much conviction as President Kennedy in threatening war if the Soviets placed missile bases in Cuba. The Peking government had only recently emerged victorious from a war against Nationalist armies supplied and supported by the United States. With American sponsorship, the Nationalists could still pose a formidable threat to Mao Tse Tung's fragile government. Some Americans today, as well as in 1950, would argue that since Mao Tse Tung's Communist regime represented an evil force in the world, it was legitimate for the forces of justice to adopt any means to destabilize and ultimately undo it. But most of America's allies, today as in 1950, find this argument unacceptable. The British, in particular, have always sought accommodation with Communist China and acknowledged the legitimacy of the People's Republic. This much granted, it was unreasonable to expect the Chinese to stand idly by while the United States deployed an army along the Yalu.

Yet the Chinese, in their turn, displayed considerable strategic naiveté. The testimony of Chinese officers makes clear that they greatly underestimated the power of a Western army. Because they had just defeated an American-sponsored and -equipped Nationalist army, Mao Tse Tung and his commanders appear to have expected the same level of performance, and the same weaknesses, in the U.S. Army itself. This view was reinforced by their early experience of fighting Americans in November and December 1950. The Chinese undoubtedly went into Korea with the limited objective of driving back the Americans to a respectable distance from the Yalu. But in December 1950, in the exultation of tactical success, they made a strategic error precisely mirroring that of the Americans a few weeks earlier: they saw an opportunity to expand a limited operation into a crushing and symbolic wider victory. Thus they drove on southward in hot pursuit of the fleeing Americans, and thus, with their supply lines overextended and their resources of everything but manpower almost exhausted, they met the full might of a Western army, regrouped under Ridgway. Throughout the two years that followed, the combatant nations felt themselves engaged in an inescapable struggle for face. Each side having rashly overreached its limited war aims, peace became attainable only after a long process during which the combatants became once more reconciled to these. The war drove China into diplomatic and economic isolation and made her an absolute dependent of the Soviet Union for a generation. "Peking's action," Dr. Rosemary Foot has written, "displayed its revolutionary zeal, inexperience in world affairs, troublemaking capacity in the immediate vicinity of its borders, and exaggerated sense of its own power."

But if China was denied its ideological triumph in Korea, the war made Mao Tse Tung's nation a great power in the eyes of the world. The impact of that first crushing Chinese victory in the winter of 1950 was never entirely lost. The spectacle of a heavily armed and armored Western army fleeing before Marshal Peng's cotton-clad divisions was not forgotten. Most men who fought against the

Chinese in Korea went home with a considerable regard for their fighting qualities, which made it all the more remarkable that, in Vietnam a decade later, a new generation of Americans proved once more reluctant to believe that Asian soldiers could match Westerners on the battlefield. In Korea, China convinced the world that she was a force to be reckoned with, after centuries in which she had been dismissed as an ineffectual society of mandarins and warlords. The chief negative cost of the war to Peking was that it prevented the Communists—perhaps forever—from gaining control of Formosa, today's Taiwan. In June 1950, Washington was weary of Chiang Kai Shek and his defeated Nationalists. Had it not been for the North Korean invasion, they would have almost certainly been left moldering on Formosa until the Communists overwhelmed them. Instead, they became a central element in America's policy for resisting Communist expansion in the Far East, the beneficiaries of vast military and economic aid, which made possible the powerful modern industrial state they created over the next thirty years.

Thousands of men who fought for the United Nations in Korea are deeply moved today by the gratitude that South Koreans still display for the salvation of their country from the Communists more than thirty years ago. Perhaps this has been enhanced by watching South Vietnam submerged into a Communist state. ''I see Koreans today, and the respect they show for us,'' said Private Bill Norris of the 27th Infantry, ''and I contrast this with the animosity I saw for us in Europe, after World War II ended. They didn't want us over there. In Korea, I see gratitude. I never felt exploited by a Korean, in the way we all were as GIs by the French and the Belgians in 1945. In the marketplace in Seoul, I could buy stuff for the same price a Korean paid for it. I felt safe there.'' Sergeant John Richardson, of 2nd Princess Patricia's Canadian Light Infantry, believed passionately that the war was worthwhile: ''In October 1983, I had the great privilege of going back to Korea. It was the thrill of a lifetime. On my return, I simply told the Calgary Branch of the PPCLI Association that I was convinced that our fallen comrades rest in a country where their sacrifice is fully appreciated.''

''We stopped communism, didn't we?'' said Bob Campbell of the 1st Marines. They did indeed. At the 38th Parallel a border persists today between one of the more advanced and one of the most backward societies in Asia. The people of North Korea have paid the bitterest price of all for Kim Il Sung's adventure in June 1950. To this day they remain the prisoners of the aging, obsessive, perhaps demented old dictator in one of the most backward societies in Asia. Fifteen years after the Chinese set about opening up a new relationship with the West, the North Koreans reject any attempt to do so, and even their relations with Peking are strained. North Korea exists in pitiful isolation, a society dominated by poverty and the cult of Kim Il Sung.

South Korea, meanwhile, has become one of the greatest economic and industrial powers in Asia. The harshest price it has paid for the war is that, even today, it remains a society under siege. The threat from the North has never receded. Pyongyang maintains a constant propaganda war and a military capability that cannot be ignored. North Korea's constant efforts to undermine the South by subversive activity, and periodically by guerrilla and terrorist operations across the border, provide the justification for the military machine that still dominates South Korea. Syngman Rhee was deposed in 1960, when the United States publicly withdrew its support from the old dictator after he had rigged one election too many. A generation after his fall a procession of more or less repressive military, or military-influenced, governments rule from Seoul. Political dissent is ruthlessly suppressed. The United States maintains a strong military presence. Washington has always tacitly accepted the tough domestic policies of South Korea's governments, maintaining the bastion against communism. Seoul won the warm approval of the United States during the Vietnam War, repaying the aid given in 1950 by sending a South Korean division to Indochina which proved one of the most formidable fighting formations in the struggle against the Communists. It also earned a reputation as one of the most savage and ruthless in its dealings with the Vietnamese. Ironically, it was the Vietnam War which gave the Korean economy its decisive boost to takeoff. South Korea today displays all the traditional qualities of its people: energy, organization, fiercely nationalistic competitiveness, ruthlessness. Much of the country the UN armies knew has vanished under unlovely steel and concrete.

Some critics regard all this, as they later regarded the shortcomings of the American-sponsored regime in Vietnam, as sufficient reason to deny the Seoul government all claim to legitimacy. Yet others—the author among them as a correspondent in Vietnam—acknowledged the failings of the Saigon or Seoul regimes while denying that these provided sufficient reason to concede victory to the Communists. The evidence of equal, indeed greater, evils wrought by the Communist forces could not be gainsaid. Rarely in the world is a choice offered between a cause of absolute virtue and one of absolute evil: even the Allied cause in the Second World War was confused for many participants by discovering the bloody hand of Joseph Stalin on the side of the democracies. In Korea, as in Vietnam, the democracies supported the cause of a flawed society. Yet they were fighting against opponents representing an even harsher tyranny. Who can doubt that if Hanoi had been defeated, South Vietnam would today enjoy the same prosperity as South Korea, and its people at least a greater measure of freedom than they can look for under communism?

Today the people of South Korea have achieved a prosperity and fulfillment that gives them immense satisfaction. In 1950, Won Jung Kil was twenty-one, an unemployed welder eking out an existence in Inchon, strongly hostile to the Rhee regime. He was conscripted in 1951 and spent six years of wretched near-starvation as a ROK army driver: "I hated the officers. They had too much of everything. Pay? We had no pay. There was just a little food. No Korean enjoyed the war." Yet today, Won can say, "It was worthwhile. We are fine, we have enough to eat. I like our life now very much." The simple, material satisfaction is very deep for people who have come such a long way in thirty-five years. They look back upon the war as a nightmare for their nation. But they reveal a real gratitude for the campaign waged by the United Nations that enabled their society to retain its independence, that made possible everything they have today. Few Westerners, looking upon the respective circumstances of North and South Korea today, can doubt that the West's intervention in 1950 saved the Southerners from a tragic fate, and indeed opened the way to a future for them infinitely better than anything attainable under Kim Il Sung. If the Korean War was a frustrating, profoundly unsatisfactory experience, more than thirty-five years later it still seems a struggle that the West was utterly right to fight.

CHRONOLOGY

1950

June 25   ·North Korean forces attack South Korean positions south of the 38th Parallel.

             The United Nations Security Council, in the absence of the U.S.S.R., adopts a resolution calling for the withdrawal of North Korean forces to the Parallel.

June 27   President Truman orders U.S. air and sea services to give support to South Korean forces. UN Security Council calls on member nations to give aid in repelling aggression in Korea.

June 29   North Korean Army seizes Seoul. Britain orders Far Eastern Fleet to give aid.

June 30   Truman orders U.S. ground troops to Korea and naval blockade of Korean coast. Authorizes U.S. Air Force to bomb North Korea.

July 1   First U.S. combat troops arrive on Korea. Major General William F. Dean placed in command of U.S. forces in Korea.

July 4	U.S. troops first meet enemy just north of Osan and are forced to retreat.
July 7	General Douglas MacArthur named Supreme UN Commander.
July 13	Lieutenant General Walton H. Walker, commander of the Eighth Army, assumes command of ground forces in Korea.
July 15	North Koreans cross Kum River.
July 18	U.S. First Cavalry and 25th Infantry Divisions reach Korea.
July 21	24th Division troops fight out of burning Taejon. General Dean missing in action.
August 1	Second U.S. Infantry Division reaches Korea.
	Yakov Malik, the Soviet delegate to the UN, ends Moscow's boycott of the organization and takes over the presidency of the Security Council.
August 2	First U.S. Marine Brigade reaches Korea.
August 8	North Koreans breach Naktong River perimeter line.
August 15	UN troops repel two attacks along Naktong.
August 29	British 27 Brigade arrives from Hong Kong.
September 3	Communist offensive threatens Taeju.
September 7	General Walker declares, "Our lines will hold."
September 15	U.S. X Corps makes successful amphibious assault on Inchon, enabling UN forces to break out of Pusan and push toward the 38th Parallel.
September 19	X Corps starts to encircle Seoul; Eighth Army sweeps north and west with Communists in flight. Filipino troops reach Korea.
September 26	Seoul falls.
September 29	General MacArthur enters Seoul with President Syngman Rhee.
October 1	South Korean troops cross 38th Parallel.
October 7	UN adopts resolution that "all appropriate steps be taken to ensure conditions of stability throughout Korea."
	U.S. troops cross the Parallel.
October 8	Mao Tse Tung secretly orders Chinese "Volunteers" to "resist the attacks of U.S. imperialism."
October 15	Truman and MacArthur meet on Wake Island.
October 18	ROK troops occupy Hamnung and Hungnam.
October 19	Eighth Army takes Pyongyang, capital of North Korea.
October 25	Chinese forces fight with ROK troops less than forty miles south of the Yalu River.
October 27	Eighth Army halted by Chinese.

October 29	X Corps halted by Chinese in northeast.
October 30	Eighth Army's 6th ROK Division overwhelmed by Chinese at Yongdu.
November 1	First Chinese MIGs appear along the Yalu.
November 3	U.S. 25th Division driven back from Yalu area.
November 6	MacArthur charges Chinese with unlawful aggression. Chongchon River line held.
November 8	Air battle over Sinuiji.
November 11	Eighth Army again attacked.
November 12	U.S. Army 3rd Division arrives in Korea.
November 16	Truman reassures China and other nations that he has never had any intention of carrying the hostilities into China. Lull in fighting.
November 24	Chinese special delegation arrives at UN Security Council. MacArthur launches offensive and troops approach Chinese border.
November 25	Chinese release fifty-seven U.S. prisoners in propaganda move.
November 26	Chinese counterattack.
November 27	Eighth Army halted by huge Chinese forces.
November 28	General Walker announces offensive at an end.
December 1	Eighth Army and X Corps begin withdrawing in face of Chinese offensive.
December 5	U.S./UN troops withdraw from Pyongyang. Chinese occupy the capital of North Korea.
December 9	X Corps forced to withdraw from Wonsan by sea.
December 11	X Corps evacuates Hungnam.
December 17	Truman declares state of national emergency.
December 22	Chinese reject cease-fire: it makes no reference to China's demands for removal of foreign troops from Korea and for a seat in the UN.
December 23	General Walker killed in jeep accident.
December 25	Chinese cross 38th Parallel.
December 27	Lieutenant General Matthew Ridgway takes over command of ground forces in Korea.

1951

January 1	Communist offensive begins.
January 4	U.S./UN forces evacuate Seoul.
January 7	Communists enter Wonju.
January 8–15	U.S. 2nd Division, with others, stops Chinese south of Wonju.
January 13	U.S. delegation votes for UN cease-fire resolution.

January 17	China rejects cease-fire proposal.
	Eighth Army reenters Suwon.
February 1	UN resolution declares China to be engaged in aggression.
February 10	Eighth Army retakes Inchon and Kimpo airfield.
February 13	Major Chinese offensive against X Corps in Central Korea.
February 15	Communists defeated at Chipyong-ni.
February 21	Eighth Army launches "Operation Killer."
March 7	"Operation Ripper" launched. Eighth Army crosses Han River east of Seoul.
March 13	Communists start to withdraw across all fronts.
March 15	Eighth Army retakes Seoul.
March 21	Eighth Army retakes Chunchon.
March 22	Eighth Army reaches 38th Parallel.
April 3	Eighth Army Divisions cross Parallel.
April 5	MacArthur's letter criticizing Truman's strategy and the concept of limited war made public.
April 11	Truman relieves MacArthur as UN commander and appoints Ridgway to succeed him.
April 15	Lieutenant General James Van Fleet takes command of the Eighth Army.
April 19	MacArthur denounces the Truman Administration before Congress for refusing to lift restrictions on the scope of the war.
April 22	Chinese begin their spring offensive.
	Start of battle of Imjin River.
April 25	Eighth Army pushed back eighteen to twenty miles.
May 1	First phase of Chinese offensive halted north of Seoul.
May 16	Chinese launch second phase of spring offensive.
May 17	2nd Division again stops Communists.
May 23	Eighth Army begins offensive.
May 28	Eighth Army takes Hwachon and Inje.
June 3	Eighth Army moves toward "Iron Triangle" in central Korea.
June 12	Eighth Army controls "Iron Triangle."
Early June	At the MacArthur congressional hearing, Secretary Acheson expresses willingness to negotiate a cease-fire near the 38th Parallel.
June 23	Yakov Malik, the Soviet Ambassador to the UN, calls for a cease-fire.
June 25	Chinese radio voices desire for cease-fire.
June 29	Ridgway offers to meet the Communist commanders to discuss cease-fire and armistice.
July 1	Kim Il Sung, commander of the North Korean forces, and

Peng Teh-huai, commander of the Chinese "Volunteers," agree to begin armistice discussions.

July 10	Armistice negotiations begin at Kaesong.
July 26	Agreement on the agenda for the armistice talks reached.
August 23	Communists suspend negotiations after alleged UN violation of the neutral zone at Kaesong.
October 25	Cease-fire discussions resume at Panmunjom.
November 13	U.S. Administration proposes acceptance of current line of contact, provided other issues outstanding at the truce talks are settled within thirty days. U.S./UN ground action permitted to continue.
December 27	Thirty-day limit reached after establishing demarcation line on November 27. No progress on other issues made, so line invalidated.

1952

January–April 7	Disorder in prison camps as screening of prisoners begins.
April 19	UN delegation informs the Communists that only 70,000 of 132,000 prisoners of war are willing to return home.
May 2	Communists reject UN proposals over question of voluntary repatriation.
May 7	Prisoners at Koje-do hold General Dodd hostage until May 11. Both sides announce stalemate over prisoner-of-war issue.
May 12	General Mark Clark succeeds Ridgway.
June 23	U.S. Air Force bombs Yalu River power installations to induce a more cooperative attitude at the truce talks.
August 29	Heaviest air raid of the war launched against Pyongyang.
October 8	The final offer on the prisoner-of-war question is rejected by the Communists and an indefinite recess is announced.
October 24	Eisenhower announces that if he is elected President, he will go to Korea.
November 4	Eisenhower elected President with 55 percent of the vote. He visits units in Korea for three days beginning December 5.
November 10	Van Fleet announces the mobilization of two new South Korean divisions and six regiments.

1953

February 10	General Van Fleet retires. General Maxwell D. Taylor assumes command of the Eighth Army.
February 22	Clark proposes an exchange of sick and wounded prisoners.

March 30	The Chinese agree and propose that prisoners unwilling to be repatriated be transferred to a neutral state.
April 20	Exchange of sick and wounded prisoners begins at Panmunjom.
April 26	Armistice negotiations resume.
May 13	Clark authorized to mobilize four more South Korean divisions.
May 20	The National Security Council decides that if "conditions arise," air and ground operations will be extended to China and ground operations in Korea will be intensified.
May 28	The U.S./UN negotiating team presents its final terms and threatens to break off the talks if these are rejected. Chinese attack outposts of U.S. 25th Division.
June 8	Prisoner-of-war question resolved and principle of voluntary repatriation accepted.
June 10	Chinese open assault on ROK II Corps near Kumsong. By June 16, ROK II Corps pushed back to new main line of resistance.
June 15–30	Chinese attack U.S. I Corps.
June 17	Revised demarcation line settled.
	President Rhee orders South Korean guards to release North Korean prisoners who do not wish to be repatriated.
July 20	New main line of resistance established on south bank of Kumsong River.
July 27	Armistice signed at Panmunjom.

NOTES AND REFERENCES

Publication details of all titles cited in the Notes are given in the Bibliography.

Prologue: Task Force Smith

1. Unless otherwise attributed, all direct quotations in the story of Task Force Smith are taken from the author's interviews with survivors: Lieutenant Colonel George Masters; Major Floyd Martain; Corporal Ezra Burke; Corporal Robert Fountain; Lieutenant Carl Bernard.
2. Donald Knox, *The Korean War, an Oral History*, p. 21.
3. Ibid., p. 23.

Chapter One: Origins of a Tragedy

1. The narrative of the arrival of the American advance party is based on an author interview with one of the participants, Lieutenant Ferris Miller, U.S.N., December 10, 1985.
2. Dennett quoted Bruce Cumings, *Origins of the Korean War*, p. 103.
3. October 3, 1943, quoted Cumings, op. cit., p. 114.
4. Ibid.
5. Miller, loc. cit.
6. Cumings, op. cit., p. 138–39.

7. U.S. National Archive, Foreign Relations of the United States, 1945, 6:1049–53.
8. Miller, loc. cit.
9. Edgar Kennedy, *Mission to Korea,* p. 14.
10. FRUS, op. cit., 6:1049–53.
11. FRUS, 1945, 6:1070–71.
12. FRUS, 1945, 6:1061–1065, Benninghoff to Secretary of State.
13. FRUS, 1945, 6:1023.
14. Author interview, Roger Makins (Lord Sherfield), October 1, 1986.
15. FRUS, 1945, 6:1122–24.
16. History of the United States Armed Forces in Korea, Vol. II, Chap. 1, p. 11.
17. FRUS, 1945, 6:1133–34.
18. FRUS, 1945, 5:1144–48.
19. HUSAFIK, op. cit., Vol. III, Chap. 4, Pt. 1, p. 1.
20. Author interview, General Paek Sun Yup, October 1985.
21. Author interview, Minh Pyong Kyu, October 1985.
22. Author interview, Kap Chong Chi, October 1985.
23. Miller, loc. cit.

Chapter Two: Invasion

1. Public Record Office (PRO), F0371/84076.
2. U.S. National Archive Defense Records, OPS 091, RG319 G-3, Box 121.
3. Nikita Khrushchev, *Khrushchev Remembers,* p. 367.
4. Allen Whiting, *China Crosses the Yalu,* p. 77.
5. William Manchester, *MacArthur: American Caesar,* p. 543.

Chapter Three: The West's Riposte

1. Narrative based upon an author interview with Han Pyo Wook, October 1985.
2. Christopher Mayhew, conversation with the author, May 1985.
3. Dean Acheson, *Present at the Creation,* p. 248.
4. U.S. National Archive, Record of JCS Action relative to Korea, pp. 12–13.
5. Truman Papers, PSF, quoted Rosemary Foot, *The Wrong War,* p. 59.
6. Douglas MacArthur, *Reminiscences,* p. 331.
7. *The New York Times,* September 7, 1950.
8. Author interview with Lord Franks, August 1985.
9. Ibid.
10. Manchester, op. cit., p. 548.
11. Ibid., p. 4.
12. Author interview with Colonel Fred Ladd, October 1985.
13. Ibid.
14. Ibid.
15. Author interview, Colonel George Masters, April 1985.
16. Ladd, loc. cit.

17. Paek, loc. cit.
18. Miller, loc. cit.
19. Author interview, Lee Chien Ho, October 1985.
20. Author interview, Suk Bun Yoon, October 1985.
21. Author interview, Won Jung Kil, October 1985.

Chapter Four: Walker's War

1. Knox, op. cit., pp. 38–39.
2. William F. Dean, *General Dean's Story,* p. 25.
3. Martain, loc. cit.
4. Rosalyn Higgins, *United Nations Peacekeeping 1946–67,* Vol. II, p. 179.
5. Author interview, General John Michaelis, April 1985.
6. Masters, loc. cit.
7. Author interview, Patterson, April 1985.
8. Author interview, Avery, April 1985.
9. Author interview, Handler, October 1985.
10. Author interview, Sorensen, October 1985.
11. Author interview, Alton, April 1985.
12. Author interview, Fore, October 1985.
13. Author interview, Taplett, November 1985.
14. Author interview, Waters, November 1985.
15. Author interview, Pearson, July 1985.
16. Minh, loc. cit.
17. Kap, loc. cit.
18. James Cameron, *Point of Departure,* pp. 106–7.
19. Author interview, Mayo, October 1985.
20. Author interview, General Paul Freeman, May 1985.
21. Saturday Evening Post, October 23, 1950.
22. Ibid.
23. Cameron, op. cit., p. 109.

Chapter Five: Inchon

1. Shepherd oral history transcript, U.S. Marine Corps Museum.
2. Author interview, General Alpha Bowser, May 1985.
3. Author interview, General Ellis Williamson, May 1985.
4. Ladd, loc. cit.
5. Taplett, loc. cit.
6. Smith oral history transcript, U.S. Marine Corps Museum.
7. Ibid.
8. Shepherd transcript, op. cit.
9. Author interview, Sheldon, May 1985.
10. Williamson, loc. cit.

11. Cameron, op. cit., p. 137.
12. Author interview, Brigadier General Ed Simmonds, October 1985.
13. Cameron, op. cit., p. 140.
14. Smith transcript, op. cit.
15. Michaelis, loc. cit.
16. Williamson, loc. cit.
17. Shepherd transcript, op. cit.
18. *Daily Telegraph,* 26.ix.50.
19. David Rees, *Korea: The Limited War,* p. 90.
20. Simmonds, loc. cit.

Chapter Six: To the Brink: MacArthur Crosses the Parallel

1. Shepherd transcript, op. cit.
2. PRO CAB 128/18.
3. MacArthur, op. cit., p. 214.
4. Paek, loc. cit.
5. U.S. National Archive, FR7:1108–9.
6. Quoted Foot, op. cit., p. 94.

Chapter Seven: The Coming of the Chinese

1. Author interview, Simon, May 1985.
2. Mitchell, op. cit., p. 80.
3. U.S. National Archive, NSC Minutes, 10.11.50.
4. U.S. National Archive, FR7: 1205–6.
5. John Gittings, *The Role of the Chinese Army,* p. 43.
6. *People's Daily,* August 23, 1950.
7. Kavalam M. Pannikkar, *In Two Chinas: Memoirs of a Diplomat,* p. 163.
8. This version of the circumstances in which Marshal Peng assumed command of the "Volunteers" is that given to the author by Chinese veterans in Peking in 1985. It must be treated with caution, and viewed against the background of Lin Piao's disgrace. But some sinologists consider it plausible.
9. Quoted Samuel B. Griffith, *The Chinese People's Liberation Army,* p. 135.
10. Author interview, Li Hebei, January 1985.
11. Author interview, Yu Xiu, January 1985.
12. Author interview, Li Hua, January 1985.
13. To the author, May 1985.
14. Author interview, Mario Scarselleta, April 1985.
15. Author interview, Bill Shirk, April 1985.
16. Quoted Griffith, op. cit., p. 145.
17. Fortune, loc. cit.
18. Author interview, James Waters, May 1985.

Chapter Eight: Chosin: The Road from the Reservoir

1. Smith transcript, op. cit.
2. Ibid.
3. Author interview, Andrew Condron, August 1985.
4. Letter to the author, August 1985.
5. McAlister letter to the author, August 1985.
6. To the author, September 1985.
7. Bowser, loc. cit.
8. Ibid.
9. Taplett, loc. cit.
10. Simmonds, loc. cit.
11. Ladd, loc. cit.
12. Shepherd transcript, op. cit.
13. Williamson, loc. cit.
14. Author interview, Robert Tyack, October 1985.

Chapter Nine: The Winter of Crisis

1. Freeman, loc. cit.
2. Schultz letter to the author, March 1985.
3. Bernard, loc. cit.
4. Author interview, Karl Morton, April 1985.
5. Ladd, loc. cit.
6. *Crossbelts,* regimental magazine of the Royal Irish Hussars, Spring 1951.
7. Paek Sun Yup, loc. cit.
8. Author interview, Moon Yun Seung, October 1985.
9. Cooper, loc. cit.
10. Martain, loc. cit.
11. Quoted Walter Karig, *Battle Report,* p. 353.
12. Author interview, Hu Seng, February 1985.
13. Li Xiu, loc. cit.
14. Li Hebei, loc. cit.
15. PRO London, W0216/836.
16. Ibid.
17. Ibid.
18. Uncataloged British records.
19. Ibid.
20. James Cardinal, private correspondence loaned to the author.
21. Fountain, loc. cit.
22. Harry S. Truman, *Years of Trial and Hope,* p. 385.
23. Acheson Papers, quoted Foot, op. cit., p. 103.
24. U.S. National Archive, FR7:1330.
25. MacArthur interview with *U.S. News & World Report,* quoted Joseph C. Goulden, *Korea: The Untold Story,* p. 393.

26. Truman, op. cit., p. 381.
27. PRO London, W0216/836.
28. *U.S. News & World Report,* op. cit.
29. PRO London, CAB128/180.
30. Alan Bullock, *Ernest Bevin,* Vol. II, p. 821.
31. Franks, loc. cit.
32. PRO London F0371/83018 8.12.50.
33. Schnabel and Watson, *History of the Joint Chiefs of Staff,* Vol. III, Pt. 2, 6.12.50.
34. Ibid.
35. Richard F. Haynes, *The Awesome Power: Harry S. Truman as Commander-in-Chief,* p. 95.
36. U.S. National Archive Records of Army Staff G3 091 Korea TS 5.7.51, Box 38a, RG319.
37. FRUS: 1326.
38. Foot, op. cit., p. 132.
39. U.S. National Archive, Foreign Policy of the United States, 7:192–3.
40. Matthew B. Ridgway, *The Korean War,* p. 86.
41. Ibid., p. 88.
42. PRO London W0216/63 836.
43. To the author, May 1985.
44. Michaelis, loc. cit.

Chapter Ten: Nemesis: The Dismissal of MacArthur

1. Manchester, op. cit., p. 617.
2. Author interview, General Charles Bolté, October 1985.
3. Schultz, loc. cit.
4. Uncataloged British records.
5. PRO London W0216/728.
6. Ridgway, op. cit., p. 121.
7. Courtney Whitney, *MacArthur: His Rendezvous With History,* p. 363.
8. Minutes of British COS meetings, uncataloged records.
9. Ibid.
10. Author interview, Air Marshal Sir John Nicholls, April 1985.
11. Williamson, loc. cit.
12. Freeman, loc. cit.
13. Ridgway, op. cit., pp. 147–49.
14. Manchester, op. cit., p. 646.
15. Kennedy, op. cit., p. 134.
16. Sheldon, loc. cit.
17. Ladd, loc. cit.
18. Uncataloged British records.
19. Ibid.
20. Isaacson and Thomas, *The Wise Men,* p. 263.

Chapter Eleven: The Struggle on the Imjin

1. All quotations in this chapter, unless otherwise attributed, are based upon author interviews with participants.
2. P. J. Kavanagh, *A Perfect Stranger,* pp. 104–5.
3. Ibid.
4. S. J. Davies, *In Spite of Dungeons,* pp. 18–19.
5. *Crossbelts,* regimental magazine of the Royal Irish Hussars, Autumn 1951, p. 17.
6. Anthony Farrar-Hockley, *The Edge of the Sword,* p. 89.
7. Ibid.
8. Davies, op. cit., p. 23.
9. Farrar-Hockley, op. cit., p. 93.

Chapter Twelve: The Stony Road

1. The Second Indianhead Division in Korea, p. 141.
2. To the author, May 1985.
3. Ridgway, op. cit., p. 157.
4. Bullock, op. cit., p. 792.
5. Author interview, St. Clair Tisdall, June 1985.
6. U.S. National Archive, Ridgway to JCS, 21.6.51.
7. Ibid., Ridgway to JCS, 14.7.51.
8. Ibid., FRUS 1951, Galleys 418–19.
9. Uncataloged British records.
10. Ibid.
11. PRO London, F0371/92847.
12. Ibid.
13. Ibid., F0371/92848.
14. Kauffroth letter to the author, July 1985.
15. Author interview, General Sir William Pike, April 1985.
16. Snider, loc. cit.
17. Suk Bun Yoon, loc. cit.
18. Quoted Melvin B. Vorhees, *Korean Tales,* p. 150.
19. Avery, loc. cit.
20. Handler, loc. cit.
21. Author interview, Robert Sebilian, October 1985.
22. Author interview, Gordon Gayle, October 1985.
23. Simmonds, loc. cit.
24. Author interview, William Norris, April 1985.
25. U.S. National Archive Department of Military History, ACMH 626.

Chapter Thirteen: The Intelligence War

1. Lee Chien Ho, loc. cit.
2. William Ellery Anderson, *Banner Over Pusan,* p. 96.

3. Author interview, William Ellery Anderson, July 1985.
4. Anderson, op. cit., p. 115.
5. Ibid., p. 182.
6. Goulden, op. cit., p. 463.
7. Author telephone interview, General Jack Singlaub, October 1985.

Chapter Fourteen: The Battle in the Air

1. For a more detailed discussion of these issues, see the author's *Bomber Command,* Michael Joseph, 1979.
2. Freeman, loc. cit.
3. Author interview, Air Marshal J. E. Johnson, September 1985.
4. Author interview, General John Sloane, August 1984.
5. Author interview, General Oliver Lewis, October 1985.
6. Author interview, Jim Low, April 1985.
7. General William Momyer, *Air Power in Three Wars,* p. 74.
8. Author interview, Roy Watson, June 1985.
9. Low, loc. cit.
10. Author interview, Joe Hilliard, October 1985.
11. Ibid.
12. Momyer, op. cit., p. 53.
13. Quoted George F. Futrell, *The United States Air Force in the Korean War,* p. 468.
14. Ridgway, op. cit., p. 279.
15. Quoted Momyer, op. cit., p. 170.
16. Alexander Seversky, *Victory Through Air Power,* p. 102.
17. Vorhees, op. cit., p. 170.

Chapter Fifteen: The War on the Hills

1. Author interview, James Stuhler, August 1985.
2. Author interview, Tom Pentony, April 1985.
3. Author interview, Alan Maybury, June 1985.
4. Commonwealth Division report, 26.10.52, Staff College Library.
5. Ibid.
6. Commonwealth Division report to War Office Director of Intelligence, 21.9.52. Staff College Library.
7. Author interview, Li Ben Wen, January 1985.
8. Author interview, Wang Zhu Guang, January 1985.
9. Patterson, loc. cit.
10. Paul Sheehy, private correspondence loaned to the author.
11. PRO London, W0216/720.
12. Ibid.
13. Pike, loc. cit.
14. Ibid.
15. Avery, loc. cit.
16. Pentony, loc. cit.

Chapter Sixteen: The Prisoners

1. Pamphlet loaned to the author by a British veteran.
2. Davies, op. cit., p. 29.
3. Scarselleta, loc. cit.
4. Avery, loc. cit.
5. Condron, loc. cit.
6. Author interview, Graham Cockfield, April 1985.
7. Author telephone interview, Walt Mayo, October 1985.
8. Cooper, loc. cit.
9. Erricker private correspondence loaned to the author.
10. Davies, op. cit., p. 68.
11. Ibid., p. 70.
12. Fortune, loc. cit.
13. Author interview, Captain John Thornton, U.S.N., April 1985.
14. Majury, loc. cit.
15. Condron, loc. cit.
16. Eugene Kinkead, *Why They Collaborated,* pp. 153–54.

Chapter Seventeen: The Pursuit of Peace

1. Author interview, Alan Maggio, October 1985.
2. Ibid.
3. Author telephone interview, Robert Hoop, October 1985.
4. Bouchier to War Office, 10.5.52. Uncataloged British records.
5. PRO London F0371/99640.
6. Ibid.
7. Ibid.
8. PRO London F0371/99641.
9. Ibid.
10. Schnabel and Watson, *History of the [U.S.] Joint Chiefs of Staff.*
11. August 12, 1952.
12. Ronald Caridi, *The Korean War and American Politics,* p. 253.
13. U.S. National Archive, minutes of the NSC meeting, 11.2.53.
14. Ibid., FR15:827.
15. Eisenhower Papers, March 31, 1952, quoted Foot, op. cit., p. 215.
16. Han Pyo Wook, loc. cit.
17. Author interview, General William Livsey, May 1985.
18. Snider, loc. cit.
19. Author interview, General Arthur Trudeau, October 1985.
20. Maybury, loc. cit.
21. Fore, loc. cit.
22. Wang Zhu Guang, loc. cit.
23. Fortune, loc. cit.

Chapter Eighteen: Hindsight

1. All quotations in this chapter are based upon author interviews with veterans unless otherwise stated.
2. Foot, op. cit., pp. 239–40.
3. "A Reminiscence of the Chinese People's Volunteers in the Korean War," *China Quarterly,* No. 98, June 1984, pp. 303–4.
4. Ibid.

SELECT BIBLIOGRAPHY
AND A NOTE ON SOURCES

The principal sources for this book have been oral interviews with participants in the Korean War and those familiar with its diplomatic and political aspects, together with the relevant files in the Public Record Office, London, and the National Archive, Washington, D.C. I have also consulted records and reports at the Staff College, Camberley, and personal correspondence preserved privately. The National Military Museum in Peking contains a large Korean section, and much visual material, but no important documentation is available to a foreign researcher. There are major oral-history transcript collections at the U.S. Marine Corps Museum, Washington, D.C., and at the U.S. Army's Military History Institute at Carlisle Barracks, Pennsylvania. The list of secondary sources below does not include unit and formation histories, which exist for almost every fighting element on the UN side in Korea. I have drawn upon the contemporary files of major British and U.S. newspapers, together with some locally published wartime English-language newspapers in Korea.

Acheson, Dean. *Present at the Creation*. Hamish Hamilton, 1969.
Ambrose, Stephen E. *Eisenhower: The President*. Allen & Unwin, 1984.
Anderson, William Ellery. *Banner Over Pusan*. Evans, 1960.
Barclay, C. N. *The First Commonwealth Division*. Gale & Polden, 1954.
Barker, A. J. *Fortune Favours the Brave*. Leo Cooper, 1974.
Bartlett, Norman, ed. *With the Australians in Korea*. Australian War Memorial, 1954.

Biderman, Albert D. *March to Calumny*. Macmillan, 1963.

Blumenson, Martin. *Mark Clark*. Jonathan Cape, 1985.

Bohlen, Charles E. *Witness to History, 1929–1969*. Norton, 1973.

Bradbury, William C., Samuel M. Meyers and Albert D. Biderman. *Mass Behavior in Battle and Captivity: The Communist Soldier in the Korean War*. University of Chicago Press, 1968.

Bradley, Omar N., and Clay Blair. *A General's Life*. Simon and Schuster, 1983.

Bullock, Alan. *Ernest Bevin*, Vol. II. Heinemann, 1983.

Cameron, James. *Point of Departure*. Arthur Barker, 1967.

Carew, Tim. *The Commonwealth At War*. Cassell, 1967.

Caridi, Ronald J. *The Korean War and American Politics: The Republican Party as a Case Study*. University of Pennsylvania Press, 1968.

Chae, Kyung Oh. *Handbook of Korea*. Pageant Press, 1958.

Chafe, William H. *The Unfinished Journey*. Oxford University Press, 1985.

Collins, Lawton J. *War in Peace*. Houghton Mifflin, 1969.

Cumings, Bruce. *Origins of the Korean War*. Princeton University Press, 1981.

Curtov, Hwang B. *China Under Threat*. University of California Press, 1956.

Cutforth, Rene. *Korean Reporter*. Heinemann, 1951.

Davies, S. J. *In Spite of Dungeons*. Hodder & Stoughton, 1955.

Dean, William F. *General Dean's Story*. Viking, 1954.

Deane, Philip. *Captive in Korea*. Hamish Hamilton, 1953.

Donovan, Robert J. *Tumultuous Years*. Norton, 1982.

Dulles, John Foster. *War or Peace*. Macmillan, 1950.

Eisenhower, Dwight D. *The White House Years: Mandate for Change, 1953–56*, Vol. I. Doubleday, 1963.

Farrar-Hockley, Anthony. *The Edge of the Sword*. Frederick Muller, 1954.

Felton, Monica. *That's Why I Went*. Lawrence & Wishart, 1953.

Field, James A. *History of U.S. Naval Operations Korea*. Naval History Division, Washington, 1962.

Foot, Rosemary. *The Wrong War*. Cornell University Press, 1985.

Foreign Affairs, Her Majesty's Secretary for. *Survey of Events Relating to Korea*. Her Majesty's Stationery Office, London, 1950.

Futrell, George F. *The United States Air Force in the Korea War*. Office of Air Force History, Washington, 1983.

George, Alexander L. *The Chinese Communist Army in Action*. Columbia University Press, 1967.

Giesler, Patricia. *Valour Remembered: Canadians in Korea*. Department of Veteran's Affairs, Ottawa, 1982.

Gittings, John. *The Role of the Chinese Army*. Oxford University Press, 1967.

Goulden, Joseph C. *Korea: The Untold Story*. McGraw-Hill, 1982.

Griffith, Samuel B. *The Chinese People's Liberation Army*. Weidenfeld & Nicolson, 1968.

Grist, Digby. *Remembered with Advantage*. Barton Press, 1976.

Gugeler, Russell A. *Combat Actions in Korea*. Office of the Army Chief of Military History, Washington, 1970.

Harriman, W. Averell. *America and Russia in a Changing World*. Doubleday, 1971.

Heinl, Robert Debs. *Victory at High Tide*. Leo Cooper, 1972.

Hermes, Walter G. *Truce Tent and Fighting Front*. Government Printing Office, Washington, 1966.

Higgins, Marguerite. *The War in Korea*. Harper & Row, 1951.

Higgins, Rosalyn. *United Nations Peacekeeping 1946–67*, Vol. II. Oxford University Press, 1970.

Higgins, Trumbull. *Korea and the Fall of MacArthur*. Oxford University Press, 1960.

Holles, Robert. *Now Thrive the Armourers*. Harrap, 1952.

Howarth, T. E. B. *Prospect And Reality*, Collins, 1985.

Hoyt, Edwin P. *The Pusan Perimeter*. Stein & Day, 1983.

———. *On to the Yalu*. Stein & Day, 1984.

———. *The Bloody Road to Panmunjom*. Stein & Day, 1985.

Isaacson, Walter, and Evan Thomas. *The Wise Men*. Simon and Schuster, 1986.

Johnson, Air Vice Marshal J. E. *The Story of Air Fighting*. Hutchinson, 1985.

Joy, C. Turner. *How Communists Negotiate*. Macmillan, 1955.

Karig, Walter, Malcolm W. Cagle, and Frank A. Manson. *Battle Report: The War in Korea*. Holt Rinehart, 1952.

Kavanagh, P. J. *A Perfect Stranger*. Heinemann, 1966.

Kennan, George F. *Memoirs 1925–1950*. Little, Brown, 1967.

———. *Memoirs, 1950–1963*. Little, Brown, 1972.

Kennedy, Edgar. *Mission to Korea*. Derk Verschoyle, 1952.

Khrushchev, Nikita. *Khrushchev Remembers*. Little, Brown, 1971.

Kie-Chiang Oh, John. *Korea: Democracy on Trial*. Cornell University Press, 1968.

Kim, Chong Ik and Han-Kyo. *Korea and the Politics of Imperialism*. University of California Press, 1967.

Kinkead, Eugene. *Why They Collaborated*. Longman, 1960.

Knox, Donald. *The Korean War, an Oral History: Pusan to Chosin*. Harcourt Brace Jovanovich, 1985.

Kohn, Richard H., and Joseph P. Harahan, eds. *Air Superiority in World War II and Korea*. U.S.A.F. Warrior Studies, 1983.

Langley, Michael. *Inchon: MacArthur's Last Triumph*. Batsford, 1979.

Linklater, Eric. *Our Men in Korea*. Her Majesty's Stationery Office, 1954.

Lowe, Peter. *The Origins of the Korean War*. Longman, 1986.

MacArthur, Douglas A. *Reminiscences*. Heinemann, 1965.

McGuire, F. R. *Canada's Army in Korea*. Historical Section, General Staff, Army Headquarters, Ottawa, 1956.

McLellan, David S. *Dean Acheson: The State Department Years*. Dodd Mead, 1976.

Manchester, William. *MacArthur: American Caesar*. Hutchinson, 1978.

Marshall, S. L. A. *The River and the Gauntlet*. Morrow, 1953.

———. *Pork Chop Hill*. Morrow, 1952.

Melady, John. *Korea: Canada's Forgotten War*. Macmillan of Canada, 1983.

Mitchell, Colin. *Having Been a Soldier*. Hamish Hamilton, 1969.

Momyer, General William W. *Air Power in Three Wars*. New York, 1978.

Montross, Lynn, and Nicholas A. Canzona. *U.S. Marine Operations in Korea 1950–53,* Vols. I–V. Historical Branch, U.S. Marine Corps, Washington, 1957.

Morgan, Kenneth. *Labour in Power.* Oxford University Press, 1984.

Pannikkar, Kavalam M. *In Two Chinas: Memoirs of a Diplomat.* Allen & Unwin, 1955.

Pogue, Forrest. *George C. Marshall,* 3 vols. Viking, 1963–73.

Porter, Brian. *Britain and the Rise of Communist China 1945–54.* Oxford University Press, 1967.

Rees, David. *Korea: The Limited War.* Hamish Hamilton, 1964.

———, ed. *The Korean War: History and Tactics.* Orbis, 1984.

Reeves, Thomas C. *The Life and Times of Joe McCarthy.* Stein & Day, 1982.

Ridgway, Matthew B. *The Korean War.* Doubleday, 1967.

Rovere, Richard H., and Arthur M. Schlesinger, Jr. *The MacArthur Controversy and American Foreign Policy.* Noonday Press, 1965.

Russ, Martin. *The Last Parallel.* Signet, 1957.

Scalpino, Robert A. *North Korea Today.* Praeger, 1963.

Schaller, Michael. *The American Occupation of Japan.* Oxford University Press, 1985.

Schnabel, James F., and Robert J. Watson. *History of the Joint Chiefs of Staff,* Vol. III, Pt. 2. Historical Division, Joint Secretariat, 1979.

———. *The U.S. Army in the Korean War,* Vols. I and II. Office of the Chief of Military History, Washington, 1972, 1984.

Seversky, Alexander. *Victory Through Air Power.* Simon and Schuster, 1942.

Stone, Isidor F. *The Hidden History of the Korean War.* Monthly Review Press, 1952.

Stueck, William. *The Road to Conflict: U.S. Policy Towards China and Korea.* University of North Carolina Press, 1981.

Suk, Lee Hyung, ed. *History of UN Forces in the Korean War,* five vols. Korean Ministry of National Defence, 1973.

Taylor, Maxwell D. *Swords and Plowshares.* Norton, 1972.

Thompson, Reginald. *Cry Korea.* Hodder, 1951.

Thorne, Christopher. *Allies of a Kind.* Hamish Hamilton, 1978.

———. *The Issue of War.* Oxford University Press, 1985.

Thornton, Captain John. *Believed to Be Alive.* Eriksson, 1981.

Truman, Harry S. *Years of Trial and Hope.* Doubleday, 1956.

Vatcher, William H. *Panmunjom.* Atlantic Books, 1958.

Vorhees, Melvin B. *Korean Tales.* Secker & Warburg, 1953.

Watt, D. C. *Succeeding John Bull: America in Britain's Place.* Cambridge University Press, 1984.

Whiting, Allan. *China Crosses the Yalu: The Decision to Enter the Korean War.* University of California Press, 1970.

Whitney, Courtney. *MacArthur: His Rendezvous with History.* Knopf, 1956.

Whitson, William W. *The Chinese High Command.* Macmillan, 1973.

Willoughby, Charles A., and John Chamberlain. *MacArthur, 1941–1951.* McGraw-Hill, 1968.

Young, Kenneth. *Negotiating with the Chinese Communists: The United States Experience 1953–1967.* McGraw-Hill, 1968.

APPENDIX

Summaries of Offers of military assistance for Korea by UN members as of 15 January 1952. Many of those marked "Acceptance deferred" were never taken up: most conspicuously, Nationalist China's offer of three infantry divisions.

GROUND FORCES

Country	Date	Details of Offer ·	Status
Australia	3 Aug. 1950	Ground forces from Australian Infantry Force in Japan	In action
		Additional battalion of Australian troops	
Belgium	13 Sept. 1950	Infantry battalion	" "
	3 May 1951	Reinforcements	" "
Bolivia	15 July 1950	30 Officers	Acceptance deferred
Canada	14 Aug. 1950	Brigade group, including three infantry battalions, one field regiment of artillery, one squadron of self-propelled anti-tank guns, together with engineer, signal, medical, ordnance and other services with appropriate reinforcements.	In action
China	3 July 1950	Three infantry divisions	Acceptance deferred
Colombia	14 Nov. 1950	One infantry battalion	In action
Costa rica	27 July 1950	Volunteers	Acceptance deferred
Cuba	30 Nov. 1950	One infantry company	Accepted
El Salvador	15 Aug. 1950	Volunteers	Acceptance deferred
Ethiopia	2 Nov. 1950	1,069 officers and men	In action

365

Country	Date	Details of Offer	Status
France	20 Aug. 1950	Infantry battalion	" "
Greece	1 Sept. 1950	Unit of land forces	" "
	2 July 1951	Additional unit of land forces	Transmitted to Unified Command
Luxembourg	15 Mar. 1951	Infantry company integrated into the Belgian forces	In action
Netherlands	8 Sept. 1950	One infantry battalion	" "
New Zealand	26 July 1950	One combat unit	" "
Panama	3 Aug. 1950	Contingent of volunteers ⎱ Bases for training ⎰	Acceptance deferred
Philippines	10 Aug. 1950	Regimental combat team consisting of approximately 5,000 officers and men	In action
Thailand	23 July 1950	Infantry combat team of about 4,000 officers and men	In action
Turkey	25 July 1950	Infantry combat force of 4,500 men, later increased to 6,086 men	In action
United Kingdom	21 Aug. 1950	Ground forces	" "
	Official information communicated on 12 June 1951	Two brigades composed of brigade headquarters	" "
		Five infantry battalions	" "
		One field regiment	" "
		One armored regiment	" "
United States of America	Official information communicated on 8 June 1951	Three Army Corps ⎱ With supporting One Marine Division ⎰ elements	" "

NAVAL FORCES

Country	Date	Details of Offer	Status
Australia	28 July 1950	Two destroyers	" "
	29 July 1950	One aircraft carrier	" "
		One frigate	" "
Canada	12 July 1950	Three destroyers	" "
Colombia	16 Oct. 1950	One frigate—*Almirante Padilla*	" "
France	19 July 1950	Patrol gun boat	Withdrawn
Netherlands	5 July 1950	One destroyer—*Evertsen*	In action
New Zealand	1 July 1950	Two frigates—HMNZ *Tutira* and HMNZ *Pukaki*	" "
Thailand	3 Oct. 1950	Two corvettes—*Prasae* and *Bangpakon**	" "
United Kingdom	28 June 1950	Naval forces in Japanese waters diverted to Korea	" "
	Official information communicated on 12 June 1951	One aircraft carrier	" "
		Two cruisers	" "
		Eight destroyers	" "
		One Survey Ship	" "
United States of America	Official information communicated on 8 June 1951	A fast carrier task group with a blockade and escort force, an amphibious force, reconnaissance and antisubmarine warfare units	" "

* Destroyed on grounding.

Country	Date	Details of Offer	Status

AIR FORCES

Country	Date	Details of Offer	Status
Australia	30 June 1950	One RAAF Fighter Squadron	" "
		One air communication unit	" "
		Base and maintenance personnel	" "
Canada	21 July 1950	One RCAF Squadron	" "
Union of South Africa	4 Aug. 1950	One fighter squadron, including ground personnel	" "
United Kingdom	Official information communicated on 12 June 1951	Elements of the Air Force	" "
United States of America	Official information communicated on 8 June 1951	One Tactical Air Force, one Bombardment Command, and one Combat Cargo Command, all with supporting elements	" "

MATERIAL

Country	Date	Details of Offer	Status
Philippines	3 Aug. 1950	17 Sherman tanks and one tank destroyer	In action

TRANSPORT

Country	Date	Details of Offer	Status
Belgium	28 Sept. 1950	Air transport	" "
Canada	11 Aug. 1950	Facilities of Canadian Pacific Airlines between Vancouver and Tokyo	" "
		Dry Cargo Vessels (10,000 tons)	" "
China	3 July 1950	Twenty C-47s	Acceptance deferred
Denmark	22 July 1950	Motor ship *Bella Dan*	Withdrawn
Greece	20 July 1950 13 Oct. 1950	Eight Dakota transport planes	In action
Norway	18 July 1950	Merchant ship tonnage	" "
Panama	3 Aug. 1950	Use of merchant marine for transportation of troops and supplies	" "
Thailand	3 Oct. 1950	Transport *Sichang* to be attached to Thai troops	" "
		Air transport	" "
United Kingdom	Official information communicated on 12 June 1951	Seven supply vessels	" "
United States of America		Air transport supply vessels	" "

MEDICAL

Country	Date	Details of Offer	Status
Denmark	18 Aug. 1950	Hospital Ship *Jutlandia*	" "
India	29 July 1950	Field Ambulance Unit	" "
Italy	27 Sept. 1950	Field Hospital Unit	" "
Norway	6 Mar. 1951	Surgical Hospital Unit	" "
Sweden	20 July 1950	Field Hospital Unit	" "
United Kingdom	Official information communicated on 12 June 1951	Hospital Ship	" "

Country	Date	Details of Offer	Status
United States of America		Large-scale hospital facilities	" "

MISCELLANEOUS

Country	Date	Details of Offer	Status
Costa Rica	27 July 1950	Sea and air bases	Accepted
Panama	3 Aug. 1950	Bases for training	Acceptance deferred
		Free use of highways	Accepted
		Farm lands to supply troops	Pending
Thailand	2 Feb. 1951	Treatment for frostbite	"

ACKNOWLEDGMENTS

Thanks are due to a host of Korean veterans in Britain, the United States, Korea, and China who not only contributed written or taped accounts of their experiences but in many cases met and entertained me in the course of my researches. To all of them I should like to express my gratitude and my hope that they do not feel too exasperated or disappointed by the narrative that I have built around their stories and comments. The list below includes only field ranks and above and omits decorations, which would otherwise overwhelm these pages.

Clyde Alton, Professor Eugene Alvarez, William Ellery Anderson, A. F. Antippas, Warren Avery, Tom Bagnall, A. D. Barnes, Moe Beaudin, Keith Bennett, Carl Bernard, D. O. Blackmon, Major General P. Bogert, General Charles Bolté, Colonel Donald W. Boose, Commander J. H. G. Bovey, John Bowler, General Alpha Bowser, Major General Thomas Brodie, Ezra Burke, D. S. Caldwell, James Cardinal, John F. Carney, Deirdre Chappell, Graham Cockfield, Andrew Condron, Major William Cooper, James Coulos, C. W. Crossland, Harvey E. Dann, L. A. Davis, Kenneth G. Dibble, A. H. Donaldson, William Drummond, Matthew Dukes, Tony Eagles, Hamish Eaton, Captain John Ellis, Jerry Emer, Robert Erricker, E. Esslinger, Colonel M. G. Farmer, Peter Farrar, General Sir Anthony Farrar-Hockley, Eric G. Fazan, Robert Flaherty, Richard A. Fleckenstein, Clyde Fore, Major J. A. Foulis,

Captain Robert Fountain, R. W. Fox, C. W. Franklin, Lord Franks, General Paul Freeman, Jack Gage, T. J. Gallagan, Brigadier General Gordon Gayle, Tom Glenn, Pip Wook Han, Selwyn Handler, Lawrence J. Hansen, Colonel E. Denis Harding, Clyde A. Harriman, C. J. Harrold, Clifton W. Hastings, J. L. S. Haughton, Brian Hawkins, Commander R. Hennessy, Michael Hickey, Charles E. Higgins, Joe Hilliard, Charles F. Home, Robert Hoop, Seng Hu, Xiang Huan, J. Husher, William Jacob, Air Marshal J. E. Johnson, P. C. Jones, Brigadier Amos Jordan, Bok Suh Kang, Chong Chi Kap, Arthur Karma, S. M. Kauffroth, P. J. Kavanagh, Bernard Loch, Christopher Mayhew, Walt Mayo, Colonel George Masters, Don McAlister, John McQueen, John Merrick, General John Michaelis, Ferris Miller, Patrick Min, Pyong Kyu Minh, Alan Moody, Yun Seung Moon, Karl R. Morton, John Mosse, Stan Muir, William Muncaster, Bill Myers, Fred Nelson, Air Marshal Sir John Nicholls, William Norris, Henry O'Kane, Captain David Omer, Lieutenant Colonel Paul D. Orwoll, Nam Kyu Paek, General Sun Yup Paek, Bill Patterson, Roy Pearl, John C. Pearson, Major Tom Pentony, General Sir William Pike, E. J. Plaisance, Lieutenant Lloyd Pulton, Julio Ramon, Colonel George Rasula, Alistair Rattray, Barry Reed, J. Richardson, S. Richardson, Lieutenant Colonel G. P. Rickord, Bernard Rock, Mario Scarselleta, Ronald Schaffer, Peter F. Schultz, Robert Sebilian, Paul Sheehy, Bill Shirk, W. F. Showen, General Peter Sibbald, Brigadier General Ed Simmonds, General Jack Singlaub, John Slackpark, Major Lester A. Sliter, Major General John Sloane, John J. Slonaker, George F. Smith, Brigadier Chris Snider, Brigadier Snow, Bill Sorenson, Robert W. Steffy, Captain W. J. H. Stuart, James Stuhler, Bun Yoon Suk, Lieutenant Colonel Robert Taplett, Paul E. Tardiff, Raymond Tauszik, Bill Taylor, Brigadier G. Taylor, Timothy P. Taylor, Andre Thiry, Captain John Thornton U.S. Navy, Commander I. P. Thorne, St. Clair Tisdall, Thomas L. Tomlinson, Eric Townsend, General Arthur Trudeau, Robert Tyack, J. W. L. Tyler, Albert Van Alstyne, Albert Varley, Mark Villanueva, Brian Wall, Melvin C. Walthall, Zhu Guang Wang, Major Guy Ward, James Waters, Roy Watson, Philip Welton, Lieutenant Colonel E. Williams, General Ellis Williamson, Major General Sir John Willoughby, Brigadier David Wilson, Blair Winer, B. Woodhouse, Willis J. Wood, Tom Worthington, Jung Kil Won, Professor Suk Bun Yoon, Major General Allan Younger, Xiu Yu.

INDEX

Acheson, Dean, 180
  on China policy, 49, 51, 69, 135, 177,
    181, 184, 186
  on dismissal of MacArthur, 202–3, 207
  Korean policy and strategy of, 57–63,
    116, 117, 316
  MacArthur's behavior irritating to, 121
  on Nationalist Chinese participation in
    Korea, 69
  on NSC-68, 50
  on prospects for peace, 230
  public disapproval of, 184
  on use of atomic weapons in Korea,
    183–84
  on Wake Island meeting, 122–23
Advisory Council, South Korean, 35
Air Force, U.S., 69, 73, 77, 234, 249
  atomic bomb and, 254
  B-29 bomber operations of, 263–65
  casualties in, 262–63, 264
  during Chinese winter offensive,
    171–72
  close support role of, 256
  daylight bombing missions of, 263–64
  dogfights of, 260–61
  F-86 Sabre jet fighters used by, 258–64
  in Korean War, 255–69, 322
  morale in, 265
  new equipment and techniques used
    by, 257–58
  night bombing operations of, 257, 264
  ordnance carried by, 257, 262, 264
  rescues of downed pilots of, 261–62
  tactical bombing role of, 256–57,
    263–65, 267–69, 275–77, 322
Air University, 255
Alexander, Harold, 272
Allen, Leven, 189
Allison, John, 117
Almond, Edward M., 66–67, 69–70,
  111, 140, 153

battle for Hagaru and, 160
battle for Seoul and, 112–13
Inchon landing force commanded by,
  103–6
in invasion of North Korea, 119–20,
  126
northern drive strategy of, 147–49, 154
Smith's relationship with, 103–4, 110,
  147–49, 156, 160–61
withdrawal from Chosin and, 157, 161
Alton, Clyde, 84
American-Soviet Joint Commission on
  Korean Trusteeship, 37
Anderson, William Ellery:
  background of, 245–46
  intelligence operation run by, 246–50
Angier, Pat, 214–16
Ansung, 128–29
Army, British, 129
  in battle of Imjin River, 209–27
  in battle of Pusan Perimeter, 85, 89
  hill warfare engagement of, 111–12,
    274–75, 277–80, 283
  Korean porters attached to, 240–41
  PLA encounters with, 131, 142–44,
    145, 209
Army, South Korean (ROK), 112,
  139–41, 208–09, 228–29
  ARVN compared to, 334
  in battle of Pusan Perimeter, 86, 95–96
  brutality of, 242
  capabilities of, 46–48, 73
  casualties of, 73, 329
  Chinese entrance into war and,
    129–31, 137–38
  expansion of, 318, 322
  invaders delayed and damaged by, 76
  in invasion of North Korea, 119–21,
    125–26
  Japanese Army ties of, 39
  as militarily untrustworthy, 239, 242

About the Author

Max Hastings' prize-winning books include *Overlord, The Battle for the Falklands* (coauthor), *Das Reich* and *Bomber Command*. He has written for *The London Standard*, London *Spectator* and the *Daily Express*. He is currently the editor of *The Daily Telegraph* in London.

THE KOREAN WAR
MAX HASTINGS

It was a bloody, bitter siege, the first war we could not win. At no other time since World War II have two superpowers met in battle. At no other time since World War II, except in the Cuban missile crisis, has East-West nuclear war been so close. The Korean War cost the U.S. 142,000 lives in three years, just under the number lost during ten years in Vietnam. Yet Korea has been neglected by historians and too long misunderstood by the American public.

Now Max Hastings, preeminent military historian and author of *Overlord: D-Day and the Battle for Normandy,* takes us back to the struggle to restore South Korean independence after the Communist invasion of June 1950. Hastings dramatically recounts the sequence of great military dramas that formed the war—the invasion itself, the huge U.S. losses in the first year, the defense of the Pusan Perimeter, MacArthur's triumphant landing at Inchon, which cut off the North Koreans, the drive to the Yalu, and the Chinese retribution.

As he demonstrated in *Overlord,* Hastings' particular genius is getting us *inside* the experiences of the fighting men. Using personal accounts from interviews with over 200 vets—*including the Chinese*—Hastings follows real officers and soldiers through the battles, showing us how it was in the thick of the raging action.

And Hastings brilliantly captures the big picture—the Cold War crisis at home, the strategies and politics of Truman, Acheson, Marshall, MacArthur, Ridgway, and Bradley. He shows how Korea served as a prelude to Vietnam and how its lessons—the difficulty of using air power against a primitive economy,